Contents

W9-BXZ-507

A PARENTS' GUIDE
to
Special Education
for
Children with Visual
Impairments

Susan LaVenture, Editor

AFB **PRESS**

American Foundation for the Blind

Printed in the United States of America

Library of Congress Cataloging-in-Publication Data

A parents' guide to special education for children with visual impairments / Susan LaVenture, editor.
    p. cm.
   Includes bibliographical references and index.
   ISBN 0-89128-892-9 (pbk. : alk. paper)—ISBN 0–89128–893–7 (ascii disk)
   1. Children with visual disabilities—Education.   2. Special education.   3. Parents of children with disabilities.   I. LaVenture, Susan.

HV1626.P63 2007
371.91'1—dc22

2006102495

Photo Credits: Photos courtesy of Chicago Lighthouse for People Who Are Blind or Visually Impaired, pp. 36 and 90; Columbia Lighthouse for the Blind, p. 244; Perkins School for the Blind, by John Kennard, pp. 60 and 126; HumanWare, p. 170; L. Penny Rosenblum, pp. 2 and 138; Natalie Knott, p. 200; The New York Institute for Special Education, p. 292.

The American Foundation for the Blind—the organization to which Helen Keller devoted her life—is a national nonprofit devoted to expanding the possibilities for people with vision loss.

(∞)™

It is the policy of the American Foundation for the Blind to use in the first printing of its books acid-free paper that meets the ANSI Z39.48 Standard. The infinity symbol that appears above indicates that the paper in this printing meets that standard.

To my three children, who have been my best teachers while I was raising and loving them, and especially to my son, Alex, who introduced me to the world of vision.

Preface

This book is meant to be a guide for you. It is intended to help you understand the important information families need to know about education and their children who are blind or visually impaired. When a child has a visual impairment, learning and development may need to be helped along the way. Intervention, encouragement, and special educational planning therefore become an essential part of the school years. Often, children require some training and instruction from teachers who specialize in working with blind and visually impaired students. Your child might also need certain accommodations and arrangements, like books or materials in a format like braille, or a seat near the front of the class, in order to participate fully in the classroom and in extracurricular activities. The authors of this book, experienced parents who have walked down the educational road successfully and specialists in the vision field, have provided the information they feel you should know as a parent to help you proceed down this road. Every child is an individual and has unique needs and strengths, and there is no one formula that fits for every child's successful education. But there is an educational process, and knowing what it is and what it can offer can lead to educational success. The process works, but it needs you. Parents play the most important and influential role in their child's education. This book is a means to help you in this role and through this process.

Not very long ago, at a parent meeting of the New York City Affiliate of the National Association for Parents of Children with Visual Impairments (NYC-NAPVI), Carl Augusto, President and CEO of the American Foundation for the Blind (AFB), gave a presentation about his life growing up with a visual impairment and advice to parents from his perspective. Carl is recognized as a prominent national leader in the vision field and among nonprofit organizations and is a father of two grown children. His remarks to our parents were so genuine, insightful, and practical that I thought the families reading this book would appreciate them and find them useful. Here they are:

"Being a parent is a tough job, but it's probably the best job in the world. Many parents also work outside the home, have more than one child, and may even be a single parent. Therefore, being a parent of a blind or visually impaired child may seem overwhelming.

Here is some advice:

1. Have the right attitude about blindness and visual impairment. Blindness doesn't need to be 'the end of the world' or a tragedy. Your child should be encouraged to accept blindness as a characteristic but not a barrier. Don't be preoccupied with what your child can't do or see. Focus on what he or she can do now and in the future with training and development. And don't be embarrassed about having a visually impaired child; be proud of his or her accomplishments.

2. Have high expectations for your child, even if your child has multiple disabilities. His or her potential is probably greater than you think.

3. Treat your child the way other children are treated. When he or she is old enough, encourage your child to engage in different activities. Your child should be responsible for doing chores around the house and should clean up his or her room after play, just as sighted children do.

4. Try not to lose sight of key priorities. Make sure your child develops social skills, a good personal appearance, adaptive skills like braille (if it is feasible and recommended), travel skills, and personal adjustment skills (like how to identify clothing, cook, shave, or apply cosmetics), and uses technology. Technology is revolutionizing the way blind and visually impaired people function. As the years progress, talk to your child about your expectation that he or she will work. And teach your child to be an advocate for himself or herself—encourage your child to cope with his or her problems and make decisions independently. You'll want your child to be as independent as possible after you are no longer able to take care of him or her.

5. Know your rights and the rights of your child and be prepared to fight for them. Know the law, like the Individuals with Disabilities Education Act and the Americans with Disabilities Act.

6. Get services for your child. There are many organizations of and for the blind. You can find that information on the web site of the American Foundation for the Blind (www.afb.org).

7. Interact with other families. Get to know parents of other visually impaired children; you can learn so much from each other. Be active in the National Association for Parents of Children with Visual Impairments. You can gain much support, information, and encouragement from this organization. You can also help others in the process.

Being a parent of a visually impaired child will be a challenge. But the following will help:

1. Perseverance—don't quit. Continue to advocate for your child.

2. Be patient with yourself and with your child. Change may not happen every day, but it will happen over time if you are persistent and patient.

3. Show your love for your child. You may not do the 'right' things at all times but your love will be recognized by your child, and it is what he or she especially needs."

Susan LaVenture
Executive Director
National Association
for Parents of
Children with Visual
Impairments

Beginning the Adventure: An Introduction

Going through an overstuffed closet to weed out things for the trash before the movers came, I discovered a dusty box of old cassette tapes. Curious about what they might contain, I began to listen to them one by one. Within a few minutes, I found a recording of my mother reading materials from my seventh-grade social studies class, a textbook entitled *Cultures* by David C. King. As I listened, I was struck both by how young she sounded and by how tired she sounded. And then, something happened that grabbed me by the throat emotionally: I heard a clock strike in the background. I remembered that my father loved grandfather clocks, and years before had found one that chimed differently for the AM and PM hours. As my mother continued to slog her way through reading my boring middle-school textbook, which her son who was blind could not otherwise have read, the grandfather clock chimed 2:00 AM. I know I now appreciate so much my mother's dedication in making sure I had a meaningful education, but I wonder how much I appreciated it at that time, when I was a young teenager who didn't want to do his homework.

In many ways, you are starting on an adventure that is not unlike the task captured on the tape I found in my closet. If you are a parent or guardian of a child with vision loss, let me first congratulate and thank you for taking the time to read this book. If you are reading these words, I want to assure you that, because you are making the commitment to learn about the educational opportunities for your child, the adventure you and your child are embarking on together, no matter how steep the up-hill climb might sometimes feel, will be a successful one. By dedicating time to discover how you can be an effective partner and advocate in the education of your child, you have already demonstrated that you have the basic ingredients for success. Be encouraged, and take heart also in the knowledge that you are not alone. As you make your way through this adventure, be aware that with persistence, some occasional pushiness, and a good measure of faith in your child and in your own efforts, good things will come. Hold out for the happy ending to this adventure, which is really the beginning of the rest of your child's life.

I call this journey you are taking an adventure for several reasons. Because your child has a disability like visual impairment, you will encounter people, personalities, bureaucracies, cool gadgets and technology that will amaze you, and philosophies about living with disability—in short, a whole world of experiences that most parents do not have the opportunity to see for themselves. You also have the chance of a lifetime to change that world, if only for one person, namely the child you care about. In order to do that, though, you need some knowledge of the tools and techniques for maneuvering in this sometimes strange world, and the law, and that's what this book is about.

Although the chapters you are about to read reflect some of the latest changes in the law, it will be helpful for you to know that, in many ways, there is no such simple thing as "the law." We have many federal statutes, pages and pages of federal and state regulatory requirements, technical assistance and policy guidance papers issued by the U. S. Department of Education and rulings by its Office of Civil Rights, and numerous instances of litigation. In addition to the Individuals with Disabilities Education Act (IDEA), which is mentioned in the chapters that follow, other laws that can provide your child with additional rights include Section 504 of the Rehabilitation Act and the Americans with Disabilities Act (ADA). This volume of information can be overwhelming, and applying it to your child's particular circumstances can take patience and persistence. This book is not meant to be a legal handbook—information on legislation and law is readily available from many sources. It is intended to introduce you to the topic of special education and the educational needs and rights of students who are visually impaired. In its pages, you can become acquainted with the concerns of families like yours and the vocabulary you need to begin to make your own translation.

The American Foundation for the Blind (AFB) can help you as you get oriented to this environment. One quick way to stay on top of developments in vision-related special education is to stop by our web site, www.afb.org, and see if we can point you in the direction of other resources that might answer your questions or spark solutions. There is, however, no substitute for learning from other parents and advocates for children with vision loss. The National Association for Parents of Children with Visual Impairments (NAPVI) can put you in touch with parents from around the country, with whom you can compare notes, share your frustrations, celebrate the large and the small successes along the way, and join hands and voices to both work and call for change to improve the world of special education for all children with disabilities. Now, that's an adventure worthy of your child's potential, no matter what your child's abilities may be. So, let's begin.

Mark Richert, Esq.
Director, Public Policy
American Foundation
For the Blind

Acknowledgments

With my heartfelt gratitude, I would like to recognize the numerous parents, professionals, agencies who specialize in the vision field, and schools for blind students who have contributed their expertise and experiences to this book written for parents:

Carl R. Augusto, President and CEO, and Maureen Matheson, Vice President of AFB Press and Information Services, of the American Foundation for the Blind (AFB), for demonstrating their belief in both the significant role parents have in their children's lives and in the importance of supporting parents and equipping them with knowledge through their commitment to the publication of this book—and their patience in waiting for its completion.

Natalie Hilzen, Director and Editor in Chief of AFB Press, with whom I have thoroughly enjoyed working in tandem, from the conception of the content outline of this book, throughout the entire process of creating it, and continuing through the tireless work involved, down to the final editorial details, in making this publication the most comprehensive guide to special education available specifically for parents of children with visual impairments.

AFB Press staff—specifically, Ellen Bilofsky, Sharon Baker-Harris, Jenese Croasdale, and Beatrice Jacinto—for all their contributions to the refinement, production, and promotion of the book, and Celia Hartmann, for her thoughtful editing.

Ana Maria Quintana, National Association for Parents of Children with Visual Impairments (NAPVI) Associate Staff, for supporting me at the NAPVI national office so that I could concentrate on working on the manuscript.

Steve Perreault, Hilton-Perkins Advisor to NAPVI, and the entire staff of the Hilton-Perkins National and International Programs for their belief in NAPVI and in parents. The partnership between NAPVI and the Hilton-Perkins National and International Programs has been invaluable. Steve has touched my life since my first involvement with NAPVI, when I was a young mother in need of support and connection with an association of other parents having similar experiences.

All the NAPVI Board members and parent leaders who have consistently given of themselves by offering support to new parents who are in need, and who have in addition been contributing authors and reviewers of this book: Kate Aldrich (CA); Jeannette Christie (NY); Patricia Cox (OK); Sheri Davis (FL); Mary Fuller (NH); Kris Kiley (VA); Judith Lesner (CA); Kevin E. O'Connor (IL); Alison Rickerl (TX); Susan Singler (AZ and TN); Julie Urban (AZ); and Mary Zabelski (IL).

Carol B. Allman, former Program Director of Exceptional Student Education at the Florida Department of Education, for reviewing the original manuscript and providing invaluable editorial contributions; and Kay Alicyn Ferrell, Professor at the School of Special Education and Executive Director of the National Center on Low-Incidence Disabilities (NCLID) at the University of Northern Colorado, for her consultative advice and review and for allowing us to include material from NCLID in this book.

Sue Rawley and Kate Aldrich, parents, for their valuable reviews and insightful comments.

Kathleen Boundy, Attorney and Director of the Center for Law and Education in Boston, Massachusetts, a tireless advocate for parents and children with disabilities who has the special education law written on her heart, for validating the information on the Individuals with Disabilities Education Act (IDEA) that we have included in the book.

Tom Miller, Supervisor of Educational Services, Perkins School for the Blind, for providing his expertise on IDEA as it relates to early intervention services.

Frank Simpson, Superintendent of the Lavelle School for the Blind, for his ideas, contributions, and early support of the book.

Amy R. McKenzie, Assistant Professor, Program in Visual Impairments, Florida State University at Tallahassee, for her expert compilation of a sample Individualized Education Program (IEP).

And all the contributing photographers, individuals, and organizations who provided photographs that reflect the intent of the book:

The Mak family of Brooklyn, New York, for giving us permission to publish their photograph on the cover of the book, and Judy Evans, AFB Communications staff, for coordinating the photo shoot; L. Penny Rosenblum, Assistant Professor in the Department of Special Education, Rehabilitation, and School Psychology at the University of Arizona in Tucson; Marianne Riggio, Educational Consultant, Hilton/Perkins Program, and Stephanie Sullivan, Administrative Assistant, Perkins School for the Blind; Antoine Johnson and Andrea Noel, Columbia Lighthouse for the Blind, Washington DC; Mary Zabelski, Chicago Lighthouse for People Who Are Blind or Visually Impaired; Kim Benisatto and The New York Institute for Special Education; HumanWare and Dominic Gagliano, Vice President of Blindness Sales; Erika Musser, parent; and Natalie Isaak Knott, orientation and mobility specialist and teacher of students with visual impairments.

About the Contributors

Susan LaVenture is Executive Director of the National Association for Parents of Children with Visual Impairments (NAPVI) in Boston, Massachusetts. A leader in the development of nonprofit parents' organizations and advocate on behalf of families of children who are visually impaired, she initially became involved in working with other parents almost 20 years ago when her youngest son was diagnosed with retinoblastoma, a rare form of infant eye cancer. She lectures at Harvard Medical School and is a presenter in this country and abroad on the significant role of parents in their child's development and education. Through NAPVI's partnership with the U. S. Department of Education Office of Special Education Programs, she has led a national effort to provide education training workshops to parents throughout the United States on the Individuals with Disabilities Education Act (IDEA).

Kate Aldrich is a nurse practitioner and former board member of the National Association for Parents of Children with Visual Impairments in Santa Rosa, California. She has presented at numerous conferences for parents of children with visual impairments and other disabilities and is the parent of a son with who is visually impaired and has multiple disabilities.

Carol B. Allman is a consultant and author in the area of special education and educational programming for students with visual impairments, focusing on accessible testing nationwide. Retired as Program Director of Exceptional Student Education at the Florida Department of Education, she has been a teacher and school administrator and is the coauthor of *Seeing Eye to Eye* as well as recipient of a Lifetime Achievement Award from the Florida Chapter of the Association for Education and Rehabilitation of the Blind and Visually Impaired (AER).

Sheri Davis is a teacher of students with visual impairments in Tampa, Florida, former Secretary of the National Association for Parents of Children with Visual Impairments, and currently President of Florida Families of Children with Visual Impairments. A speaker at numerous conferences for parents and families, she is the parent of a son who is visually impaired.

Jane N. Erin is Professor and Coordinator of Programs in Visual Impairment in the Department of Special Education, Rehabilitation, and School Psychology at the University of Arizona, Tucson. A nationally known researcher, author, and presenter, she is coeditor of *Diversity and Visual Impairments,* coauthor of *Visual Impairments and Learning,* and former editor-in-chief of the *Journal of Visual Impairment & Blindness.* The author of *When You Have a Visually Impaired Student with Multiple Disabilities in Your Classroom: A Guide for Teachers,* she is the recipient of the 1996 Mary K. Bauman Award for contributions to education in visual impairment from the Association for Education and Rehabilitation of the Blind and Visually Impaired (AER).

Mary E. Fuller is an advocate for children who are visually impaired and their families and Regional Representative of the National Association for Parents of Children with Visual Impairments in Concord, New Hampshire. A former high school chemistry teacher, she is the parent of a daughter who is visually impaired.

M. Beth Langley is Special Education Diagnostician in Pinellas County, Florida, who serves as a countywide developmental evaluation specialist for children and youths with significant disabilities, including visual impairment, for the Pinellas County Schools. The author of the *Individualized Systematic Assessment of Visual Efficiency (ISAVE)* materials published by the American Printing House for the Blind and of numerous other publications on the topics of assessment, multiple disabilities, and developmental issues, her background includes training in the areas of speech pathology, mental retardation, elementary education, and the assessment of students with dual sensory impairment and other multiple disabilities. She is the parent of Eric, an award-winning athlete who is blind from retinopathy of prematurity and has cerebral palsy, a seizure disorder, and severe cognitive challenges.

Tami Sue Levinson has worked as both a classroom and an itinerant teacher of students with visual impairments, including infants and preschoolers.

Donna McNear is a teacher of students with visual impairments and a certified orientation and mobility specialist at the Rum River Special Education Cooperative in Cambridge, Minnesota. A contributor to numerous publications including *When You Have A Visually Impaired Student in Your Classroom* and *Foundations of Education,* she is past President of the Division on Visual Impairments of the Council for Exceptional Children and the recipient of the Outstanding Service in Education award by the Minnesota Chapter of the Association for Education and Rehabilitation of the Blind and Visually Impaired (AER).

Kevin E. O'Connor is a leadership consultant, professional speaker, teacher, and author and is Senior Lecturer at Loyola University in Chicago and at Columbia College, Chicago's performing arts school. A former President of the National Association for Parents of Children with Visual Impairments, he is the recipient of the CSP designation as Certified Speaking Professional, a distinction held by fewer than 500 persons in the world for excellence in public speaking. The author of several books, including *Present Like a Pro: A Field Guide to Mastering the Art of Business, Professional, and Public Speaking*, and contributor to several publications on visual impairment, he is the parent of a son who is visually impaired and currently a student at George Washington University in Washington, DC.

Susan Singler is a registered nurse in Springfield, Tennessee, and past President of the Tennessee Association of Parents of the Visually Impaired. An author and advocate on behalf of families of children who are visually impaired, she is the parent of a son who is visually impaired with additional disabilities.

Karen E. Wolffe is Director of Professional Development and Career-Connect for the American Foundation for the Blind. A nationally known speaker and author on such topics as career education, transition, and employment for youngsters and adults who are visually impaired and an adjunct faculty member at the University of Arkansas at Little Rock, she is coeditor of *Teaching Social Skills to Students with Visual Impairments*, editor of *Skills for Success*, coauthor of *Navigating the Rapids of Life: The Transition Tote System* and *Transition Issues Related to Students with Visual Disabilities* and author of *Career Counseling for People with Disabilities*.

Mary Zabelski is Director of Educational Services at the Chicago Lighthouse for People Who Are Blind or Visually Impaired and has been working in this capacity for the past 20 years. A former special education and early childhood teacher, she is the parent of an adult daughter who is blind and President of the National Association for Parents of Children with Visual Impairments (NAPVI). The cofounder of the Illinois Association for Parents of Children with Visual Impairments (IPVI) in the 1980s, she continues to provide support to parents and families throughout the country as a parent, teacher, and advocate for specialized services for children with visual impairments and other disabilities.

CHAPTER 1

Special Education Services: What Parents Need to Know

Susan LaVenture with Carol B. Allman

When a child is born with a visual impairment, or acquires one through illness or injury, his or her parents may feel shocked, bewildered, and frightened. All of us, including the parents of children who are visually impaired, sometimes find ourselves dealing with a situation that we didn't expect and for which we feel unprepared.

For most people, visual impairment is an abstract concept—most people don't have a visual impairment and don't know someone who does. Visual impairment is in fact what is known as a low-incidence disability. That is, the number of visually impaired people in this country, and in the world at large, is relatively small in relation to the size of the population as a whole. Although estimates vary, approximately 100,000 students are receiving special education services related to their visual impairment in this country.[1] For this reason, parents of children who are visually impaired may need to learn what visual impairment is and what it may mean for their children and their education. They may often find that immediate family members, local doctors, and their own neighborhood schools are unfamiliar with the implications of visual impairment for a child's learning and education, and may not understand what the family may be experiencing emotionally or know how to help them.

However, parents of visually impaired children are not alone. A number of national organizations in this country are dedicated to the well-being of visually impaired children and adults, and they are important sources of a wide variety of information and support for them and their families. (The Resources section at the back of this book provides an extensive listing of these organizations.) Other sources of help and

FINDING CONNECTIONS WITH OTHER FAMILIES

My son was my third born, a happy 10.6-pound baby boy, a picture of health. Alex had a great temperament, ate well, slept well, and went to all his pediatrician visits without any problem.

At home, my husband and I started noticing an unusual glare that reflected from his eyes when he looked at us. At first we didn't think much about it because Alex seemed so healthy and active. As the glare from his eyes shining back at us seemed to appear more frequently, I made an appointment with our pediatrician, who referred us to an ophthalmologist. At that visit, we didn't expect what we were about to learn about our son. The ophthalmologist was very concerned and said he was sad to tell us that he believed Alex had an extremely rare childhood malignant eye cancer called retinoblastoma, which appeared in 1 in 20,000 births. The reflection we were seeing was from a tumor that had grown behind Alex's retina. Alex was blind in his right eye and would need to have immediate surgery and treatment to save his life. Within days, my 10-month-old son had his right eye removed, and we were told he would need to undergo medical treatment for the next five years to save his remaining vision and his life as well. We were devastated.

We felt guilty—was there a way we could have prevented this from happening? We were angry—why hadn't this been detected earlier during Alex's routine medical visits? We felt very alone and isolated. We had never heard of this rare medical condition called retinoblastoma and didn't know anything about it. At that time, it was difficult to find information on the disease. As parents, we felt a strong need to connect with other families who had had a similar experience and could understand what we felt and what we were going through. We asked if there was a retinoblastoma association to communicate with other families that had experienced this. But we were told that there was no such thing—retinoblastoma was too rare, and it was too difficult to organize such a small number of families. As a mother, I wanted to know how my son's visual impairment would affect him. What did I need to know as a parent? My quest began to search for the information, the resources, the experts, and other families.

Susan LaVenture
Mother of a 20-year-old son with retinoblastoma
Executive Director, National Association for
Parents of Children with Visual Impairments
Watertown, Massachusetts

information include specialized schools for students who are blind or visually impaired and their experienced staff; special education professionals in state education departments and local school districts; and state vision consultants, who are involved in coordinating the efforts of teachers who specialize in working with visually impaired children.

Parents can also find support and assistance at parent information centers, which provide parents of children with disabilities with training about this country's special education law and about parents' role in the special education process. Located in most states, these centers are federally funded and serve families statewide. The information they provide concerning special education law is approved by the U.S. Office of Special Education Programs (OSEP) in Washington, D.C. In addition, most parent centers are sources of help from parent advocates, who can accompany parents to important meetings such as Individualized Education Program (IEP) team meetings, which are described in Chapter 4. Contact information for reaching these centers through the PACER Center, which houses the National Technical Assistance Center for State Parent Centers throughout the country, is also provided in the Resources section of this book. (Sources of help and information are highlighted in this chapter in "Help at a Glance.") Another source of assistance, Pilot Parents groups, can be found in many states throughout the country. Pilot Parents are groups of parents of children with special needs who help other parents by providing them with support, information, and referrals to community services and special programs. These groups can be located via the Internet or, in many cases, through the state department of education's web site area for parents.

Sometimes it can seem as though the only people who understand what we're going through are people who have been there too. The validity of this feeling shouldn't be overlooked. Other parents of visually impaired children, either individually or in organized groups, can offer informed advice, excellent information, and ongoing support for parents. The National Association for Parents of Children with Visual Impairments (NAPVI), also listed in the Resources section, can assist you with networking with other families through its national database of parents and parent support groups.

Because of the impact that a visual impairment can have on a child's overall growth and development, and on the family as a whole, it can be useful and sustaining for you as a parent to become connected with parent support networks and early intervention services early in your child's life. Knowing that resources are available to you can be reassuring as well as strengthening and can help keep you from feeling alone. There are many ways in which you as a parent can learn about how your child's visual impairment affects his or her development and education. This chapter provides an introduction to some of the basic principles parents will

Help at a Glance

If you need additional information or support, one place to begin is the office of the director of special education for your school district. In addition, most states have the following agencies, which are primary sources of information:

■ your state's special school for students who are visually impaired (there is more information about these schools in Chapter 7)

■ the state department of education, and in particular the consultant from this state department who specializes in the education of students who are visually impaired, often referred to as "the state vision consultant"

■ the state commission for persons who are visually impaired, or a unit focusing on people who are visually impaired within the state department of rehabilitation or vocational rehabilitation, departments that focus on education, training, employment, and rehabilitation issues for visually impaired individuals

To get specific contact information for your state, you can contact the American Foundation for the Blind (AFB) through its help-line number, (800) 232-5463, in the United States, or consult the *AFB Directory of Services for Blind and Visually Impaired Persons in the United States and Canada,* available in print in many libraries and on AFB's web site at www.afb.org under the "Where Can I Find?" service finder.

In addition, a national network of parent information, support, and assistance centers and groups are available to help. The organizations described in this chapter and in the Resources section of this book offer a wide range of services and assistance. One place to start is the Pacer Center at (888) 248-0822 (or, in Minnesota, [952] 838-9000) or www.pacer.org.

Adapted from S. J. Spungin, Ed., *When You Have a Visually Impaired Student in Your Classroom: A Guide for Teachers* (New York: AFB Press, 2002), p. 6.

want to know about the education of their child with a visual impairment that are established in the special education law of the United States. Later chapters in this book explain in more detail how these principles relate to the education of students who are visually impaired.

VISUAL IMPAIRMENT: WHAT DOES IT MEAN?

Effects of Visual Impairment

A parent whose child has a visual impairment may wonder what effect vision loss will have on his or her child. No one answer to that question applies to all children. Your child's specific visual condition, the presence of

From a Parent's Perspective

STOP AND TAKE A BREATH

Teachers and doctors are experts in their respective fields. You are the expert in knowing your child. Look to teachers and doctors to add their knowledge to yours. Early intervention is helpful and necessary for both the parents and the child.

If you are like most parents when faced with your child being diagnosed as blind or visually impaired, and then perhaps subsequently with developmental disabilities, you may become overwhelmed. I believe it is important at this time of your adjustment *to stop and take a breath.*

Stop and just enjoy your child for a period of time: maybe an hour, maybe a week, or maybe a month. If possible, take a break from all the appointments and get to know your child again. Get on a schedule. Get up at the same time every day, feed your baby at the same times every day, bathe your baby at the same time every day. Setting routines allows your baby to understand how the day works; he or she learns to predict and look forward to certain times of the day, to feel comfortable, and begins to know "what comes next." Routine and structure are important to children who are blind or visually impaired. Routine and structure provide security and offer a sense of control. But routine and structure do not mean rigid. It's okay to break away, too.

Susan Singler
Mother of a 24-year-old son with retinopathy
of prematurity and additional disabilities
Nashville, Tennessee

any additional disabilities, his or her personality and temperament, and many other factors will all influence how he or she reacts to a particular visual impairment. Children who are visually impaired are as unique and as varied as any other group of children. Furthermore, no two people who experience vision loss see in the same way. There is a tremendous range in the way people see, even if they have the same visual diagnosis. In addition, because of elements including fatigue, lighting in the environment, and how a person may feel at any given moment, the same person's vision can actually vary at different times during the same day.

Important Educational Principles

Despite this variability, however, one overall statement does apply to most children who are visually impaired: A child with a visual impairment will typically learn about the world in a different way from a child without a visual impairment. Depending on his or her individual circumstances, a visually impaired child may not be able to rely on his or her sight to obtain information, and therefore may need to use senses other than vision for receiving information.

A child with limited vision will usually need particular kinds of attention from infancy in order to acquire and hone skills that sighted children acquire as a matter of course by watching people and objects around them and imitating what they see. Children who are visually impaired typically need to have clear explanations provided for them, sometimes repeatedly. Direct experiences need to be set up for them consciously and with thoughtfulness, so that they have a chance to learn about what other children learn spontaneously through vision in their daily lives. For example, your visually impaired child may need to be able to pet the neighbor's dog from head to tail and to spend time touching the dog's entire body in order to understand the animal referred to in a story as "a dog" and to determine what a dog really is. He or she may need to help stir the batter for a batch of cookies, help put them in the oven, and be told that the good smell coming from the kitchen is the cookies baking—and then taste the cookies—in order to make the connections between the process of baking and the food he or she eats. Limitations on the ability to receive information from the world around us can have far-reaching effects on your child's ability to understand concepts, learn language, move about freely with confidence, and develop and grow in a variety of ways. For this reason, the families and teachers of children with visual impairments use alternative methods and strategies for teaching them to read, write, interact socially, and perform various daily activities. The effect of visual impairment on children and the way in which they may experience the world as a result is described in "What's Different About the Way Children Who Are Visually Impaired Learn?"

What's Different about the Way Children Who Are Visually Impaired Learn?

Blindness and visual impairment affect *how a* child learns, not *what a* child learns. One of the most important things to remember about your child who is blind or visually impaired is that he or she can learn almost anything that anyone else learns—but he or she has to learn it in a different way.

Think about the way children who are blind or visually impaired experience the world. Because their vision is limited, they rely on other sensory information. If you are sighted, you might walk into a room and look around, scanning it visually to determine how big the room is, where the furniture and food table are, and who is there. A person who is blind or visually impaired will need to listen to voices and other sounds to get an idea of the size of the room. He or she will need to explore the room physically to know where the furniture is, perhaps smell the food to tell where it is located, and rely on everyone present to identify themselves. What occurred for you almost instantaneously and automatically takes longer, and requires input from others, for the person who is blind or visually impaired.

Something else happened, too. When you walked into that room, you had an immediate, complete picture of what was going on. Once you had that overview, you could pay more attention to the individual parts: who was with whom, what different kinds of food were being served, and which chairs were empty. For the person who is blind or visually impaired, the opposite occurs. He or she receives information in bits and pieces, from several sources (touch, smell, hearing, and so forth), and somehow has to put that information together into a whole. The process is not easy; it's something like putting together a jigsaw puzzle without knowing what it's supposed to look like.

Children who are blind or visually impaired learn differently from sighted children for no other reason than the fact that in most cases they cannot rely on their vision to provide information. The information they obtain through their other senses is *inconsistent* (things do not always make noise or produce an odor), *fragmented* (comes in bits and pieces), and *passive* (not under the child's control). It takes practice, training, and time to sort all this out.

Parents and professionals who work with your child need to understand the following principles.

(continued on next page)

MAKE NO ASSUMPTIONS

You cannot assume that children who are blind or visually impaired have learned something simply because they have been exposed to it. Most sighted children learn incidentally, without specific instruction, because they have watched someone else do something, or because they associate what they have seen with what they have heard. Children who are blind or visually impaired do not have this advantage and often must be specifically taught what other children learn incidentally. For blind or visually impaired children, learning cannot be left to chance.

REMEMBER THAT LEARNING PROCEEDS FROM PARTS TO WHOLES

Sighted people learn by looking at the whole picture before examining the parts. People who are blind or visually impaired learn the other way around. They are forced to rely on many discrete pieces of information and are limited by what can be touched, felt, or heard at any point in time. Think of a cow. The child who is blind or visually impaired can easily understand that a cow, like other animals, has four legs, a tail, two ears, two eyes, and a mouth. But how do you explain an udder, or how a cow chews cud, without allowing the child to touch and examine the cow? It is difficult to get close enough to a cow to permit such exploration, but even if you do, the child's experience is limited to what the hands can feel; depending on the size of the hands, you can only feel so much at once. Somehow, all of these little pieces of information have to fit together to form the concept of "cow." With this concept in place, the child can move on to other concepts, such as cud-chewing mammals, the origin of milk, and the food chain.

This example makes it clear why children who are blind or visually impaired often seem to have inadequate or inappropriate concepts. Their instruction needs to be systematic, clear-cut, and concrete; if it is not, they will not be prepared for higher levels of learning.

USE CONCRETE OBJECTS

Blindness or low vision limits the opportunities to develop symbolization, which is the process by which one thing stands for another. The acronym "NAPVI" stands for "National Association for Parents of the Visually Impaired" [now the National Association for Parents of Children with Visual Impairments], but it also stands for the larger concept of a group of families working together on behalf of children who are blind or visually impaired. This is abstract thinking, but it is at the heart of all learning and begins very early in life. The sighted child can see that one object (a stuffed cat, for example) stands for another object (a living, breathing, animal). But from the point of view of the blind or visually impaired child, the two items share very few characteristics. The confusion that results when symbols are introduced too quickly is not worth the relearning that has to occur later. Of course, it is not always possible to use real objects rather than representations of objects. But it is important to understand that the process cannot be taken for granted.

ADOPT THE CHILD'S POINT OF VIEW

Because sighted people rely on their vision so much and so naturally, they are often not even aware of other simultaneously available sensory information. If you are sighted, when you go to the shopping mall, for example, you are aware of a multitude of visual cues that help to keep you oriented and find your way around. The child who is blind or visually impaired experiences something entirely different, usually in the form of a multitude of auditory and olfactory cues. You *see* the bakery; your child *smells* it. You *see* the video arcade; your child *hears* it. You *see* the department store; your child *smells* the perfume counter. You *see* the pet store: your child *hears* and *smells* it. Every store has a characteristic odor or sound that can be utilized to help the child who is blind or visually impaired understand more about the design and layout of the mall—that is, if you interpret these sensory stimuli for your child and help him or her make some sense out of all the simultaneous information. But *you* have to be aware of them first.

The same principle applies to any learning task. Teachers are primarily trained to use visual methods of instruction and often do not realize the importance of using a multisensory approach with children who are blind or visually impaired. It requires a different way of thinking about a lesson: thinking about it from the child's point of view. Relating the lesson to the child's own experience can make the difference between rote memorization and true understanding.

In a lesson about weather, for example, a teacher who is trying to make the lesson more concrete for a student who is blind or visually impaired might be tempted to use cotton to represent clouds. But, this is really *a visual* representation, based on the sighted person's experience. The concept of clouds that the child who is blind or visually impaired would acquire from handling cotton halls would not be accurate. On the other

(continued on next page)

hand, if the teacher tried to explain clouds by comparing them to what fog feels like, the child who is blind or visually impaired would have a more accurate concept of the composition of clouds. Granted, this is not easy. It requires planning and divergent thinking, but it can make all the difference in the world to the student who is blind or visually impaired.

ADDRESS CHILDREN BY NAME

It is difficult for a child who is blind or visually impaired to know if he or she is the person being addressed and is therefore expected to respond, or if someone else is. While other children can use eye contact to get this information, children who are blind or visually impaired cannot. Use your voice to provide clues, set limits, and establish expectations.

ALLOW TIME

It often takes longer for children who are blind or visually impaired to do everyday tasks. It is important that they be given the time to accomplish things on their own.

USE THE BODY AS A REFERENCE POINT

Children who are blind or visually impaired will know their own bodies better than the rest of their environment. It helps to use body parts as a reference point for other activities. Instead of pointing to a location, or guiding the child to it, you can say, "The coffee mugs are on the shelf to your right, about shoulder level."

CAPITALIZE ON PAST EXPERIENCES

If possible, try to remind the child who is blind or visually impaired about a previous action when telling him or her about something new. For example, "The trash can is over by the door where you came in, to the right." Or, "To make this computer game work, you use the mouse the same way you do with the word processor."

MAKE DOERS, NOT DONE-TO-ERS

Because children who are blind or visually impaired must process so much information, it is often tempting (and sometimes quicker) to assist them by doing things for them—whether it's tying a shoe, buying lunch, or typing a term paper. It is equally tempting for the child to allow this to be done. But it is also risky, since it can sometimes lead to dependency and, in turn, a low self-concept.

Children who are blind or visually impaired are children, first, with the same demands, desires, dreams, and delights that all children have. But there is no doubt that they require a different style of education—one that creates opportunities to learn, rather than waiting for the opportunities to create themselves.

Kay Alicyn Ferrell, Ph.D.,
Division of Special Education
University of Northern Colorado

Reprinted with permission from K. A. Ferrell, "What Is It That Is Different about a Child with Blindness or Visual Impairment?" in P. Crane, D. Cuthbertson, K. A. Ferrell, & H. Scherb, Eds., Equals in Partnership: Basic Rights for Families of Children with Blindness or Visual Impairment (Watertown, MA: Hilton/Perkins Program of Perkins School for the Blind and the National Association for Parents of the Visually Impaired, 1997), pp. v–vii. ©1997. All rights reserved.

EDUCATION FOR STUDENTS WITH VISUAL IMPAIRMENTS

When the effects of a visual impairment interfere with his or her learning, a child is eligible for special education services in this country. As explained later in this chapter, children are entitled to a variety of educational services under the federal law known as the Individuals with Disabilities Education Act (IDEA), and these services will be described throughout this book. However, in order for you as a parent to know whether your child is receiving the services that he or she needs, it is important for you to understand the nature of your child's visual impairment and how it affects him or her. You will also find it useful to know what the educational needs of visually impaired children in general may be.

Early Intervention

Infants begin developing their knowledge of the world around them almost immediately. They begin forming impressions and concepts of people and objects based on their experiences and interactions, and these concepts in turn help them begin to acquire language as a way of referring to the world at large. When a child is unable to gather information through his or her sense of sight, it is essential to help the child obtain that information in other ways. It is also essential for this learning to take place as early in the child's life as possible, so that he or she can begin to develop ideas, concepts, and knowledge and the ability to move and explore the surrounding environment just as other children with unimpaired vision do. Early intervention is the term used to de-scribe professional assistance whose purpose is to help your child and your family learn these other ways as soon as possible. Because early intervention can be of crucial importance to a child's growth and devel-opment, you as the parent of an infant or young child may want to seek out early intervention services as soon as you learn that your child is visually impaired. Under IDEA, a process referred to as "child find" is undertaken by the states, in which children with disabilities and who are in need of special education and related services are identi-fied to determine if they are currently receiving needed services. Infants and toddlers with disabilities, from birth until their third birthday, and their families, receive early intervention services under IDEA Part C. Chapter 2 of this book provides more detailed information on early in-tervention.

Expanded Core Curriculum

Visually impaired children need to learn the same things in school that sighted children do. From how to tell time to how to do long division, they need to study what is called the core curriculum: the general edu-cation curriculum that all students are expected to master, including language arts, science, mathematics, and social studies. However, in or-der for them to be able to study these and other subjects, and to learn how to live and work independently, children who are visually impaired usually need to learn an additional set of skills. These skills have been identified and described by educators specializing in work with visually impaired children, but they are not mentioned specifically in IDEA. They are known as the expanded core curriculum, because they form an addi-tional set of studies for visually impaired children; they are also some-times called disability-specific skills because they are the skills needed by a child as a result of being visually impaired. (These skill areas are listed in "The Expanded Core Curriculum.") They include such activities as knowing how to read and write without the use of printed materials, for example, by learning braille; learning how to move about in the en-vironment safely and independently, which is known as orientation and mobility (O&M); knowing how to use technology devices such as spe-cialized computer equipment designed for individuals with visual im-pairments; and learning ways in which to use what vision they have effectively and efficiently.

The classroom teacher is responsible for teaching your child the gen-eral education core curriculum. However, because the expanded core cur-riculum is a specific body of knowledge and skills that covers the unique, specialized needs of visually impaired students, the subjects included within it need to be taught by a teacher who specializes in working with

The Expanded Core Curriculum

The following areas constitute the expanded core curriculum: the subjects and skills that students who are visually impaired need to learn in school because of their disability in order to be able to study the rest of the educational curriculum along with their sighted classmates.

- Compensatory academics—critical skills that students need to be successful in school, such as concept development, organizational skills, speaking and listening, and communication skills.

- Orientation and mobility—skills to orient the child to his or her surroundings and travel skills to allow him or her to move independently and safely in the environment, such as human guide techniques; use of standard and adaptive canes; recognition of cues and landmarks; movement through space by walking, creeping, or moving a wheelchair; and directing others or requesting assistance.

- Social interaction—skills needed to access social situations appropriately and prevent social isolation of students with visual impairments, such as shaking hands or turning toward others when speaking or being spoken to; using language to make a request, decline assistance, or communicate a need; expressing emotion and affection appropriately; and adjusting social responses according to the expressions of others.

- Independent living—skills needed to function in school and at home as independently as possible, such as personal grooming, time management, cooking, cleaning, clothing care, and money management.

- Recreation and leisure—skills to ensure students' enjoyment of physical and leisure-time activities, including making choices about how to spend leisure time; actively participating in physical and social recreational activities; trying new leisure activities; following rules in games and activities at an appropriate level; and maintaining safety during leisure activities.

- Visual efficiency—these skills include skills needed to use low vision devices, magnifiers and other optical and nonoptical aids that help people make maximum use of their vision; environmental cues; and recognizing when to use other nonvisual senses.

(continued on next page)

■ Use of technology—skills to use devices such as computers or electronic equipment that will make school, home, and work easier places in which to live and function.

■ Career education—special skills that focus on the student moving toward working as an adult, including exploring and expressing preferences about work roles; assuming work responsibilities at home and school; understanding concepts of reward for work; participating in job experiences; and learning about jobs and adult work roles at a developmentally appropriate level.

■ Self-determination—skills to be used in advocating for one's own needs and desires.

students with visual impairments. This teacher is a pivotal member of the educational team that works with your child.

THE EDUCATIONAL TEAM

The concept of the team is central in the education of students with disabilities. Parents are critical members of this team. Students who are visually impaired and other students with disabilities have a wide range of unique and specialized needs that a regular classroom teacher does not have the expertise to address. No one person can have all the necessary skills and specialized knowledge to meet all of a child's special needs. For this reason, a variety of professionals typically work with children who are visually impaired to deliver educational services. They may include

- a regular classroom teacher
- a teacher of students with visual impairments
- an orientation and mobility instructor
- a psychologist
- an occupational therapist
- a physical therapist
- a speech and language therapist
- a paraeducator
- an audiologist
- an ophthalmologist
- an optometrist

Roles and Responsibilities of Professionals Who Work with Visually Impaired Students in the Schools

Many school personnel and other professionals may have occasion to work in school with students who are visually impaired, depending on the students' needs. However, certain professionals have primary responsibility for doing so: the student's general education teacher or teachers; the teacher of students who are visually impaired; and an orientation and mobility (O&M) instructor, if the student's Individualized Education Program (IEP) calls for instruction in this area. In addition, a paraeducator may also work closely with the student.

The roles and general responsibilities of each of these professionals are outlined here

GENERAL EDUCATION TEACHER

- Teaches academic and social curricula for all students in the class, including the student who is visually impaired, and is responsible for grades and discipline for all students.

- Provides textbooks and instructional materials to the teacher of visually impaired students in a timely manner so that the material can be prepared in alternate formats needed by the student, such as in braille, large print, or an audio or electronic format.

- Communicates regularly and schedules time to meet with the teacher of visually impaired students to discuss the student's progress and plans for meeting his or her future educational and social needs.

- Creates a classroom climate that is comfortable for all students, including the student who is visually impaired.

- Serves on the team that prepares and monitors the student's IEP, as explained in Chapter 4.

TEACHER OF VISUALLY IMPAIRED STUDENTS

- Teaches disability-specific skills and other aspects of the expanded core curriculum, such as reading and writing in alternate media like braille or large print; the use of magnifiers and other optical devices; speech access software for the computer; and independent living skills.

(continued on next page)

- Conducts various assessments of students who are visually impaired to determine their abilities and needs, including how they use any existing vision (a functional vision evaluation or assessment) and what method of reading and writing would work best for them (a learning media assessment).

- Serves on the team that prepares and monitors the student's IEP.

- Prepares or obtains textbooks, instructional materials, and examinations in the appropriate accessible format (such as braille, large-print, audio, or electronic format) for use by students who are visually impaired at the same time as their classmates.

- Analyzes the classroom and other environments for access and safety related to a student's visual impairment or blindness, and communicates how best to organize the classroom and materials to others on the educational team (this sometimes overlaps with the responsibilities of the O&M instructor).

- Schedules time to meet with the general education teacher, family members, and other members of the educational team to discuss the student's progress and provide strategies for making the instructional environment accessible, including appropriate accommodations and adaptations for the student.

- Provides suggestions and strategies to the general education teacher, family members, and other school personnel to include the student who is visually impaired to the greatest extent possible in all school, classroom, and extracurricular activities.

- Works with family members in various ways, such as helping them understand the development of students with visual impairments; assisting them to learn skills they need to teach their child; and helping them obtain appropriate recreational and rehabilitation services, such as camp activities and pre-employment experiences.

- Makes referrals for additional services, when necessary, such as for O&M instruction or clinical low vision services.

- Provides in-service training for teachers, paraeducators, and other school personnel on effective instructional strategies for teaching students with visual impairments.

O&M INSTRUCTOR

- Orients students who are visually impaired to the school environment.

- Teaches indoor and outdoor orientation and skills for safe and independent travel in the community.

- Consults with the general education teacher, the teacher of students who are visually impaired, school personnel, and family members to provide suggestions and strategies for reinforcing safe and independent travel skills.

- Teaches concepts about the body, space and direction, movement, and the physical environment.

- When appropriate, teaches students to use the long cane, optical devices, and/or their vision and other senses to move about the community independently, including crossing streets and traveling on public transportation.

- Provides in-service training to teachers, paraeducators, and other school personnel in orientation, the sighted guide technique, and other travel skills required by students who are visually impaired.

- Serves on the team that prepares and monitors the student's IEP.

PARAEDUCATOR

Some local educational agencies assign paraeducators (who are also called teachers' aides, paraprofessionals, school aides, or teaching assistants) to certain classrooms as part of particular programs. In some cases, paraeducators are assigned to classrooms in which there are students with disabilities to assist the general education teacher; in other cases, they are assigned to work with individual students who are visually impaired. In either situation, the paraeducator, with guidance from the teacher of visually impaired students, often has the duties described here:

- Under the supervision of the general education teacher and with direction from the teacher of students with visual impairments and the O&M instructor, supports and reinforces classroom instruction.

- Prepares or arranges to obtain modified instructional materials and textbooks in braille, large print, or electronic or audio format.

(continued on next page)

■ Helps students who are visually impaired practice skills that have been taught by the teacher of students with visual impairments and the O&M instructor.

■ Works with a student who is visually impaired, following the instructions of the general education teacher and sometimes the teacher of students who are visually impaired or the O&M instructor, and encourages the student to complete assignments or tasks independently.

■ Balances the need to maintain proximity to the student who is visually impaired for safety reasons with the need to maintain an appropriate distance to give the student the opportunity to interact socially with other students and adults and to develop independence and self-advocacy skills.

■ Serves on the team that prepares and monitors the student's IEP.

When working with students who are visually impaired, it is important for paraeducators to resist providing too much assistance or supervision because doing so can interfere with the student's ability to develop independent skills.

Adapted from S. J. Spungin, Ed., *When You Have a Visually Impaired Student in Your Classroom: A Guide for Teachers* (New York: AFB Press, 2002), pp. 12–15; and J. N. Erin, *When You Have a Visually Impaired Student with Multiple Disabilities in Your Classroom: A Guide for Teachers* (New York: AFB Press, 2004), pp. 14–16.

• a special education teacher who has specialized in a particular area of disability
• an adaptive physical education teacher.

The roles and functions of these different professionals are described in "Roles and Responsibilities of Professionals Who Work with Visually Impaired Students in the Schools."

When it comes to instruction in the classroom, the staff who will work most often and intensely with your child may be the regular classroom teacher; the teacher of students with visual impairments (you may hear this teacher sometimes referred to as "the vision teacher"), who is certified in the education of visually impaired students; and a paraeducator. The regular classroom teacher is the person who teaches academic subjects to all students in his or her class. He or she will work together with the teacher of students with visual impairments, who teaches the student

ASSERTIVE ADVOCACY, EFFECTIVE COMMUNICATION, ADVANCE PLANNING

Our journey to and through school with our son Corbb began with a "birth to 3" program. Looking back, I can't remember a time when we were not in "school" in some form. Early intervention was what we were told was important, and we did what we were told, especially in those early years when we knew very little.

We met teachers who were specialists in a world in which we were new and felt like aliens. They did things other teachers never did. They listened, they worked one on one, and they even gave us their home phone numbers. They were wise enough to know that they were not only teachers of children who were visually impaired; they were also teachers of the parents of children who were visually impaired.

These earliest teachers taught us the importance of three things: assertive advocacy, effective communication, and advance planning. Regardless of the schools to which our son went over the next 18 years, we honed these skills at every turn.

To be assertive in our advocacy meant that we should consider taking a proactive approach to what was recommended and what we wanted. We kept a three-ring binder with notes, doctors' letters, and school information. We worked cooperatively with the teachers and administrators in a variety of ways. We kept the lines of communication open. We asked questions of the people whose specialty would most likely give us the answer. We never sat next to each other at IEP meetings so as to better see what was going on and allow us to sit closer to the teachers. We brought our son to every meeting, and we brought food there as well! We debriefed with the teachers and ourselves after every meeting, and we networked with other parents. When it came time for our son to use a dog guide, Corbb worked with the principal and arranged to have a spot at the faculty in-service training session so they would be fully trained not to touch the dog, but still treat Corbb as a normal student. Each advocacy step included Corbb as much as possible, not because we were so smart, but because the teachers told us to do so. And, in doing so, we were allowing Corbb to learn to advocate for himself.

One day, during a challenging IEP meeting, when our son was quite young, the school district's representative came to the meeting. Our

(continued on next page)

hunch was that the district was going to curtail some services. This was also at a time when laptop computers were just coming into widespread use. Corbb was about 5 years old at the time. We sat down for the meeting, the district representative opened her laptop, and we were ready for a disagreement. Then Corbb went over to her and asked to see the computer. She let him climb up in her lap and the two of them had a great time while our teachers outlined what they and we wanted. In response, she said "Sure, whatever!"

That day I understood that feelings could play an important role even during a federally mandated meeting. Ever since, we have allowed the discussion of feelings or reminded professionals of the feelings. When a physician is busy and rushed and perhaps a bit brusque, I know that I can say, "Doctor, I really need your help and understanding for just one more moment. We have waited a long time to see you and I know you are busy. I also want you to know that we trust you. Can you spare us just a moment more?" We also as parents processed each meeting with some version of, "How was that for you?" It seems simple, but it worked to help us process the data and the feelings, the hope and the grief, the victories, the speed bumps, and the roadblocks.

Advance planning was a godsend for us. We didn't know we were supposed to plan any more than six months or a year ahead until the teachers did. In sixth grade we were already beginning to talk about high school. In seventh we were planning for a nondriving version of drivers' education, even though Corbb could never drive. The team believed that his participating would accomplish three important things: social networking, learning how to be a better passenger, and allowing him to come on his own to an understanding of why he should not drive. His use of braille was evaluated regularly, as were technical aids. Each step looked ahead to the next few steps, always with the thought of Corbb taking over these decisions as appropriate.

We did all of these three things when we chose schools, right up to the university Corbb chose. We also allowed him to teach himself and to do these things for himself. We allowed him to work out his misunderstandings with teachers when he wanted to do it alone, and we intervened, always with his permission, when needed.

Despite the differences that blindness has made in our lives and in our schools, we found that the more we followed Helen Keller's advice, the better it worked: "A person who is severely impaired never knows his hidden sources of strength until he is treated like a normal human being and encouraged to shape his own life."

Kevin E. O'Connor
Father of an 18-year-old son with Leber's congenital amaurosis
Long Grove, Illinois

who is visually impaired the subjects and skills of the expanded core curriculum. In addition, this teacher serves as a consultant to the regular classroom teacher and to other members of the educational team and school staff. He or she helps the visually impaired student understand the visual concepts involved in lessons and adapts materials for the student so that they are provided in a form other than a visual one or in a form the student can use. This allows a visually impaired student to participate along with the rest of the class. The role of the paraeducator and the activities he or she performs can vary from school district to school district or even from school to school and are also a topic of continuing debate among educators. If a paraeducator is assigned to the classroom, this person works under the supervision of the regular classroom teacher and the teacher of visually impaired students. He or she acts as an assistant who may help the visually impaired student with items such as obtaining adapted materials, such as a large-print worksheet, for a lesson. The paraeducator may be assigned to help other students in the class as well.

In addition to providing instruction, members of a student's educational team also serve on the IEP team that plans his or her educational program and the services the student receives. They are responsible for assessing the student's strengths and needs, setting educational goals on the basis of these assessments, and providing the services that will help the student meet these goals. Chapters 3, 4, and 5 describe many of the activities undertaken by the student's educational team and, in particular, the members of the IEP team.

The primary roles played by central members of the team are outlined in "Roles and Responsibilities of Professionals Who Work with Visually Impaired Students in the Schools," and additional information on the professionals who may be working with many students with visual impairments is provided in Chapter 8. However, under IDEA, the student and his or her family are also vital members of a student's IEP team, and it is essential for parents to understand the crucial role they play in the education of their visually impaired child. In addition to acting as their child's first and best teachers, as all parents do, the parents of children who are visually impaired have the right to provide information on their children's needs to other members of the IEP team, to request necessary services, to help create the educational goals and programs for their children, and to advocate on their behalf. They are powerful and vital players under the special education law in this country.

IDEA: THE LAW

Provisions for specialized instruction, educational services, and accommodations for students with visual impairments are mandated—that is, legally required—by special education law in the United States. The Individuals with Disabilities Education Act (IDEA), the federal law that ensures the provision of special education, was initially enacted in 1975 under the name of the Education for All Handicapped Children Act. Since that time it has undergone periodic revisions (known as reauthorizations). Parents need to be aware of the critical importance of becoming familiar with the law, with the fact that it undergoes review and possible change every several years, and with any changes enacted during its periodic reauthorizations. (It is also important for them to know about other legislation such as Section 504 of the Rehabilitation Act and the Americans with Disabilities Act [ADA], which also protect certain rights.)

Parents of children with disabilities, individuals with disabilities, and national organizations who serve people with disabilities were the driving forces behind the development of concepts and language in this law. These national organizations and resources can provide the families of children who are visually impaired with updated information about IDEA. (The Resources section at the back of this book lists numerous organizations, publications, and web sites that are key sources of information for families.)

It is essential that families understand the role that IDEA has in determining the services that their children are entitled to and will ultimately receive in the classroom. Becoming familiar with the law is a key way in which to understand what special education services a child is entitled to and what to ask for to ensure that he or she receives them. Although IDEA has many provisions (the full wording of the law can be found at www.ed.gov or http://idea.ed.gov), six basic principles are embodied in the law, which are explained in more detail here:

1. free and appropriate public education
2. comprehensive evaluation

3. individualized education program

4. education in the least restrictive environment

5. participation of parents and students in making decisions

6. procedural safeguards.

Free and Appropriate Public Education

In general, IDEA protects the inclusion of students with disabilities in public education. Before IDEA, no federal law protected children's right to a free and appropriate public education (often abbreviated as FAPE) in local public schools. Before the law was enacted, many children with disabilities were excluded from schools, and many more were denied adequate and appropriate opportunities to learn. This legislation has done much to help children with disabilities to be integrated into society and to participate in school and working life in a way that was unknown many decades ago. Today there are a variety of possible school programs for children who are visually impaired: in regular classrooms with the support of a teacher of visually impaired students; in neighborhood schools with specialized rooms and instruction for children with disabilities; and in special state schools for visually impaired students (these are explained in Chapter 7). In addition to guaranteeing children with disabilities the right to a free, appropriate public education, IDEA requires that specialized vision-related services by qualified professionals and the modifications and accommodations needed by students to learn and participate actively in school are identified and put in place for each child.

Comprehensive Evaluation

Evaluation is the process used under IDEA to determine whether a child has a disability and needs special education and related services. Even though your child's visual impairment may seem obvious to you, your child needs to be evaluated to document his or her disability in order to start the special education process. The information from an evaluation can help you and the school system develop an appropriate plan, called an Individualized Education Program (IEP), which will include the types of accommodations and specialized services your child needs to benefit from his or her education. Other types of evaluation that are important in developing your child's IEP are conducted with the teacher of students with visual impairments taking the lead. One type of evaluation, known as a functional vision evaluation or assessment, includes a close look at how your child is able to use vision that he or she might have. It also provides some judgments about the best way for your child to begin to access print material—that is, to obtain the information presented visually in print. The method that your child uses may be braille, large print, regular print using special optical devices such as magnifiers, special computer equipment, or any combination of these.

The terms "evaluation" and "assessment" are ordinarily interchangeable. However, under IDEA, a comprehensive evaluation consists of a collection of different types of assessments designed to carefully examine your child's strengths, abilities, and unique learning needs. The various types of assessments that your child may undergo are described in Chapter 3 on assessment and Chapter 6 on accommodations and adaptations. Under IDEA, students with disabilities are entitled to have a reevaluation of their strengths and needs at least once every three years at no cost to their families. This is referred to as a full and individual evaluation (FIE). It must include an assessment of any area in which disability is suspected, not just visual impairment, and at a minimum should include a functional vision evaluation or assessment to determine the way in which a child uses vision, a learning media assessment, which determines the primary way in which a child obtains information, an orientation and mobility (O&M) assessment, an eye report, and a functional, developmental, and academic assessment.

As Chapter 3 explains, it is very important for qualified professionals with specialized expertise to perform these assessments. It is equally important for parents to know that if they disagree with the findings from the original assessment arranged by their child's educational team, they have the right to request an independent educational evaluation conducted by an expert of their choice in order to obtain a second opinion. An assessment of this kind can be especially useful in any cases in which school or educational staff and a child's parents do not agree on the extent of specialized services that the child needs and that the school district is willing to provide.

Individualized Education Program

The IEP is the road map to your child's education, and it is put together by a group of people known as the IEP team. Parents are integral and equal members of that team. Most of the people on the team will work directly with you and your child in providing educational services. Your child, when appropriate, may also be a member of the IEP team. Chapters 4, 8, and 10 provide more detailed information on IEPs.

Given the unique needs of every student with visual impairments, it is important for parents and educators to work in partnership to make sure that effective educational planning and services are provided for your visually impaired child. As a parent you instinctively know your child best and have the benefit of observing his or her developmental progress and behaviors over a period of time. These observations are crucial for assessing his or her abilities and needs. Professionals trained in the education

From a Parent's Perspective

ESTABLISHING GOALS

Knowing the services to which your child is entitled is only half the battle. Getting those services is another matter altogether. For a child with vision problems and additional disabilities, it is sometimes difficult for educators to determine the child's primary disability. If an educator does not consider your child's lack of visual ability to be a primary problem, getting vision services for that child can be difficult. Teachers of students who are visually impaired are key providers for children with vision impairments and additional disabilities.

How does a parent of a child with many needs go about obtaining all the services he or she needs? Establishing your goals for your child is helpful, since it provides a map for the future. Naturally, those goals will change, based on your child's progress. Establishing goals will help identify the services needed to meet them, especially when there are many needs.

Kate Aldrich
Mother of a 24-year-old son with retinopathy
of prematurity and multiple disabilities
Santa Rosa, California

and rehabilitation of students who are visually impaired have the necessary specialized knowledge and skills to assess and instruct students. When their efforts are combined with yours, it is of great benefit to the child.

Some of the specialized areas you can expect to be on your child's IEP include learning special skills in the expanded core curriculum, discussed earlier in this chapter. Your child's IEP needs to be based on a consideration of his or her needs in these important areas. Chapters 4, 5, 8, and 9 discuss special skills and related services that might be appropriate for your child.

Least Restrictive Environment

IDEA states that, to the maximum extent appropriate, children with disabilities are to be educated in the regular classroom with children who are not disabled. This may be done by providing special education, related services, other supplementary aids, assistive technology services, and accommodations that the IEP team determines necessary. A child's educational placement needs to be based on answers to questions including: Does the child need to be provided with instruction in the use of braille? What are the child's communication needs? Does the child need specialized technology or assistive technology devices and services in order to work within the general curriculum, such as magnifiers or computers with synthetic speech? Does the child require special accommodations for testing? Special classes, separate schooling, or other situations in which children with disabilities are removed from the regular educational environment should be used only if the nature or severity of the child's disability is such that education cannot be provided in regular classes with the use of supplementary aids and services.

Most children who are visually impaired attend school in their neighborhood communities, although this was not always the case in the past. A range of possible educational placements is available for students with disabilities. These are outlined in Chapter 7 on placement options. These possibilities may include placement in a regular classroom, special classroom, or special school. The placement that is best for your child is determined annually by his or her IEP team. Tips on advocating and negotiating for appropriate placement for your child and other related issues are discussed in Chapters 7 and 10.

Parents' and Students' Input into Educational Decisions

As you come to understand the way in which your child's visual impairment affects his or her activities in your daily lives, you can also become knowledgeable about how the visual impairment influences your child's educational needs and experiences. Having this knowledge enables you to make important contributions to the process of planning for your child's education. IDEA protects your role as a parent to be a full participant in the decision making that goes into educational planning for your child.

This planning is formalized through an Individualized Family Service Plan (IFSP) for children usually from birth to their third birthday and through an IEP for students from age 3 to 21 years. (There is more information on IFSPs in Chapter 2 and on IEPs in Chapter 4). An IFSP or IEP team is established to be responsible for the special educational planning process for your child. You as a parent are by law a member of these teams and thus play a significant role, providing critical information about the unique needs of your child. It may at first seem intimidating or daunting to be an active participant in your child's educational planning. But you know your child better than anyone and can become a powerful resource and advocate for his or her development and education. And as they mature, students with visual impairments can learn to be advocates for their own needs and desires and participate in the decisions made about their own educational programs, as provided for in IDEA.

Procedural Safeguards

Under the law, procedural safeguards protect the rights of children with disabilities and their parents. Among these are procedures that state and local educational agencies are required to establish to ensure that parents of students with disabilities can enforce their child's right to a free and appropriate education. Other procedures keep parents informed of decisions affecting their child's education. For example, you as a parent have a right to examine all records relating to your child and to participate in meetings related to his or her evaluation and educational placement, and you have the right to obtain an independent educational evaluation of your child. Procedural due process safeguards—the right to receive reasonable notice in writing of proposed changes to your child's educational program or placement, and the right to seek informal resolution of complaints through negotiation and mediation or formal resolution through an administrative due process hearing and appeal to a proper court—help ensure fairness for children and families. A copy of IDEA's procedural safeguards is made available to parents of a child with a disability by the child's school one time per year. In addition, a copy is provided when a child is initially referred for services, an evaluation is initially made, a complaint is filed by a parent, or a parent requests this information. A full explanation of the procedural safeguards is given, written in an understandable manner and in the parent's native language, unless it is clearly not feasible to do so. Chapter 10 provides additional information on these safeguards.

Changes in the Law

Many laws in the United States, including the laws that affect education and in particular special education, are reauthorized every several years—that is, they are reviewed by Congress to see if they will continue as law or will be amended. During this process, provisions of the law can be changed. In addition, regulations concerning the implementation of the law are issued. States' special education laws and regulations must be consistent with federal law; they may provide students and parents greater, but not less, protection than federal law. For these reasons, it is important for parents to stay current about both law and policy. An effective way of remaining aware of the law as it applies to special education is to contact a parents' organization such as NAPVI. Also check with your child's teacher and other school personnel on a yearly basis. In addition, a number of sources of information, including web sites such as www.ed.gov/IDEA, http://idea.ed.gov, www.wrightslaw.com, and others listed in the Resources section of this book, provide current information on the law and educational issues.

It is also important for parents to be aware of the impact of other legislation signed into law in 2002, called No Child Left Behind (NCLB, which is the most recent version of the federal Elementary and Secondary Education Act). Some provisions of this legislation seek to address the gap in test scores among populations of children in this country. NCLB expects all students—including those with disabilities—to meet state standards of proficiency, based on state assessments. This has resulted in schools' paying extensive attention to testing and the resulting scores. NCLB has mandated stronger accountability on the part of schools and has emphasized the use of proven educational methods.

Whereas IDEA specifically affects the rights of you and your child in regard to education, NCLB is directed at systemic change by schools and school districts. The influence of this legislation varies across the country, as schools use their resources in different ways to address its requirements. (The U.S. Department of Education's NCLB web site is at www.ed.gov/nclb/landing.jhtml.) It is therefore important that parents understand how both NCLB and special education legislation influence the services that their children are entitled to receive. It is important to become aware of practices in your local school district. Expanding your understanding of IDEA and NCLB can be extremely valuable in helping you become more effective in requesting the special educational services your child needs to achieve the standards expected for all children under NCLB.

STRATEGIES FOR SURVIVAL—AND SUCCESS

When someone in a family experiences vision loss or another disability, it can seem overwhelming. If you feel this way, you're not alone. Reacting to a child's visual impairment with a range of strong, sometimes negative, feelings is understandable. It is an experience shared at first by just about everyone in this situation. Although having a child with a visual impairment may mean adjustments for the entire family, parents need to know that their visually impaired children can lead successful lives and have promising futures. In trying to regain some equilibrium, and when it comes to school and educational issues in the life of your child, a number of strategies can help you balance your life and your concern about your child. They can help you to learn about educational services that are important and how to obtain them, and can help you begin building a path to the future for your child.

Take Care of Yourself

Do your best to pay attention to what matters to *you*, even though you may sometimes feel too tired to do so. You're entitled to take care of your own life without feeling guilty. Taking care of *yourself*—eating what's good for you, sleeping as much as you can, relaxing or doing activities that are important to you—is an important one of your many jobs. It can help you maintain your spirits and strength and in that way help your family and your child as well.

Keep in Touch

Emotional support from people who care about you is crucial. When we feel less than perfect, many of us tend to withdraw from friends and sometimes from family, too. Although you may be tired, try to stay in touch with friends, family, and other people who can boost your spirits and provide assistance.

Allow Time

Allow yourself, your family, and your child time. It is the element that often makes the difference in life. Learning about visual impairment and adjusting to it are part of a continuing process. In many ways, we're all in constant transition, and it may be helpful to remember that.

Work with Knowledgeable Professionals

Try to locate and consult with professionals who are knowledgeable about your child's eye condition, and establish continuing relationships with a physician, eye care specialist, or other service providers you feel you can trust. Friends, family, other parents, your own doctors, and many of the organizations listed in the Resources section of this book can be sources of information for finding such professionals. University-affiliated hospitals, professional organizations, and national organizations in the field of visual impairment can provide valuable suggestions.

Become informed about your child's eye condition and about services and help that may be of use to you and your family. Most people are aware that the Internet is a great source of information, and you can find out about a wealth of resources by using it. You may not be aware, however, of the variety of national organizations that offer information, support, and referrals for visually impaired people and their families. In addition, a number of publications offer invaluable advice.

When you are talking to your child's doctor, don't be hesitant about explaining politely that you might need several minutes to ask a few questions and make sure you understand what is being said. Answers to questions such as these are important for you and your family to know:

- What is the diagnosis of my child's eye condition?
- What caused the condition?
- How will the condition affect my child's vision now and in the future? What can my child see?

• Can the condition be treated? If so, what is the treatment? What are the benefits? How successful is any available treatment? What are the risks and side effects associated with it? When will it start, and how long will it last?

• Should I watch for any particular symptoms and contact the doctor if they appear?

• How often should my child see an eye care professional?

• What other professionals might be helpful in treating my child? These might include a low vision specialist, who can evaluate your child's vision and advise you on how your child can make the best use of any vision he or she has.

Numerous resources can help you learn about your child's visual impairment and how you can encourage your child's growth and development. For example, the Hadley School for the Blind offers free correspondence and online courses for parents of visually impaired children, and the American Foundation for the Blind's AFB Press and other organizations listed in the Resources section publish many materials that can help and inform parents.

Connect with Other Families

Become connected with other families who have had a similar experience. Many parent groups and electronic mailing lists and discussion groups that can be found on the Internet are great sources of support and information. Often, national networks and associations that focus on specific disabilities and specific eye and medical conditions have state and local chapters that sponsor activities such as conferences and programs for families. Many parents who have raised a child with a visual impairment have become experts that you can rely on for finding contacts, current medical and educational information, and useful resources.

Seek Out Early Intervention Services

This chapter and Chapter 2 explain the importance of early intervention. These services can make a world of difference for your child's growth and development and, because early intervention focuses on the needs of the family too, they are a great support and source of information for you and your family.

Keep Good Records

Try to find a place in your home where you will maintain files on your child's medical condition and school status. You may find it helpful to separate medical from school files, but any system that helps you keep important information safely and within reach is valuable. Save copies of doctor's reports, reports from other consultants or specialists such as your child's early interventionist, and correspondence between your family and any educational and medical program or agency with which you have had contact. Copies of your child's IEPs and results of any assessments are especially important.

Stay Up to Date on the Law

Knowing what your child is entitled to under IDEA, and under your state law as well, can be invaluable to you in understanding what to ask for and how to proceed in order to make sure your child receives appropriate services. Try to pay attention to any current changes in the law as well. For example, you may see the term "IDEA 2004," or the Individuals with Disabilities Education Improvement Act, which amended IDEA when the law was reauthorized.

Request the Services of a Teacher of Students with Visual Impairments

If your child's educational team doesn't include a teacher certified in the education of students with visual impairments, request the services of such a teacher. There is a national shortage of teachers who specialize in working with visually impaired students. If you are told that no such teacher is available, contact your local school district and its director of special education as well as the state department of education with your request. Your state's special school for visually impaired students (or a neighboring state's, if your state doesn't have one), your state vision consultant in the state department of education, and parent groups such as NAPVI can offer suggestions and advice on making sure that your child receives the services of an appropriate teacher. Request other services that you think are important for your child.

Work with Your Child's Educators

Get to know the important people in your child's educational life and work to foster good relationships with them. The classroom teacher, teacher of students with visual impairments, paraeducator, school principal, special education director, and school district staff are key individuals who play pivotal roles, directly or indirectly, in your child's educational program.

Know Your Legislators

Don't forget to learn the name of your local and state legislators who represent your area and the contact information for their neighborhood offices. Both the legislator and the office can be very helpful when you are trying to obtain services for your child and need information and assistance on whom to contact or the extent of your rights under the law.

COLLABORATIVE EFFORTS

A number of national issues that relate to the education of students with visual impairments are of concern to families. These include a shortage of expert teachers and O&M specialists, and difficulties in some parts of the country with visually impaired students obtaining in a timely way reading materials that they can use effectively with their eye condition. This book is intended to be a practical and useful tool to help you understand key areas and issues related to your child's education.

Many concerned parents have found it important and effective for parent associations to join forces with other national organizations representing the visually impaired community as well as statewide agencies and coalitions for the protection and improvement of educational services for children with visual impairments. Organizations including NAPVI, the Council of Schools for the Blind, the Association for Education and Rehabilitation of the Blind and Visually Impaired (AER), and the American Foundation for the Blind (AFB) work together to eliminate inequities faced by blind and visually impaired individuals in the United States and to protect services for children and adults and their families. These efforts are strengthened when many organizations join together to rally for or against certain policies concerning children with visual impairments. It is particularly powerful for parents to form associations with their local school and agencies serving people who are blind or visually impaired so they can have a strong voice in influencing policy and the improvement of services for children.

The idea for this book came from parents wanting to share their experiences and help other parents. It was inspired by the belief that parents' knowledge and advocacy are critical to the education of their children with visual impairments. The chapters that follow provide additional information and support on specific topics to families to assure them that their children's education can lead to successful, independent, and satisfying lives.

Note

1. Estimates derived by the American Foundation for the Blind Policy Research Department from a study described in C. Kirchner and S. Diament (1999), "USABLE Data Report, Estimates of the Number of Visually Impaired Students, Their Teachers, and Orientation and Mobility Specialists: Part 1," *Journal of Visual Impairment & Blindness*, 9 (3)

(1999), pp. 600–606; and from the U.S. National Center for Health Statistics' 2005 National Health Interview Survey data. Data available at http://www.cdc.gov/nchs/about/major/nhis/quest_data_related_1997_ forward.htm.

For More Information

American Foundation for the Blind, *AFB Directory of Services for Blind and Visually Impaired Persons in the United States and Canada*, 27th edition (New York: AFB Press, 2005).

C. Cortiella, "NCLB and IDEA: What Parents of Students with Disabilities Need to Know and Do" (Minneapolis, MN: National Center on Educational Outcomes, University of Minnesota 2006).

P. Crane, D. Cuthbertson, K. A. Ferrell, and H. Scherb, *Equals in Partnership: Basic Rights for Families of Children with Blindness or Visual Impairment* (Watertown, MA: Hilton/Perkins Program of Perkins School for the Blind and National Association for Parents of the Visually Impaired, 1997).

J. N. Erin, *When You Have a Visually Impaired Student with Multiple Disabilities in Your Classroom: A Guide for Teachers* (New York: AFB Press, 2004).

M. C. Holbrook (Ed.), *Children with Visual Impairments: A Parents' Guide*, second edition (Bethesda, MD: Woodbine House, 2006).

M.C. Holbrook and A. J. Koenig (Eds.), *Foundations of Education,* Vols. 1 and 2 (New York: AFB Press, 2000).

R. L. Pogrund and D. L. Fazzi (Eds.), *Early Focus: Working with Young Children Who Are Blind or Visually Impaired and Their Families,* second edition (New York: AFB Press, 2002).

S. J. Spungin (Ed.), *When You Have a Visually Impaired Student in Your Classroom: A Guide for Teachers* (New York: AFB Press, 2002).

P. W. D. Wright and P. D. Wright, *Wrightslaw: From Emotions to Advocacy: The Special Education Survival Guide* (Hartfield, VA: Harbor House Law Press, 2002).

P. W. D. Wright and P. D. Wright, *Special Education Law*, second edition (Hartfield, VA: Harbor House Law Press, 2006).

CHAPTER 2

Start at the Beginning: The Importance of Early Intervention

Mary Zabelski

As a parent, you may have received the news that your child had a visual impairment right after he or she was born. Or, you may have noticed something unusual about your child's eyes or vision, something no one else noticed, but that you became more and more concerned about. Both of these possibilities are the kind of experiences that parents of visually impaired children typically may have.

After the realization that a visual impairment exists come a wide variety of reactions. However, no matter what you may be feeling when you receive word that your child is visually impaired, common thoughts for parents are, "What does this mean for my child? How will this affect my child's development? And what do I need to do now?" In the case of infants and very young children, early intervention services can provide some answers.

EARLY INTERVENTION: A DEFINITION

The term "early intervention" has a literal meaning—intervening in a child's development to provide support at an early time in his or her life. At its best, early intervention identifies a child in need of special services as early as possible in order to support and promote his or her growth and development. Why is this early identification important? Because like all children, youngsters who are visually impaired need to learn about the

WE ALL LEARN FROM EACH OTHER

Investigate an early intervention program through your pediatrician and/or state department of health, and/or your local school district. The ideal program should involve a blend of time spent at the early intervention center, with other children, and home visits from the teacher of students who are visually impaired to work with your child and with you.

It is important for everyone to remember that you, the parent, are your child's primary teacher, and that you need to learn also. Stimulate your baby as much as you can. Talk all the time so that your baby knows where you are. Babies are great listeners!

"Jameyanne is in the living room and Mommy's in the kitchen. I'm coming to get you!"

"Mommy is going to turn on the coffee grinder—here it goes now." (This is an important one, because some sounds can be frightening if they are not anticipated.)

"Mommy is going to carry you down the hall to your room to change your diaper."

"Let's dance from the kitchen to the living room."

These are the first steps to orienting your child to him- or herself and to his or her place in the surrounding environment. Teach your baby your own home—your familiar home is the best place to start orientation. Call your baby from one room to another—keep calling as she crawls toward you to keep her following your voice—reward him with kisses and he'll give them back. Keep singing and dancing with your baby. Make it fun: It's going to be a long dance.

I encourage you to get involved with other parents through early intervention and a parents' group such as the National Association for Parents of Children with Visual Impairments (NAPVI). We learn so much from one another, parents and children. Keep talking to your child. Your talking will have an impact, so be sure that it is positive. Your tone will tell it all: Let your self-esteem shine through your voice and enrich your child.

Mary E. Fuller
Mother of a 15-year-old daughter with
aniridia glaucoma
Concord, New Hampshire

world around them but are not able to rely on their sight to the extent that sighted children do. The sooner the process of exploring the world begins, the sooner your child's growth, development, and learning can be encouraged and helped to take place. Often, a child born with blindness or visual impairment may need extra assistance to grow and develop in the ways other children do. An effective early intervention program can help target specific needs or problems, plan positive strategies assisting in development, and help your family to feel comfortable and confident as you raise your child. Expert intervention and appropriate educational and family services during early childhood can help ensure that your child with a visual impairment will enter kindergarten or first grade with the skills he or she needs to start on a successful life in school. For this reason, parents who suspect that their children have vision problems should bring this to the attention of their pediatricians, who should be able to refer them to a pediatric ophthalmologist. Signs of a possible problem include a lack of eye contact, eyes that appear to wander, eyes that do not seem to align, a lack of visual response to lights being turned on, sensitivity to light, and the inability to look at objects placed nearby. Depending on the condition, a child may also need to be examined by a low vision optometrist—a professional knowledgeable about evaluating the need for special lenses and other devices to help maximize the use of vision in people who are visually impaired—who specializes in working with children.

WHY INTERVENTION?

Although the effects of visual impairment can range from mild to severe, any degree of vision loss can affect all aspects of learning. Many children who are blind or visually impaired may exhibit delays in motor and language development within the first few months of their lives. These delays may be due in large part to a lack of visual stimulation.

As noted in Chapter 1, much early learning is acquired incidentally as toddlers watch other children and adults interact with the environment and imitate their actions. Incidental learning is learning gained by observing persons and activities around us within our immediate environment. Babies begin to attach names or words to objects as they see their parents using familiar items, and this process encourages their language development. Therefore, much of early learning is attached to visual experiences, as is much of early motor development. Children who are blind or visually impaired may not move toward an object in the immediate environment because they may have no knowledge of its presence, unless perhaps the object makes itself known by a sound or in some other way or unless someone else calls their attention to it. As a result, the motivation to crawl or walk may be delayed for many visually impaired children, with the result being a delay in their motor skills. Overall, since so much early learning is acquired through visual experiences, an infant or toddler who is blind or visually impaired can miss out on many opportunities for incidental learning unless he or she is provided with early stimulation that has been deliberately and thoughtfully planned and carried out.

Children who are blind or visually impaired may also miss social opportunities, since they may be unable to watch the ordinary play and behavior of other children. However, their families can play a critical role in helping them learn and participate in relationships with others. For these reasons, early intervention services that provide families with guidance on specific, specialized strategies to help their children have experiences that other children regularly participate in can be invaluable.

Through play, by providing stimulating experiences and describing people, objects, and events, with the help of trained professionals, you can teach your child to explore the surrounding environment and become aware of what is around him or her. You can learn how to encourage the development of natural curiosity, often untapped in a child who is blind or visually impaired. And you can be shown ways of providing your child with direct information about the world and its objects that can help him or her develop an understanding of them. This in turn leads to the growth of concepts and language—known as concept development and language development—that your child can use to describe the world.

The term "early interventionist" is broad, and in general is used to describe professionals who work with infants from birth through age 36 months who have disabilities and their families. Early interventionists come from a variety of backgrounds and have a range of expertise in such fields as child development, special education, occupational and physical therapy, and speech and language therapy. Early intervention programs whose staff includes a teacher of students with visual impairments, an orientation and mobility (O&M) instructor, and an early childhood specialist knowledgeable about multiple disabilities and specifically trained to work with children who are blind or visually impaired offer expert services targeted to meet the needs of children who require extra help in finding out about the world. Your child may also benefit from the services of an occupational therapist, physical therapist, or speech pathologist for assistance in overall growth and development. A comprehensive program can help you and your family learn parenting skills designed to be especially supportive of your child's educational and developmental needs.

EARLY INTERVENTION STARTS AT HOME

You are your child's first and best teacher. No one knows your child the way you do. You know what he needs when he cries, or makes certain facial expressions. You know what makes her happy, anxious, fearful, or confident. Only you can offer your child this expertise. It is the first step in beginning the educational process for your child, and seeing yourself as your child's teacher.

Your baby's cries, her "goos," her physical gestures are her language. It's the way she communicates nonverbally with you. You respond with verbal communication in your words to her, the tone of your voice. Your actions are the beginning of her language development, and the communication of her needs to you. It's "early intervention" and "education." Your child learns that when she cries, you will respond; it's one of the first cause-and-effect relationships a child learns.

You understand your child as no one else does. *Even though you may not realize it right now, you are the expert,* and you will be called upon to offer your expertise to help educators and medical professional care for and teach your child.

Take time to cuddle your baby, play verbal rhyming games, and allow your child to play with soft toys that make squeaky noises. Put on some children's music and sing to your child or with your child. Keep rhythm with your baby, using his feet or hands to make marching and drumming motions. Laugh and make funny noises, respond to any response you receive from your child. It's natural!

While you and your child are laughing and singing, you are practicing "early intervention." Everything you do together in play is a learning experience for both of you. Early intervention, done by parents with simple play, intuitive touches of love, or banter of words and sounds, is a natural process between parent and child. It happens as a matter of course. It's how all babies learn.

It is no different with your child who has a visual impairment or other disabilities. What is different for the child who is visually impaired or multiply disabled is the importance of this type of play. Any activity that provides your child with sensory experiences—involving her senses of touch, sound, smell, and taste—to create a reaction as a direct result from her action, helps her understand from her earliest experience that she is capable, productive, and able to do what others can.

Susan Singler
Mother of a 24-year-old son with retinopathy
of prematurity and additional disabilities
Nashville, Tennessee

THE LAW AND EARLY INTERVENTION

Early intervention services in this country are typically provided to infants and toddlers with disabilities from birth to 3 years of age. These services are delivered in various programs and most, if not all, states throughout the country. Programs vary in the types of services provided. Usually, they are run through a state department or agency, but often are offered through a local school district or sometimes through a local hospital. Specialized programs run by various organizations for children and adults with disabilities may also include early intervention services in many parts of the country.

Part C Programs

As Chapter 1 explained, the Individuals with Disabilities Education Act (IDEA) is the federal legislation that ensures services to children with disabilities throughout the United States. Under the provisions of IDEA, infants and toddlers with disabilities from birth up until their third birthday and their families receive early intervention services; the provisions governing these services are found in a section of IDEA entitled Part C. For this reason, you may sometimes hear early intervention programs in this country referred to as "Part C programs." In general, children and young adults between the ages of 3 and 21 years receive special education and related services under IDEA Part B. (However, IDEA was amended in 2004 to permit states to extend their early intervention programs to allow children, with the parents' consent, to continue to receive early intervention services after they turn 3 until they are eligible to enter kindergarten.) Under Part C regulations, children under age 3 who have developmental delays or any physical or mental conditions that are likely to cause developmental delays or special needs that may interfere with their education are entitled to receive early intervention services. The purpose of early intervention is to provide services, education, and support that lessen the effects of disability or developmental delay. Services are intended to identify and meet a child's needs in five primary areas: physical development, cognitive development, communication, social or emotional development, and adaptive development.

IDEA Part C provides states with funding to sustain statewide programs of early intervention services for infants and toddlers and their families. Each state participating in the Part C program is required to designate a lead agency in charge of early intervention for the state. These agencies, often referred to as "Part C agencies," vary from state to state. They may be located within the state department of health, human services, education, or rehabilitation. Parents who wish to locate the Part C agency in their state can do so by contacting their state department of health or education and making inquiries, or can consult the *AFB Directory of Services for Blind and Visually Impaired Persons in the United States and Canada*, which is available in print and on the web site of the American Foundation for the Blind (AFB) at www.afb.org under the "Where Can I Find?" service finder. A parents' organization such as the National Association for Parents of Children with Visual Impairments (NAPVI; see the Resources section at the back of this book for contact information) can also help you to locate the appropriate agency.

In recognition of the importance of intervening on behalf of a child as early as possible, states are also required to conduct a process known as "child find." This process is intended to identify, locate, and evaluate all children with disabilities from birth to age 21, who are in need of early intervention or special education services. Your child find agency may not be the same as the Part C agency in your state. In general, the child find agency may be what is known as the local education agency, or local school district, operating under your state department of education. To obtain services and information, parents can contact their local school district office or their Part C agency to begin the early intervention process.

Assessment and Planning

Essential services under IDEA Part C include assessment, also referred to as evaluation, a process that involves a team of specialists called a multidisciplinary team who are experienced in various areas of child development, such as early development, physical therapy, and speech and language therapy. (Chapter 3 contains more information on assessment.) This team will gather information about your child to determine whether he or she is eligible for early intervention services and to identify his or her special needs. When a child is found to be eligible for early intervention, the needs that have been identified are described in a document called an Individualized Family Service Plan (IFSP), which must be created as part of the process outlined under IDEA. The plan indicates the services needed to support a child's development and to help the child's family in its efforts to assist the child's development as well. It explains why intervention is needed, what kind of intervention it will be, who will provide it and how often, and where the services will be provided. (For more on IFSPs, see Chapter 4.) Assessment is a critical part of special education planning and, depending on the practices and policies of the local school district, will take place at various intervals to determine a child's progress and need for services.

The IFSP needs to indicate the child's current levels of physical, cognitive, communication, social or emotional, and adaptive development. This description includes the areas of fine and gross motor skills, vision, hearing, and overall health; information on the family's concerns, priorities, and resources for promoting the child's development; the main outcomes expected for the child and ways in which the child's progress will be measured; the specific services that will be provided, their frequency, and how they will be delivered; the natural environments (such as the home, a child care center, or other setting) in which services will be provided; the dates and duration of services; and steps that will be taken to support the child and family's transition or movement out of early intervention services. In addition, as part of the early intervention process, a service coordinator is assigned to help the family by making sure that the IFSP is put into effect and to coordinate the services outlined in the plan.

SERVICES PROVIDED, SERVICES TO REQUEST

A wide range of services may be provided through early intervention, including audiological services; vision services; occupational and physical therapy and speech and language therapy; special instruction services; medical and nursing services; psychological and social work services; health services necessary for the child to benefit from other early intervention services; family training, counseling, and home visits; and transportation to enable the child and family to receive early intervention services.

Although IDEA requires that all special education services include input and participation from family members, early intervention particularly emphasizes the essential importance of the family's role, needs, and concerns in determining a child's educational program. A baby's needs cannot be separated from the needs of his or her family. In recognition of this, early intervention services are designed to support the family as well as the child. Other reasons why early intervention so strongly involves the family include the recognition that parents are their child's best teachers (see "Early Education: Parents as Teachers") and the critical fact that the family needs to continue working with the child at home on the lessons and skills that the early intervention team may have introduced. This process is called reinforcement. With the repetition of such activities as providing stimulation and information to your child in a certain way, he or she will continue to be stimulated, to learn new activities and information more effectively, and to develop new skills.

It is therefore important for parents not to hesitate to make the most of early intervention. You may want to think about what is important for your child to do and to learn, and to discuss this with your family. Then you will want to communicate it clearly to the service coordinator and other professionals working with your child. You may want to write down these items and also to write down any questions that occur to you, especially when you are at home with your child. You may also want to ask these professionals about other sources of information that you think you need.

Once your child is in an early intervention program, comprehensive assessment of his or her needs will take place. Assessment gives an indication

Early Education: Parents as Teachers

As a parent, you are your child's first and most important teacher from infancy through the preschool years. Just about all your interactions—playing, talking, putting on clothes, feeding—are natural teaching experiences for you and learning opportunities for your child. In your role as teacher, keep in mind that:

- Every child, whether visually impaired or not, is a learner.
- The family is the most significant influence in the life of a young child.
- Children have different learning styles and, therefore, effective teaching approaches should be geared to their individual needs.

What makes you a natural teacher?

- **You know your child** better than anyone else does and have a better idea of what he or she is ready to learn.
- **You spend more time with your child** than anyone else does. Therefore you're able to take advantage of the many ordinary events—things that happen throughout the day in the normal course of family life—that are opportunities to teach your child something.
- **You give your child toys** and common, everyday objects to help him or her learn in natural situations that can be applied to other situations outside the home.
- **You provide opportunities** for your child to practice what he or she has learned and a chance to experience the world under your guidance.
- **You act as a role model.** By starting early, you teach your child behaviors and good habits that will last a lifetime.
- **You involve your child in family life** so that friends and relatives learn how to interact with your visually impaired child and he or she learns how to act with others.

Visually impaired children learn by touching, listening, smelling, tasting, moving, and using whatever vision they have. You teach your child by talking, touching, and playing during natural interaction times. You

(continued on next page)

are also teaching when you give your child toys and ordinary household objects that vary in texture, weight, smell, sound, and color. The more sensory experiences you provide—experiences that have your child use his or her senses and learn how to obtain information through them—both one at a time and simultaneously, during everyday routines and special family occasions, the better. Your creative, on-the-spot teaching is an essential part of your child's education.

Early intervention services can help you expand your natural teaching skills to help your toddler or preschooler be ready for more formal learning experiences in school. But do not underestimate the value of your own everyday, natural activities with your child. Every moment you spend with your child is a teaching moment. It might be playing, or talking, or running errands, or just being—but you are teaching your child just the same.

Reprinted from K. A. Ferrell, *Reach Out and Teach: Meeting the Training Needs of Parents of Visually and Multiply Handicapped Young Children* (New York: American Foundation for the Blind, 1985), pp. 10–11.

of how your child is developing in various areas, such as movement, communication, social skills, cognitive skills, self-help skills, and sensory areas (that is, learning to use the information gathered by our senses). It is important to determine during this process whether your child's visual impairment or other disabilities have affected his or her development so that a remediation plan can be put into effect. The extent of the services planned and the number of hours per week depend on the degree of the disability and your child's needs. He or she may only need services from a teacher of students with visual impairments, a specially trained and certified teacher whose skills and role are discussed in more detail in Chapter 1, or may need a variety of services, such as occupational therapy, speech therapy, nursing, and vision services, depending on the level and extent of his or her disability.

Services for children with visual impairments are specialized and may be very scarce in some parts of the country. Critical services may include those of the teacher of students with visual impairments, whom you may hear referred to as a vision specialist, vision teacher, "v.i. teacher," or itinerant vision teacher, to provide special training and adaptations, to encourage the use of all your child's senses, and to teach basic self-care skills. These adaptations might include using strong color contrasts in the environment; presenting items at a certain distance or within the child's visual field so they can be seen; or providing toys and educational materials paired with information given through sound, touch, smell, and taste (called a multisensory approach). Also, preliteracy skills, which help prepare your child's interest in and ability to read, are another very important focus for this teacher. For example, children who are visually impaired can explore shapes and numbers tactilely, through the sense of touch, and should be encouraged to explore the environment through their other senses. By listening, touching, tasting, and smelling, our children become familiar with objects in the environment even if they cannot see them. If the team of early interventionists for your child does not include a teacher with certification in teaching children who are blind or visually impaired, you will want to request specifically the services of such a teacher, in writing. If your child has a diagnosis indicating a visual impairment, you can also request a functional vision assessment or evaluation, which the school district should provide at no cost. This assessment focuses on the way your child uses vision and is explained in more detail in Chapter 3.

Your child may also need the services of an orientation and mobility (O&M) instructor, who can teach your child about his or her body; about body position in space; about basic spatial concepts and directions, such as in, on, under, up, down, left, and right; about skills such as trailing, or touching the walls with one hand to determine one's position while walking; and other activities that can increase your child's ability to move about and travel safely in the environment. Your child may also need occupational therapy to improve hand function, and to help in the learning of daily living skills (from eating with utensils and drinking from a cup, to washing hands and bathing, toileting, grooming, and dressing independently). Physical therapy may also be helpful to stimulate motor development and improve posture; and speech therapy, to encourage language development and oral motor skills necessary for speech.

Sometimes a child's inability to obtain information visually and perform certain tasks can be misunderstood if the professionals working with him or her are not experienced or trained in the effects of visual impairment. For example, the effect of vision loss may be mistaken for a cognitive limitation. For this reason, it is essential that a teacher who is trained to work with infants and toddlers who are blind or visually impaired be part of your child's early intervention team. To locate a specialized teacher, parents can contact the state school for visually impaired children (in their state or a neighboring state if their own state does not have one); their state department of education; or their state's vision consultant, who works within the state department of education. Other sources of help and information are local agencies that provide services to persons with visual impairments. Additional information on locating professional help can be obtained from the national organizations listed in the Resources section of this book and described in Chapter 1.

SETTINGS FOR SERVICES

Early intervention programs vary greatly throughout the country, but the delivery of services should be designed to meet the needs of the child and family. An effective early intervention program should be family centered: The family's needs and desires are addressed and the family should be treated as an equal participant, choosing the type and frequency of service delivery, the specific related services, and the service provider from a range of options. These options can include services provided by a professional who visits you in your home, or services provided in a school or in the community in locations such as hospitals or day care centers, Head Start programs, or specialized clinics. Therefore, services are usually referred to as "home based" or "center based," depending on where they are received. Some children will receive a combination of home- and center-based intervention. "Program Models" describes the main locations of early intervention and preschool programs.

IDEA indicates that to the maximum extent appropriate for the needs of a child, early intervention services need to be delivered in what are called natural environments, which are defined in the law as settings that are natural or normal for other children of the same age who do not have any disabilities. Natural environments include the home as well as community settings such as day care centers that children without disabilities also attend. When your child attends a program with other children who are not visually impaired and with staff who are not specifically trained in working with young children with visual impairments, it is important for you to be aware of the need to request specialized services and accommodations that your child may need.

Home-based programs are often used when a child is very young or has medical conditions that may prevent him or her from participating in a program outside the home. They allow the early intervention specialist to come directly to your home, which is the most natural environment for a small child, for scheduled visits, during which he or she will work directly with your child and can share information and suggestions with you on how you can encourage your child's development. Center-based programs, in which you can bring your child to receive services, may serve children with visual impairments only, or may also serve children with other disabilities or without any disabilities. Because they can be housed in various places, ranging from schools to churches to day care centers, and may be operated by federal or state agencies, school districts, or private agencies, they are diverse but give your child an opportunity to learn alongside other children and to socialize with them as well. The time your child spends in a center-based program will depend on his or her IFSP.

There are pros and cons to each type of program setting. In general, services provided in your home may help you to understand how to adapt

Program Models

Early intervention and preschool programs work with families using one or more of the delivery methods described here.

- Home-based services: Teachers, counselors, or consultants come to your home on a regular basis. All activities take place in your home. These teaching/training visits usually last about an hour; they can occur as often as four times a week or as infrequently as once a month, depending on how well staffed your local program is, how many families it serves, and how far staff members have to travel to reach all families.

- Center-based services: You and your child travel to a central location. All teachers, consultants, and counselors are located at the center and work with children there individually and in small groups. Depending on how old your child is, you may be able to drop your child off for a class and return when class is over. Or you may be asked to help out in the classroom, or to join a parent discussion group.

- Home- and center-based services: Some activities occur in your home and sometimes you and your child go to the center to receive services.

Regardless of which type of services or environment your program offers, it should provide the following effective practices:

- A certified teacher of visually impaired students and an orientation and mobility (O&M) specialist, if not directly on staff as teachers, are at least involved in assessment, planning, and consultation. No other teacher is trained to understand how visual impairments affect development, or how a child can learn to compensate for the visual impairment.

- An occupational or physical therapist should be available to answer questions about your child's motor development and how he or she moves, and to work directly with your child if your doctor prescribes it. If a therapist is not available, the program can refer you to one.

- You are involved in the choice of which program your child receives and what goals your child works on.

(continued on next page)

- The program asks your permission to assess your child, to obtain copies of medical records, and to take pictures of your child, and you are given a copy of any permission forms you sign. All records and files concerning your child are confidential.

- You are given copies of your child's assessment report and Individualized Family Service Plan (IFSP) and, later, Individualized Education Program (IEP), described in Chapter 1 and Chapter 4.

- You are kept up to date on how your child is doing, including receiving ideas and suggestions for activities you can work on with your child at home.

- You have a chance to meet with other parents, either in a formal meeting or informally, over coffee or refreshments.

- The curriculum—what your child is taught—covers motor development, visual development, self-help skills such as toileting, language and communication, social and emotional development, mental or intellectual or cognitive development, O&M, and sensory development (dealing with the use of touch, smell, hearing, and taste to learn about the environment).

- A variety of support services—extra but necessary services that add to the quality and completeness of the program—are available. Some examples are services from social workers and speech therapists, low vision examinations, access to toy libraries, transportation, and other services such as those from pediatricians, ophthalmologists, and psychologists.

The program you find may not follow all these practices, but you can select a program on the basis of how many of these practices it includes. Also, you can work together with the program's staff to try to have them include these elements and see that they are in place in the future. Every program learns from the people who are part of it, so share your ideas.

Adapted from K. A. Ferrell, *Reach Out and Teach: Meeting the Training Needs of Parents of Visually and Multiply Handicapped Young Children* (New York: American Foundation for the Blind, 1985), pp. 24–26.

your home, such as by changing the lighting in certain rooms, how to guide your child in certain activities within your own circumstances, and how to create a multisensory environment for your child within your own home with your own toys and household objects. In addition, being at home can be comforting and reassuring to both you and your child. However, center-based programs offer the benefit of providing your child with the company of other children and also provide you with the opportunity to spend time with other parents and with center staff. Some families may choose a combination of home- and center-based services. For example, you may take your child to an agency such as Easter Seals for speech and occupational therapy, and then receive home-based services in which a teacher of students with visual impairments works with you and your child.

TRANSITION TO PRESCHOOL

As Chapter 9 explains, movement from one school environment to another is often called "transition." Transitions involve a move from one phase of life to another and are usually important times in the life of an individual and family. Because they typically involve many significant changes that can have a substantial impact on everyone involved, they call for preparation and thoughtful planning. Because the move out of early intervention services marks a critical point in a child's life, it is essential that this move and the arrangement of subsequent services for the child be carefully planned.

As your child approaches his or her third birthday, the time when early intervention typically ends, a number of activities need to take place. A determination needs to be made of whether your child is eligible for special education services. Based on eligibility, a transition from Part C early intervention services to services covered by Part B of IDEA needs to begin. And an Individualized Education Program (IEP) needs to be written to identify the special education services that your child will receive after the transition occurs.

Under IDEA, the law requires that if a child is eligible to receive Part B services, preparation for the child's transition should begin around the age of 30 to 32 months and no less than three months before the child's third birthday, the time when early intervention will end (unless the option to continue under Part C until kindergarten is exercised). A transition planning meeting arranged by your child's early intervention program is held with the local school district to discuss next steps, particularly how to prepare your child for the transition out of early intervention. The school district in which you live is required to provide a free and appropriate public education for all children with disabilities from 3 through (in most cases) 21 years of age, and your local school district will need to provide special education services beginning on your child's third birthday if he or she has been found to be eligible. The assessments and evaluations that your child participates in up to his or her third birthday will determine whether your child requires special education services, which specific services, and how often. The IEP team will make the overall determination of services, and you as a parent are an equal team member with the other specialists. Written copies of their reports and an updated functional vision assessment should be among the documents collected before the first meeting to write your child's IEP. The IEP written at a meeting with the local school district and the family will outline the goals and objectives to address your child's special education needs. As Chapter 1 and Chapter 4 explain, the IEP is the blueprint for services to be arranged for your child during his or her school years. If your child turns 3 during the summer months, the team writing the IEP will decide when the district's services to your child will begin.

WHAT FAMILIES CAN DO

Families of children who are visually impaired can take a number of steps during this time to help their children move successfully to an appropriate educational program that supports their growth and development. Providing information about their children's needs during the processes for determining eligibility for services and creating the IEP needs to be a primary focus of efforts. Gathering accurate medical reports and other information for the planning meeting and for the team that conducts the initial evaluation under Part B to review will be extremely important. Information to help the team understand your child's academic and functional needs, including needs for accommodations such as preferential seating—that is, seating that allows your child to see materials like books or lessons written on a chalkboard clearly—large print, braille, or use of a closed-circuit television (CCTV) or other equipment, for example, is also vital. These accommodations should be recommended within the functional vision assessment performed by a low vision optometrist or teacher of students who are visually impaired.

The functional vision assessment provided by a teacher of students with visual impairments can provide critical information related to a child's evaluation for eligibility for a special education program at the preschool level. If the school district cannot or will not provide a person to perform such an assessment, parents can obtain a low vision exam for their child. Such an exam evaluates the vision a child may have and how the child uses vision and is typically performed by an optometrist specializing in low vision, that is, visual impairment severe enough to interfere with activities of daily life. Recommendations for adaptations and accommodations in the classroom can be provided as a result of this exam. Parents can also seek an independent evaluation by a teacher certified in the field of visual impairments and used to working with young children. (A learning media assessment, described in Chapter 3, is another specialized assessment that can identify the kinds of adaptations and accommodations most effective for your child.)

As early intervention ends, the purpose of the evaluation is to determine if your child has a disability that will make him or her eligible for special education services, and, if so, what services would be appropriate. Before your child is evaluated, you can ask whether the school district has experience testing a child who is blind or visually impaired and whether it has specialized evaluation tools available. You can also make sure that the district is planning to consult with a teacher specializing in working with visually impaired students about the testing. If the school district is inexperienced in dealing with visually impaired children, you can point out the importance of understanding the impact of visual impairment on a child and the effect of vision loss in determining your child's needs. You can also contact the special school for visually impaired children in your own or a neighboring state, which usually provides specialized assessments and consultation throughout the state for children with visual impairments, and ask for help and advice. (These schools can be found through the state department of education or through the *AFB Directory of Services for Blind and Visually Impaired Persons in the United States and Canada.*) You can contact the director of special education in your school district and your state department of education and request the involvement of a professional who specializes in work with visually impaired children. If necessary, you can get an independent evaluation or contact the state board of education and file a complaint regarding the local school district's inability to provide an experienced or appropriate person. You can also contact national parents' groups (see the Resources section) for support and information.

As Chapter 3 explains, it is important that the person or persons testing your child be familiar with visual impairments in order to understand the responses your child is making and to be able to determine accurately your child's needs for services. A familiarity with the effects of vision loss on the ability to learn is essential. In addition, many tests that are used to evaluate children do not provide a full and accurate picture of a visually impaired child's capabilities, because they have been designed to be used to test children with unimpaired sight. Some tests in fact require a child to have functional vision because the questions asked require the child to see well in order to perform a task, or they may contain pictures or graphics that a child with vision loss cannot see clearly or at all. For these reasons, it is critical that the persons administering the tests are aware that your child has a vision problem and may need special accommodations during testing, such as large print or descriptions of pictures that are shown, in order to respond to his or her full potential.

Parents can play the key role in informing these persons about their child's needs, in person-to-person conversations and in writing, and can provide other information essential to an accurate assessment of their children. Copies of your child's most recent medical reports, especially any reports from ophthalmologists or other eye care providers, are vital. You will want to prepare an explanation of how your child uses his or her vision or what kind of adaptations work best for him or her during various activities. Making a list of any visual accommodations that you may have in your home and presenting it to the assessment team provides concrete information about your child's needs. In addition, bringing along a professional from the early intervention team to assist you during the IEP planning meeting can be an effective support for you and can be invaluable in helping people unfamiliar with your child become informed about his or her visual impairment and any other factor that may have a significant effect on his or her learning.

PLANNING A SUCCESSFUL PATH TO PRESCHOOL

Once a child has been found eligible for special education services and an IEP has been developed, an appropriate preschool program needs to be determined for the child. Although the child's educational team makes this determination, you are an important part of the team and need to provide critical input. In preparing for the next phase of school life, parents of children who are eligible for preschool programs providing special education can ask their local school district for an opportunity to visit and review local preschools. There may be various options available, and you will want to visit and observe preschools before accepting any placement for your child. But whether or not your child will be in a preschool program with special education services provided, a number of considerations can help you decide whether a program is appropriate for your child and will be effective in meeting your child's needs and supporting his or her development consistent with your child's IEP. (Factors to consider when evaluating whether a placement is an effective, high-quality environment for your child are outlined in more detail in Chapter 7.) Visiting a program with a list of questions you have prepared in advance so that you can get all the information you need is an essential first step. Some questions you will want to ask are the following:

- How long is the school day?
- How many days per week is the program offered?
- How many children are in a class? What is the maximum number of children allowed in a program?
- What is the staff-to-student ratio—how many staff members are there to work with the children in class?
- What is the background of the teachers and other staff who will work with your child? Are they professionally certified?

- Do any of the teachers who will work with your child have experience with children who are blind or visually impaired?

- Will the local school district send a teacher certified in working with students who are visually impaired to consult with the classroom teacher and provide advice, suggestions, information, and other technical assistance?

- Will the school district provide direct services in the classroom from the teacher of students with visual impairments? Will your child be provided with any specialized adaptations, such as large print, he or she needs to develop important skills? These might include skills that will help prepare him or her to learn how to read or how to use braille, if braille is appropriate to your child's needs.

In addition to these questions, you may want to take into account a number of other considerations:

- Is the program licensed by the state, and does it have a good reputation?

- Is the location of the program safe and clean, and is it accessible for people with disabilities?

- Is the location convenient to your home or place of work?

- Are transportation arrangements suitable for your child's needs? Are the vehicles accessible for wheelchairs and other necessary equipment, and do the scheduling and the pick-up and drop-off locations fit your family's needs?

- What services are available to children and families in the program?

- Do staff have a supportive, welcoming attitude to the children and their families?

- Will your child have a chance to interact with children with and without disabilities?

- Are visits from parents and family members permitted and welcome?

- Are references from other parents available? Do other parents recommend the program?

Once your child's preschool has been selected and you have agreed, having a teacher of students with visual impairments provide information to the preschool classroom teacher is of crucial importance. This teacher can act as a consultant to explain how your child's vision loss affects his or her behavior and ability to learn and how to adjust the classroom environment so that your child can perform to his or her utmost potential. For instance, the teacher of visually impaired students can discuss accommodations such as appropriate lighting levels to allow your child to use his or her vision comfortably and efficiently; behaviors that your child

~~may be using to compensate for a vision loss, such as head turning or tilt-~~ing; and ways to organize the classroom to ensure your child's ability to move safely and to understand where materials and specific areas are located.

The visual impairment or diagnosis that your child has may require specific adaptations in the classroom. These may include the following, which you and the teacher of visually impaired students can discuss with the preschool classroom teacher:

- Preferential seating next to the teacher during story time so that books can be best seen by your child, or inspected by touch, with extra verbal descriptions included for your child.

- Presentation of materials in a clear and simple format with strong outlines.

- Use of different contrasting colors when arranging or selecting classroom materials.

- Definition of classroom space or special areas such as the reading area by the use of such materials as markers, borders, colored tape on the floor, or rugs.

- Specific verbal directions provided out loud during transitions or movement from one place or activity to another.

- Use of the buddy system, in which children in the class are paired when traveling in and out of the building.

- Clear announcements of destinations to the class before beginning to travel.

- Placement of braille or large-print labels (when appropriate) around the classroom to increase your child's exposure to written language— an important support for reading readiness for all children.

- Placement of materials such as color charts and number charts down at the floor level, where children can access them as they explore and play. Children with additional disabilities may be comfortable in various positions, such as on beanbags, wedges, or mats on the floor, rather than sitting in chairs or wheelchairs for most of the day; a physical or occupational therapist can recommend effective positioning.

- Use of real objects or realistic models, such as a real bunny in a cage or fuzzy toy bunny when reading a story about rabbits, whenever possible to support development of ideas and concepts.

- Allowance for additional practice in skills and extra time to finish activities.

Almost any visual condition—whether it be central or peripheral field loss, depth perception problems, light sensitivity, the use of only one eye, or any of a number of other visual impairments—requires specific teaching strategies, accommodations, and classroom modifications. In order for your child to navigate the preschool setting successfully in a safe and positive atmosphere, input from a teacher with experience and understanding of how vision affects learning is invaluable. In addition to providing preschool staff with information that can address your child's specific needs, this teacher can also explain that behavior possibly mistaken for a learning difficulty of some kind may in fact be the result of inadequate classroom accommodations and teaching methods that need to be adapted for a visually impaired child.

Transition to preschool is a very important step in your child's life. It means moving into new educational programs as well as new activities in your neighborhood and community. For parents, working with an early intervention team and then moving a child into preschool is in many ways the beginning of a continuing career as the child's educational coordinator and advocate. Many of the steps that a family can take when a child is very young—learning as much as possible about the child's visual impairment and abilities and needs, gathering information about educational issues and special education law and services, developing good working relationships with service coordinators and other helpful professionals, and connecting with other parents, parents' groups, and concerned national organizations—will be repeated, refined, and improved upon as family members accompany the child through his or her school career. The strategies outlined in Chapter 1 and this chapter and those provided in the chapters that follow can help you and your child have a successful and satisfying journey through the school years.

For More Information

D. Chen (Ed.), *Essential Elements in Early Intervention: Visual Impairment and Multiple Disabilities* (New York: AFB Press, 1999).

N. Chernus-Mansfield, D. Hayashi, Marilyn Horn, and L. Kekelis, *Heart to Heart, Parents of Blind and Partially Sighted Children Talk about Their Feelings* (Los Angeles: Blind Children's Center, 1986).

N. Chernus-Mansfield and L. Kekelis, *Talk to Me, I and II: A Language Guide for Parents of Blind Children* (Los Angeles: Blind Children's Center, 1984).

S. A. Goodman and S. H. Wittenstein (Eds.), *Collaborative Assessment: Working with Students Who Are Blind or Visually Impaired, Including Those with Additional Disabilities* (New York: AFB Press, 2003).

L. Harrell, *Touch the Baby, Blind and Visually Impaired Children as Patients: Helping Them to Respond to Care* (New York: American Foundation for the Blind, 1984).

M. C. Holbrook (Ed.), *Children with Visual Impairments: A Parents' Guide*, second edition (Bethesda, MD: Woodbine House, 2006).

D. Hug, N. Chernus-Mansfield, and D. Hayashi, *Move with Me: A Parent's Guide to Movement Development for Babies Who Are Visually Impaired* (Los Angeles: Blind Children's Center, 1987).

R. L. Pogrund and D. L. Fazzi (Eds.), *Early Focus: Working with Young Children Who Are Blind or Visually Impaired and Their Families*, second edition (New York: AFB Press, 2002).

NOTES

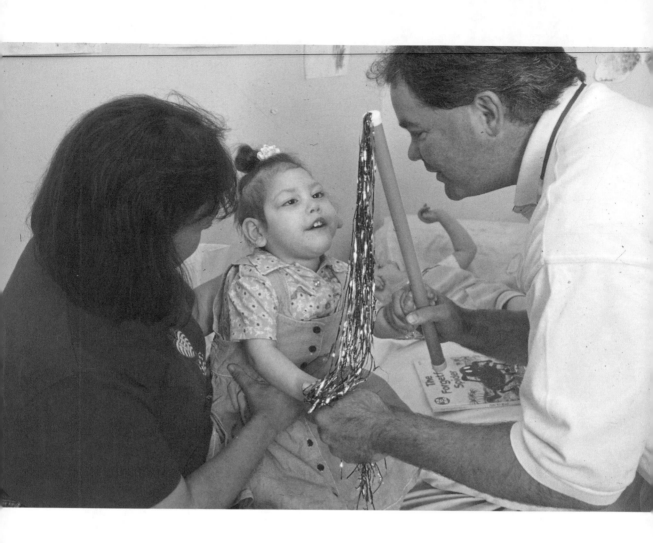

CHAPTER 3

Assessment: Identifying Your Child's Needs

Jane N. Erin and Tami Sue Levinson

Before a child of any age who has a visual impairment can begin to receive appropriate support and assistance, an assessment has to be done to find out what special services—if any—he or she needs. Although many people associate the word "assessment" with taking tests in a classroom with paper and pencil, thinking about time passing, and worrying if they will perform at their best, assessment encompasses many things in addition to written exams.

For example, the parents of 3-year-old Nathan were apprehensive before their son's evaluation by his local school district, because sometimes he did not talk to strangers, and he could not even write his name yet. They were afraid that he would not cooperate for testing. They bought him a new shirt for the meeting and told him to be sure to answer all the questions that were asked. When they arrived at the meeting, they were surprised that the woman encouraged Nathan to play with some toys on the floor while she spoke with them about his eye condition and about what things he could do. Then she sat on the floor and played with Nathan, occasionally taking notes on a tablet and making some marks on a checklist. Finally, she asked Nathan to walk with her to the playground, and she talked with him about things he saw along the way. This was a much more pleasant experience than his parents had expected, and they wondered what had been learned through such an informal process.

For a visually impaired child, a variety of assessment tools can help the educational team understand his or her visual abilities, level of development, academic skills, and other skills such as self-care (those everyday tasks required to take appropriate care of oneself, such as getting dressed, washing, brushing teeth, and so on) that may be affected by his or her visual impairment. In a sense, assessment is at the heart of all instruction, because it determines both a child's strengths and needs, so that appropriate attention and services to address the child's needs and maximize his or her strengths can be planned.

The family has a key role in assessment, and it is important for you to understand its purposes so that you can participate in a way that will be most helpful to your child. This chapter explains some of the most common types of assessments that are used in an evaluation and addresses concerns that parents frequently have. When considering the topic of assessment, parents may find it helpful to be aware of these important points:

- The assessment of students with visual impairments is a complex task that requires careful planning and consideration and specialized knowledge, and it needs to be conducted by a team of educators and professionals with different specializations.

- Parents' input into their child's evaluation—in particular, the initial special education evaluation—is essential. A teacher who specializes in working with visually impaired students is a key member of the evaluation team. This teacher may be the person who conducts certain specialized assessments that focus on the needs of students who are visually impaired.

- Assessments used with sighted students are often used for students who are visually impaired. These typically cannot provide completely accurate information about a visually impaired student's abilities and needs. For this reason, professionals who are knowledgeable about students with visual impairments and other disabilities need to be involved in the evaluation process.

PURPOSES OF EVALUATION AND TYPES OF ASSESSMENTS

All students are assessed regularly and in a variety of ways during their school years. For students in mainstream classrooms, assessment is usually conducted with an entire class; it is intended to help the teacher evaluate students' progress in learning. When a student has specialized learning needs, the results of assessment can guide planning to address these needs. In fact, evaluation based on a variety of assessments is the very basis for the program of instruction and special services put together for all students receiving special education services.

The Team Approach

As explained in Chapter 1, a central concept in the Individuals with Disabilities Education Act (IDEA), the primary federal legislation that governs the provision of special education in the United States, is the Individualized Education Program (IEP), which is explained in more detail in Chapter 4. This document is assembled by an IEP team annually for every child receiving special education in this country. Why a team? Because the needs of children with visual impairments and other disabilities are diverse and unique, and no one individual has the expertise to assess and address all those needs. The legally mandated or required members of a child's IEP team are his or her parents; the regular education teacher; the teacher of students with visual impairments, who has specialized training and knowledge in working with visually impaired children and who may be the individual who conducts certain specialized assessment of the

---

From a Parent's Perspective

ASSESSMENTS AND THE EDUCATIONAL TEAM

Individuals included in a child's team should be (if appropriate): parents, child (if age appropriate), "vision teacher"—the teacher of students with visual impairments—orientation and mobility instructor, regular education teacher, speech and language therapist, physical and/or occupational therapists, social worker, guidance counselor, psychologist, and school or district administrator. It is very important that each individual on the team be knowledgeable about your child and the information gathered during evaluations. No one can make an informed decision about the true least restrictive environment and other important issues for a child without a strong background in interpreting evaluation results on a child with a visual impairment. Be sure to have a teacher of students with visual impairments work in tandem with the school psychologist, speech-language therapist, or other professionals involved with testing. Many concepts evaluated will be foreign to children who are blind and may be fragmented for children with low vision. Not many valid assessment tools exist or are used to measure cognitive or social and emotional levels on children with visual impairments. Be diligent about asking questions about the type of assessments used with your child.

Sheri Davis
Mother of an 18-year-old son
with Leber's congenital amaurosis
Lutz, Florida

child and who can interpret evaluation results; a representative of the school district; the child him- or herself, as appropriate; and, at the discretion of the parents or school, other persons with knowledge or expertise regarding the student, such as the paraeducator who works regularly with the child and the orientation and mobility (O&M) instructor, a specially trained professional who teaches techniques for safe and independent travel to people who are visually impaired. Other members of a student's team may include, depending on his or her needs, an occupational therapist, a physical therapist, a school psychologist, or a speech and language therapist. This team compiles and reviews pertinent information about the student's abilities and needs, including the recommendations and results of any assessments undertaken, and determines educational goals for the student and the services necessary to support him or her in pursuit of these goals. These goals and services are specified in the student's IEP, which serves as the blueprint for the student's educational program.

Identification and Eligibility

The initial evaluation for visually impaired students is usually carried out to determine whether the child's visual impairment creates an educational disadvantage, making him or her eligible for special education services. Standards for eligibility vary among states and even among individual school districts. Families who want to find out about eligibility criteria in their state can contact their state department of education or can consult the web site of the state department of education for their state regulations in special education. The *AFB Directory of Services for Blind and Visually Impaired Persons in the United States and Canada,* published by the American Foundation for the Blind (AFB) and also available on AFB's web site (www.afb.org; see "For More Information" at the end of this chapter) provides contact information for state agencies throughout the country. You can also contact the special education director in your local school district for this information.

For a child to qualify for services as being visually impaired, most state departments or school districts require or recommend a report from an ophthalmologist or optometrist that describes the child's eye condition and other information about vision, including etiology (origin of the visual impairment), visual acuity (clarity of vision), and prognosis (future effects of the condition). Many states or districts also require a functional vision assessment, an evaluation that shows how well the child is able to use his or her vision in real-life circumstances, conducted by a certified teacher of visually impaired students or an O&M specialist. Some also require a learning media assessment, conducted by a teacher of visually impaired students, which helps to identify how a child uses his or her senses to obtain information and the best ways of presenting educational materials and other information to the child. These two assessments, which are discussed in more detail later in this chapter and in Chapter 6, can help the IEP team in determining what educational needs the student has that are related to his or her visual impairment.

In addition, most schools require a psychoeducational evaluation as part of the assessment for special education services. This is conducted by a psychologist or by someone with special expertise in testing, known as a psychometrist or educational diagnostician. In most school systems these individuals have little experience with visually impaired students since the population of these students in the United States and through-out the world is small. The teacher of visually impaired children should be available to the psychologist to provide suggestions about appropriate evaluation procedures. Specialists employed at schools for visually impaired students in many states can also suggest to you local professionals who are qualified to carry out a psychological evaluation.

Sometimes parents are concerned that the fact their child is undergoing psychoeducational testing implies that there is something wrong with his or her thinking or mental stability. This not the case. A psychoeducational evaluation is actually intended to provide a more complete description of a child's learning abilities and patterns, and it reports both strengths and weaknesses. The results of this particular assessment will help the team to determine whether specialized services are needed for your child.

Intelligence Tests

Intelligence tests are usually included in a psychological evaluation when a child is referred for special education. Psychologists often administer standardized intelligence tests such as the Wechsler Intelligence Scale for Children (WISC-IV).[1] These types of tests evaluate a student's performance in areas such as vocabulary, verbal comprehension, picture sequencing, mathematical calculation, and picture assembly (putting together a picture from fragments of the whole). As in other areas in which your child may be assessed, there is no standardized intelligence test for visually impaired students in the United States that provides data that compares a child's scores with those of other visually impaired students. Although there have been attempts to create such a test in the past, the small numbers of students who are visually impaired and their varying characteristics have made it impossible to gather enough data to determine the standards of proficiency that would create an accurate measure of intelligence for children who are visually impaired.

Because no single test can accurately measure intelligence in a visually impaired child, most psychologists use several methods to gather information to reflect that child's learning abilities while taking into consideration the visual impairment. For example, the previous versions of the WISC included separate verbal and performance scales. The performance scale was inappropriate for most visually impaired students because it relied heavily on pictures and visual symbols that many visually impaired children could not see and that would need to be presented in a modified way for them. For this reason most psychologists combined it with other assessment tools to provide a more complete idea of a child's reasoning abilities and intelligence. The newest version, the WISC-IV, includes several scales that can be used with both blind and low vision students. Some of the picture-based items have been eliminated, and the memory scales have been expanded. The WISC-IV is appropriate for use with blind and visually impaired students when it is administered by a professional who is knowledgeable about visual impairment and who has consulted with the teacher of visually impaired students. Intelligence testing can help the team decide if your child may have learning difficulties other than those that may result from having a visual impairment, and it can assist in deciding if a child is eligible for special education services.

Educational Goal Setting

Various assessments are used to help decide what educational goals are important in order for the student to acquire the specialized skills needed because of his or her visual impairment. For younger children, developmental assessments are sometimes conducted to determine the child's general abilities compared to other children of the same age or grade level. These assessments are usually administered by the teacher who is most familiar with the child, with assistance from other team members. Developmental assessments may be checklists or scales that are commercially produced; some make comparisons with developmental milestones in children without disabilities, while others are created specifically to assess children with physical disabilities; a few are specifically designed for visually impaired students. Developmental assessments and skills inventories such as the Oregon Project[2] and the Reynell-Zinkin Developmental Scales[3] emphasize typical developmental patterns for visually impaired students; other scales, such as the Carolina Curriculum[4] and the Callier-Azusa Scale,[5] are for students with multiple disabilities that include visual impairments.

Some evaluators use developmental scales that have been normed on students without disabilities—that is, the standards of development or achievement have been calculated with reference to children who are not disabled. In such cases, data have been collected on large numbers of children to determine the age at which they usually acquire a skill. It may be helpful to know how a child with a visual impairment compares to children without disabilities in terms of reaching these milestones, but it is important to remember that visually impaired students may master some skills at a different pace than sighted children their age, especially skills involving movement and self-care. A delay of a few months does not necessarily indicate a problem; it may just indicate that a child has a different way of learning. Most developmental assessments are intended to be administered to children younger than six years old. Older children's development becomes more influenced by their ongoing experiences and learning, and as they grow their individual development becomes more uneven. For example, a child with an autism spectrum disorder may make very gradual progress in developing social skills while making rapid progress in his or her motor skill development. Other types of assessments such as ecological and academic assessments, described later in this chapter, are more useful as a child grows older.

Making developmental comparisons among children is a complex issue. When comparisons involving visually impaired children are made, they frequently are not valid unless those conducting the assessment were aware of the impact of visual impairment and other disabilities on development and took that information into consideration when reaching a conclusion. When professionals give information about a child's developmental age, it is helpful for parents to ask what kinds of children the instrument used was intended to evaluate. When it comes to the assessment of their children, parents of students who are visually impaired may want to make sure that someone knowledgeable about visual impairment be involved in the assessment and in the interpretation of results.

Play-Based Assessment

As the example of Nathan at the beginning of this chapter indicates, observational methods such as play-based assessment are often used with younger children. These methods allow the evaluator, usually the teacher who knows the child best along with other team members, to learn about a child from watching him or her select and interact with different toys or other materials, use objects and words in imaginative ways, use movements to discover the world around him or her, and figure out how to solve problems. Although the observation is very informal and allows the child to play as he or she chooses, an experienced evaluator will be looking for specific skills to indicate what a child understands and what he or she can learn or invent. This approach is especially useful when a child will not or cannot cooperate in a structured or formal test situation; it is a more natural and less stressful way of gathering information about the child's abilities and interests.

Ecological Assessments

Ecological assessments evaluate how a child performs a skill in real environments, such as at school, at home, and in his or her community. They can be conducted by any teaching professional in his or her area of expertise. These assessments describe how a child does the steps of a routine task and whether he or she needs assistance in any of the steps. This kind of analysis is called a discrepancy analysis, which is a comparison of how someone with a disability does a task with the way it is typically performed by a person who does not have a disability. It can help the assessment team understand how a child learns routines, anticipates new events, and solves problems. It can also provide important information on the skills that will be helpful for a child to master in order to perform tasks. An ecological assessment may also be a narrative description of how a child does a task. Although these assessments do not provide information about how a child compares to groups of children his or her age, they do provide a solid foundation for deciding on goals that will be useful to a particular family and child.

Specialized Assessments

Specialized assessments are usually administered to evaluate a child's skills in areas that are affected by his or her visual impairment, and they are discussed in more detail later in this chapter. These are usually criterion-referenced assessments—that is, they list skills to be evaluated but do not compare performances of groups of students. Specialized assessments may be conducted in such areas as O&M (the ability to move and travel independently), daily living skills, knowledge of braille, social skills, use of the abacus for mathematical calculation, and listening skills. They are usually administered by teachers or other professionals to gather information about what skills and knowledge a child already possesses and what areas he or she may need to work on in order to gain more mastery.

Academic Testing

Academic testing is a regular part of measuring any student's scholastic progress. These kinds of tests are what you may think of when you remember your own school experience or imagine your child taking tests: paper-and-pencil tests that are taken along with classmates. However, some educators are now using different methods, such as group problem solving, to measure students' progress. When classroom tests require reading and writing for sighted students, a visually impaired student should also read the test and write the answers in whatever reading medium he or she uses best. In order for this to take place, the teacher of visually impaired students will put the test into braille or large print, or the classroom teacher might put it on a computer disk, so that by using special software, the student can read it on a braille display and write his or her answers in braille or on the computer. Although reading the test to the blind or visually impaired student may be considered in exceptional circumstances, oral administration of this kind of test may not provide the same level of challenge if it does not require the student to read the material. Only when a test is designed to get information from or about students quickly, when verbal abilities are being assessed, or when a student has an identified learning difficulty in addition to his or her visual impairment should the student be routinely tested orally.

Achievement Tests

Achievement tests are standardized commercial tests designed to evaluate a student's knowledge in academic skill areas and to compare his or her knowledge to that of other children on a similar grade level. Most states require standardized tests every one to three years, and they use these to measure how students compare to those in other schools and districts and even other states. Students with visual impairments are also required to take standardized tests, and it is the role of the teacher of visually impaired students to make sure that these tests are available in a child's best reading medium. Some students may be given more time to complete these tests if that is an appropriate accommodation for them. If that is the case, this requirement should be stated on the student's IEP, as explained in the next chapter. Under the federal No Child Left Behind Act, all children must be tested regularly to determine their progress toward mastering state educational standards. If a child is visually impaired, accommodations may be provided that allow him or her to demonstrate skills and knowledge without being restricted by the effects of the visual difference. (See Chapters 4 and 6 for more information about accommodations.) A few children cannot participate in the state assessments even with accommodations, and in such cases may receive an alternate assessment, based either on regular or modified standards, to allow them to demonstrate progress.

SPECIALIZED EVALUATIONS OF VISUALLY IMPAIRED STUDENTS

Some assessments are used to evaluate students with visual impairments only. Because most school districts typically serve only a few visually impaired students, parents may need to request these assessments for their child if their school district does not offer them. Many school district personnel are not familiar with the value and purpose of these assessments because they have not worked frequently with students who are visually impaired, and the assessments provide critical information about a child's abilities and needs. In addition to the direct assessments of students that are discussed here, your child's IEP team will also consider information from a variety of other sources. These are discussed in "Other Sources of Assessment Information."

Functional Vision Assessment

The functional vision assessment, sometimes called the functional vision evaluation, is performed once a student has been referred for evaluation

Other Sources of Assessment Information

Many kinds of information need to be gathered in order to obtain a full picture of a child. In addition to information gathered by having a student take certain tests or directing the student in specific tasks (direct assessment), some information also needs to come from indirect sources, such as the student's records or observations of the student without interacting with him or her. Information that may have already been collected in other sources can be crucial to understanding a child's strengths, abilities, and unique needs. Indirect methods of assessment include reviewing previous data, reports, and other information; conducting interviews with family members and other teachers; performing surveys on student performance with team members who frequently interact with a child; and undertaking observations of the child. The following lists, which give possible sources of indirect assessment information, are useful in assessment planning to make sure that all information has been collected and reviewed and all factors that are critical to understanding how a child functions in various contexts have been considered.

FILE REVIEWS

- the student's cumulative file
- health records
- the student's special education file
- the classroom teacher's files (work samples)
- information from other agencies
- academic achievement information, including grades on assignments and tests and in classes or courses

MEDICAL DATA (FROM SCHOOL AND OTHER FACILITIES)

It is critical to have current medical information to inform the assessment process and ensure all medical conditions are considered and the implications for a child's learning process determined.

- vision screening report
- ophthalmologic exam results
- clinical low vision evaluation report

- hearing screening results
- audiological (hearing) exam report
- information on other health or disability conditions
- information on factors such as seizures, allergies, and medications

INTERVIEWS (IN PERSON, OVER THE TELEPHONE, BY MAIL OR E-MAIL)

Interviews and surveys provide a method for gathering pertinent information in real-life settings based on input from a variety of people. A well-organized survey is an efficient and effective method for obtaining information. The following list provides suggestions on whom to include in interviews and surveys.

- parents
- student
- classroom teacher
- special education teacher
- paraeducator
- other staff (lunchroom and recess staff, coaches, extracurricular staff)
- other school or related agency personnel (job-coaches, counselors, rehabilitation specialists)

ENVIRONMENTS

Observations of a child with visual impairments in real-life situations are among the most effective methods for gathering meaningful information to help determine appropriate accommodations and modifications, yet are often underutilized. The following list provides many contexts and environments that could be considered for observations.

- school
- home
- community
- workplace
- day care

ENVIRONMENTAL FACTORS

It is not unusual for children's abilities and needs to vary given the circumstances in their environment. For example, only assessing during the day the orientation and mobility needs of a child who has an eye condi-

(continued on next page)

tion that interferes with his or her ability to see in the dark would not adequately gather information to determine his or her educational needs and any necessary adaptations or accommodations. Environmental factors that may influence a student's performance and have an impact on educational needs are listed here.

- familiar/unfamiliar settings
- time of day
- lighting
- noise level in background

ADDITIONAL TEACHING AND LEARNING ACTIVITIES AND CONTEXTS

Gathering information and conducting observations about a variety of teaching and learning activities, and in contexts that are sometimes overlooked by team members, may yield pertinent information about a child's abilities and needs. Here are some examples of situations and places that may provide relevant information in the assessment process.

- structured/unstructured activities
- independent and group activities
- transitions (between locations/rooms, between activities in the same room)
- bus travel (arrival and departure)
- playground
- lunchroom
- academic instruction
- physical education
- art activities
- library work
- computer use

Donna McNear

Adapted from Evaluation Workgroup, *Assessment of Students with Visual Impairments: Minnesota Promising Practices Guidelines, Draft* (Faribault, MN: Minnesota Resource Center: Blind/Visually Impaired, April 2000), unpublished.

for eligibility as a visually impaired student. A teacher of students who are visually impaired or an O&M specialist conducts the functional vision assessment. This assessment focuses on the child's functional vision—the vision the child may have and the ways he or she uses it to perform tasks in daily life, in school, and in other typical settings. It expands on the information provided by the child's eye care specialist, which is usually obtained in the clinical or formal setting of a physician's office, by describing the child's use of vision while he or she does a variety of activities, including reading, writing, physical activities, and viewing objects from a distance.

When the IEP team meets to put together the student's educational program, as explained in Chapters 1 and 4, the functional vision assessment provides information and recommendations that are included in the IEP, the educational plan. The section of the IEP called the Present Level of Performance (see Chapter 4 for a description of the sections of the IEP) should include a statement about how the child is using vision during near tasks (performed closer than two or three feet), distance tasks (beyond three feet), and mobility tasks (during which the child is moving and may be viewing moving objects). If a need for instruction is identified in any areas in the Present Level of Performance, these areas will be targeted in the goals and objectives of the IEP. For example, the following skills might be listed as IEP objectives:

- learning to scan from left to right with a magnifier, moving the device across a line of print in a book
- learning to scan a playground visually for a piece of equipment or other object
- learning to use a video magnifier or closed-circuit television (CCTV: a device that enlarges reading material)

These are examples of skills that children may learn to make better use of their limited vision.

The functional vision assessment also identifies necessary adaptations and materials that a child may need to accomplish classroom activities successfully on a day-to-day basis as well as if he or she undergoes any statewide or district-level testing (see Chapter 6 for more information on such adaptations). Some common adaptations include

- the provision of additional lighting when your child is completing near-vision tasks such as reading or drawing
- use of a reading stand to prop up printed materials
- use of white paper and black felt-tip markers to increase the contrast of handwritten materials and make them more legible
- a longer time for completing a test than that given to sighted classmates

The functional vision assessment is an important tool in planning, but it is also an informational document for all educational personnel. It should be clearly written, with recommendations that parents and all other educational team members can understand. A sample functional vision assessment report appears at the end of this chapter.

Learning Media Assessment

The learning media assessment is conducted for two reasons. First, it is used to identify the senses—touch or hearing, for example—through which a child primarily obtains information from his or her environment. Second, based on this information, the assessment also indicates the child's primary learning medium—the format through which he or she can most effectively obtain information—which may be braille, large print, audio, or some combination of these media. Knowing the student's preferred learning channel enables the educational team to begin plans for adapting and supporting the student's curriculum. For example, if the child's primary learning channel is tactile and he or she is developmentally ready for reading, the team will probably decide that he or she should begin reading in braille.

The results of the learning media assessment are integrated into several sections of a student's IEP. The Present Level of Performance section should report the student's current learning medium (for example, braille, large print, print with a magnifier, pictures, or auditory production such as cassette tapes). The level of proficiency that the student has reached should also be included in this section of the IEP. For example, if the child can read braille at a first grade level at a speed of 40 words per minute, this should be stated in the report. If the student needs instruction in using different learning media or sensory channels, goals and objectives to achieve this should be included in the IEP. For example, instruction in braille, use of a magnifier with regular print, or use of an audio cassette player may be goals; specific objectives for instruction in a particular medium would be identified by the learning media assessment. The IEP also includes a statement about whether braille instruction is appropriate, as required by the IDEA Amendments of 1997. That decision is based on information from the learning media assessment which is mandated, or legally required to take place, by IDEA. The assessment also assists the IEP team to complete the IEP sections specifying which adaptations are appropriate for the student to use during testing of all kinds. A sample learning media assessment report appears at the end of this chapter.

Orientation and Mobility Assessment

An O&M assessment provides information about a child's ability to remain oriented in his or her environment and to travel with or without assistance.

Although children with visual impairments can learn the same travel skills as their sighted peers, they may require instruction and practice in some of the concepts and skills. An assessment should be carried out by an O&M instructor: an individual who has received professional certification in this field. This specialist may use a number of procedures to evaluate a child. He or she may ask the student to demonstrate concepts such as left and right, identify body parts and their functions, locate areas within a classroom or a familiar room, and travel through familiar and unfamiliar areas. Some specialists will use standardized assessment tools such as the Hill Performance Test of Positional Concepts[6] to record what the student has mastered and the areas in which she or he experiences difficulty. Instructors will usually observe a child traveling and will talk to him or her and the family about the child's regular travel habits. If a child uses a cane or another device, the instructor will observe how he or she holds and uses it.

Based on this assessment, the specialist will make a recommendation to the educational team about whether the child can benefit from regular O&M services. Young children and children with other disabilities should also be considered for an O&M assessment, even if they do not walk by themselves. The O&M specialist can still evaluate and instruct the child in ways to become more independent in movement and travel. Any instruction, however, should always begin with a thorough assessment.

Assistive Technology Assessment

An assistive technology assessment is often needed to determine what devices and equipment will allow a student maximum access to learning. Although the term "assistive technology" is sometimes used broadly to cover many different devices that help people with disabilities complete tasks, it usually refers to equipment, devices, and methods that provide access to the environment and print information for people with visual impairments using computer hardware and software and other electronic equipment. Assessment recommendations for a child might include the use of specialized equipment such as braille notetakers, computer systems that include software used to enlarge the images and text displayed on the computer screen, or special computer keyboards adapted for people with visual or physical impairments. Technology assessments should be performed by professionals who are proficient in the use of assistive technology in everyday settings. Often a technology assessment is best conducted by a team that includes the teacher of students with visual impairments and a technology expert. School districts and state agencies sometimes have teams of professionals whose primary role is to work on assessment and the use of assistive technology by learners who are visually impaired. IDEA requires a student's IEP team to address his or her need for assistive technology, and a comprehensive assistive technology assessment is generally the way to establish this need.

Assessment of Students with Multiple Disabilities

Students who have other disabilities in addition to a visual impairment will require careful assessment to reveal their strengths and abilities as well as areas in which they experience difficulties. A single test will not provide in-depth information on the child's abilities; extended observation is an important part of the assessment process. Because children with multiple disabilities often function best in regular and familiar routines, most evaluations will be conducted in a familiar setting with people who are known to the child. Asking the student to participate in a regular routine such as having a snack or putting shoes on and taking them off can provide a wealth of information about his or her communication skills, motor ability, motivation, and ability to pay attention.

Sometimes the purpose of an assessment is to decide whether a child has multiple disabilities. When developmental delays of more than a year exist during the preschool years, this possibility should be considered. Often additional disabilities such as learning difficulties, mental retardation, or physical disabilities are not identified until later in a child's development, while severe visual impairments tend to be identified early. Families and professionals may assume that a child's developmental delays compared with sighted children of the same age are due to the visual impairment. Therefore, specialists such as occupational and physical therapists, specialists in learning disabilities or physical disabilities, or speech and language therapists, who can address the child's other disabilities, may not become involved until a child has developed enough for delays in other areas to become evident.

Parents are vital sources of information in the assessment of all children, but their input is especially important when a child does not speak or is not able to respond to specific directions. Parents' descriptions of a child's regular activities, likes and dislikes, and ways of communicating, as well as the family's goals for him or her, help to shape the team's conclusions about the child's abilities and important objectives for learning.

It is not unusual for different team members to report that a child shows skills and abilities in one setting or set of circumstances but not in another. For example, you may notice that your son turns to a person who calls his name, but other team members may note that he does not do this at school. Your daughter may hold her own cup at school but not at home. Many children with multiple disabilities are more likely than other children to respond to specific cues and prompts that direct them to perform a particular activity in one situation and not another. When a child performs a skill only in one setting, the team will want to observe carefully to decide how he or she can learn to carry it out in other settings and under differing circumstances. When you as a parent can provide full information about the ways in which your child communicates and responds at home, it is helpful to professionals working with him or her. It also initiates an important collaboration among parents and professionals when they work together to share information and reinforce the child's development of skills.

STRATEGIES FOR PARENTS

Because assessment is a formal activity that involves technical information, parents may have many concerns and questions on this topic, such as those listed here. However, a number of suggestions may be helpful in preparing a child and family to deal with the process of assessment:

- Discuss the purpose of any assessments conducted with the members of your child's educational team, especially the teacher of visually impaired students, to understand the information that is being sought.

- Share any information that you have concerning your child's needs and abilities in writing with the professionals who assess your child and with the educational team members, especially information that can influence the way in which an assessment is conducted or interpreted. This information might include current medical and other reports as well as your own description of your child's needs. In addition, it ought to include important information about the way in which your child communicates, responds, and behaves, so that those working with your child have a better understanding of his or her responses during the assessment and the circumstances that will help your child feel comfortable.

- Ask questions about the knowledge and credentials that those conducting an assessment have concerning children with visual impairments and any other health or medical condition affecting your child. Request in writing that a professional experienced in working with visually impaired children be involved in the performance and interpretation of the assessment.

- Request that the results and implications of the assessment be explained to you. If you believe that the assessment of your child is inaccurate, or you have other concerns, you can request an independent assessment, as explained in this chapter and in Chapter 10.

Families may find that they have many questions about the assessment process, such as the following ones:

Is it important to know how my child compares to other children?

Some families want to know how their children are developing in comparison to other children. As explained earlier, various tests and checklists that are normed provide information about how old most students are when they attain a specific skill. However, comparison does not help a team in planning educational goals. If a child is very different in physical or intellectual abilities from other children of the same age, he or she may have other disabilities and learn in different ways.

A child with multiple disabilities can often lag further and further behind his or her classmates who do not have disabilities in learning over time, even though he or she is making steady progress when compared to his or her own previous level of performance. It can be discouraging for a family and a team to view normal developmental rates as an important goal. It may be far more important to demonstrate that a child has functional learning goals and can attain the skills that are most important to his or her own growth and education. Functional goals relate to skills that can be applied in real life experiences: putting on shoes, pouring a drink, participating in a ball game or other leisure activity, and using money to buy groceries. Although all children need to learn functional skills, they will require more practice and may be emphasized more strongly when a child has several disabilities.

What if I don't think an assessment is accurate?

Parents can request an independent educational evaluation by a qualified person of their choice if they do not believe the assessment of their child reflects his or her real abilities. The school district is obligated to assume the cost of this evaluation. If this reevaluation is done and the results are different from the first evaluation, the team should consider the differences in the two assessment procedures. Sometimes there are differences because the original evaluator was not familiar with testing procedures for visually impaired children or because the tests and activities were not appropriate for a child with a visual impairment. Sometimes the difference occurs because children respond differently to different people, or because the settings varied, and that variation is important for the team to consider in educational planning. If you still believe that your child has not been fairly tested, you can follow the procedures for due process that are described in Chapter 10. Often the specialized school for children with visual impairments in your state or a nearby state (see Chapter 7) can conduct independent evaluations or can recommend people who are experienced and qualified in the assessment of visually impaired learners.

Should my child receive extra time to take tests?

Some tests are meant to be completed in a specific period of time. Students with visual impairments often need more time than their sighted classmates to respond and record answers in print or braille. Often children with low vision—visual impairment severe enough to interfere with their ability to perform the tasks of daily life—who read print are given the standard time plus half, and visually impaired children who read braille will be given twice the typical time. Deciding how much time is needed is difficult, because students' reading speeds vary. Some people recommend that learners with visual impairments be given as much time as needed, but this may provide the student with an extra advantage. If other students are required to complete the test in a given time period, the visually impaired student should also have a time limit that is based on his or her reading rate. The IEP team should decide whether a student should be allowed to have additional time for testing and, if so, how much time. This information should appear in the IEP.

How can pictures and graphs be presented on tests my child takes?

If there are charts and graphs on a test, these should be available to the visually impaired student, either as a verbal description or as a raised tactile graphic that the student can feel and "read" with his or her fingers. Tactile graphics should be clear and easy for the student to interpret without assistance; if this is not possible, the information should be described in the text. Another but less desirable option is to have a reader available who is experienced in describing visual material to visually impaired students.

How can I prepare my child for an assessment?

It is important to help your child understand what to expect from any assessment, especially if it is unfamiliar. Try to obtain as much information about an assessment that will be performed and the circumstances in which your child will be assessed. Speaking with the teacher of visually impaired students, other members of the educational team, and the director for special education in your school district will be helpful. If your child will be going to a new place or working with a new person, you may want to think of ways to tell or show him or her what the situation will be like. You may want to talk with the professionals doing the assessment to find out if there are ways you can help your child be comfortable during the assessment, especially if your son or daughter is shy or changes behavior when working with others. If your child is going to complete specific tasks, it is important that he or she has the chance to do well; this means getting plenty of sleep and being alert for the activities. Sometimes an assessment involves observation, and you may want to let the team members know what things your child enjoys and what he or she dislikes, so that the team can plan to observe in a variety of situations. You may also want to ask whether the evaluators want to see a range of behaviors across many activities, or whether the assessment is intended to evaluate your child's most highly developed skills. For example, an arithmetic test is intended to reflect a child's best abilities, but an assessment of his or social skills should describe how your child typically interacts with others, even though he or she may not use all the skills he or she has learned.

What can I expect from an assessment?

As a parent, you should be aware of the purpose of the assessment. You should also be informed about the outcome of the assessment. This information may be in the form of a written report, test scores, a checklist, or another document that records what was done during the assessment and what was discovered as a result of it. For important assessments, parents should have the opportunity to talk with the professionals who conducted the assessments and to learn the results, including implications for educational services and adaptations. If you believe that an assessment has not described your child's abilities accurately for any reason, you can write a statement about your concerns that will be attached to the report in your child's files.

PARENTS' RIGHTS, RESPONSIBILITIES, AND CRUCIAL ROLE

IDEA provides for various parent and guardian rights related to the evaluation of their child. For example, prior written notice is required whenever a school district proposes to evaluate a child, which must include an explanation of why such an evaluation is believed to be necessary; a description of each procedure, assessment, record, and report on which this proposal is based; and an explanation of parents' procedural safeguards under IDEA. In addition, written parental consent must be given for a school to conduct an initial evaluation or a three-year reevaluation for eligibility for special education services. Your written consent is voluntary, and you may revoke it at any time.

As already noted, parents may request a reevaluation or an independent educational evaluation of their child, once a year, under the following conditions:

- if they are not satisfied with the quality of the existing evaluation
- if there have been changes in the child's physical or emotional condition since the evaluation was conducted

When the quality of the evaluation is in question, the reevaluation must be conducted by a certified professional who is independent from the school district. In this case, the district will pay the costs of the assessment, unless it chooses to initiate a due process hearing to show that its evaluation was appropriate. Parents can also seek an independent assessment at any time if they wish to assume the cost. Universities, psychological clinics, and professional organizations can often provide information about professionals who are qualified to conduct independent assessments. Parents who have concerns about the assessments undertaken of their children need to voice them to the members of the educational team and to their school and school district, as well as share important information about their child's needs and abilities.

Families are vital participants in assessment because they have more information about their children than anyone else does. You will best be able to contribute if you are aware of the purpose of the assessment, the procedures that may be used, and how the assessment is relevant to your child's IEP and learning goals. Only through carefully planned assessment will members of the educational team be able to determine useful and important learning goals for your child, the services and instruction that will assist him or her in pursuing these goals, and whether he or she has made progress in reaching these goals. Educational programs that effectively address a child's needs are the outgrowth of accurate and informed assessments.

Notes

1. D. Wechsler, *Wechsler Intelligence Scale for Children (WISC IV)* (San Antonio, TX: Harcourt Assessment, 2003).
2. D. Brown, V. Simmons, J. Methvin, S. Anderson, S. Boigon, and K. Davis, *The Oregon Project for Visually Impaired and Blind Preschool Children*, fifth edition (Medford, OR: Jackson Education Service District, 1991).
3. J. Reynell, *Reynell-Zinkin: Developmental Scales for Young Children* (Windsor, UK: NFER-Nelson, 1979).
4. N. Johnson-Martin, K. G. Jens, S. M. Attermeier, and B. J. Hacker, *Carolina Curriculum for Infants and Toddlers with Special Needs*, second edition (Baltimore, MD: Paul H. Brookes, 1986).
5. R. Stillman, *Callier-Azusa Scale: G Edition* (University of Texas at Dallas: Callier Center for Communication Disorders, 1978); and R. Stillman and C. Battler, *Callier-Azusa Scale: H Edition* (University of Texas at Dallas: Callier Center for Communication Disorders, 1985).
6. E. W. Hill, *The Hill Performance Test of Selected Positional Concepts* (Wood Dale, IL: Stoelting Company, 1981).

For More Information

Lists of assessments used with visually impaired students, and detailed information about them, can be found on the web site of the Texas School for the Blind and Visually Impaired, under Assessment (http://www.tsbvi.edu/Education/index.htm#Assessment), and on the web site of Lighthouse International (http://www.lighthouse.org/about/education/professionals.htm).

American Foundation for the Blind, *AFB Directory of Services for Blind and Visually Impaired Persons in the United States and Canada,* 27th edition (New York: AFB Press, 2005).

S. A. Goodman and S. H. Wittenstein (Eds.), *Collaborative Assessment: Working with Students Who Are Blind or Visually Impaired, Including Those with Additional Disabilities* (New York: AFB Press, 2003).

T. Heinze, "Comprehensive Assessment," in A. J. Koenig & M. C. Holbrook (Eds.), *Foundations of Education: Instructional Strategies for Teaching Children and Youths with Visual Impairments,* Vol. 2 (New York: AFB Press, 2000), pp. 27–59.

M. C. Holbrook, A. L. Corn, J. N. Erin, A. J. Koenig, L. B. DePriest, and I. Presley, "Specialized Assessments for Students with Visual Impairments," in A. J. Koenig & M. C. Holbrook (Eds.), *Foundations of Education: Instructional Strategies for Teaching Children and Youths with Visual Impairments,* Vol. 2 (New York: AFB Press, 2000), pp. 103–172.

C. A. Layton, "Ongoing Assessments: Informal Techniques," in A. J. Koenig & M. C. Holbrook (Eds.), *Foundations of Education: Instructional Strategies for Teaching Children and Youths with Visual Impairments,* Vol. 2 (New York: AFB Press, 2000), pp. 61–102.

S. Lewis and C. B. Allman, "Educational Programming," in M. C. Holbrook & A. J. Koenig (Eds.), *Foundations of Education: History and Theory of Teaching Children and Youths with Visual Impairments,* Vol. 1 (New York: AFB Press, 2000), pp. 218–260.

Sample Functional Vision Assessment Report

Student: John Martinez   Birth Date: 7/23/97   Age: 9
School: Midwest School for the Blind and Visually Impaired
Teacher: Anna McMillan
Assessor: Amy Flora
Dates of Assessment: November 1, 2, & 8, 2006

1. Background Information

John Martinez is currently a residential student in a multi-age middle elementary classroom at the Midwest School for the Blind. He loves science, animals, movies, video games, and talking about his interests. He is friendly and willing to engage in assessment. He has learning disabilities, and his academic achievement ranges from 1–3 years below grade level on state standardized tests administered over the past two years.

   John's visual impairment is caused by a partial retinal detachment in his right eye, and retinal folds in the left eye. Both these conditions severely impair his ability to see both near and at a distance, and he is legally blind. His right eye has better near vision, and his left eye is better for distance vision. John used to wear bifocals, but during a June 6, 2003, ophthalmological exam by Dr. Marilyn Chase, MD, of the Children's Clinic, it was determined that the bifocals were actually "hurting more than helping" his ability to see. His eyeglass prescription was changed at that time to correct for the nearsighted right eye (−3.00), the farsighted left eye (+1.00), and astigmatism (irregularities in the cornea that cause vision distortions) in both eyes. John's color vision was described as normal, and Dr. Chase indicated that his visual prognosis is stable. John was assessed at the Happy Valley Low Vision Clinic in November of 2003, when a 6X monocular and a 4X dome magnifier were prescribed.

2. Purpose of Assessment

The purpose of the assessment was to obtain current information on John's use of vision in order to make recommendations for modifications and accommodations to meet his visual and educational needs and to find out if his eyeglasses actually improve his vision.

3. Functional Vision Assessment Results

(Unless otherwise indicated, all testing was done in a classroom with overhead fluorescent track lighting.)

<u>Appearance of Eyes:</u> John has brown eyes that appear normal except for a slight right inward turn (esotropia) of the right eye and continuous horizontal nystagmus (rapid back and forth motion) in both eyes.

<u>Eyeglasses:</u> John's eyeglasses automatically assume an amber tint in bright lighting. They appear to fit him comfortably and be free from scratches. John was observed removing his glasses when working on the computer. This enabled him to move his right eye to within about 1" of the screen when necessary to look at details. He also asked to remove his eyeglasses when requested to identify unknown objects at a distance of 2–5'.

Convergence (Eyes turn in simultaneously to focus on an approaching object): John's left eye was observed to converge on a penlight at about 5" from the bridge of his nose, but convergence in his right eye was not observed.

Eye Preference: When reading, John said his right eye was his better eye. When using the computer without screen magnification, John used his right eye, without eyeglasses, to view the screen at a distance of about 1–2" when searching for detail. When asked which eye he would prefer to use with a monocular for distance viewing, he chose the left. This is consistent with previous indications that the right eye is better for near vision and his left eye is better for distance viewing.

Shifting Gaze (From one stationary object to another): John was able to shift his gaze between two 5" bright red toys held 4' apart on a horizontal plane at eye level, but he turned his head in several jerky movements in order to be able to shift his gaze both from left to right and right to left.

Tracing: John was able to use his sight to follow a curved line from beginning to end drawn with a ballpoint pen on paper.

Tracking: John could successfully follow a 3' wide and high "H" pattern traced in the air using a 6" bright red toy car. He moved his head to follow the motion and tracked across midline. His left to right movement was jerky the first trial, and smoother the second.

Peripheral Vision/Visual Fields: John's visual fields were assessed using a 3" Koosh ball. On the left he was able to see the ball in the front, side, upper, and lower fields, although he appeared to have about an 80-degree range to the side rather than the normal 90-degrees. On the right he was able to see the ball from about chest level and above both in the front and to the side (about 80 degrees). Below chest level he was unable to see the ball no matter where it was presented. Although this testing method was imprecise, John does appear to have a significant field loss on his lower right side.

Pictures on Storybooks: Wearing his glasses, from a distance of about 10", John could identify unfamiliar pictures and details down to at least ½" size in several "Spot" books. He could easily identify 2–4" high animals in photographs in a science book and notice details about the animals.

Contrast: John was successful in finding low-contrast details larger than ½" size in approximately 4"× 4"-sized photographs of animals in a science book. Wearing his glasses at about a 10" viewing distance, he could identify two blue dolphins in blue water. He was able to count three similarly colored brown dogs lying next to each other. He located a black baby chimp on its mother's back. He noticed that an adult buffalo had horns but the baby did not.

Reading: John's use of vision for reading tasks was assessed both with and without glasses in his classroom with overhead fluorescent track lighting.

He recently acquired a 4X dome magnifier that is modified with a handle so he can manipulate it (he was previously using a 2X). John's teacher says he consistently used the 2X magnifier, and is excited to have the new one. He also has a CCTV, which he operates independently when he wants to relieve visual fatigue or view details.

John's current reading book is at the early primer level. The type is about 18 point (2M), and has good spacing between the letters and words. He prefers to read it with his glasses and using the 4X dome magnifier at a viewing distance of 2–3". John was able to read his book with his eyes 6" from the magnifier on request, but he quickly returned to the 3" viewing distance when words were difficult to decode.

John was able to read his reading book without a magnifier when wearing his glasses. To do so, he brought the book about 2–3" from his eyes. When asked if he could read it without his glasses or the magnifier, he said that he couldn't because it would be too blurry. He was able to read it without his glasses by using the 4X magnifier at a distance of 6". (He started reading at 3", but moved to 6" when requested to do so.)

Formal Near Acuity (Assessed with a Sloan Double-Sided Near Vision Card at 16"):
(John turned his head about 30 degrees to the left of midline whenever reading the chart with his right eye only, both with and without his glasses. With his left eye or both eyes, he appeared to look directly at the chart.)

	With glasses	Without glasses
Right Eye (OD)	5/5 @ 20/400 3/5 @ 20/320 = 6.5 M	4/5 @ 20/320 = 6.5 M
Left Eye (OS)	5/5 @ 20/320 = 6.5 M 0/5 @ 20/250	3/5 @ 20/400 = 8 M
Both Eyes (OU)	4/5 @ 20/320 = 6.5 M	2/5 @ 20/400 0/5 @ 20/320 Worse than 20/400

Results indicated that John's eyeglasses do improve both his near vision in his left eye and that of both eyes together. It is interesting to note that his vision without his eyeglasses with both eyes was worse than both eyes separately.

Informal Distance Assessments

Whiteboard: Wearing his glasses, John could not identify any writing on the classroom whiteboard when seated at his desk, which is 15' from the board. The writing on the board was in blue dry erase marker and ranged from 2–3½" high.

For the purpose of this assessment, John was asked to start at a distance of 10' from the board and move in slowly until he could identify a letter. At 5' from the board, he was able to identify the 3½" high capital letter "T" in the word Tuesday, but not any lower case letters, which were 2" high. At 2' he could identify 2" lower case letters. Without his eyeglasses, John started at a distance of 8' from the board and had to move to a distance of 4' to be able to identify a 3" capital "W."

When sitting in a front row desk 5½' from the board, John could identify a 6" capital "C" without his glasses, but with eyeglasses he thought it was an "O." He could consistently identify 6" capital letters within words without his glasses, but misidentified some of the same letters with his eyeglasses on. He was able to identify 10" letters within words consistently when wearing his eyeglasses. John did better reading letters from the board at 5½' when not wearing his eyeglasses than when wearing them.

Identification of unfamiliar toys at distance: (The assessor started at a distance of 10' and slowly brought the toys toward John until he was able to identify them.)

Wearing his eye glasses, John identified a 5" bright red car at 8', and a 3½" bright yellow car at 2'. At 5' John called a 5" light-brown plastic dog a turkey and asked to take his glasses off. He then identified it as a pig (it does look like a pig) and asked if he could identify the rest of the toys with his eyeglasses off. Without his eyeglasses John identified a 5" long dark-brown plastic horse at 7' and a 6" pink-and-black plastic pig at 4'.

John preferred not to wear his eyeglasses when being asked to identify toys in the 6'–2' range. He saw the plastic dog more accurately at 5' without his eyeglasses. Darkly or brightly colored objects seemed easier for him to identify.

Formal Distance Acuity (Feinbloom number chart at 10'): (Testing was done in a school hallway with extra lighting directed at the acuity chart. John turned his head about 30 degrees to the left of midline whenever reading the chart with his right eye only, both with and without his eyeglasses. With his left eye or both eyes, he appeared to look directly at the chart.)

	With Glasses	Without glasses	Glasses + monocular
Right Eye (OD)	10/200	10/225	
Left Eye (OS)	10/200	10/200	2/4 @ 10/60 4/4 @ 10/80
Both Eyes (OU)	2/3 @ 10/160	10/200	

Using the Feinbloom chart, which has very high contrast thick black numbers on a white background, John's vision in both eyes at 10' was significantly better with his eyeglasses than without. He chose his left eye for the monocular. John's vision with the monocular was tested at the end of the session. It is likely that he was tired, and better results might be possible if tested when fatigue is not a factor.

Technology: John uses Zoom Text 7.0 Level 2, which has speech output in addition to screen magnification features. John needs large keys and can visually identify the enlarged keys from a distance of 4–6". He uses Talking Typer software to practice keyboarding skills, but uses an inefficient hunt and peck method because of the shortness of his fingers.

John was observed using his vision and Jaws (a software program which announces or "reads" what is on the screen), to get information from a science web site accessed by his teacher. Using standard screen sizes, John often had to bring his right eye to within 1–3" of the screen to see details.

Orientation and Mobility (O&M): John is not currently receiving O&M instruction, although he has in the past. He travels within the familiar school environment without the aid of a cane. The last O&M assessment, conducted in October of 2005 by Ken Kuo, indicated that he was able to detect obstacles and landmarks visually. According to this assessment, he used his monocular to read streets signs that he could not approach, but when possible he moved to within about 5 feet of a sign to read it.

4. Summary

John mainly uses vision to acquire information. John's glasses improve his vision for near tasks. He independently chooses a dome magnifier, and with his 4X magnifier and glasses, he can read 12-point letters at 3–4" and 18-point (2M) print at 3–6", although poor posture and visual fatigue are issues.

John can independently operate a CCTV, and is responsible enough to use it when he needs to see details more clearly, or eliminate fatigue. He chooses not to use a slant board or extra lighting. Results show that his right eye is the better eye for near tasks.

John can identify objects and see details ½" or larger in picture books. He is also able to distinguish between poorly contrasting details in pictures and photographs.

At intermediate distances (2–5'), John was better able to see letters on the whiteboard and identify a plastic animal without his glasses than with them. He could consistently identify 6" letters on the board without his glasses, and 10" letters with his glasses at a viewing distance of 5'.

With his eyeglasses on, John was able to identify a bright red 5" long toy car at 8' and a 3½" yellow car at 2'. When asked to identify large numbers from the Feinbloom Distance Acuity chart at 10' he did better with his glasses on than with his glasses off and with both eyes together (10/160) than either eye separately (20/200 left and right). His vision was considerably improved (10/80) by using a monocular with his left eye (the eye he preferred). Unfortunately, John has misplaced his monocular, perhaps as long as a year ago, and no longer has access to one.

John turns his head to the left when looking with his right eye. He appears to know where and when to turn his head, although it is not certain if further instruction in eccentric viewing techniques would improve his ability to use vision efficiently. He does not currently use a cane for travel, and currently receives no orientation and mobility instruction, although he has in the past.

5. Recommendations

Referral for Other Evaluations:

1. John's last clinical low vision exam was three years ago. It is recommended that John be scheduled for an exam to determine the most appropriate low vision devices for John at this time.

2. Further assessment of John's need for orientation and mobility instruction is warranted in light of the facts that he has a restricted visual field on the mid to lower right hand side, and that his visual acuity at all distances is severely compromised. While John is able to travel successfully without a cane throughout the familiar school campus, safe travel in unfamiliar environments is a concern.

3. Occupational therapy evaluation for the most efficient instructional method to teach computer keyboarding.

Adaptations:

Currently many successful adaptations are being implemented to aid John's visual efficiency. The following suggestions are offered for consideration:

1. If John does not have a monocular, allow him to sit in the front row of class (5' from board), and use 8" letters when writing on the board.

2. Make sure the option of extra lighting is available as an easily accessible option for John.

3. Use brightly colored markers, balls, and physical education equipment whenever possible or necessary to increase visibility.

4. John should be encouraged to use a slant board to bring material closer for near tasks to prevent postural problems in the future and to reduce fatigue. He will need instruction in using his dome magnifier with a slant board.

5. Results of this functional vision assessment show that John's distance vision was significantly improved with a monocular. If a clinical low vision assessment confirms this, John should use a monocular for distance viewing in the classroom, outdoor activities, and O&M. He should be taught to keep it in a safe place at school and home. He should be provided instruction in its proper care and use.

Amy Flora, Graduate Intern, and Anna McMillan, Classroom Teacher

This functional vision assessment was adapted with permission from an original by Cathy Fenn Mueller and Lisa Serino.

Sample Learning Media Assessment Report

Student: Tracy Kinney   Age: 11 (DOB 2/11/95)   Page 1 of 2
Date of assessment: 3/27/06   Date of report: 4/17/06
Assessor: Michael Petrofsky, TVI   School: Cranberry Elementary, Fifth grade

Background information: Tracy has low vision due to retinopathy of prematurity and cataracts. She was born at 29 weeks gestation and experienced intraventricular hemorrhages. She has mild cerebral palsy and developmental disabilities in addition to her visual impairment.

Tracy attended preschool from 1998–2000 in a special education classroom at Cranberry Elementary School, with services in visual impairment from an itinerant teacher. She currently attends fifth grade in the same school, with support services for two periods a day in the resource room for visually impaired students.

Tracy reads print using enlarged materials. Her reading level is at the mid-second grade level, according to her resource room teacher, and she typically uses 18-point print in large-print textbooks. A clinical low vision evaluation from October 2004 recommended the use of an 8X hand magnifier for reading, but the family and TVI reported that Tracy does not like to use the magnifier that was prescribed. Her corrected visual acuity was measured using the Feinbloom chart at 20/200 OU, 20/300 OD, and 20/200 OS during the clinical low vision evaluation; she wears glasses for most activities but will occasionally remove them for near tasks that require a close viewing distance.

Assessment purpose and strategies: Tracy was observed over two days on four occasions that included English, social studies, and mathematics lessons in class, a physical education class, and lunchtime in the cafeteria. The assessor also met with her in a conference room to conduct individual assessments. Observations in mathematics and physical education were documented with the *Learning Media Assessment* forms (Koenig and Holbrook, 1995). The *Johns Basic Reading Inventory* was conducted with Tracy; informal assessment was conducted with printed materials from a variety of sources including recreational books, magazines, and labels on food products.

Assessment results:

VISION The assessment indicated that Tracy uses vision as her primary sense in gathering information from the school setting; on the Use of Sensory Channels form she used vision first to acquire about 75% of needed information. Hearing and touch were used in appropriate situations and appeared to be equally meaningful as secondary media.

The *Johns Basic Reading Inventory* confirmed that she reads independently at the second grade level. For the assessment samples, her reading speed was 47 words per minute. She recognized photographs in magazine advertisements and on food labels, and she recognized words written in 8- and 10-point print on some labels when she held the material two to three inches from her eyes.

To determine when Tracy fatigues from reading, a long-term reading assessment was conducted. Tracy read from a narrative (library) book and expository (science) book. In both books, she alternated reading aloud for 2 minutes and then silently for 5 minutes to determine how quickly she tired when reading. Tracy asked to stop reading after 20 minutes when reading the library book and after 10 minutes when reading the science textbook.

TACTILE Tracy occasionally used touch to identify or confirm small objects that she could not recognize visually, such as a small paper clip on the floor and an earring left on her desk by a classmate. Tracy has been taught the braille alphabet visually, and she has been encouraged to read some simple words tactilely; she was able to recognize an l, b, c, and x and to decode the words "bag" and "ball" with letter-by-letter decoding. She had difficulty following lines of braille letters from left to right with both hands, and she was unable to find the beginning of the next line from the previous line.

AUDITORY Tracy responded appropriately to information presented orally; she retold the facts of a simple story read aloud to her, but she did not predict events based on remembered facts and she could not draw conclusions. When asked to sequence three events named from the story, she could tell which event happened first but could not recall the sequence of the last two events. She could recall specific facts when requested. She could remember up to four random syllables when they were repeated to her.

Recommendations:

1. Tracy should continue her work in a conventional reading program, with use of enlarged print for textbooks.

2. A follow-up appointment with the low vision clinic should be arranged to reassess the possible use of magnification, including the possibility of a stand magnifier, which Tracy may find easier to hold and manipulate.

3. Strategies for building reading speed using material at Tracy's independent reading level should be considered for Tracy: repeated reading, paired reading, and follow-along reading could be helpful in encouraging more rapid reading.

4. Although braille does not appear to be a useful medium for information access at this time, regular exposure to it as part of games or functional activities will establish a basic awareness and a positive attitude toward tactile learning in case there is a future need.

5. Independent access to information through auditory media should be a regular part of Tracy's learning program. Use of recording devices, including digital textbook players, should be incorporated into content subjects such as science and social studies so that Tracy can obtain information at a more complex level than her reading abilities allow. Use of screen readers such as JAWS should be considered for the same purpose to complete research and find favorite sites on the Internet. Given Tracy's tendency to fatigue quickly when reading, alternative methods and technology will give her the ability to use other resources to acquire information.

6. Instruction in handwriting with emphasis on legibility is important for short writing tasks, but Tracy will also need to work on improving keyboarding skills to allow her to produce lengthier material and to edit the material.

Summary:

Although Tracy has a significant visual impairment, she is a visual learner whose primary literacy medium is print. Her educational program should emphasize efficiency in the use of vision and should include activities to build reading speed. In addition, reconsideration of magnification for reading tasks may be of value. Combinations of visual and auditory input, as with screen readers, may improve her efficiency in gathering information.

Michael Petrofsky, Teacher of Visually Impaired Students

CHAPTER 4

The Individualized Education Program: Blueprint for Services

Carol B. Allman

Once your child has been found eligible to receive special education services because of his or her visual impairment, the process of determining your child's individual needs begins. The document that outlines these needs and services is known as the Individualized Education Program (IEP). Although "Individualized Education Program" is the term used in federal legislation and regulations, you may hear this "program" referred to in other ways. Each state has state laws that discuss the IEP, and they may refer to it by a different name. Some common names are individual educational plan, individual education program, or individualized educational plan. Regardless of the term used, what is being referred to is the IEP—the blueprint of the appropriate services that your school system will provide for your child.

If your child receives services as an infant or toddler, the document that sets out the services he or she will receive is called the Individualized Family Service Plan (IFSP). And, as your child grows toward adulthood and your family begins to plan for his or her life after school, the document is called a transition IEP. (See Chapter 2 for more on the IFSP and Chapters 9 and 10 for more on the topic of transition.) These plans are required by law, under the Individuals with Disabilities Education Act reauthorized in 2004 (IDEA, which is described in more detail in Chapter 1), and must be written by a team of persons (including the child's parent) on an annual basis. This chapter is intended to explain more about the process of developing an IEP for your child and its importance, outline the required components of the IEP, clarify what your child is entitled to receive as spelled out in the IEP document, and provide you with strategies and tips for making the IEP process a positive and productive one for you and your child.

DEFINITIONS AND IMPORTANCE OF IEPs

The legal definitions of the IEP and IFSP documents are outlined in IDEA. The full wording of the law can be found at http://www/ed.gov). The IEP consists of a written statement for a child with a disability that is created, reviewed, and revised in a meeting attended by various educational specialists, the parents, and, if appropriate, the child him- or herself. This document is crucial for your child because it outlines, on a yearly basis, the educational services he or she will receive from the school system. The IEP has a number of specific components that are required, and there are rules that must be followed in scheduling and holding the meetings to create, review, or revise an IEP.

The IFSP is a written plan for providing early intervention services to a child from birth to age 3 and the child's family. Most, if not all, states provide services for children from birth to age 3 using this plan, but the federal government does not require that these services be provided. The IFSP is important to you, your family, and your child because it outlines the services that are needed by all of you as you begin your journey to obtain educational and other needed services for your child. It is therefore in the best interests of your child and your family to be aware of the practices and policies in effect in your state (see Chapters 1, 2, and 10 for more information). As discussed later in this chapter, a transition IEP is similar to the regular IEP, but must address the services needed to prepare your child for life after high school. The transition IEP is critical to make sure that your child has a plan to support moving toward adulthood, after he or she graduates from public school. (Chapter 9 provides more information on transition and the transition IEP.)

THE IEP PROCESS

A number of essential elements are required in the IEP. There is also a defined and required process for the creation, review, and revision of the IEP. When the IEP team, described in Chapter 1, begins to think about what should be in your child's IEP, they must consider certain specific factors. You can think about some of these elements before the meeting arranged to discuss the IEP and be prepared to discuss there how each relates to your child's needs. These specific factors include:

- your child's strengths and your concerns for enhancing his or her education

- any skills (academic, developmental, or functional, that is, relating to everyday tasks) that you as a family think your child needs to address

- the results of any assessments or evaluations your child has undergone, including state- or district-wide testing

- strategies and supports that may address any specific behavior problems that impede your child's learning or the learning of others while your child is in the learning environment

- your child's language needs, if he or she has limited proficiency in English

- instruction in braille and the use of braille, if assessment of your child's current and future needs indicates a need for braille reading or writing

- communication needs of your child, such as the need for a device like a symbolic communication board if he or she is nonverbal

- assistive technology devices and services your child needs: these might include a computer with adapted software providing voice capabilities that "read" what is displayed on the screen, or a braille notetaker, an electronic device that would allow your child to take notes in braille.

When your child's IEP is written for the first time, or reviewed or revised in subsequent IEP meetings, you can expect to see a number of people present as part of the IEP team. The team members required to be there for the meeting include you (the parents), at least one mainstream classroom teacher if your child is expected to be in any mainstream, or regular education, classes; at least one special education teacher; a representative of the school who is qualified to provide or supervise special education services; and, for meetings concerning a transition IEP, your child. Other persons who might attend the meeting include other special educators who are providing services to your child, such as the orientation and mobility (O&M) specialist; representatives from agencies in your community who provide services to people who are blind or visually impaired, especially for transition IEPs; and school psychologists, if your child has recently undergone psychological assessment. You can also expect the teacher of visually impaired students to be there. You and the school system may invite other persons to attend the meeting if they have knowledge or special expertise relating to your child—for example, occupational therapists or speech and language therapists as well as persons you might invite to accompany you for support.

ESSENTIAL ELEMENTS OF THE IEP

The IEP, IFSP, and transition IEP are written on forms that include standard sections. Forms may vary from state to state and school district to school district. A specific form for the IEP is not mandated by IDEA, so the appearance of the forms used may vary. However, any form used must have certain required components, so all IEPs include certain essential information. The following sections of this chapter describe each of the IEP components and explain what you might expect to see on your child's IEP for each one. Subsequent sections explain the elements of the IFSP and transition IEP.

Present Levels of Educational Performance

A statement outlining your child's present levels of educational performance is usually found at the beginning of one of the IEP's pages. This statement describes what your child can do and what he or she knows at the time that the IEP is written. It forms the basis for completing the rest of the IEP because it describes your child's current status. One or more "present level" statements may be included, depending on the school district's requirements. For example, one present level statement may address your child's current progress in all areas of academics (the core curriculum, also known as the general curriculum, that all students follow) as well as in regard to critical skills in the expanded core curriculum that your child, as a student with a visual impairment, needs in order to pursue his or her education. (See Chapter 1 for more on the expanded core curriculum.) Although progress is the most important feature of the present level statement, you may also see statements that indicate areas of weakness for your child. These are not meant to be judgmental concerning you or your child, but help to make the IEP team aware of the areas that might need to be addressed in other portions of the IEP.

You can make an important contribution to completing this portion of the IEP by giving input about the progress you see your child making. It can be helpful for you to think about these areas before the IEP meeting and come prepared with a written list of progress you have seen. The educators at the meeting will most likely come prepared with their own progress notes or present level statements, and these will be based on results of tests and other evaluation methods they have used to chart your child's progress during the school year. The IEP's present level statement is based on assessments and tests done at school and on parents' reports and teachers' observations. You are a vital team member in the accurate creation of this important statement.

You might expect the statement on present level of educational performance to read something like the following examples:

- Based on Maria's results on the district math test, she understands basic math problems using addition, subtraction, and multiplication at the fifth-grade level. Maria uses the abacus to do math calculations and can complete calculations in the same time allotted to other students in her class. Her reading comprehension is at the fourth-grade level and she needs extra time to complete reading assignments in her preferred mode of reading (braille).

- Based on teacher and parent reports, Tom can move around his classroom comfortably but needs help in moving to rooms outside of the regular classroom where he spends the majority of time.

Measurable Annual Goals

Measurable annual goals set forth what the IEP team considers to be the priorities that need to be addressed so that your child can progress in the general curriculum and other goals designed to help your child learn as independently as possible (for example, the use of taped materials for large amounts of reading required). The general curriculum is the academic curriculum (core curriculum) that all students in the school system are being taught, regardless of their level of ability or disability. Your child may be working on grade level with his or her classmates or may be working at a different grade level on alternate achievement standards, which address the skills your child needs to work toward the state's standards for all children.

Annual goals will often address other educational needs that result from your child's disability. For example, your child may need special instruction in several important areas called the expanded core curriculum, which covers skills needed because of vision loss and to live independently and productively. These areas include skills in compensatory academics (concept development, organizational skills, speaking and listening), social interaction, recreation and leisure, O&M, independent living, career education, effective use of vision, use of technology, and self-determination (being able to express and explain one's own needs and advocate for oneself). The annual goals will address the critical skills your child needs to participate in the academic curriculum in order to receive an appropriate education, as well as other functional or daily living skills he or she needs. These goals give you a picture of what the school will be working on for your child as it relates to his or her experience with the general curriculum.

You should not ordinarily expect to see academic skills that are part of the school district's regular academic (core) curriculum listed as annual goals on your child's IEP. These curriculum goals are the same for all children in the school system. What you should expect to see are goals that address how to help your child to participate in the regular academic curriculum (core curriculum) with his or her classmates, and goals to address specific concerns that result from his or her specific visual impairment (expanded core curriculum).

Annual goals are based on the present level statement—usually they address the needs and weaknesses that have been identified. They describe what your child should learn in one year. Annual goals must be measurable: You must be able to know when your child has mastered the goal. Here are some examples of annual goals for Maria and Tom based on their present level statements described previously:

- By the end of the school year, Maria will improve her braille reading rate so that she can finish assignments with no extra time on 95% of the class assignments.

- By the end of the school year, Tom will travel to his music classroom without assistance on four out of five consecutive days.

Benchmarks and Short-Term Objectives

Benchmarks or short-term objectives are only required on the IEP if your child is being evaluated with an alternate assessment based on alternate standards in the state- or district-mandated assessment of student achievement. If they apply to your child's circumstances, they describe what your child will be able to accomplish at various intervals throughout the school year as he or she works toward the annual goals. They are the small steps on the way to the big step of an annual goal. There will usually be at least two benchmarks or short-term objectives listed for each annual goal, but there may be more depending on the nature of the annual goal. Some examples of benchmarks and short-term objectives for the annual goals listed above for Maria and Tom are:

- Maria will increase her braille reading rate by 50% (from 30 words a minute to 45 words a minute) as measured on timed observations once a week.

- Maria will write correct answers to assignments using her braillewriter (a machine similar to a typewriter that types braille) or Braille 'n Speak (an electronic typewriter that displays braille that has been typed) with 95% accuracy.

- Tom will use appropriate cane techniques on two out of five consecutive days at school.

- Tom will ask for assistance as needed in two out of five situations.
- Tom will use appropriate cane techniques on three out of five consecutive days at home and at school.
- Tom will ask for assistance when needed in three out of five situations at home and at school.

Description of Report of Child Progress

During the school year you will want to know how your child is doing and if he or she can be expected to master the annual goals set out in his or her IEP within the school year. This is important to know because it helps you and the IEP team identify specific reports and time periods when your child's progress toward those goals will be reported. You should expect to receive this information at least as often as report cards or other periodic reports are sent out for children without disabilities. You may want to encourage the school to send this information to you on a more frequent basis so that you can keep up with daily progress on a skill that needs special attention. The IEP must indicate how the goals will be measured and when periodic reports will be sent to inform you of your child's progress toward the goals. You will be able to check on your child's progress by following some of the suggestions offered under "What You Can Do After the IEP Meeting," later in this chapter. Some examples of progress reporting related to Maria and Tom's goals noted previously are:

- Maria's braille reading progress will be noted on her report card that will be sent home every 6 weeks.
- Tom's progress on cane travel to the music room will be noted in monthly written reports to his parents.

Related Services, Supplementary Aids, Program Modifications, and Supports for School Personnel

Once the annual goals are written, the IEP team will then determine what supports and services your child needs so that he or she will make progress in the general curriculum (core curriculum) and the expanded core curriculum, and on the annuals goals set out in his or her IEP. Services might include instruction in reading braille, small-group instruction, social skills training such as how to hold appropriate conversations with classmates, O&M training, speech therapy, transportation that is provided outside of the normal bus schedule set up by the school district, counseling, assistive technology services, school health services (when medication needs to be administered at school, for example), or community-based instruction such as help from a teacher in a work setting to make sure the child learns how to do a job well.

Any services the team decides as a group will best prepare your child to meet his or her goals can also be included in this section of the IEP. For your visually impaired child, it is imperative that he or she spend time with a teacher trained to teach children with visual impairments. The teacher of visually impaired students has the expertise to teach braille, use of technology such as a Braille 'n Speak, independent living skills, social skills, and other necessary skills from the expanded core curriculum that your child will need to master. The services of such a teacher need to be part of the educational program for a child who is visually impaired. If there is a shortage or absence of such teachers in your school district, it is important to request these services in a formal way.

Supplementary aids and services that your child might need to benefit from his or her education include assistive technology (for example, a Braille 'n Speak or specialized computer software), braille or large-print textbooks, or help from an instructional aide.

Examples of services that Maria might receive that relate to her annual goal are instruction in braille reading or instruction in use of the Braille 'n Speak. Tom's IEP might list special education services that include individual or small-group instruction in cane travel.

Program modifications and supports for school personnel will include any modifications that may need to be made in teaching or testing your child. While the term "modifications" is used in the wording of IDEA, you may also hear these changes referred to as "accommodations." Although these terms mean something slightly different, each describes changes that need to be made to the way your child is taught or tested compared with how his or her sighted classmates may be taught or tested.

In general, accommodations change *how* your child is taught or tested. Some examples include having extra time to complete assignments, using braille or large-print materials, having assignments or tests broken up into smaller parts, or completing assignments in a quiet setting away from other students.

Modifications describe changes to *what* your child is learning or tested on. Some examples of modifications include being taught material at a lower grade level, being tested at a lower grade level, or being taught fewer skills in the curriculum at the same grade level. (See Chapter 6 for more information on accommodations and modifications.)

Sometimes the teachers who work with your child, other than the teacher of visually impaired students, will need support themselves that will, in turn, benefit your child's learning. Examples of support to school personnel are specific training for the classroom teacher in basic O&M skills to reinforce mobility that your child is learning, changes to the classroom such as lighting or special equipment (perhaps a desk area with plenty of space for equipment and materials), or orientation about the need to provide to the teacher of visually impaired students the worksheets and handouts used in the classroom so that he or she can provide them in a timely fashion in braille or large print for a visually impaired child.

Although specialized terminology such as related services, supplementary aids, and program modifications can at times be difficult to differentiate, the important point is that the IEP team identifies what your child needs and documents this in the IEP.

Initiation, Duration, Frequency, and Location of Services

When the IEP is written, the IEP team will also indicate when, for how long, and where your child will receive each of the special education and related services, accommodations and modifications, support, and supplementary aids and services that he or she needs. When the services will be provided is indicated by dates marking the beginning and end of service during the current IEP—what are called the initiation and duration dates. How long the services will be provided represents the amount of time your child will be receiving particular services over the course of the IEP. For example, your child may receive O&M services twice a week for an hour during the first school semester, or the teacher of visually impaired students may work with your child on improving braille skills four times a week for 45 minutes each time. Where the services will be provided is called the service location; services generally are delivered at what is called your child's placement, the specific setting or physical place where your child will receive his or her education. (See the following sections and Chapter 7 for more on options for placement.) Services are provided in a variety of ways, and your child may be served through any one or a combination of the following settings:

- in the general education classroom, within a neighborhood school, with the teacher of visually impaired students assisting the regular education teacher
- in a specialized resource room within the school for part of the day with the teacher of visually impaired students
- in the community with an O&M specialist or in a work-study program with a special education teacher
- in a special education classroom with some assistance from the teacher of visually impaired students
- in the home or in a hospital setting with assistance from the teacher of visually impaired students
- in a day care facility with assistance from the teacher of visually impaired students
- in a residential school for students who are visually impaired

This is not an exhaustive list of service placements, and different combinations of these options may be appropriate for your child, depending on his or her needs and the services that have been identified on the IEP. Placement is determined every year when the IEP is readdressed and may (in some cases, should) change yearly, depending on the services that your child needs on an annual basis. The team may also indicate the name of the teacher who will provide the services, although this is not required. You may ask for this information as this part of the IEP is put together.

Extent of Participation with Nondisabled Children

During the development of the IEP, the IEP team will talk about the times during the day when your child will participate in academic learning in class with nondisabled students and when your child will receive instruction from a special education teacher in other expanded core curriculum skills apart from his or her nondisabled classmates. Both kinds of instruction are critical because they ensure that your child receives appropriate academic instruction as well as instruction in the special skills he or she needs for life and for learning. The IEP team will also indicate the time needed for special, related, and supplementary services.

Removal from Programs with Nondisabled Children

If your child's placement involves his or her removal from the regular education classroom or from nonacademic activities such as lunch and extracurricular activities for any amount of time during the school day, or if your child will take an alternate assessment to a mandated state or district assessment, the IEP team must explain on the IEP the extent to which your child will be removed from participating in school and the regular assessments with his or her nondisabled classmates. The decision to do this or not will be based on your child's individual needs. Overall, if your child can learn academic subjects in the general education classroom, he or she should probably be part of that class even if accommodations and some assistance from a teacher of visually impaired students will be needed from time to time. Some regular education courses and classes can be adapted to meet the special needs of your child. You will want to be part of the discussion of this point, so that you are clear about what your child will be taught, where, and with what differences from the experience of his or her sighted classmates.

Testing Accommodations

The IEP team is required to write on the IEP the accommodations that your child will need when taking any state or school district assessments (tests). The accommodations should be similar to those used by your child in classroom instruction, as listed under the program modifications section of the IEP. Some IEP forms may combine information on testing accommodations with the program modifications section, but it should be clear to you what accommodations are to be used when your child undergoes state or district testing.

The IEP team may determine that the state or district test is not appropriate and that your child needs an alternative assessment. This decision is made on the basis of the curriculum and skills that your child is being taught. However, the purpose of state testing is to see if your child is learning the curriculum and skills based on state standards, so your child's curriculum should match the state standards. The IEP must include a statement addressing this testing that indicates the accommodations, the reason why the student cannot participate in the regular assessment, and the alternative assessment procedure to be used for your child.

Other Information That May Be on Your Child's IEP

The IEP must include all the components that have been described. It may also include items such as:

- a description of the school system's invitations to you for the IEP meeting
- health or medical information about your child
- the kind of diploma that your child is expected to receive at graduation (this can change from year to year)
- school and post-school outcomes (long-term plans for your child that help guide the IEP team)
- the primary language used by your family if it is other than English.

An IEP can be substantial in length. A sample portion of an IEP, detailing one goal and related information for a student, is shown in the appendix at the end of this chapter.

INDIVIDUALIZED FAMILY SERVICE PLANS

The IFSP has a slightly different focus—it addresses the needs of both the family and the child—so its components vary slightly from those just described for the IEP. As explained in Chapter 2, early intervention efforts focus on the developmental needs of the young visually impaired child but also on needs and desires of the child's family for support, their goals for the child, and information on how the family can help promote their child's development.

Some components that differentiate the IFSP from the IEP include the following:

- Certain specific areas of development—physical, cognitive, communicative, social or emotional, and adaptive development—are addressed in the statement of present level of performance.

- A statement of the family's resources, priorities, and concerns is included. This statement does not relate to your financial resources, but rather to the access that you have to support that will assist you in raising your child.

- The major outcomes to be achieved for the child and the family; the criteria, procedures, and timelines used to determine progress; and whether modifications or revisions of the outcomes or services are necessary are indicated.

- Specific early intervention services necessary to meet the unique needs of the child and the family, including the frequency, intensity, and the method of delivery are described.

- A statement addressing the natural environment in which early intervention services will be provided appears. This statement is intended to require the IFSP team to look at providing early intervention to your child in the setting that he or she might be in if your child had no disability. The setting might be a day care facility, a preschool, a private home care setting, or your home.

- Identification of a service coordinator is required, who is responsible for ensuring that the services specified are provided and that there is coordination with other agencies and persons as needed to carry out the IFSP.

- The projected dates for initiation of services and their anticipated duration are indicated.

- Steps to support the child's transition to preschool or other appropriate services are outlined. (See Chapter 2 for more on IFSPs.)

TRANSITION IEPS

The process and components of writing transition IEPs are similar to the ones detailed in this chapter. Transition IEPs also include these types of information:

- beginning not later than the first IEP to be in effect when the child turns 16 (or younger, if determined appropriate by the IEP team), and updated annually, measurable postsecondary goals—goals for the student's life beyond high school—are indicated, based upon age-appropriate assessments of the student's needs for training, education, employment, and where appropriate, independent living skills

- transition services (including courses of study such as specific courses needed to prepare for college or enrollment in a vocational educational program) needed to assist the child in reaching those goals are specified

Transition services are critical to a student's successful movement into adult life. Your son or daughter will be a vital part of the transition IEP team, and it is required that he or she be invited to the IEP meeting. The team decides on the needed transition services, which may include college or university programs, continuing and adult education programs, vocational training, employment, adult services from various agencies, independent living programs, and community participation. Your child's participation in this plan is important to ensure that post-school goals are discussed and his or her likes and interests are considered as the transition IEP is being written. Some students at this age may want to play an active role in their transition IEP meeting and actually run the meeting. This kind of involvement is called self-advocacy or self-determination and is a skill that many young people learn as part of the expanded core curriculum. (For some resources for further developing this skill, see "For More Information" at the end of this chapter; see Chapter 9 for more on transition IEPs.)

KEY POINTS ABOUT THE IEP

The IEP process is important for your child, and it is therefore important for parents to take it seriously. The IEP outlines the services that your child will receive during the school year that the IEP is in effect. Some essential points to remember about the IEP and the IEP process include the following:

- The IEP is written at the IEP meeting, but members of the IEP team may come to the meeting with written notes and ideas about your child.

- The IEP is written for your child as an individual and describes the special education and related services he or she will receive for one year (or less). A new IEP must be written at least every 12 months.

- You and the school system have the right to invite anyone to the IEP meeting whom you believe can provide information about your child that will help the team develop the IEP. For example, a school system might choose to invite a social worker who has worked with your child and your family in the past. As a parent you might want to invite the person who takes care of your child after school and who has important information to add to the IEP discussions. People invited to any IEP meeting should have knowledge about the child and have something important to add to the writing of the IEP. In general, a collaborative and cooperative approach with members of your child's educational team is recommended as the most effective way of ensuring that your child obtains the services he or she needs. If you are having difficulty with your school system over issues related to receiving services for your child, it is wise to seek mediation before the IEP meeting is held so that some agreement and resolution can be reached and the meeting itself can be a productive one. (See Chapter 10 for more on advocacy and negotiation.)

• When you sign an IEP, it does not mean that you either agree or disagree with what is written on the IEP form. Your signature only means that you were present at the IEP meeting. In fact, signatures are not required on an IEP. It *is* required that a list of the persons who participated in the meeting be included on the IEP form. If, however, you do not agree with the IEP you may indicate that on the IEP.

• The most important components of the IEP are the present levels of performance statements, measurable annual goals with benchmarks or short-term objectives, and the way in which your child's progress toward the goals will be measured. These components are all related and form the basis for the other components of the IEP.

WHAT IS YOUR CHILD ENTITLED TO RECEIVE?

As noted throughout this book, federal law entitles your child to receive a "free, appropriate public education." "Free" means that there is no cost involved other than the typical items that schools sometimes ask for help in obtaining, such as admission fees for field trips, extra project materials, or other unusual costs that generally are not included in the school budget. You are not required to pay for something the school asks for if you choose not to do so. "Appropriate" means that the education provided meets the standards set by the state to include preschool, elementary, and secondary school education. It also means that the education provided is in compliance with the IEP. "Public" means that the educational services are provided under the public school system's supervision and direction.

It is important to know that nowhere in the law is the quality of a free and appropriate public education described or required. "Quality" is a term that can have multiple meanings depending on whom you ask. Although any parent may want to campaign to improve the quality of education a school offers, this effort cannot be justified on the basis of your rights under IDEA. However, if you feel that your child is not receiving the free, appropriate public education that is required and is your child's right, you can seek a remedy to that situation through a parent-school conference, an IEP meeting, mediation, or a due process hearing (described in more detail in Chapter 10).

EFFECTIVE STRATEGIES FOR THE IEP PROCESS

The IEP is a document, but it also reflects a process; and there are many elements that can and should happen as part of that process. Some effective strategies to help you and your child throughout this process are presented here that include actions to take before, during, and after the IEP meeting. (See also "12 Strategies for IEP Day" for some additional ideas.)

In addition to following the suggestions that are listed, it is often helpful to talk to other parents who have children who are visually impaired, either individually or in support groups, and to contact national organizations that offer information and assistance (these are described in Chapter 1 and in the Resources section at the back of this book). You might also want to consider attending the IEP meeting with a spouse, other family member, or supportive friend. Keeping accurate records of your child's education will also help you at all stages of the IEP process throughout your child's school years (see "Keeping Records of Your Child's Education").

What You Can Do Before the IEP Meeting

A number of steps can help you prepare for an IEP meeting:

- Watch your child in a variety of activities, including doing schoolwork, playing, being in social situations, eating out, and interacting in the community. Make note of tasks and activities he or she has mastered and those with which you think he or she needs help.

- Talk to your child and make note of his or her interests, likes, and dislikes. Begin discussions about "what you will be when you grow up" early. Conversations like these let your child know that you have high expectations for him or her. They also help your child begin to explore options to be considered as he or she gets older. These discussions are particularly important as your child becomes a teenager and in preparation for working on his or her transition IEP.

- Review records and reports from school that indicate your child's progress.

- Visit your child's class and observe him or her at work and play.

- Observe other classes at the school to get an idea about how children in other classes work and play.

12 Strategies for IEP Day

Here are some suggestions for a successful experience on IEP day:

1. Have a vision—a dream—for your child.

2. Share that dream with your child's teachers and your child.

3. Write your educational ideas down, and brainstorm with your child's teacher before the IEP meeting.

4. Remember, the education of a visually impaired child, with or without additional disabilities, doesn't mean just learning to read and write braille. It also means learning to play games, ride bikes, swim, and take care of oneself.

5. Be specific about what you want your child to accomplish during that school year.

6. Include in the plan opportunities for interaction with both nondisabled and disabled peers as part of the IEP. Friendships are important for all children.

7. Be organized. Get a three-ring binder and a three-hole punch and remember to take them with you to the meeting. Keep all the paperwork generated at the meeting in the binder. It will be easy to organize and reorganize, to store, and to find when you need it. The binder can also be personalized to your child: You can make it fun and special by adding school pictures and other memorabilia that are meaningful to both of you.

8. Be open and ready to listen. IEP days are hard. Remember that, with few exceptions, everyone at the meeting wants the same thing: what's best for your child.

9. Remember that it's okay to cry at IEP meetings.

10. Remember that it's okay to laugh at IEP meetings.

11. Remember that it's okay to be frustrated, but work to focus on a solution.

12. Remember that it's okay to agree not to agree at IEP meetings.

Susan Singler

Keeping Records of Your Child's Education

Keeping good records of your child's education is important for you and a valuable part of your role on the IEP team. Among the documents you may want to keep copies of are the following:

- all final copies and draft copies of IEPs from each year
- any amendments to the IEP
- all types of evaluations or assessments that your child may have undergone (see Chapter 3 for more information on assessments)
- any letters or other communications exchanged between you and your child's school and any independent evaluators
- any handouts or signed papers distributed at IEP meetings
- your notes (remember to date them) from IEP meetings and any other meetings with school personnel or evaluators that you attend.

The records can be useful in a number of ways:

- They provide a historical record of your child's educational experience.
- They are available for you to refer to whenever you need them.
- They are a great help in your preparation for the IEP meeting.
- If you move, or your school can't locate your child's records, you have a copy at hand.
- In the event that you take any legal action, the records will document any decisions or outcomes.

Susan LaVenture

- Write down the services you would like to discuss that you think are needed by your child. Think about your reasons for wanting him or her to receive these services.
- Collect any current medical information on your child that might be helpful to the IEP team in determining needed services.
- Also collect any handouts or information you may have on the needs of visually impaired children from parents' groups or national organizations to share with team members.
- Know what the components of the IEP are and be prepared to give your input on each area.

- Sign and return the form inviting you to the IEP meeting, so that school personnel know you have received the invitation and are coming to the meeting. If you want to have the meeting scheduled at another time, you need to tell the school so arrangements can be made to schedule the meeting at a time that is good for all team members. The school is required to give you at least two invitations to the scheduled IEP meeting. If you have received these and do not respond to either invitation, school personnel can go ahead and conduct the IEP meeting without your being present.

- Read invitations and other materials that come to you from the school. If you have questions about them, call the school principal or guidance counselor.

- Ask for a copy of the IEP form so that you can be familiar with it.

What You Can Do at the IEP Meeting

On the day of the IEP meeting, keep the following points in mind:

- Arrive on time or, if you cannot, let the school know that your plans have changed.

- If it is appropriate for your family situation, attend with your child's other parent. If it is not appropriate, consider asking a close family friend, relative, or parent advocate for support. (As Chapter 1 explains, support from a parent advocate is available from several sources.)

- Bring any notes you have prepared for the meeting, as well as paper and a pen.

- Share your ideas and information about your child.

- Ask questions when you don't understand something.

- Bring a copy of the previous IEP and/or copies of any evaluations of your child that will be discussed at the meeting.

- Bring a copy of any articles, books, or suggested references to share with the IEP team, as appropriate, for the topic discussed at the meeting.

- Be polite but assertive at the meeting. Do not be afraid to offer your suggestions or to persist with your point of view if others disagree. Explain the reasons why you believe something is important for your child.

- Listen to others who disagree, and think carefully about why they feel the way they do. Being defensive or emotional without carefully considering what is being discussed is usually not an effective way of persuading others to your point of view.

IEP DAY: THE WAY IT WAS

After more than 15 years of attending my son's IEP Day, I consider myself a professional. But, I'm not. I'm the Mom. I don't have the professional detachment that allows the other team members to sit at the conference table and see all my child's abilities and deficiencies laid out in black and white, without emotion, and without experiencing the loss they mean to me.

IEP Day is always a stressful day for me, no matter how many times I've attended, no matter how well planned. That's because I'm not allowed just to focus on my child's accomplishments: I also must look at the disability, stare it in the face. Living with my son, day to day, I forget about his disability. It's secondary to who he is, although it's a part. I'm familiar with it and comfortable, until I have to see it in writing on IEP Day.

I've finally learned to see the positive things identified and discussed on IEP Day. I take pride in my child's hard work and accomplishments. I swallow hard and come up with suggestions to strengthen the identified weaknesses. He's mature enough now to participate on IEP Day and offers suggestions of his own.

Most important, I've learned to give myself time afterward to grieve if I need to, to cry, to celebrate, and to process the information I received until I'm comfortable with it. That way I can help him be comfortable and feel good about the information we've received. I've learned to schedule the day off from work on his IEP Day.

On that day we always schedule some other activity, too, that we both enjoy: maybe stopping on the way home from school for a soda or ice cream, playing in a different park, or anything to feel "normal" again. There we talk about his day, praise his hard work and accomplishments, and remind each other of the areas he needs to improve. We reconnect and both feel better. Life for us is back to normal—until the next IEP Day.

Susan Singler
Mother of a 24-year-old son with retinopathy
of prematurity and additional disabilities
Nashville, Tennessee

- Make your points clearly, and provide rationales and any documentation you have to back up your point. This might include educational and other recommendations from your child's evaluations, information from experts on the topic, and similar information.

- Listen carefully to the other team members and their ideas about your child. Take notes if you want to share information with other family members after the meeting. Date your notes, and keep them together.

- Be realistic about the abilities of your child. Work with the IEP team to determine the placement that will be most effective for your child's learning.

- Despite his or her visual impairment, expect that your child will learn as his or her cognitive and intellectual level allows. Work with the IEP team to maintain a high level of expectation for your child. In general, children often respond to others' expectations, and low expectations will not be helpful to your child.

- Ask about the different kinds of high school diplomas your state confers and what you can do to help your child work toward the goals you have for him or her for after high school.

- If you disagree with something that is said at the IEP meeting, voice your opinion, but do so in a helpful way. Explain why you disagree, and give suggestions for alternatives for anything with which you disagree. Some sample responses to statements that you might hear when you are discussing your child's need for special services appear in "Ready Responses for School Meetings" at the end of this chapter.

- The IEP will be written at the meeting; make sure that you receive your free copy of the IEP.

Chapter 8 discusses other important steps parents of children with multiple disabilities can take, and many of them are helpful for all parents. In addition, Chapter 9 discusses steps that are especially important for meetings relating to a child's transition IEP.

Questions to Ask at the IEP Meeting

The meeting that is held to write your child's IEP is a good opportunity to ask pertinent questions about what your child will be learning, the outcomes that can be expected (including what type of diploma your child is working toward), and other school-related issues. Some questions that you might ask include:

- Is my child learning the general curriculum (core curriculum) of other students in the school, or is there a special curriculum for my child?

- What special skills (expanded core curriculum) will my child be learning because of his or her disability?

- What diploma track is my child on?

- How will my child's progress be measured?

- When should I expect to get information about my child's progress?

- Who will be instructing my child in the academic areas (core curriculum) and special skill areas (expanded core curriculum)?

- Who should be my point of contact if I have issues or problems with my child's program of study?

What You Can Do After the IEP Meeting

- Look at your child's schoolwork and talk to him or her about school activities.

- Send your child to school on time every day.

- Make sure your child is eating and sleeping well so that he or she is prepared for the school day.

- Help your child be prepared for school by reviewing homework, asking questions about the next day's activities, and providing a place for your child to do homework or other school-related work and to keep his or her school materials.

- Schedule a teacher conference with various persons who might be providing services to your child on a regular basis—about every other month is a useful interval.

- As time permits, volunteer to help out at your child's school or in his or her classroom.

- Look at information that your child brings home from school and sign any forms as requested.

- Let your child's teacher know about any unusual behavior that your child displays at home.

- Be willing to implement some goals from the IEP in your home. For example, you can help with some dressing or eating skills that have been identified as goals for your child. Giving your child opportunities to repeat certain skills helps reinforce his or her learning of them.

- If at any time you feel that the school is not addressing your child's IEP, ask for another IEP meeting or talk to the school principal or a person familiar with special education services in your child's school.

- Ask a friend, other parents, or a parent group to talk through with you any issues you have with the implementation of your child's IEP.

- If you think you need mediation services to solve issues that you have with the implementation of your child's IEP, ask for these services, which are to be offered to you at no cost. Mediation can help you and the school resolve any issues that arise in a productive and nonconfrontational way.

Understanding the IEP process and its components will help you work closely and productively with the school system to obtain the educational services that will be important to your child. Remember that your knowledge and help are important to share with persons at your child's school who work with him or her. Your continued participation in and understanding of what a free appropriate public education entails for your child is crucial to his or her educational success. It is equally valuable to the school system, which needs you as a partner in your child's experience of the educational process.

For More Information

S. Field and A. Hoffman, "Promoting Self-Determination through Effective Curriculum Development," *Intervention in School and Clinic,* 30 (3) (1995), pp. 134–141.

M. C. Holbrook (Ed.), *Children with Visual Impairments: A Parents' Guide,* second edition (Bethesda, MD: Woodbine House, 2006).

S. Lewis and C. B. Allman, "Educational Programming," in M. C. Holbrook & A. J. Koenig (Eds.), *Foundations of Education: History and Theory of Teaching Children and Youths with Visual Impairments*, Vol. 1 (New York: AFB Press, 2000), pp. 218–259.

G. S. Pugh & J. Erin (Eds.), *Blind and Visually Impaired Students: Educational Service Guidelines* (Watertown, MA: Perkins School for the Blind in cooperation with the National Association of State Directors of Special Education, 1999).

State Department of Education   Page __1__ of __4__

Individual Educational Program

IEP Development Date _11/2/06_ Student Name _Samantha Smith_ Sex M Ⓕ

Grade _7_ School _Anytown Jr. High_ Birth Date _12/1/93_ ID# _123-45-6789_

Exceptionality (ies) _____Visual Impairment_____

Evaluation/Reevaluation Date _11/3/08_ Date of Last IEP _11/3/05_

Desired Outcome   School __X__ Post-School_____

> To be completed for all students. Desired school outcomes may include those regarding involvement in the general curriculum, school programs, courses of study, and extracurricular activities. Desired post-school outcomes may include postsecondary education, employment, living arrangements, community participation, recreation and leisure, and social activities 3 to 5 years after graduation.

The student desires to _continue to advance from grade to grade and graduate from high school. Samantha would like to join the student council this school year._

Is this a Transition IEP?   ____ YES   __X__ NO

General Factors

Strengths of the child _academic achievement, thoughtful & caring personality_

Results of the most recent evaluation (include results of student's performance on any state or districtwide assessments) _Samantha is currently reading 90 wpm in braille, with 90% comprehension at the 7th grade level. Samantha experiences challenges in the ECC areas of social skills, independent living and self-determination. Teachers report Samantha being overly aggressive in advocating for her needs. Additionally, Samantha is not able to perform common age-appropriate independent living activities such as matching & selecting her clothing, folding laundry, making her bed, setting the table & preparing a snack or simple meal. Samantha's O&M skills are on target for her age. On the state-wide assessment, Samantha scored a passing grade on both math & reading last school year._

What concerns for their child's education have the parents expressed? _____

Special Factors

Special factors have been considered for this student. CHECK (✓) ALL identified needs addressed in this IEP:

❏ Need for positive behavior intervention or strategies   ☑ Braille needs
❏ Language needs (limited English proficient students)   ❏ Communication and language needs
☑ Need for assistive technology devices and services   ❏ Need for extended school year services
❏ Need for specially designed/adaptive physical education   ❏ Need for special transportation services

Check (✓) the instructional structure (i.e., domains, transition services activity areas) you will use and the areas within the structure in which present level of educational performance statements and measurable annual goals, including benchmarks or short-term objectives, will be written. Transfer the domains or areas checked to the following page(s).

☑ Domains   ❏ Transition Services Activity Areas
✓ Curriculum and Learning Environment __Instruction   __Post-school Adult Living
✓ Social and Emotional Behavior   __Related Services   __Daily Living Skills
✓ Independent Functioning   __Community Experience   __Functional Vocational Eval.
✓ Communication   __Employment

This sample IEP was adapted by Amy R. McKenzie.

Measurable Annual Goals, Including Benchmarks or Short-Term Objectives
(additional pages as needed)

Present Level of Educational Performance for _Social Skills_

Specify the domain or transition area checked on the previous page. Identify the sources of information about the student; the student's strengths; how the student's disability affects involvement and progress in the general curriculum, or for prekindergarten children with disabilities, how the disability affects the child's participation in appropriate activities; and the priority educational needs that result from the disability.

Based on _Samantha has been observed by peers, teachers and her parents to have_ _appropriate body language in social situations. The independent Living Curriculum_ _assessment tool indicates that she can generally sustain relationships with a_ _limited number of peers (2) but has difficulty being conversational with a larger_ _group of peers._

Effects of disability _Social skills are often not developed naturally when one has a_ _visual impairment and cannot observe the interactions of others._

Priority educational need _Appropriate social skills are critical to adult life as students_ _progress on to higher education or work experience._

Measurable Annual Goal

Measurable annual goals, including benchmarks or short-term objectives, must relate to meeting the student's needs that result from the disability to enable the student to be involved in and progress in the general curriculum and meeting each of the student's other educational needs that result from the disability.

Samantha will increase her circle of friends with whom she can have a _meaningful conversation. Through direct instruction she will practice starting a_ _conversation, listening to a conversation, asking appropriate questions, and making_ _comments appropriate to the subject and of interest to her peers._

Assigned Instructional Duties for This Goal:

Responsibilities may include planning, implementing, documenting student performance, consulting, etc.

Lead Teacher/Staff _TVI_ Other _O & M instructor_

Title/Position of Person(s) Responsible   Title/Position of Person(s) Responsible

Benchmarks or Short-Term Objectives   **Results**

No benchmarks or short-term objectives are needed for this activity.

Evaluation Plan

The evaluation plan includes a statement of how the student's progress toward the annual goal will be measured.

Samantha will self-monitor her conversational skills, report to the TVI regarding _conversations that she has initiated and sustained, and ask questions of the TVI_ _and O&M instructor to clarify her success. She will also ask her closest_ _friends if her social behavior seems appropriate._

The student's progress toward annual goals and the extent to which progress is sufficient to enable the student to achieve the annual goal by the end of the year will be reported to the student's parents:

_____ with report cards every _____ weeks   _X_ through written reports every 12 weeks
_____ through conferences every _____ weeks   _____ other (specify)

Exceptional Student Education

Services, modifications, and supports are provided for the student to advance appropriately toward attaining the annual goals, be involved and progress in the general curriculum, participate in extracurricular and other nonacademic activities and be educated and participate with other students with disabilities and nondisabled students in activities.

Special Education	Dates: Initiation	Duration	Frequency	Location
Direct instruction from a TVI in ECC areas	11/2/06	11/1/07	1 hour, 5 times per week	School & community

Related Services	Dates: Initiation	Duration	Frequency	Location
Direct instruction from a COMS	11/2/06	11/1/07	1 hour, 1 time per week	School & community

Program Modifications/ Supports for School Personnel	Dates: Initiation	Duration	Frequency	Location
Inservice for staff	8/20/07	8/21/07	1 x 1 year, 4 hours	School
Consult w/ all teachers	11/2/06	11/1/07	45 min, 1 x 1 week	School/ classroom
Consult w/ parents	11/2/06	11/1/07	1 hr, 1 x 1 month	Home
Central location for books & equipment	11/2/06	11/1/07	Daily	School
Preferential seating – front	11/2/06	11/1/07	Daily	Classroom
Extended time on tests, 1.5 x	11/2/06	11/1/07	Daily	Classroom
Desk copies–braille	11/2/06	11/1/07	Daily	Classroom
Hands on experiences w/ demonstration	11/2/06	11/1/07	Daily	Classroom

Supplementary Aids and Services	Dates: Initiation	Duration	Frequency	Location
Braillewriter & paper	11/2/06	11/1/07	Daily	Classroom/ school/home
Braille class materials	11/2/06	11/1/07	Daily	Classroom/ school/home
Braille textbooks (Math, science, foreign language)	11/2/06	11/1/07	Daily	Classroom/ school/home
Digital textbooks (history, English)	11/2/06	11/1/07	Daily	Classroom/ school/home
Slate & Stylus	11/2/06	11/1/07	Daily	Classroom/ school/home
DAISY Player	11/2/06	11/1/07	Daily	Classroom/ Home/School
JAWS	11/2/06	11/1/07	Daily	Classroom/ Home/School
Braille embosser	11/2/06	11/1/07	Daily	Classroom/ Home/School
BrailleNote	11/2/06	11/1/07	Daily	Classroom/ Home/School
Abacus	11/2/06	11/1/07	Daily	Classroom/ Home/School
Tactile graphics/diagrams	11/2/06	11/1/07	Daily	Classroom/ Home/School
Talking calculator	11/2/06	11/1/07	Daily	Classroom/ Home/School
Adapted science equipment	11/2/06	11/1/07	Daily	Classroom/ Home/School
Braille ruler & protractor	11/2/06	11/1/07	Daily	Classroom/ Home/School

State and Districtwide Assessment Accommodations/Modifications

Participation in state and districtwide assessment program(s) __*x*__ Yes _____ No _____ NA

If yes, describe needed accommodations/modifications for each *Braille test booklet, braille answer sheet, braillewriter, abacus, talking calculator, extended time – 1.5x*

If no, explain why each assessment is not appropriate and describe each alternative assessment _____

_____

Participation in Regular/Vocational Education	Percent of Time	Purpose
General Education	*83%*	*Academics*

Removal from Programs with Nondisabled Students

Explain the extent, if any, to which the student will NOT participate with nondisabled students in the regular class and extracurricular and nonacademic activities. *Direct services from a certified Teacher of students w/ Visual Impairments & Certified Orientation & Mobility specialist*

Placement (Based on percent of time with nondisabled students)

__*x*__ Regular Class (more than 79% with non-ESE)
_____ Resource Room (more than 40%, but less than or equal to 79% with non-ESE)
_____ Separate Class (less than or equal to 40% with non-ESE)
_____ Hospital/Homebound
_____ Separate Day School
_____ Residential Facility
_____ Juvenile Justice Program

Specialized Transportation Services

CHECK (✓) the statement describing the condition that qualifies for weighted funding for specialized transportation services.

__✓__ 1. Medical equipment is required (e.g., wheelchair, crutches, walkers, cane, tracheotomy equipment, positioning or unique seating devices).
_____ 2. Medical condition requires a special transportation environment as per physician's prescription (e.g., tinted windows, dust-controlled atmosphere, temperature control).
_____ 3. Aide or monitor required due to disability and specific need of student. Describe:
_____ 4. Shortened school day is required due to disability and specific need of student. Describe:
_____ 5. School assigned is located in an out-of-district school system. Describe:

PARTICIPANTS

LEA Representative *Malinda Freeman*   Regular Education Teacher *Josh Gaines*
                                         (if appropriate)

Parent(s) *Susan Smith*   Student *Samantha Smith*

ESE Teacher *Judy Bennett*   Evaluation Interpreter_____

Other IEP Team Members

Jane Heard, O & M; Max Rollins, Blind Services Counselor

Ready Responses for School Meetings
Mary Zabelski

Whenever we feel the stakes are high, we often feel anxious, too. If you are concerned about your next meeting with members of your child's educational team, you are probably feeling the way most families do. But there are many ways in which you can prepare yourself for the meeting (they have been described in detail in Chapter 4). Talking with your family, friends, other parents, representatives of parent and national organizations, and your child's teacher of visually impaired students can also help you feel more comfortable and even more confident.

When you're unsure about how to address statements with which you may disagree at a meeting, or you think the school system is avoiding the delivery of important services for your child, it can be helpful to have some effective and appropriate responses thought out so that you feel better prepared.

The following are some scenarios that you might encounter at an IEP meeting. Each starts with a statement that you might hear when you are discussing your child's need for special services. For each one, some background information is presented that puts the statement in context, and some possible replies are provided that you can offer in response. (A longer series of statements and possible replies, along with helpful steps that you can take, is presented at the end of Chapter 10.) The replies may be useful in other discussions and conversations about your child, too, not just in IEP meetings.

"Sorry, we don't have the money."

Background Information

Many school districts are struggling with shrinking budgets and underfunded mandates (IDEA has never been fully funded by the federal government). However, the law states that your school district must provide a free, appropriate public education for your child. If you are advocating for something that you think your child needs, and it is going to cost the school district money, the issue of where the money comes from is not your problem as a parent.

Possible Responses

"I can appreciate the dilemma you face in these tough times of tight budgets. But what we really need to focus on right now is the need for accessible classroom materials for Bradley. He still needs to access the regular classroom materials with a closed-circuit TV" [or substitute your child's need here].

"It's really a matter of prioritizing the money that the district does have. For our conversation today, this issue isn't about money; this is about equal access. Bradley needs adapted computer technology to work in the computer lab with the other students in his class."

"We're not convinced that your child needs . . ."

Background Information

This statement can create an "us against you" scenario. The reason the other members of your IEP team may not be convinced about the need for a service may be because of other issues unrelated to your child's needs. (These might include lack of money, bias against a particular service or program that you are requesting, or lack of knowledge, among others.) Whoever makes a statement similar to this should be able to define clearly the reasons why he or she is "not convinced" of the necessity of the program or service to meet your child's needs. Make sure you are open to their reasons—they might be valid. If you only get more excuses (such as "we've never done that before"), bring the conversation back to exactly why you think your child needs what you are asking for. Prepare yourself so you can articulate clearly why your child needs the service or program you are requesting.

Possible Responses

"Why do you feel that Janelle doesn't need an O&M instructor? She's very afraid of walking on her own outside, and she frequently trips when she enters the building or tries to go up steps. I'm afraid for her safety. I'd like to request that she have an orientation and mobility evaluation, and I will put that in writing to you and sign any paperwork that will make the evaluation happen. Perhaps that'll give us the information we need to decide whether she needs this service added to her IEP."

"It takes Janelle hours to do her homework because she reads at such a slow pace. Her eyes frequently hurt her, and she often gets headaches. Since the prognosis for her vision is poor, I'd like her to begin learning braille, along with reading large print. Can't the vision teacher evaluate her using a functional vision assessment? If she's a good candidate for braille instruction, her reading scores may go up."

"I have 400 other children in this building."

Background Information

This response usually comes up when a parent is advocating for a child, and the principal, teacher, or special education director is feeling the pressure of meeting the needs of all the children for whom she or he is responsible. How is he or she to maintain a focus on the "big picture?" Don't get into that conversation. Remember the reason why you are all meeting: Your child has been determined to need an individualized plan, and you are there to provide him or her with it.

Possible Responses

"I know that part of your job is to look at the 'big picture' and make sure that every student has his or her needs met, but we're here to discuss my child's individual plan for education. Miguel needs specialized services because of his visual impairment. Without these services provided by a teacher of visually impaired students and an O&M instructor, plus the necessary adaptations and modifications to compensate for his visual limitations, he won't be able to work at the same level as his classmates."

"The general education teacher couldn't be here today."

Background Information

You show up at your IEP meeting, and there is no general educator (regular classroom teacher) present. The team members who are there might just say that they couldn't get the schedule together to have everyone there. IDEA notes with strong emphasis that the general education teacher should be present at the IEP meeting. If this teacher will be the primary educator interacting with your child in the classroom on a day-to-day basis, it is crucial that he or she attend all IEP meetings, at least for the portion of the meeting that discusses academic learning skills and the accommodations needed to access those skills.

Possible Responses

"I notice that the general education teacher isn't here today. So I assume we'll consider this meeting a 'pre-planning' session for our real IEP meeting, when the general ed teacher can be here."

"I really believe that we all want to plan an educational program that specifically targets Rekha's academic needs. There's really no point in spending all this time talking about it without the entire IEP team present. This meeting is really our chance to all be on the same page about her educational services and goals."

"Kofi can read large-print magnification on the closed-circuit TV and on his computer. We don't feel that he needs to learn braille at this time."

Background Information

Although Kofi can read the magnified large print, it takes him more than twice as long as the other students to read the same materials. He's falling behind on his homework assignments and can't seem to keep up with his classwork. He often complains that his eyes hurt. His pediatric ophthalmologist has indicated that his vision will not improve and may further deteriorate. The district may not want to provide more direct-service minutes of the teacher of visually impaired students' time to Kofi because she has a very large caseload of students. Instruction in braille would require adding more direct-service minutes of instruction each week to Kofi's IEP.

Possible Responses

"I know we all feel that it's important for Kofi to keep using his remaining vision, but he's falling further behind in reading and in his other classroom assignments. His grades have dropped this year since he has more homework, and the volume of reading is increasing. Shouldn't his needs be evaluated through a learning media assessment in order to make an effective decision for him? I'd like to have this added to the IEP right away."

"We can continue his use of large-print magnification, but learning braille can only help, not hurt his ability to read. This is especially true if it will decrease his eyestrain and headaches and help him finish his homework in a reasonable time. I'd like to try this option to see what the outcome is."

"Let us get back to you on how that might work."

or

"I don't have the authority to make that decision."

Background Information

There might be some good discussion going on in your child's IEP meeting, but unless these discussions actually get written down as services specified in the IEP, the law does not require that the services be implemented. The reason the members of the IEP team are defined in the law is so that the provisions decided upon by the team members can first be documented and then put into effect. If the team member who makes this statement has a legitimate reason for needing to get additional information or permission before writing the service down in the IEP, establish clear protocol on who will "get back to you" on this and when.

Possible Responses

"This is a really important service for my daughter. Whom do you need to talk to in order to get additional information? How will it influence the decision we make here as a team? When can you get the information back to me on what it will take to get this written into her IEP? I'd like to reconvene this meeting as soon as you can get this information for me."

"Your child is doing great compared to other students who are blind or visually impaired."

Background Information

What is this kind of statement really saying? If it is given in response to educational delays in your own child's performance, the goals for your child need to be very clear. For your child to be provided with an appropriate education and meet the standards for his or her grade level, the standard of success is what every child in that grade should know, not comparisons to the outcomes for students who are blind or visually impaired, which possibly have been poor in the past.

Possible Responses

"Well, that's interesting to know. But let's keep our focus on the standards for Manuel's goals and what he's supposed to learn and know in the eighth grade. How can we continue to ensure that the goals and services we're talking about today will help him achieve what the state standards require all eighth graders to know?"

"Thank you for this information about Manuel's achievement compared to other visually impaired students. I was wondering if we could discuss this assessment in relation to his own classmates and how he compares to the other students. Have the tests you administered been given to typically sighted students in his class?"

"Sorry, but our school is not equipped with the computer technology that your daughter needs."

Background Information

Equal access to technology is a right to which children with disabilities are entitled. The school is mandated by law to provide the necessary assistive technology within the classroom and the school to ensure that a student who is blind or visually impaired can compete with sighted peers, at no cost to his or her family. Unfortunately, this does not always happen.

Most states have instructional materials centers where equipment such as braillewriters, closed-circuit televisions (CCTVs), textbooks in braille or in large print, and other materials for students with visual impairments are available for the school districts to order. Students needing specialized technology such as adapted computers with braille displays, screen magnification, large-print software, speech output, or tactile graphics are entitled to these adaptations by law (through the Individuals with Disabilities Education Act [IDEA] and Section 504 of the Rehabilitation Act). Special education departments in each school district are aware of this. The school district is responsible for the cost of the technology needed to meet the educational needs of children under its jurisdiction.

Possible Responses

"Since you don't know how to adapt the school computers for my daughter's use, I'm requesting in writing an assistive technology evaluation so we can determine what her needs are and what technology she would benefit from. She should have the same opportunity to access the computer technology as her sighted classmates."

"Although you don't have specially adapted computers with a refreshable braille display and speech output, you're responsible for providing this technology since Ying is totally blind. Her assistive technology evaluation specifically addresses her technology needs, and provides recommendations for specific programs. I'm sure that we, as the IEP team, want what is best for Ying so that she can keep up with her classmates. I'd like this documented in her IEP, including specific training on the equipment for Ying and her classroom teacher."

"We can provide your son's textbooks on tape or CD, so we don't need to teach him braille skills."

Background Information

Although Alan's school textbooks may be reproducible in an audio format such as on cassette or CD, listening to classroom materials is not the same as reading them. All children need the opportunity to be taught to read in a format that is most accessible to them, whether visual or tactile. Reading is a literacy skill. Unless Alan learns to read, he will be considered illiterate and may not be employable as an adult. This critical literacy skill needs to be addressed at an early age—at the same time as his sighted classmates are learning to read.

Possible Responses

"Using books on tape or CD occasionally is one thing, but these are listening materials, not reading materials. Alan needs to know how to read, and at this point he can't read print—he needs to learn braille. The other students receive their textbooks in regular print because they can read print; Alan needs to receive his textbooks in braille."

"I have eye reports from Dr. Menendez, Alan's pediatric ophthalmologist, and Dr. Soo-Chow, his low vision optometrist, describing his vision at this time. The functional vision assessment report from Alan's teacher of visually impaired students specifically recommends braille instruction because of his inability to read print in a meaningful and functional way. With his extremely limited vision, braille needs to be his primary reading medium. I'd like this documented by a learning media assessment and would like this skill added to his IEP at this time."

"We took the liberty of filling out a 'draft' IEP. Please sign here."

Background Information

School personnel, realizing the limited amount of time in the IEP meeting, may draft an IEP for the student ahead of time. The problem is that if it was not created in the context of the discussions, concerns, and priorities of the parents and other IEP team members, it is out of compliance with the law. A draft IEP is only a list of proposed recommendations that the educational personnel happen to put on the actual form. It carries no weight until the considerations of the draft have been discussed and agreed upon by the entire IEP team, including the parent. It is true that to discuss, agree upon, and write the IEP in one meeting that lasts only an hour or two is usually impossible. Beginning to see the IEP "negotiations" as a series of meetings, e-mails, and telephone calls is probably more in line with reality. As long as you are involved in creating the draft, it does make sense to work ahead of time on the IEP.

Possible Responses

Plan to be in touch with your child's teacher a month or so before the IEP meeting and ask: "If you'll be creating a draft of Nicole's IEP, could I get a copy of the draft 10 days before the meeting? That way I can come to the meeting prepared to talk about the recommendations in the draft. Better yet, let's set up a time to work on the draft together."

If you get to the meeting, and a draft is presented that you didn't know had been created, you might say: "Because I didn't have time to look at this draft ahead of time, let's have a discussion about each of the elements, and as a team, we can incorporate the parts of the draft we determine are needed for Nicole into the one we write today."

"Your child is two years delayed in his language development. Due to his blindness, we really can't expect more than that."

Background Information

What is this kind of statement really saying? If it is given in response to documented educational delays in your child's performance, the abilities and needs of your child and appropriate goals need to be discussed and clarified. In order to meet the standards for the grade level your child is in, the "measurement" of success is what every child of that age should know, not what every sighted child of that age should know. In order to have clear and appropriate expectations set, your child's strengths and weaknesses need to be clearly defined in the IEP, based on the results of appropriate evaluations. Also, you need a clear understanding of your child's cognitive ability and whether a delay in his or her progress is due to cognitive limitations or the inability to use classroom materials visually. Low expectations for students who are blind or visually impaired have frequently been at the root of poor outcomes for these students in our schools for many years.

Possible Responses

"What are the steps we need to build in here to get Kumar to his next level of performance? Let's look again at his strengths and weaknesses. How are we going to put goals in his IEP to make sure he is moving toward his grade level expectations, so he won't remain behind? What about summer school? Tutoring? Extra direct service minutes from his teacher of students who are visually impaired?"

"Let's look at Kumar's IQ scores again and compare them to his test performance in school. His IQ scores indicate that he has average intelligence, but his test scores are below average. Can we discuss the accommodations and test formats he needs to make sure that his tests measure his knowledge rather than penalizing him for being visually impaired?

"When I read the test questions to Hannah, she usually answers them correctly, but I don't have the time to give her individual attention when she's taking tests with her fourth-grade classmates. I'm sorry, but I have to give her failing grades because of her poor written test performance."

Background Information

Students with visual impairments may require testing materials in regular print, large print, braille, tactile graphics, audio formats, or some combination of these formats. The provision of a test and related materials should be based on whatever medium is used by the student, as identified on his or her IEP. Students who are blind or visually impaired can, and must, be made part of the state's assessment program through use of accommodations that allow them to demonstrate their knowledge and skills without being penalized for their visual impairment. Accommodations in setting and scheduling may also include individual test administration, different lighting, space for testing materials and tools, extended time for test sessions, several brief testing sessions and tools such as magnification devices, "talking" (with speech output) or large-print calculators, tape recorders, and computers. Many regular classroom teachers and other service providers have no experience in testing students with visual limitations. The test administrator is responsible for ensuring that all tests are available in the format that the individual student needs. The teacher of students with visual impairments should be consulted to make sure that the student will have equal access to testing materials and that the appropriate accommodations are in place for his or her individual needs.

Possible Responses

"I know that we all want Hannah to demonstrate her knowledge of the classroom materials and do well on her tests. Allowing her to have extra time, large print, or a reader may level the playing field and give her opportunities to succeed along with her classmates."

"At her last eye examination, which I gave you a copy of, Hannah's pediatric ophthalmologist and low vision optometrist recommended that she receive her tests magnified to 18-point print, with double the time to complete her work. I'd like her teacher of students who are visually impaired to evaluate her need for these accommodations in learning and assessment. Also, she may need a person to record her answers since she can't identify the small grid spaces on the answer sheet. If she doesn't get these accommodations, she may not be able to demonstrate her true knowledge of the materials."

CHAPTER 5

Related Services: Addressing Additional Needs

Carol B. Allman

When children have a visual impairment or other disability, providing them with special education services—such as instruction from a teacher of visually impaired students—often is not sufficient. They may need additional support or services before they can truly benefit from the education they are receiving. Such additional services might include, for example, orientation and mobility (O&M) training so that the student can get around to his or her classes in school, or physical therapy to help a child with physical disabilities maintain a position in which he or she can see the chalkboard. The term "related services" describes a variety of such supportive educational services, which may be provided to students as part of their special education program. It is important for parents to be aware of the availability of such services for their child's education.

Although related services are different, in definition, from special education services and from supplementary aids and services, which were mentioned in Chapter 4, sometimes it is difficult to tell when a service is special education and when it is a related service or a supplementary aid or service. The general definitions provided under IDEA are:

- Special education means specially designed instruction, at no cost to the parents, to meet the unique needs of a child with a disability.
- Related services are those required to assist a child with a disability to benefit from special education. Such services are described in more detail in this chapter.

127

- Supplementary aids and services refer to supports that are provided in the regular education class and other education-related settings (for example, where extracurricular activities like band or writing clubs take place) to enable children with disabilities to be educated with nondisabled children to the maximum extent appropriate.

The differences in these definitions may seem difficult to understand, but the important point to remember is that whatever services your child requires for his or her education need to be identified. This chapter will define related services, explain why they are important, discuss who should provide them, and explain how they are related to the Individualized Education Program (IEP).

WHAT ARE RELATED SERVICES?

A full range of services is available to students who are classified as eligible to receive them, at no cost to their parents, and based on the individual student's educational need. Schools must provide those related services that are necessary for a child to learn and to participate in his or her school program and receive a free, appropriate public education, and to enhance his or her experience of it. No limit can be put on the number of related services a child receives, provided they are all necessary. In addition, the amount of time the service is offered must be sufficient for the child to get the help he or she needs. Related services are listed in the student's IEP, including the amount of time per week the child will receive each service and the expected length of time over which the service will be required: weeks, months, and so on, as appropriate.

The Individuals with Disabilities Education Act (IDEA) defines related services as "transportation and such developmental, corrective, and other supportive services as are required to assist a child with a disability to benefit from special education." Related services must, in particular, be considered when a transition IEP is being created to prepare a student for the next stage of life beyond high school (for more on this, see Chapters 4 and 9). Such services can be crucial in coordinating the young person's various activities as he or she moves into life after high school. For example, a student may need transportation to and from the workplace for supported employment or O&M training at a potential work site or the college campus she or he is attending.

The related services areas specifically identified and defined in IDEA appear in the list that follows. Other services may be offered if they are required for a child to benefit from his or her special education program. For the definitions of related services as they appear in the regulations that implement the law, see "Legal Definitions of Related Services in IDEA."

Legal Definitions of Related Services in IDEA

The following definitions of related services are from the federal regulations that support IDEA. This information can be useful to refer to if you have to document your child's need for a specific related service.

Audiology Services: (i) identification of children with hearing loss; (ii) determination of the range, nature, and degree of hearing loss, including referral for medical or other professional attention for the habilitation of hearing; (iii) provision of habilitative activities, such as language habilitation, auditory training, speech-reading (lip-reading), hearing evaluation, and speech conservation; (iv) creation and administration of programs for prevention of hearing loss; (v) counseling and guidance of pupils, parents, and teachers regarding hearing loss; and (vi) determination of the child's need for group and individual amplification, selecting and fitting an appropriate aid, and evaluating the effectiveness of amplification.

Counseling Services: services provided by qualified social workers, psychologists, guidance counselors, or other qualified personnel.

Early Identification and Assessment of Disabilities in Children: the implementation of a formal plan for identifying a disability as early as possible in a child's life.

Interpreting Services: For children who are deaf or hard of hearing, oral transliteration services, cued language transliteration services, sign language transliteration and interpreting services, and special interpreting services for children who are deaf-blind.

Medical Services for Diagnostic or Evaluation Purposes: services provided by a licensed physician to determine a child's medically related disability that results in the child's need for special education and related services.

Occupational Therapy: (i) improving, developing or restoring functions impaired or lost through illness, injury, or deprivation; (ii) improving ability to perform tasks for independent functioning if functions are impaired or lost; and (iii) preventing, through early intervention, initial or further impairment or loss of function.

(continued on next page)

Orientation and Mobility Services: services provided to blind or visually impaired students by qualified personnel to enable those students to attain systematic orientation to and safe movement within their environments in school, home, and community.

Parent Counseling and Training: assisting parents in understanding the special needs of their child and providing parents with information about child development.

Physical Therapy: services provided by a qualified physical therapist.

Psychological Services: (i) administering psychological and educational tests, and other assessment procedures; (ii) interpreting assessment results; (iii) obtaining, integrating, and interpreting information about child behavior and conditions relating to learning; (iv) consulting with other staff members in planning school programs to meet the special needs of children as indicated by psychological tests, interviews, and behavioral evaluations; (v) planning and managing a program of psychological services, including psychological counseling for children and parents; and (vi) assisting in developing positive behavioral intervention strategies.

Recreation, Including Therapeutic Recreation: (i) assessment of leisure function; (ii) therapeutic recreation services; (iii) recreation programs in schools and community agencies; and (iv) leisure education.

Rehabilitation Counseling: services provided by qualified personnel in individual or group sessions that focus specifically on career development, employment preparation, achieving independence, and integration in the workplace and community of a student with a disability. The term also includes vocational rehabilitation services provided to a student with disabilities by vocational rehabilitation programs funded under the Rehabilitation Act of 1973, as amended.

School Health Services: services provided by a qualified school nurse or other qualified person.

School Social Work Services: (i) preparing a social or developmental history on a child with a disability; (ii) group and individual counseling with the child and family; (iii) working with those problems in a child's living situation (home, school, and community) that affect the child's adjustment in school; (iv) mobilizing school and community resources to enable the child to learn as effectively as possible in his or her educational program; and (v) assisting in developing positive behavioral intervention strategies.

Speech-Language Pathology: (i) identification of children with speech or language impairments; (ii) diagnosis and appraisal of specific speech or language impairments; (iii) referral for medical or other professional attention necessary for the habilitation of speech or language impairments; (iv) provision of speech and language services for the habilitation or prevention of communicative impairments; and (v) counseling and guidance of parents, children, and teachers regarding speech and language impairments.

Transportation: (i) travel to and from school and between schools; (ii) travel in and around school buildings; and (iii) specialized equipment (such as special or adapted buses, lifts, and ramps), if required to provide special transportation for a child with a disability.

- **Audiology services:** services to identify and diagnose children with hearing loss and determine what measures need to be taken to help the child participate in learning (such as hearing aids and auditory training).

- **Counseling services:** services provided by qualified personnel such as social workers, psychologists, and guidance counselors to help a child with problems in school or in planning for the future.

- **Early identification and assessment of disabilities in children:** services related to the requirement for each state to implement a formal plan to find children with disabilities as early as possible, usually through a preschool screening program.

- **Interpreting services:** communication services for students who are deaf or hard of hearing, including transliteration (exact translation) or sign language, as well as special interpreting services for students who are deaf-blind.

- **Medical services for diagnostic or evaluation purposes:** services delivered by a physician to determine the nature of a child's disability and its implications for his or her special education program.

- **Occupational therapy:** services to help children develop fine motor coordination and daily living skills necessary to their success in school and the community.

- **Orientation and mobility services:** services and training provided by qualified O&M specialists who teach students who are visually impaired techniques for moving about safely and independently.

- **Parent counseling and training:** services to help families understand their child's special needs and how they may relate to typical child development.

- **Physical therapy:** services to develop and promote a child's gross and total body movements, muscle tone, coordination, and balance and equilibrium.

- **Psychological services:** services involved in conducting assessments, making interpretations and recommendations based on those assessments, working with students individually or in small groups, and providing consultation to teachers, other school personnel, and parents.

- **Recreation, including therapeutic recreation:** services involved in evaluating a child's functioning during leisure time and providing programs that encourage appropriate body movement, such as running on a track, either in school or through community agencies.

- **Rehabilitation counseling:** services and training relating to advocating for oneself and to pursuing careers and employment.

- **School health services:** services provided by a school nurse or other qualified staff, which may include vision and hearing screenings and maintenance of current medical records.

- **Social work services in schools:** services aimed at helping teachers and families locate appropriate community resources and implement effective educational programs.

- **Speech-language pathology:** services for the identification and diagnosis of speech and language difficulties and with providing therapy to the child as well as consultation to school personnel.

- **Transportation:** services supporting travel from home to school, as well as any specialized equipment necessary to transport a child safely, such as adapted buses, lifts, and ramps.

Federal law specifically indicates that *all* related services may not be required for an individual child and that the list the federal documents define is not an exhaustive one. Related services may include other "developmental, corrective, or supportive services," such as artistic and cultural programs; art, music, and dance therapy; nutrition services; or independent living services to help students learn to take care of their own everyday needs. Often these services relate to the unique set of skills called the expanded core curriculum for children with visual impairments, which is described in Chapter 1. The teaching of the expanded core curriculum would not be listed as related services on the IEP, but would be considered special education services because these unique services are taught by the teacher of students who are visually impaired.

WHY ARE RELATED SERVICES IMPORTANT?

Related services are important because they represent services that the school system can provide that make the total educational program for your child an effective and appropriate one. It may be crucial for children

---

From a Parent's Perspective

. . . AND CANE MAKES THREE

I so well remember driving to day care after my day of teaching high school. I turned the corner at Elm Park and saw a young lady walking with a little girl who was holding a small cane. It was a minute until I realized, with a lump in my throat and a few tears in my eyes, that that little girl with the cane was my little girl.

I pulled over to watch. My little girl needed that cane. It was the first time I saw it, and it was hard for me. I wept and wept. I felt so badly for her . . . and for me. After I dried my eyes, I went along to the day care center and parked the car and walked back toward them. As I approached, I called out to Jameyanne and ran to her. "Wow—look at that neat cane! You're doing a great job! Show Mommy what you do with it. Can we bring it home to show Daddy?" Stephanie and Jameyanne decorated the cane during the year for Christmas, Easter, July 4th, and Halloween! Jameyanne's brother, Michael, wanted one too!

My father, especially, refused the cane. God would cure her; she didn't need that thing. God knew how I understood him. So Jameyanne and my Dad and I went to the mall together, and I left them. I asked my Dad to help her and make her click her way through the mall. I reminded him that she did need the cane, but more so, she needed him to like the cane. He understood, and they spent that time together—all three of them.

Mary E. Fuller
Mother of a 15-year-old daughter with aniridia glaucoma
Concord, New Hampshire

ORIENTATION AND MOBILITY: MAKING IT WORK

Orientation and mobility (O&M) instruction must be meaningful to your child. The school system is now in charge of giving your child appropriate services by a trained and qualified O&M instructor. The skills he or she is to acquire and master must be taught in a sequential manner in the widest range of appropriate environments. A child with a visual impairment will need to be taught what sighted children learn from their environment. A visit to a pediatric optometrist is appropriate at this time to obtain information about your child's functional vision and any low vision devices that he or she might utilize while traveling. Instruction in using tactile maps and in making maps can assist in orientation. Basic skills in mobility should be practiced in familiar, relevant, and safe environments and move on in a continuum to more complex situations.

A guideline for what your child should be doing comes from looking around at what her sighted peers are doing: Where they are traveling? This age-appropriate travel should be the goal of the child's O&M training. Some school systems interpret these needs too narrowly to include travel only within the school environment. The O&M specialist has an obligation to challenge your child beyond that narrow space to a higher level of independence in the widest range of the child's relevant travel. Techniques like sighted guide travel and the incorporation of protective technique should be taught consistently and sequentially until your child has mastered them.

Indoor and outdoor travel objectives could include traveling to places such as the grocery store, locating a particular store at the mall, and mapping a route from home to a friend's house and traveling to it. Along the way, instruction can occur in cane technique, use of low vision devices for helpful sightings, and exposure to possible obstacles. Polite and safe travel skills in crowded and uncrowded areas should be addressed. Analysis of traffic patterns should be taught in a safe environment while working toward independence. Independence will come slowly, and mastery of travel will take time. The long-term goals and objectives for your child are to be safe and independent in the widest range of environments in order to prepare him or her for a lifetime of independence in travel.

Mary E. Fuller
Mother of a 15-year-old daughter with aniridia glaucoma
Concord, New Hampshire

with visual impairments to receive O&M, rehabilitation counseling, parent counseling, or medical and health services, for example, as related services in order to participate fully in educational activities and benefit from them.

The IEP team must carefully consider the related services that are needed in order for your child to benefit from special education services. It is therefore very important that participants in the IEP process be aware of the different related services that could be provided. The list of related services that appears in this chapter is not intended as a shopping list of services from which to choose those that might be useful. Rather, you need to consider the goals and objectives of your child's IEP and consider which related services may be necessary to help your child achieve them.

WHO SHOULD PROVIDE RELATED SERVICES?

The persons who deliver the various related services will vary, depending on the services to be provided. The federal definitions of counseling, medical services, occupational therapy, O&M, physical therapy, rehabilitation counseling, and school health services specify the use of a qualified person to provide the service. Since various licensing and certification requirements apply for these services, you would expect to have persons with the appropriate credentials provide related services to your child. For example, O&M training would be provided by an O&M specialist, and medical services would be provided by persons certified to carry out the medical procedures needed.

If you feel that the person providing a service to your child does not have the required expertise or is not properly qualified, you have the right to address this issue with school personnel. You can request a conference with the school principal or guidance counselor, another IEP meeting with the IEP team, mediation (which would be set up through contact with the school principal), or a due process procedure (which would be the last resort and set up through the school principal or his or her designee) to address your issue with any related service. (Being an advocate for your child is discussed in greater detail in Chapter 10.)

HOW ARE RELATED SERVICES CONNECTED TO THE IEP?

When the IEP team meets every year, from the time your child is 3 years old through age 21, part of the team's task is to consider whether your child will need any related services. The annual goals and other parts of the IEP formulated for your child will guide the team in making decisions about the related services that your child needs. Related services are only required if they will assist your child in benefiting from special education and are necessary for him or her to receive a free, appropriate public education. The IEP team decides which related services should be provided. That decision, in turn, is based on the components of the IEP, including present level of educational performance, annual goals and short-term objectives or benchmarks, and special education services needed to meet the goals and objectives (or benchmarks). You would therefore expect to see a natural connection between the parts of the IEP and the related services provided. For example, if your child's present level of educational performance refers to your child's need for travel skills, then you would expect that O&M would be provided as a related service to teach those skills.

You can become familiar with related services areas by talking to your child's teacher of visually impaired students, special education personnel in your area, other parents, or parent or national organizations (see Chapter 1 and the Resources section at the back of this book for more information). Your knowledge about related services will be helpful to you and your child as he or she progresses through school and will be particularly useful during IEP meetings as your child's needs are being addressed by the educational team.

For More Information

P. Crane, D. Cuthbertson, K. A. Ferrell, and H. Scherb, *Equals in Partnership: Basic Rights for Families of Children with Blindness or Visual Impairment* (Watertown, MA: Hilton/Perkins Program of Perkins School for the Blind and National Association for Parents of the Visually Impaired, 1997).

Florida Department of Education, *An Introduction to Exceptional Student Education: For Parents of Florida's Students with Disabilities* (Tallahassee, FL: Florida Department of Education, 2001).

Florida Department of Education, *Parents' Educational Records: For Parents of Florida's Students with Disabilities* (Tallahassee, FL: Florida Department of Education, 2001).

M. C. Holbrook (Ed.), *Children with Visual Impairments: A Parents' Guide,* second edition (Bethesda, MD: Woodbine House, 2006).

NOTES

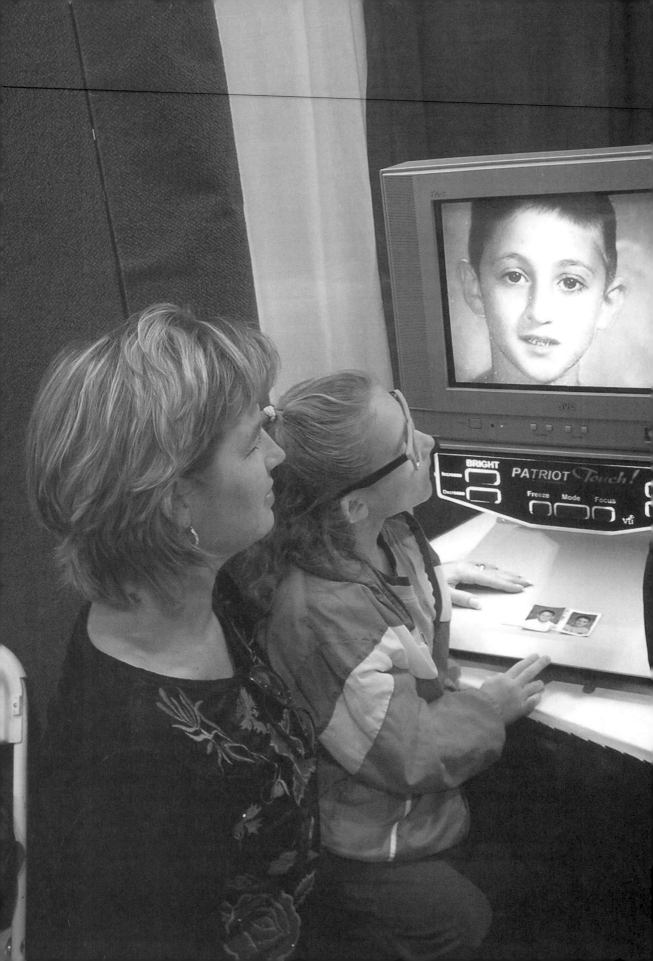

CHAPTER 6

Accommodations and Adaptations: Gaining Access to the Curriculum

Donna McNear

The nature and extent of visual impairment, and the effects, differ from person to person. Two people with the same kind of vision loss may see differently from each other and, as noted in Chapter 1, some people who are visually impaired may see differently at different times during the same day. Because of this variability it is difficult to make general statements about the educational needs of children who are visually impaired. However, one reality does not vary: A visual impairment affects the ability of a child to obtain information from the environment. In the school setting, this means that in order to participate in learning and the full range of activities that are part of going to school, your child needs to learn to obtain information in different ways from children without visual impairments. In addition, information and experiences have to be provided to your child in ways that are designed to meet his or her needs.

It is important to keep in mind that a visual impairment does not prevent someone from living a full and productive life. Children who are visually impaired can participate in all school activities, including instruction in academic subjects, physical education, field trips, and extracurricular activities. Not only are they are entitled to do so, but it is essential that they do. For a visually impaired child to learn to lead an independent, satisfying life, he or she is best served by living and working as independently as possible as early as possible—and that means now, in school as well as at home and in the community.

FREQUENTLY USED ADAPTATIONS FOR STUDENTS

People who are visually impaired can do virtually all the activities and tasks that sighted people take for granted, but they often need to learn to do them in a different way or using different tools or materials. They may need to learn braille to read and write or to learn to walk with a long cane or a trained dog guide. Wearing eyeglasses with special tinted lenses if they are sensitive to light or using a magnifier to read small print on a map are other examples of how people with visual impairments use adapted techniques to live comfortably, learn, and perform the tasks of daily life. There is an established body of knowledge about such alternate techniques that children can be taught, ranging from simple changes to highly specialized techniques requiring specific training. Your child will most likely learn about such adaptations from vision professionals such as his or her teacher of students with visual impairments or orientation and mobility (O&M) instructor.

Depending on your child's abilities and needs, he or she may need such adaptations to have access to—to make use of, to obtain information about and understand, and to participate in—the curriculum and various activities in school, as well as to instructional materials. Such adaptations in school are usually referred to by the terms "accommodations" and "modifications." For instance, a child may need reading materials in braille rather than in print or may need to examine a "real life" example of a concept instead of a picture or other representation—that is, may need the opportunity to touch and examine a live rabbit with his or her hands, rather than be presented with a picture in a book. Other examples are arranging a classroom to allow a student the flexibility to sit close to a teacher who is demonstrating a science experiment, or allowing a student extra time to complete a test that the whole class is taking.

In addition to adaptive techniques, visually impaired students may use a variety of devices to participate in school learning activities. As explained in Chapter 3, the term "assistive technology" includes equipment and devices—including optical devices like magnifiers, incorporating special prescribed lenses—that help students with disabilities complete tasks that they would otherwise have difficulty completing without them. A student who is visually impaired and has a physical disability may have difficulty handling books and might use an easel to hold a text; a student who is blind might use special equipment known as refreshable braille to read what is displayed on a computer's screen. Optical devices, sometimes referred to as "low vision devices," that use special lenses may be prescribed by an ophthalmologist or optometrist to help a visually impaired person make the maximum use of his or her functional vision. As explained in Chapter 3, functional vision refers to the way in which someone makes use of his or her existing sight to perform tasks in daily life.

Optical devices include magnifiers to hold over reading materials to enlarge the print, and video magnifiers, also known as closed-circuit televisions (CCTVs), which combine a video camera that projects an enlarged image of reading material and a computer monitor that displays the image. All these devices are examples of assistive technology.

Different school systems attach different meanings to the terms accommodations and modifications. *Accommodation* usually refers to a change in a learning activity that does not change the standard of learning or performance or the requirements that a student needs to meet for a learning task. For example, the use of braille instead of print for learning tasks would be an accommodation, as the student still needs to do the same reading and writing tasks that the rest of the class does, but using a different medium. *Modification* commonly refers to a change in a learning activity that *changes* the standard of learning or performance or the requirements that a student needs to meet for a learning task. A reduction in the number of items that a student needs to complete on a test would be an example of a modification. Because these terms are not used in the same way in all school districts, it will be helpful for you to learn how your school district defines them.

As a parent, you will want to know what accommodations and modifications are appropriate for your child, how that is determined and by whom, and how they are used during your child's school day. These questions are usually determined through the assessment or evaluation process, which is covered in more detail in Chapter 3.

When accommodations and modifications are identified for your child, his or her needs have to be examined in a variety of areas: whether he or she needs materials in special formats like braille; environmental adjustments such as enhanced or filtered lighting; or assistive technology such as synthetic speech and other specialized computer hardware. And, it is important to keep in mind that your child may need different adapted techniques and devices in different situations—no one device or technique may be the "answer" to everything.

ACCOMMODATIONS FOR READING AND WRITING

One of the essential areas of accommodations for your child relates to the way in which he or she reads and writes. Success in school for all students, including those with visual impairments, depends to a great degree on their access—their ability to understand, use, and read—instruction and materials. If a child cannot obtain information from print materials easily and efficiently, these materials need to be provided in a format that the child can use, and the child needs to develop skills in using them. Results of the learning media assessment, which is discussed in Chapter 3, will provide the information to determine what sorts of accommodations your child might need for reading and writing. Many children who are visually impaired read and write print, but others cannot make out printed text or images unassisted. For that reason, a student may need to access printed information with optical or low vision devices or enlarged print. At other times, that same student may need to access material in braille, in a recorded format, or in an electronic format that he or she can work on from a computer screen.

Although the entire educational team will be involved in decisions about accommodations, it is the primary responsibility of your child's teacher of students with visual impairments to make sure that your child has access to instructional materials, such as textbooks, handouts, and online materials, in the format that he or she needs to read most efficiently. This teacher will also determine your child's need for specific equipment or modifications to existing equipment that will support your child as he or she receives instruction. A critical part of the job of the teacher of students with visual impairments, therefore, is to ensure that materials in an appropriate format are available so that the visually impaired student can participate in class along with his or her classmates. If a child does not have materials in a form that he or she can read—whether through the use of vision, touch, hearing, or other means—and at the same time that other children in the class have them in print, he or she is at a serious educational disadvantage (see "Providing Accessible Materials").

As you work with your child's educators to meet his or needs for accessible materials, you can obtain information and assistance from your child's teacher of visually impaired students, parents' groups, and national organizations concerned with the education and well-being of people who are visually impaired. The Resources section at the back of this book provides extensive information on such organizations.

AREAS FOR ACCOMMODATIONS AND MODIFICATIONS

Typically, students may require accommodations and modifications during the school day for various activities, in the broad areas of

- instruction
- materials
- assignments
- classroom testing
- assistive technology
- the environment
- other activities

Providing Accessible Materials

To address the critical issue of ensuring that students who are blind or visually impaired receive their adapted educational materials at the same time as other students receive their books and other materials, parents, teachers, and advocates for children with visual impairments have focused on the Individuals with Disabilities Education Act (IDEA) and requirements for what is known as access to instructional materials. In the past, materials needed by visually impaired students, such as books transcribed or converted into braille, were not always available to students at the start of the school year, resulting in serious educational disadvantages.

As a result of amendments that were passed in 2004, IDEA, for the first time, included language that will help ensure that children who are visually impaired receive their textbooks and classroom materials on time and in the accessible format they need. The new provisions establish a system for the publishers of textbooks to provide electronic files for these students in a standardized electronic format known as the National Instructional Materials Accessibility Standard (NIMAS), which can be converted into books in accessible formats such as braille, large print, or electronic text. States must adopt these standards, and a central repository known as the National Instructional Materials Access Center (NIMAC) has been established. This center is responsible for receiving, maintaining, and distributing electronic copies of the instructional materials it receives and is located at the American Printing House for the Blind in Lexington, KY. Here teachers, school districts, and state education departments can obtain the electronic files necessary to generate materials for their visually impaired students. (See the Resources section of this book for more information.)

As indicated in Chapter 1, federal legislation and regulations relating to special education services change because they are reviewed and re-funded every several years by Congress. For this reason, it is important for parents to be aware of what the law requires and how those requirements may be interpreted and put into effect in their states. Services and practices can vary across the country. In regard to instructional materials, each state has the option of using the central repository or, if it does not, of assuring the U. S. Secretary of Education that it will deliver accessible textbooks to students with print disabilities in

(continued on next page)

a timely manner. If states opt to use the central repository, they need to require that publishers of textbooks provide copies of all newly purchased instructional materials in the NIMAS format. As an alternative, a state may purchase publisher-produced instructional materials in formats that are accessible to students who cannot use print or that can be converted into those formats.

These areas are illustrated in the following sections through examples of accommodations or modifications that you might expect to see in your child's classroom or other school environment. "Accommodations and Modifications at a Glance for Students with Visual Impairments" at the end of this chapter provides examples of accommodations and modifications that may be helpful for students in each of these areas.

Instruction

Accommodations and modifications can help a student understand the instruction provided by the teacher in the classroom. It is important that children with visual impairments have access to both written and oral instruction and to demonstrations in all subject matter. For example, in a preschool classroom, the teacher is reading *Goldilocks and the Three Bears* and teaching the concepts of small, medium, and large using pictures of three different-sized bears. For Monique, who is visually impaired, the teacher also has the storybook available in braille, along with three stuffed toy bears in three sizes. These will enable Monique to learn through nonvisual methods the concepts, such as relative size, that the teacher is presenting and be exposed to braille in the same way that her sighted classmates are exposed to print.

A young child, such as Monique, needs accommodations during story time and instruction in concept development for beginning reading and math skills. As students who are visually impaired move through the grades, they may need accommodations to access the teacher's instruction in a large-group setting, where students are seated at a distance from the teacher. Teachers frequently use a whiteboard or chalkboard to write directions, provide examples, and illustrate concepts and use written and visual materials to explain ideas. Students may need a variety of accommodations to access this instruction as presented in the classroom, such as using assistive technology to read visual information from a distance or a portable notetaking device to take notes on what the teacher is saying. In a class such as physical education, the student may need to be close to the teacher to observe how he or she is demonstrating how to dribble a basketball or receive individual instruction in dribbling.

Materials

Instructional materials need to be put into an accessible format for visually impaired students, and it is important that accommodations to all materials be considered. For example, Jorge, who reads braille, will need to have his classroom reading materials in braille and to receive them at the same time as his sighted classmates who read print. These materials will include, in the area of reading, his textbook, worksheets, and all supplemental reading materials. The curriculum content in each subject area, such as science, mathematics, social studies, and language arts, also needs to be reviewed so that access to all print materials is provided to Jorge in braille. In addition, diagrams, maps, and models that are used to present concepts in mathematics and social studies also need to be put into a tactile format that Jorge can read. In art class, a variety of tactile materials (textured paper, small objects, and tactile writing devices) may be needed to produce a tactile drawing. And when pictures and photos are used in teaching activities, students may need manipulatives such as cubes and beads and real objects such as coins, adapted rulers, and clocks to understand concepts being presented.

Alicia, who has low vision—severe visual impairment that interferes with her ability to perform daily tasks—and uses magnification tools to read and gather information, will need those devices to use the printed maps required in her fifth-grade social studies unit. She may also need the flexibility to use enlarged printed maps if it is difficult for her to access visual information due to low contrast and visual clutter in the materials that may make them difficult for her to read. At the high school level, when demands increase in reading and writing tasks, supplemental materials in an auditory format can support a student's access to information.

Assignments

Accommodations and modifications may be necessary to complete assignments both in class and at home. Andrei, a first-grade student who has low vision, uses braille to complete most of his reading and writing assignments. But he also uses print for math computation and benefits from using graphic materials such as photographs and charts that are enlarged or viewed with magnification tools. He has a video magnifier (CCTV) available at home and at school that he uses for some print reading and writing activities. While Andrei is developing the ability to read in both braille and print, his classroom assignments in mathematics are modified until he has mastered Nemeth numbers (numbers used in braille for reading and writing math problems). Andrei is required to complete some of his math problems in the Nemeth code at school and then complete the assignment at home using the video magnifier and print.

To maximize their learning, students need to be responsible for all classroom and homework assignments. Andrei is completing all his classroom and homework assignments, but modifications in the form of additional time are necessary while he is mastering a variety of skills to participate in all curriculum activities. When an assignment is a visual task, such as drawing a plant cell viewed through a microscope in a biology lab or interpreting a visual artist's masterpiece in art history, a student may need accommodations and modifications. Working with a partner and adapting the partner's verbal descriptions into a written paragraph, or using extra time to create a tactile drawing, may be appropriate.

Classroom Testing

Different types of accommodations and modifications can help visually impaired students take their class tests along with their sighted classmates. Ahmed, who is in third grade, has low vision and cerebral palsy and reads and writes more slowly than his classmates. To have the same opportunity as the rest of class to complete all the items on his class tests and to take the tests independently, he will need to be allotted more time than the other students. Ahmed, who can write independently, also benefits from working in a small group for testing so he does not "feel pressured" by the working pace of his classmates. Another accommodation he uses (depending on the length of the test) is taking the test in shortened segments so that he can take a break every 20 minutes.

Some students who have additional disabilities benefit from a "scribe." This is a person who records the student's verbal responses on the answer sheet to a test. Some students with low vision struggle with answer sheets requiring small shapes to be filled in with a pencil. These students frequently record their answers directly on the test form. Many tests are now administered on computers, and it is important to ensure that the material is accessible to visually impaired students through such accommodations as enlarging the font on the computer or using refreshable braille.

Assistive Technology

As noted earlier, different students may need different assistive technology tools to learn or to communicate with others. For example, Sakura, an eighth grader who is blind and reads and writes in braille, needs portable braille writing tools to take notes in braille in her class. She uses a portable braille notetaker, sometimes called a personal digital assistant (PDA)—similar to a laptop computer on which a student can both read and write in braille—that can receive e-mail and can connect to both a braille embosser and a regular printer to read information from her teachers and to communicate immediately in braille and in print with sighted teachers and classmates. Frequently students with low vision need access to visual information presented at a distance, and a variety of assistive technology devices can be helpful. Monocular telescopes prescribed by an eye specialist allow a student to see print information at a distance. To access visual information projected at a distance, such as a videotape, video magnifiers designed for distance viewing can assist.

The Environment

Students who are visually impaired often cannot perceive information directly from their environment, but accommodations and modifications help them do so. In a rural high school, Alberto, who has low vision, took Advanced Placement Spanish through distance video technology, and the distance learning environment created additional challenges for him. He was unable to access lecture information at a sufficient rate using his usual methods: a monocular telescope and a laptop. Also, since the teacher was off site, he did not have the opportunity to confer with the teacher after the lecture to get additional notes and ask individual questions. To ensure that Alberto has the same access and learning experience as his sighted classmates, the teacher provides him with individual copies of the materials and notes that are used during the lectures through e-mail and postal mail before each class. This arrangement gives him the opportunity to preview the lectures.

Education environments need to be examined for learning challenges they may pose for students who are visually impaired, and solutions to these challenges need to be devised. A common environmental accommodation, such as preferential seating (flexibility to sit in close proximity to instruction), may meet a student's need, or altering the physical arrangement of the environment may be needed, such as additional furniture, shelving, or access to electrical outlets for the operation of specialized equipment.

Other Activities

Students with visual impairments need to be able to participate in all the educational activities school offers, not just those that take place in the classroom. For example, Natasha, a blind high school student, participates in marching band. Special methods allow her to participate as independently as possible in the band routines and competitions. Physical accommodations (a bar and cord), acceptable to the rules of band competition, "connect" Natasha to the band member next to her, enabling her to stay in line and in step by following the movements of her classmate. Other school activities such as field trips, emergency procedures, and events outside of the typical school day need to be reviewed to ensure appropriate and safe participation by students with visual impairments.

By considering your child's needs in each of these areas and asking questions about them of the other members of the educational team, you can make sure that you are thinking about all the situations your child will experience in school and that you are able to contribute to the important decisions about how those needs will be met. Other aspects of your role in this process are discussed later in this chapter. Although the best way to meet your child's needs in some of these areas may seem obvious, in other areas these needs can only be determined through a systematic process of collecting and analyzing information, known as an assessment.

WHY ASSESSMENT?

Determining a specific child's need for accommodations and modifications in the particular settings of the classroom and other school environments is done by collecting information, analyzing it, and using it to make informed decisions. In general, the process of assessment, described in Chapter 3, focuses on your child's needs in a variety of areas. The discussion in this chapter focuses specifically on assessment of a student's needs for accommodations and modifications.

Assessment is a careful examination of your child's strengths, abilities, and unique needs that allows the educational team that puts together your child's Individualized Education Program (IEP) to identify the accommodations and modifications that will enable him or her to have access to an appropriate education. The assessment should result in a clear statement of educational needs for accommodations and modifications that will allow your child to have equal access to school activities in the areas of instruction, instructional materials, classroom assignments, classroom testing, assistive technology, the physical environment, and other activities, as noted earlier.

Assessment is important because changes in your child's teaching and learning activities should be based on his or her specific needs, not on what is available in the school or convenient for the classroom teacher, or on what has been effective for other children with visual impairments who are enrolled in the school. Changes in teaching and learning activities through accommodations and modifications are provided to children with disabilities so they can achieve and reach their own individual potential. The intent of accommodations and modifications is *not* to lower educational standards, avoid requirements, or grant favors because your child has a disability. The purpose is to create an appropriate and individualized teaching and learning environment where high expectations are maintained for your child and he or she can learn and develop to the maximum possible extent. High expectations are critical because they communicate to everyone, including your child, that he or she

From a Parent's Perspective

THE ONLY CONSTANT IS CHANGE

I remember one IEP meeting, perhaps it was middle school, when my son's vision teacher said that he would be evaluated again for braille. Again? My son knew braille, but wasn't using it on a regular basis since he had some usable vision. She said it was a new legal requirement and commenced a fairly detailed discussion of the pros and cons of more or less braille instruction at that point in my son's life. Although it was a legal requirement, she positioned it as a good thing for him and for us also.

At first I thought it silly to go through an extensive evaluation of something we all knew well. (Later I learned that a need and a skill can change from year to year.) In fact, because of this incident, it was the beginning for me of something I have tried to do each year since, even beyond IEP meetings. The lesson for me was to not assume that things stay the same. Vision fluctuates. Even the effect of total blindness fluctuates based on the person and his or her skills, current attitudes, successes, and challenges. Social skills also fluctuate. What was needed in first grade will change by fifth. High school brings new demands and new challenges. And all of this was and is about the future.

We adopted a strategy to try to understand the present and the future. We decided to let our son teach us. We tried to learn braille ourselves, but did better when we were just attentive and listening to him telling us about his braille lesson. The same was true with his reading large print as well as his textbooks and tapes. The more one or both of us allowed him to talk to us about his work, the more we learned, and the better we were able to understand the accommodations he might need.

Kevin E. O'Connor
Father of an 18-year-old son with Leber's congenital amaurosis
Long Grove, Illinois

is capable but may benefit from changes to support his or her individual needs. Parents play a vital role in the assessment process by thinking critically about their child's needs, asking questions, and making informed decisions that are appropriate for their particular child.

The following case study illustrates some of the complexities that parents and educators face in making these decisions and putting them into practice.

Joseph, who has low vision, moved into a new school district at the beginning of sixth grade. Most of the members of his educational team, including several of his classroom teachers and his parents, thought he should have access to all his reading material in large print because they believed large print to be useful for all students with visual impairments. The teacher of students with visual impairments reminded them that adequate assessment information had not yet been collected to make this decision, so that it could not yet be determined whether using large print for all reading material was an appropriate accommodation for Joseph. Joseph's IEP therefore stipulated that he would receive his reading materials in large print, and that the teacher for students with visual impairments would conduct ongoing assessment to make sure appropriate accommodations and modifications were in place.

As the year progressed, Joseph participated in further assessments and received new prescription reading spectacles for reading and other near vision tasks. Additional assessment included interviews with Joseph's parents and other educational team members. During the interview process Joseph's parents stated that since getting his new reading glasses, Joseph checked out regular print books from the library and read them all the time without difficulty. They also commented that he was reading more magazines in regular print. The information collected during the ongoing assessment revealed that Joseph had a faster reading rate with regular-size print text than with enlarged print, and adequate comprehension as well.

After a team meeting, Joseph's IEP was changed to indicate that his reading materials should be in regular print with access to enlarged materials when appropriate, especially for graphic material such as maps and charts. Results of the ongoing assessment also determined that he should have testing accommodations (additional time) and the use of a talking dictionary (a handheld electronic device, available commercially, that allows Joseph to type in a word and hear the correct spelling and definition read aloud).

In this case, Joseph's initial educational program did not reflect his unique needs because it was based on assumptions and not on information from a completed assessment. Initially, he was therefore not receiving appropriate services to meet his individual needs and maximize his participation in all learning activities. After he participated in an appropriate assessment, his IEP was modified to reflect his specific needs, although these could be expected to change over time, as those of students tend to.

THE ASSESSMENT PROCESS FOR ACCOMMODATIONS AND MODIFICATIONS

Assessment for accommodations and modifications is not a one-time occurrence. Rather, it is a continuing process. As your child grows and learns and faces new and different situations, his or her needs and abilities will change, and the need for accommodations will change. Continuing assessment includes the steps outlined here.

- The initial collection of information about your child's strengths, abilities, and needs helps determine appropriate accommodations and modifications. This step includes gathering information about your child's abilities and needs in the broad areas of instruction, materials, classroom testing, assignments, assistive technology, the environment, and other activities throughout the school day. The teacher of students with visual impairments will lead this process and collaborate with other team members as needed. For example, this teacher will observe your child in his or her classroom, such as during a mathematics lesson, to collect information about how your child is accessing information written on the chalkboard for students in the class. The teacher of students who are visually impaired will then discuss with the classroom teachers, in this case the mathematics teacher, his or her observations about how your child is able to access information written on the board as well as other instruction. Information from you, the parents, will be gathered to learn about activities that are going well and any concerns that may not be apparent in school.

- The information that was collected and the implications for your child's participation in teaching and learning activities throughout the school day are discussed and interpreted. During an evaluation team meeting, which includes your child's educational team members, the teacher of students with visual impairments will lead a discussion about the results and interpretation of the information gathered. For example, the team would discuss how your child accessed information from the board during the mathematics lesson and determine that your child was not able to read the math equations independently as the teacher wrote them on the board. They would review information provided by the mathematics teacher, who might report that although your child said he or she could see the board, your child seemed to rely on listening skills. You as parents might have reported that your child did not always know how to solve new equations and that he or she was trying to review math problems from the textbook at home. The discussion might reveal that your child's visual functioning was affecting his or her ability to benefit from instruction presented on the board in class.

- Your child's need for accommodations and modifications to participate in other school activities and areas would be further identified.

- Based on the identified needs, appropriate accommodations and modifications for your child's educational program would be indicated in your child's IEP.

- The accommodations and modifications specified would be implemented throughout your child's school day.

- Assessment would continue over time to evaluate and determine the appropriateness of your child's educational program and the accommodations and modifications being used.

Your child's teacher of students who are visually impaired is crucial to the assessment process and should plan and conduct the assessment with the other members of the educational team. Other team members are involved in contributing information about your child's performance, including yourself, other family members, classroom teachers, and others who are familiar with your child's abilities and needs.

Collecting Information

It is important that the assessment process for determining appropriate accommodations and modifications take into account the following basic information, as explained in Chapter 3:

- Medical information about your child's vision, such as the diagnosis of your child's eye condition, medical implications, and prognosis that can influence decisions about your child's educational needs.

- Reports from a clinical low vision evaluation to determine if low vision devices will enhance your child's ability to see in different learning environments and for reading and writing and other learning activities.

- Reports from a functional vision assessment to see how your child actually uses his or her vision in real-life familiar and unfamiliar situations, enabling observers to suggest appropriate accommodations and modifications. Family members can also provide information about how a child uses his or her vision in other activities and settings, such as watching television, playing board games, and shopping for groceries.

- Reports from a learning media assessment conducted to select the appropriate learning and literacy medium or media for your child. This information indicates whether your child will learn best by reading and writing using regular print, large print, braille, audio or electronic formats, or other formats and materials. The teacher of children with visual impairments conducts this assessment, and is typically the professional, along with a certified O&M instructor, who would conduct the functional vision assessment as well.

- Assessment reports concerning the areas of the expanded core curriculum. As explained in Chapter 1, the expanded core curriculum consists of the additional knowledge and skills that children who are visually impaired need develop in order to lead independent and successful lives, including those relating to communication modes (such as braille), O&M, social skills, independent living skills, recreation and leisure skills, career education, use of assistive technology, and visual efficiency skills. The teacher of children with visual impairments conducts the assessment in the areas of the expanded core curriculum, along with a certified O&M specialist and other team members who know the child's skills in other areas (such as a career counselor) or have knowledge in a particular area such as assistive technology.

It is important that when your child's functional vision assessment, learning media assessment, and assessment of knowledge and skills in the expanded core curriculum are conducted, consideration is given to each of the seven areas already noted as being important for accommodations and modifications in school activities (instruction, materials, assignments, classroom testing, assistive technology, the environment, and other activities), to make sure that all educational situations are taken into account. It is critical that all assessments are conducted in ways that provide meaningful information in a variety of settings, contexts, and environments. Information should be collected in the context of the child's actual school activities—in reading and art class, for example, during class changes in the hallway, and in the cafeteria. Only in this way can the IEP include appropriate decisions that reflect your child's need for accommodations and modifications in all the school environments he or she encounters. Gathering information from a variety of family members and school staff, both past and present, is also critical to form a complete picture of your child's abilities and needs in all settings, as the following case study about Marta illustrates.

Marta is a fifth-grade student with low vision. Last year, in elementary school, she received instruction from one teacher for all of her academic subjects: reading, math, social studies, and science. In middle school she now has seven teachers for all instruction in both academic and nonacademic classes. Early in the school year, her educational team conducted an educational evaluation of Marta at her school that included a functional vision assessment, a learning media assessment, and assessment in the expanded core curriculum.

The teacher of students with visual impairments tested her for two hours in an available conference room. The results showed that Marta was accessing all information for teaching and learning activities and did not need any additional accommodations and modifications.

As the year went on, Marta struggled in math, social studies, and physical education, as well as in the lunchroom. Her parents and teachers were concerned about her progress; they requested an additional assessment. This new assessment included surveys to gather information from all team members, including her parents and all her classroom teachers, and an interview was conducted with her fourth-grade teacher. Team members conducted observations in all Marta's classrooms, as well as in other educational settings, including the lunchroom, and a learning media assessment was conducted to gather more information.

This time the assessment revealed that Marta was having difficulty completing assignments and tests in the allotted time, especially in math, where the class was doing a unit on graphing that required Marta to be able to see points and lines plotted on the graphs. Survey information and observations made in her social studies class revealed that she could not access the information on maps that were used in the classroom. Through observations, the teacher of students with visual impairments also discovered that Marta was uncomfortable in the lunchroom. The learning media assessment indicated that she was experiencing fatigue when reading long assignments that were now required in her fifth-grade language arts class. Her parents reported that it was taking her an unusually long time to complete homework assignments. Marta's fourth-grade teacher reported in addition that she had been making accommodations for Marta to have extended time on tests and had enlarged some graphic materials for her use. This information had not been in Marta's school records or reported previously by her teacher, but her parents were made aware of the changes by the fourth-grade teacher through phone calls and parent-teacher conferences. The results from the clinical low vision exam included prescriptions for magnification devices for near vision tasks and a monocular telescope for accessing information at a distance.

Marta's first middle school assessment did not adequately address her need for accommodations and modifications, even though it appeared to be an appropriate assessment. It did not include information collected in her actual classrooms and in other school settings or from all of the school personnel who interacted with her. Nor did it include clinical low vision exam results and information from her parents and from her fourth-grade teacher.

As a result of the current assessment, it was determined that Marta would benefit from the following accommodations and modifications: use of magnification devices for visual tasks requiring the interpretation of fine detail in graphic material, extended time on assignments and tests involving fine detail, and use of a monocular telescope for reading the menu in the lunchroom. The team agreed to continue collecting information to determine if these accommodations and modifications were adequate.

Interpreting Assessment Information

After assessment information is collected, it is essential that the information be interpreted accurately. Sometimes it is difficult to determine why a child exhibits a particular behavior or struggles in a specific learning task or environment because of the complexity of the issues that affect the learning process for each individual student. Therefore, it is important to refrain from seizing upon quick answers and to learn to feel comfortable with not knowing all the answers at once. The following case study about Erin demonstrates this reality.

Erin is a second-grade student with low vision who was experiencing reading difficulties. Her classroom teacher believed this was due to her visual impairment. Assessment information had not been gathered since the beginning of first grade when Erin was a beginning reader. The current educational team conducted a thorough assessment, which included gathering information from Erin's parents, classroom teacher, reading specialist, and teacher of students with visual impairments. When the team met to review the assessment information, it still was not clear why Erin was experiencing difficulties in reading. The team decided it was not important to know why, but chose to implement an educational program that would provide more intensive reading instruction and use diagnostic teaching methods to determine further teaching and learning. Diagnostic teaching methods combine assessment and instruction by formulating possible factors that influence student learning and including those factors during instruction to determine what influences a student's learning and the accommodations needed for his or her visual impairment. In Erin's case, the teacher of students with visual impairments was going to use a variety of accommodations and modifications and collect data on a continuing basis to determine if the strategies and accommodations had an effect on Erin's reading skills. The team decided to meet in one month to discuss Erin's progress.

Sometimes questions about a child's learning behavior cannot be quickly answered or easily understood. In Erin's case, it was important to refrain from making possibly invalid assumptions. Instead, the team decided to engage in continuing assessment and diagnostic teaching to gather more data and information to help in future decision making. In this situation, it is important for the parent to know how ongoing assessment and diagnostic teaching are going to occur, how reporting will be completed, and when the team will reconvene to discuss the issues and new information collected.

Interpreting assessment information is not a rigid and uniform process, and there is not a "right way" to do this. Interpretation of the information is dependent on all the team members, including the parents or family members, sharing information about the child. A team process is important so that conversation can occur that is open and honest. All team members need to share information they have gathered during the assessment process and participate in a discussion based on questions and comments from all team members. Parents are very important in this process. The teacher of students with visual impairments likewise has a critical role. The information you share about your child's ability to participate in activities at home and in the community is essential. Also, your perspective on how your child is reacting to the school environment and completing homework assignments is information that school personnel may not have. When participating in discussions, if you are not clear about what others are saying or reporting about your child, try to ask questions. Rather than everyone getting "stuck" on why a child may exhibit a certain learning behavior, such as in Erin's case, it is more effective to identify the best way to help the child have success and have the same opportunity to participate in school activities as his or her classmates.

Through this team process, a collective understanding of your child's strengths, abilities, and unique needs will evolve, and the team can form a clear picture of your child's need for accommodations and modifications. Agreement can usually be reached about your child's needs, even when there are difficult issues involved and when team members have varying viewpoints. Whatever decisions are reached, making sure that assessment is a continuing process, so that decisions are frequently reevaluated, will help to confirm the decisions or suggest the need for change.

SELECTING ACCOMMODATIONS AND MODIFICATIONS

The team evaluation process should reveal where your child needs accommodations and modifications: perhaps he or she cannot read at a distance written information projected onto the classroom wall or cannot access information shown as pictures on handouts or in books.

If this is the case, for your child to participate in teaching and learning activities using projected materials and pictures, he or she will need specific accommodations and modifications that address these identified needs.

The specific accommodations and modifications that are chosen can vary and are based on the individual needs of each child. Your child may need an accommodation for accessing print materials that is very different from the way another child with a visual impairment will access print materials. Again, the team process is critical in this phase of decision making: It is discussion among team members that helps yield appropriate solutions. The guidance, knowledge, and skills provided by the teacher of students with visual impairments will continue to be very important at this stage.

The chart provided at the end of this chapter, "Accommodations and Modifications at a Glance for Students with Visual Impairments," can assist throughout this process by providing specific examples of accommodations and modifications. It is organized according to the seven areas of school experience in which accommodations and modifications are frequently made for children with disabilities. The chart lists a number of representative accommodations and modifications for each of these areas and provides examples of each to give parents and professionals an array of choices and to stimulate additional ideas.

IMPLEMENTING APPROPRIATE ACCOMMODATIONS AND MODIFICATIONS

It is essential that the accommodations and modifications that the team has identified are documented in the IEP. Documentation ensures that your child will receive the accommodations and modifications that he or she needs. The IEP includes a section where the student's accommodations and modifications are typically recorded (the form itself and the placement of this section can vary from state to state).

It is also important to have a method for communicating the accommodations and modifications identified in your child's IEP to all teachers and staff members who are responsible for the child's teaching and learning activities. It is sometimes helpful if a person is designated to undertake this communication and follow up to ensure that the appropriate accommodations are being made in the settings and environments where they are needed. Sometimes this person is the child's case manager, the teacher of students with visual impairments, or another teacher who works closely with the child. A case manager is a person designated by the school district who is responsible for ensuring that your child's rights under special education laws, regulations, and procedures are met.

Nat's case, which follows, illustrates the importance in communication in implementing a child's accommodations and modifications that are identified in the IEP.

> Nat is an eighth-grade student with low vision. After the assessment process, it was determined that he did not need any accommodations in testing situations, even though the team decided that accommodations were needed for accessing print information at a distance. Nat also received weekly support from a teacher of students with visual impairments to assist with a goal in his IEP related to advocacy skills. Statewide testing was being conducted in his school district and, without anyone's knowledge, the district testing person ordered a test in large print for Nat. The morning of the test, Nat was given a large-print test and told to take the test to a separate classroom for administration. He was confused by this and was not pleased about the situation.

In Nat's case, even though testing accommodations were not identified in his IEP, the staff person responsible for testing thought it was a "good idea" to order the large-print test for Nat and arrange for a separate testing room. This happened because of a lack of communication to other staff members about the accommodations that were noted in Nat's IEP.

The teacher of students with visual impairments or your child's case manager should communicate with all teachers and staff about your child's accommodations and modifications. Communication can occur in a variety of ways and usually depends on the age of the child, the school setting, and other factors influencing communication styles. Information can be shared in the following ways: in special meetings with school personnel at which information is shared and explained (sometimes called in-service meetings), distribution of the IEP, handouts specifically addressing a child's accommodations and modifications, e-mail, phone calls, and individual meetings with teachers and staff. Other team members can also participate in this communication, including parents, and, when appropriate, students themselves. It is important for parents to ask how the accommodations and modifications needed by their child will be communicated to all of their child's teachers and other appropriate personnel.

Depending on the extent of the accommodations and modifications, teachers and staff may need some additional training in strategies and techniques to put the accommodations into practice. The teacher of students with visual impairments will determine this and be responsible for providing that training.

After the necessary accommodations and modifications have been communicated to teachers and staff and training provided if appropriate, the teacher of students with visual impairments or your child's case manager needs to monitor your child's educational program to ensure that appropriate teaching and learning activities are occurring. This can be done through observations and discussions with the student, teachers, and other staff. Monitoring and follow-up are very important in the assessment process. Through communication with your child's teachers and case manager, you can determine if everyone is providing the appropriate accommodations and modifications for your child. If you have any concerns about whether this is taking place, expressing your thoughts and requesting that your child's identified needs be met are part of your important role.

EVALUATING THE SUCCESS OF MODIFICATIONS AND ACCOMMODATIONS

After accommodations and modifications have been implemented, it is crucial that assessment be conducted on a continuing basis to ensure that appropriate decisions have been made and that the accommodations and modifications are in place in all appropriate situations. The teacher of students with visual impairments will gather information and collaborate with others in a variety of ways to determine the success of the accommodations and modifications. This is not considered a formal evaluation, but an informal process similar to that used to collect information daily or weekly to monitor a student's progress in the curriculum. Again, information should be collected in all settings, contexts, and environments to make sure that the decisions documented in the IEP are reflected in teaching and learning practices. Information gathering can be accomplished through conducting observations, collecting student work samples, reviewing grades, and communicating with all team members. Matthew's story highlights this issue.

> Matthew, who is blind and in second grade, reads and writes in braille for all reading and writing tasks. His IEP states that he should have access to all classroom materials in braille. His teacher of students with visual impairments provides instruction in braille reading and writing activities for two hours every day, after which she leaves to teach in other schools. Part of this instruction occurs during reading time in his second-grade classroom, and part of the instruction is in a separate classroom. Matthew's teacher knew she needed to provide ongoing assessment of his educational program

and determine his participation in all teaching and learning activities, and therefore scheduled a Friday morning to observe Matthew for one-half day. During this observation, she observed him taking a math test that was read to him by a teaching assistant. After a discussion with the math teacher, she learned that the math test was not available in braille.

The teacher's ongoing assessment during Matthew's actual school activities revealed that he was not receiving all his classroom materials in braille and that the accommodations and modifications identified in his IEP were not in place. These follow-up observations showed the teaching staff where changes in Matthew's educational program were needed.

Ongoing assessment can not only discover gaps in implementing the recommendations of the IEP but also can reveal changes that should be made in the accommodations and modifications that have been selected for a student. Many factors can influence the need for changes. Sometimes children's learning needs change with their development, or there may be a change in the materials used in class. A field trip may be planned unexpectedly, or a child may gain skills in an area that eliminate the need for an accommodation. Ongoing assessment can also determine whether the original decisions were appropriate and whether further changes are necessary. Regardless of what is discovered, ongoing assessment of your child's need for accommodations and modifications will ensure that appropriate decisions have been made and are being implemented.

YOUR IMPORTANT ROLE IN YOUR CHILD'S EDUCATION

As a parent, you play a vital role in the process of choosing the specific accommodations and modifications that your child needs to participate in teaching and learning activities. Following are some suggestions about how to contribute to the process and monitor your child's use of accommodations and modifications.

Understand the Range of Accommodations and Modifications Possible

It can be difficult for any one person to have a complete understanding of the full range of accommodations and modifications that may benefit your child in all settings, especially in the area of assistive technology. Because of the broad range of possible accommodations and modifications, finding information about them from just a few sources is challenging. Exploring the sources of information in the Resources section of this book and communicating with all your child's educational team members, especially the teacher of students with visual impairments, will assist you in learning about different accommodations and modifications. In addition, publications like *AccessWorld*, the online magazine about technology for people with visual impairments, published by the American Foundation for the Blind and available at www.afb.org, can provide helpful information.

Share Information

As Chapters 1 and 3 (and this book in general) explain, you know your child better than anyone. Providing information about your child's needs, including medical, assessment, and other reports, to members of the educational team is essential.

Know Whom to Contact

The principal at your local public school is responsible for providing parents with information about services to children with disabilities. You can contact him or her if you think your child should be assessed for accommodations or modifications (if this has not previously occurred). You can also contact the regional director or administrator in special education in your school district, the teacher for students with visual impairments, or your state's department of education or parent advocacy center (see Chapter 1) if you think additional assessment is necessary to determine appropriate accommodations or modifications for your child.

Try to Resolve Differences

It is important to communicate with the person most responsible for your child's IEP, who might be an assigned case manager or other professional on the educational team. No one can be aware of your concerns if you do not communicate them. If you run into obstacles determining or implementing your child's accommodations and modifications, you can ask others to help you by participating in team meetings and following up with requests. Someone who knows your child well or is knowledgeable about the process of implementing accommodations and modifications can be of assistance in communicating the importance of the accommodations and modifications for your child. To help advocate for your child's needs, you can share information that you have gathered from this book, for example, and from the resources suggested in it, as well as providing information from assessments and other sources about your child's needs. Continue to ask questions until you are satisfied. Other team members may have the same questions.

Make Sure All Your Child's Needs Have Been Considered

As your child's advocate, try to make sure that all of his or her needs have been considered. Ask questions based on the information in this chapter. Think about your child's functioning and needs in the seven areas commonly needing accommodations and modifications. Review the different types of assessment and the list of information to gather in the assessment process (described in Chapter 3). Ask if your child's needs have been considered in all teaching and learning activities and in all the activities and settings that he or she experiences in a school day.

Stay Informed

Once an IEP has been written to include accommodations and modifications for your child, don't assume the job is done. Review your child's IEP to make sure the appropriate accommodations and modifications are clearly stated. If not, ask that the IEP be changed so that they are clear for everyone on the team. Find out who will be responsible for implementing your child's accommodations and modifications, how and by whom the information will be communicated to teachers and other staff, and how your child's program will be monitored. Ask how often information will be reported to you and by whom.

Children's needs for accommodations and modifications will evolve and change as they grow and progress through their school years. The need for changes will be driven by their growth and development as well as changes in the teaching and learning process and the materials and tools used in education, especially technology. It is fortunate that more and more parents and educators understand the needs of children with visual impairments and that the capacity of school systems to meet their needs is increasing. Paying attention to the specific accommodations and modifications that individual children need to participate in teaching and learning activities will help them achieve and reach their goals with independence and success. A partnership among parents and educators in the assessment, planning, and implementation process will enable children to receive appropriate special education services so that they can participate in all of the educational activities available to children, regardless of their visual impairment or other special needs.

For More Information

A. L. Corn and A. J. Koenig (Eds.), *Foundations of Low Vision* (New York: AFB Press, 1996).

N. Levak (Ed.), *Low Vision: A Resource Guide with Adaptations for Students with Low Vision* (Austin: Texas School for the Blind and Visually Impaired, 1994).

Overbrook School for the Blind, *Technology for All: Assistive Technology in the Classroom* (Philadelphia, PA: Towers Press, 2001).

M. Smith and N. Levack, *Teaching Students with Visual and Multiple Impairments: A Resource Guide,* second edition (Austin: Texas School for the Blind and Visually Impaired, 1996).

S. J. Spungin (Ed.), *When You Have a Visually Impaired Student in Your Classroom: A Guide for Teachers* (New York: AFB Press, 2002).

M. L. Thurlow, J. L. Elliott, and J. E. Ysseldyke, *Testing Students with Disabilities: Practical Strategies for Complying with District and State Requirements* (Thousand Oaks, CA: Corwin Press, 1998).

Accommodations and Modifications at a Glance for Students with Visual Impairments

This guide is intended to provide parents and other members of the IEP team with a tool for planning accommodations and modifications for students who are visually impaired. It lists a number of adaptations in each of the seven areas of accommodations and modifications used in this chapter, along with explanations and examples, to stimulate discussion and suggest ideas for possible solutions. The items listed are only representative samples of the accommodations and modifications that may be appropriate for students with visual impairments, based on an individual student's specific needs.

Instruction

Adaptation	Explanation and Examples
Hands-on experiences	Real-life examples of pictures or actual objects are used in instruction, for example, real coins are provided when pictures of coins are shown in a book.
Models	Models of objects that are primarily visual are used, such as objects rather than pictures to represent the planets in the solar system.
More easily readable visual aids	The student receives his or her own copy of information that will be displayed on an overhead or whiteboard or chalkboard.
Clear directions	Explicit language is used when giving directions; such as "Pass your papers to the right," rather than "over here."
Peer (classmate) note taker	A classmate takes notes of material written on the board and provides a copy to the student with visual impairments.
Extra time for responses in class	A student may require extra time to respond to class discussions because he or she needs more time to read an assignment.
Oral description or narration	Oral descriptions are provided of visual display material; for example, an exhibition of fine art would be described, or portions of a video or film would be narrated during times when there is no dialog.
Experiential learning	The student has the opportunity to experience concepts directly that others may view in pictures or from a distance; for example, if the

Verbalization of writing	class is learning about farm animals, the child with visual impairments might visit a farm.

Information that is being presented on a whiteboard or in an overhead is spoken aloud as it is being written. |

Materials	
Adaptation	*Explanation and Examples*
Braille	Textbooks, worksheets, and all materials used in instruction are provided in braille.
Tactile graphics	Printed maps, diagrams, and illustrations are provided in a tactile format.
Audiotape materials	Books and other print materials are provided on tape.
Electronic access	Materials are provided in an electronic format to be accessed with a computer or electronic notetaker, for example, a student uses an online encyclopedia to do research for a term paper or reads a textbook in digital format.
Print book for parents	A student who reads in braille receives a print copy of a textbook for use by his or her parent or guardian.
Highlighting	Markers and highlighting tape are used to enhance the important parts of a student's text.
Large print	Large-print books are used for instruction or portions of books, such as a map, are enlarged as needed.
Manipulatives	Physical items (such as small toys, buttons, or beads) are used to demonstrate mathematical concepts or used in art classes to complete a tactile drawing.

Assignments	
Adaptation	*Explanation and Examples*
Extra time for completion	A student may need extra time because of his or her reading or writing speed or the kind of tools required for reading or writing.

(*continued on next page*)

Descriptive response	A student may provide a written description of a project instead of a visual representation. For example, the class assignment might be to make a drawing of a cell viewed through a microscope. The student who is blind instead provides a written description of the cell rather than a drawing.
Use of models	The student provides a model for an assignment rather than a visual representation.
Reduction of copy work	If an assignment requires copying text or problems, a worksheet is provided so the student can write answers directly on the worksheet and does not need to re-copy the assignment. For example, the teacher might write ten mathematics problems on the board for the students to copy and solve in their notebooks, but the visually impaired student works on a worksheet instead.

Classroom Testing

Adaptation	Explanation and Examples
Extended time	A student may need extra time because he or she reads or writes slowly, or because of the tools he or she uses for reading or writing.
Use of manipulatives	A student may use manipulatives to demonstrate understanding, rather than responding in writing to a question, for example, a first-grade student demonstrates an understanding of time by using a braille model of a clock to show the answers on a test.
Spelling tests for braille readers	A student who uses contracted braille (which uses a number of contractions and shortened forms to write words) should also take spelling tests using uncontracted braille to make sure they can also read and write in standard English.
Dictation of responses to a scribe	The student verbally reports an answer, and a sighted person records the answer on the answer sheet.
Screen access to tests administered on a computer	Depending on the student's need to read in print or braille, appropriate screen access to text may be needed through enlarged text, refreshable braille, or a copy of the test in hardcopy braille.

Assistive Technology	
Adaptation	*Explanation and Examples*
Low vision devices (near)	Magnification devices for viewing or completing near vision tasks.
Low vision devices (distance)	Telescopes for viewing or completing distance vision tasks.
Braillewriter	A mechanical tool resembling a typewriter that is used for writing or "embossing" braille.
Slate and stylus	A portable tool for writing braille made up of two flat pieces of metal or plastic that are used to hold paper and a pointed piece of metal used to punch or emboss braille dots.
Electronic braillewriter	An electronic device for writing braille, incorporating a braille keyboard, which frequently has additional features, such as a calculator.
Personal digital assistant (PDA)	An electronic device for organizing and managing data, often integrated with an electronic notetaker.
Notetaker (braille)	A portable device for reading and writing in class, with braille output, often integrated with the features of a PDA.
Notetaker (speech)	A portable device for reading and writing in class with speech output, often integrated with the features of a PDA.
Computer	A tool for literacy and learning activities and access to information, especially when equipped with specialized software and hardware.
Refreshable braille	A device that is connected to (or integrated into) a computer or notetaker and that represents braille text by means of pins that can be raised or lowered to form braille cells.
Speech access software	Computer software that enables a computer to "speak" the text on the screen through the use of synthetic speech that announces what is displayed on screen.
Braille translation software	Computer software that translates print into braille and braille into print.
Large monitor for computer	A monitor that, by virtue of its size, provides larger images for students with low vision.

(continued on next page)

Adaptation	Explanation and Examples
Scanner	A device that copies print material and uses software to translate it into an electronic format so that it can be converted into a preferred reading medium.
Magnification software	Software that enlarges text displayed on a computer or other screen.
Braille embosser	A printer that embosses (prints) braille.
Print printer	A regular printer to provide print text for sighted teachers and classmates.
Tactile graphics maker	A tool that makes print images into tactile format that can be "read" through the fingers.
Word processor	A computer software program for writing and manipulating text.
Electronic mail (e-mail)	Electronic mail sent through computers and other devices that is a communication medium for students to receive and return classroom assignments.
Talking calculator	A device that provides speech access to a calculator.
Large-print calculator	A calculator with large numbers on the keys to provide access for students with low vision.
Talking dictionary	An electronic device that provides a dictionary with speech access.
Tape recorders	A device for recording auditory information and listening to materials provided auditorily on tape.
Digital players	A portable device to access digitally recorded audio books and materials.
Alternative computer access	A number of methods that allow a person with physical disabilities to use a computer, such as adapted keyboards and voice recognition technology.
Augmentative and alternative communication devices	Special communication devices for students who may have hearing disabilities or other limitations in communication. For example, some of these devices play prerecorded messages at the push of a button.
Adapted devices for daily living	A wide variety of devices adapted for use by people who are visually impaired, including measuring devices, kitchen utensils, games and toys, and writing aids.

The Environment	
Adaptation	*Explanation and Examples*
Preferential seating	A student is allowed to sit in the classroom wherever it is most beneficial, for example, where he or she has the best view of the board, away from a light source to reduce glare, or near a power outlet needed for an assistive technology device.
Flexibility to move within a room	A student with low vision is given flexibility to move closer to visual activities in the classroom, such as a demonstration being given.
Additional desk or work space	Some students (especially those who read and write in braille) require extra space to place materials needed to complete classroom tasks.
Additional shelving or storage space	Braille books and additional equipment require storage space, and adequate shelving should be provided for materials.
Appropriate lighting	Some students benefit from additional lighting for literacy tasks; others are very light sensitive (photophobic) and require reduced lighting.

Other Activities	
Adaptation	*Explanation and Examples*
Subscriptions	A student may benefit from special subscriptions to materials that are difficult to access, such as newspapers. Some subscriptions are available by telephone.
Mobility tools	Students may use a long white cane for travel or other travel tools or devices.
Adapted equipment for physical education	Students may use adapted equipment, such as balls that beep, to help them participate in physical education classes and other physical activities.
Organizational tools	A variety of products can help students organize and manage their time and school materials, including notebooks, planners, and PDAs.
Emergency procedures	Procedures need to be created for the student and others to follow in the event of emergencies, such as the need to evacuate the school building.
Use of a sighted reader	Students may need to learn to work with a sighted reader to have access to print materials.
Other health accommodations	Students may need other accommodations or modifications because of related health concerns, such as use of protective eye wear or head gear.

From Regular Classroom to Specialized Program: Exploring the Options for Your Child

Jane N. Erin

The history of the education of students with visual impairments in this country is a rich and fascinating story that began to take more formal shape in 1829, when the first special school for blind students was established in the United States. A number of such schools—called residential schools—were opened in the years that followed. They were based on European practices, in which children who were blind were sent away from home to receive specialized instruction. Various factors made the use of specialized residential schools a logical step here and abroad. First, the number of students with visual impairments was, and continues to be, relatively small in proportion to the rest of the population. Second, although the number of students was relatively small, their educational needs were unique and required informed, specialized attention. By gathering these students in one place, specialized teachers experienced in their education could work with them in a continuing and consistent way. Necessary equipment, materials, and other resources could be assembled in centralized locations as well. The placement of visually impaired students in residential schools therefore reflected efforts to deliver high-quality and effective educational services.

To this day, most states in the United States have a residential or specialized school for students who are visually impaired. However, these schools have in many instances also become learning centers that provide special assessments, consultation, and other services to schools across the state. Many of their students are youngsters who are visually impaired and have multiple disabilities who live at the school during the week and go home on weekends.

Most visually impaired students today attend their local school along with other children who do not have any disabilities, and they receive special education services of various kinds within that setting. Depending on the student's educational needs and the local school district's arrangements, a student may work in a regular classroom most of the time but go to a special resource room in the school for part of the day or a few times a week. In other instances, he or she may work in the regular classroom but receive support and instruction from a teacher of students with visual impairments who is not on staff at the school and who visits the student periodically. This teacher is sometimes referred to as an "itinerant teacher" because he or she is not based within any particular school but travels from school to school within a district or region to provide special services to students with visual impairments. This teacher may see a student as often as several times a week or as infrequently as once a month, in accordance with the needs and goals outlined in the student's Individualized Education Program (IEP). (See Chapters 1 and 4 for more on IEPs.)

One of the more difficult decisions for parents centers on what kind of school or educational program will be best for their visually impaired child, as illustrated in the following situation.

> Kristen is a lively 4-year-old attending a private preschool near her home. Her parents have been pleased with the preschool, especially with the small class that allows Kristen to get plenty of attention and be well supervised. Kristen, who is visually impaired, has learned to read some printed words in her classroom, but her parents realize that braille will be a faster way for her to read. This year the teacher of visually impaired students has been working with Kristen for three hours each week to introduce braille and other special skills that will help her to be successful.
>
> Next year Kristen's class will move on to kindergarten, which is located in the local elementary school. Her parents know that the classes will be larger and that more time will be spent on academic work. Kristen is a shy child who often plays alone, and they wonder if she will play easily with others and if she will have enough time to work on braille reading in this new setting. The state school for the blind is only an hour's drive from home, and they wonder if it would be better for Kristen to go to school there until she has learned to read. The teacher of students who are visually impaired will put Kristen's parents in touch with some other parents and bring them

> some materials about the school to read that will help them decide what is best for Kristen. They have talked to some parents of other visually impaired students and are surprised to discover that each family has different reasons for deciding what placement they prefer for their child.

Like so many other things in life, every possibility has its advantages and disadvantages. One setting or program may require a child to travel a longer distance to school but provide more specialized instruction than is available in the neighborhood school, another may offer more contact with nondisabled children, and a third may provide immediate access to related services such as occupational therapy and orientation and mobility (O&M) necessary for a particular child. As members of their child's educational team, parents are the most important participants in the decision about where their child will be educated.

A CONTINUUM OF CHOICES

Educators of students who are visually impaired frequently refer to the need for a "continuum of choices" for a child. When they use that phrase, they are referring to the fact that a variety of possible school placements—from residential schools to local neighborhood schools—exist for visually impaired students. However, they are also referring to the fact that a child's needs may change over time and may call for different placements or programs at different times in a child's life and development.

> Mario, who is 12 years old and has low vision, has been educated at his local school through fifth grade. He has taken most of his classes with other students and has received specialized instruction several times a week to teach him skills in the use of low vision devices as well as other skills related to his visual impairment. Even with this support, his grades have dropped during the past two years from Bs to Cs and Ds, and his slow reading speed has made it difficult for him to compete with his sighted peers; in addition, the time he spends on homework makes it difficult to find time to participate in student activities that encourage socialization. His parents and the other educational team members have decided that he needs more time to learn specialized skills, with emphasis on technology, increasing his reading speed, and organizational skills. Next year during middle school he will be enrolled in a resource room for visually impaired students that meets at a nearby middle school, but it is not the school that other children in his community attend.

TWO SIDES OF "LEAST RESTRICTIVE ENVIRONMENT"

The term *least restrictive environment* has two sides. My husband Stewart and I have advocated at times for our son's placement in specialized settings for students with visual impairments, such as a school for students who are blind or visually impaired and a self-contained classroom. Many other parents fight for the opposite for their child. Some parents want their child fully included from the start of their education, with all the necessary services provided either in the classroom or a pull-out setting within their local pubic school.

IDEA essentially states that unless the IEP of a child with a disability requires some other arrangement, he or she is educated in the school that he or she would attend if nondisabled. In the selection of the least restrictive environment, consideration is given to any potential harmful effect on the child or on the quality of services that he or she needs. A child with a disability, it continues, should not be removed from education in age-appropriate general education classrooms solely because he or she requires modifications in the general curriculum. According to IDEA, therefore, least restrictive environment is not literally a place but, rather, a setting where all necessary services can be provided along with exposure to nondisabled peers, as close to home as possible.

Unfortunately, in our experiences with Matthew, this setting is very difficult to find. There is usually some sort of compromise. Something is usually given up in order to get something else. Matthew has given up opportunities to learn daily living skills, have extensive O&M training, and get occupational and physical therapy services in order to get appropriate academics and exposure to nondisabled peers. As he has grown up, I realized that the brunt of the responsibility for daily living skills must fall on my husband and me. Cooking, laundry, transportation, money skills, personal hygiene must all be addressed in the home where the skills will be used.

Finding the most appropriate educational setting for your child can be one of the most challenging tasks for parents of children with a disability, particularly a visual impairment. Research, observation, and questioning are useful tools in the search for the optimal place for your child.

> Remember what the spirit of the law says: that your child is entitled to a free and appropriate education in the environment that best meets his or her needs, whether in a school for the blind or a regular education classroom, or any setting in between. You are part of the team that makes these very important decisions, and your voice must be heard.
>
> *Sheri Davis*
> *Mother of an 18-year-old son with Leber's congenital amaurosis*
> *Lutz, Florida*

Although this is a more restrictive environment, his team believes it is needed for him to learn important skills. The team will reconsider the placement each year at their meeting, and more often if needed; if Mario makes significant progress in the skills he needs, he may return to his neighborhood school in the future.

Educational settings—residential schools, resource rooms, and mainstream (general education) classrooms supported by visits from an itinerant teacher—exist along a continuum, from less restrictive (visually impaired students in classes with nondisabled students) to more restrictive (visually impaired students in classes with other students who require special education). A central principle in this country's special education legislation is the importance of educating students with disabilities in the least restrictive environment, as explained in Chapter 1 and later in this chapter. In the rest of this chapter, placements are described in the categories of mainstream or general education public school classrooms, special education classrooms, specialized schools for students who are blind or visually impaired, and home instruction. Placements can be and often are combined according to a student's individual needs. For example, a student at a specialized school might attend a public school nearby for some classes, or a preschool student might attend a regular preschool in the morning and a special class in the afternoon. A creative analysis of the choices that exist for a child's placement can help educational team members consider what would be most effective and comfortable for each specific child.

During this process, parents need to consider the pros and cons that each option offers for their child. A specialized school may offer expert, in-depth attention to a student's educational needs, but residential placement will take a child away from home and family and will also segregate him or her from students who do not have disabilities. Some educators and parents believe that integrating students who are disabled with students who are not—a concept originally referred to as mainstreaming—is the ideal in a society in which children need to learn from each other about diversity, tolerance, and acceptance. Attending school with nondisabled students is also regarded by many as an effective way for disabled students to learn good social skills and how to interact skillfully in social situations. However, it has also been observed that students who have disabilities and attend specialized schools offer each other supportive social relationships and an acceptance and camaraderie not always found in local neighborhood schools for students who may be regarded as "different." "Choosing a High-Quality Educational Setting" lists some characteristics you might want to look for in evaluating a possible placement or setting for your child who is blind or visually impaired.

Choosing a High-Quality Educational Setting

Many of the features of an effective educational setting for a child who is blind or visually impaired are similar to those that would be desirable for a child who does not have a disability. Parents trying to determine an appropriate placement for their child are best served by making time to observe a classroom in each setting that they are considering, and asking to speak with a teacher there. However, the educational team identifies a setting, not a particular teacher.

These are some factors you may want to think about in considering placement options for your child. It is important to remember that the best learning environment for one child may not be the best for another.

CLASSROOM AND SCHOOL

- The classroom has leisure and play materials that are directly accessible for all children during free time.
- Each child has a designated space for keeping personal belongings (usually a cubby hole or personal shelf).
- In specialized settings, braille materials are available; in a public school setting, the administration and staff are interested in ensuring braille access and the teacher of visually impaired students is willing to work with the school staff on this matter.
- There is a clear routine for each day. The schedule and classroom rules are posted in a format that students as well as visitors can understand.

- The classroom is well organized, with different areas for different purposes. Some classrooms have separate reading and play areas; others have a specialized area for technology.
- Furniture is the right size for the children in the class.
- The lighting and temperature are comfortable in different parts of the school.
- The school and classrooms are neat and kept free of litter.
- Student work is displayed prominently in the school and classrooms.
- There are books and writing materials in many places, and they are displayed to attract and interest children.

STAFF

- The classroom staff members are willing to answer your questions when their time permits. If they are too busy to talk to you when you observe, they offer to find another time to talk or to locate someone who can answer your questions.
- Paraeducators in the classroom are involved in learning activities or preparation for activities. They move smoothly from one task to another, and they seem to know what they should be doing.
- Adults who are working with children make sure that rules are followed and that there is a consequence when a rule is not followed. However, they do not criticize children or become angry when a rule is broken.
- Adults and children smile often and occasionally laugh together.
- Children are encouraged to assist and work with other children.
- Teachers have the appropriate teaching certifications for the children with whom they work (check with administrators about this).

ADMINISTRATORS AND SCHOOL STRUCTURES

- Administrators are willing to make the time to meet with you and be sure that your questions are answered.
- There is a clear plan for student classroom assignments within the school and for advancement to the next level of learning.
- There is a curriculum in place that is appropriate for your child. This may not be a single written document, especially in specialized

(*continued on next page*)

schools where children have widely varying needs. However, the administrators should be able to describe the framework for instruction for children in the school whose needs are similar to your child's.

- Related services that are needed for your child are available.

- The schedule and procedure for IEP meetings can be described clearly.

- There is a parent group within the school that actively participates in school decision-making. Parents are encouraged to become involved in other ways, as volunteers, advocates, or parent support personnel.

- There is at least one staff member who has a major role in communicating with parents. This may be an assistant administrator, social worker, or lead teacher.

- Administrators can show you how their curriculum meets the state standards for education in your state.

PLACEMENT OPTIONS FOR VISUALLY IMPAIRED STUDENTS

General Education Classrooms in Public Schools

Mainstream or general education classroom settings include those in which children receive no special education services, those in which there is consultation from a teacher of students with visual impairments, and those in which children receive direct instruction from a teacher of visually impaired students.

Students who spend some time with classmates their age who are not disabled have the opportunity to participate in typical classroom activities and to interact with many other children of similar age. They can learn from the behaviors of others, and they have access to the variety of academic subjects and extracurricular activities that are offered to all students. Specialized needs related to their visual impairment can be addressed by an itinerant teacher of visually impaired children, who works with the child or classroom team, which includes classroom teachers, paraeducators, related service personnel, and anyone else who works directly with the child in school. This teacher plays many roles, from directly instructing the student to acting as a consultant with other teachers and staff (see Chapter 1 for more information on the role of this teacher).

The student's IEP should describe the type and amount of service that the teacher of visually impaired students will provide.

Some visually impaired children do not need specialized educational services to be successful in school. Often these are high school students with low vision who use regular texts and materials in print and who by this time know how to adapt to their own visual impairment. For example, they may take responsibility for talking with the classroom teacher about any adaptations they need, such as a specific seat position near the front of the class and away from window glare, or the use of low vision devices such as magnifiers.

Other students are in the regular classroom but receive indirect support through consultation with a teacher of visually impaired students, known as the consultative model of services. In such cases, an itinerant teacher will work with the classroom team to implement appropriate adaptations for the child's learning. Examples of such adaptations are ordering texts in braille or enlarged print, obtaining specialized equipment such as computer software or tangible maps, recommending appropriate lighting or positioning for the child in the classroom, or working with the family to arrange a clinical low vision evaluation to determine appropriate low vision devices. The teacher of visually impaired students may participate frequently when the student begins in a new program and will have less contact with the team after they become familiar with the child's visual impairment. The consultative model with the classroom team is often the most appropriate way of addressing educational needs in regard to visual impairment for many students with severe and multiple disabilities because they learn best in consistent and familiar environments. For students with cognitive disabilities, instruction several times a week with an unfamiliar person may not result in learning that can be transferred to routine activities. Instead, the teacher of visually impaired students can be most effective with these students by working with the classroom team so that all staff who have daily contact with a child can make adaptations for his or her visual impairment during regular activities.

When a team is considering consultative services from the teacher of visually impaired students, family members should have a clear understanding of what will be included in the service. Since consultation can mean many things, it is important that all team members understand how often the teacher of visually impaired students will be in contact with the classroom team and whether the services will be regularly scheduled or will occur only in response to a specific question or challenge.

Direct instruction from a teacher of visually impaired students will be needed when the student needs to learn a skill that is not part of the regular classroom curriculum. Such skills might include learning braille, the use of low vision devices, daily living skills such as labeling materials or preparing food, planning transportation, or using technology such as a video magnifier or electronic brailler that is needed because the student is visually impaired.

The teacher of visually impaired students does not teach academic subjects such as reading or mathematics, because these are taught by the general education classroom teacher (see Chapter 1 for more on this topic). In certain cases, the teacher of visually impaired students may teach a special skill related to the student's visual impairment using the materials and curriculum from the regular classroom. For example, a student who reads braille at a very slow rate may work on increasing reading speed while reading the social studies lesson assigned to the student in his or her regular classroom. A student with multiple disabilities who needs to work on using his or her vision to locate objects may do so by locating materials used in a game played in the regular classroom.

Services by a teacher of visually impaired students in the regular classroom allow a student to spend the classroom day with peers, working on the standard curriculum; this arrangement provides a more natural learning setting and allows a child to work toward required standards that are needed for high school graduation. In addition, it provides the child with experiences in adapting to an environment with sighted classmates, which will be relevant as the child enters the world of work and college. The parent whose child is served in this setting needs to make sure that the services are appropriate for the child. For example, a young child who is a braille reader will probably need services from the teacher of visually impaired students for an hour or two a day, while an older child who is familiar with a school and doing well academically and socially may need only occasional consultation. Families should be sure to ask why professionals are recommending a specific amount of service. The response should address the needs of the learner and should not be based on the school district's ability to provide a given amount of service.

Special Classrooms

Students who are visually impaired might receive instruction in special classrooms in their neighborhood school for part of the time that they attend school, for most of the time, or for all of the time, for the reasons detailed in the next sections.

Many public schools have specialized classrooms where students who need special education can receive instruction designed to meet their specific needs. Most often, these classrooms are for students with disabilities unrelated to visual impairment that affect their academic progress. A few larger school districts have specialized classes especially for students with visual impairments. There is usually only one such classroom at the elementary or secondary level (middle school, junior high school, or high school) in a school district because the number of visually impaired students in general is small.

These classrooms may be referred to as "resource rooms" or "self-contained classrooms." In a resource room, students come and go throughout the school day. A student may come for one or two class periods for specialized instruction in an area such as braille or use of a video magnifier or closed-circuit television system (CCTV), or he or she may come more often to work on academic subjects that require significant adaptation. For example, a student who is taking advanced mathematics may need a combination of a video magnifier and human reader service to access the text, since mathematical figures are often closely placed and small in size. The amount of time that a student spends in the resource room and the goals to be worked toward there should be specified on the student's IEP.

When a student spends most or all of the day in a separate classroom, it may be referred to as a self-contained classroom. The student in the self-contained classroom may go to the regular classroom for a few periods a day, often for nonacademic subjects such as physical education or art. However, most of his or her daily work is carried out in the separate classroom where his or her education can be more individualized.

The terms "self-contained" and "resource room" are used flexibly. Some schools refer to a room as a resource room even when students are there for most of the day. Some visually impaired students who have other disabilities need adaptations related to several educational needs. For example, a student who also has a learning disability may need specialized instruction and practice in using phonetic rules for decoding words. Children with a variety of individual needs may benefit from the smaller class size and more individualized instruction that a special classroom can offer. Sometimes a school district will recommend that a visually impaired child receive services in a special classroom for students with other disabilities. Families may want to ask about the number of students who will be receiving services, the learning abilities and behaviors of other students, and the teacher's qualifications to work with visually impaired students in the class. If the teacher is not qualified to work with students with visual disabilities, the student should also receive services from an itinerant teacher of visually impaired students.

When the educational team recommends a separate classroom for a student, they should have a clear understanding of the student's goals in the special class and how the skills learned there will be generalized to the regular classroom. For example, a child who is taught to use a monocular (a handheld telescope) by the teacher of visually impaired children in a distraction-free room outside the classroom must learn to use it in other settings, such as the regular classroom or outdoors when looking for his bus number at the end of the school day. In some instances, the child's schedule in the resource room is flexible, and the regular teacher and teacher of visually impaired students arrange for times when the child needs to work on new skills. In other cases, the student attends the special classroom at specific times during the week and works on goals related to a skill area, for example, braille reading or use of a monocular. This plan is most effective when the regular teacher and the teacher of visually impaired students who is the instructor in the resource room can communicate regularly about a child's learning needs and successes.

Specialized Schools

Students who attend a school for students who are blind or visually impaired might also spend time in class at their local school, spend the full educational day at a specialized school, or receive services there in a residential program.

About 90 percent of students with visual impairments are now educated in their local schools, and only a few go to specialized schools for students with visual impairments.[1] Even though the trends have changed over the last 50 years, many parents prefer a specialized school because they believe that their child receives more attention there to the skills he or she needs because of a visual impairment. In the 1950s, most visually impaired children attended specialized schools, but changes in legislation have supported educational opportunities for students with disabilities in local schools; in most states 80 to 90 percent of visually impaired students attend a public school in their own district.

There are about 52 specialized schools for students with visual impairments in 42 states.[2] These schools were previously called residential schools, but now many students attend the special schools during the day and return to their own homes at night. The term "residential" is not appropriate for all students because they may not live at the school. For that reason, they are referred to as specialized schools in this chapter.

Some students are able to attend a local public school for some subject areas and the specialized school for others. For example, a high school student who has recently become blind might attend a public school to take U.S. history, biology, and advanced English, and might come to the specialized school to take braille classes, technology, or mathematics, which often require significant adaptations such as tactile materials, enlarged materials or computer software for enlargement, or instruction on specialized braille codes such as those used for mathematics and foreign languages. This kind of arrangement allows the student to maintain contact with his or her peers and continue to work on regular academic subjects but also to learn the skills he or she will need because of being blind. Because students rarely live in a community where there is a specialized school, they will usually attend the public school that is most conveniently located near the specialized school and will also reside at the specialized school.

Other students spend their entire educational day at a specialized school. The educational team may make this decision for a variety of reasons: the need for intensive adaptations or instruction, lack of services from a teacher of visually impaired students in the local district, or the need for a specialized curriculum that includes skills specific to visual impairment such as daily living skills and O&M may be considerations. For example, a student who has difficulty with self-care skills may attend a specialized school with a residential component so that instructors can work with the student on dressing, eating, or food preparation. In some instances in which parents have appealed the original placement decision of their child's educational team before they succeeded in having their child enrolled in a residential setting, they have been successful because courts recognized that daily living or self-care skills could better be taught in an environment that extended beyond a seven-hour school day.

Some specialized schools now accept students for short-term enrollment based on a student's individual goals as established on the IEP. This may mean that a student will attend a specialized school for a few months, a year, or 2 years based on the skills he or she needs to learn. The role of the specialized school in short-term programming is very different from the traditional approach to specialized schools, in which students were often enrolled throughout their educational years until they graduated from high school.

Specialized schools are very different from one another. One school may primarily educate visually impaired students with additional disabilities; another may emphasize academic programming and technology for secondary level (middle/junior high or high school) students. It is important for parents considering specialized schools to obtain information about the school they are looking at and to talk with administrators about the school's mission as part of making their decision. Some schools are private and receive some funding from the state in proportion to the numbers of children they educate, and others are directly under the oversight of the state government. Depending on the state, specialized schools are supported through a combination of state funds, school district payment, and private contributions. Regardless of the administrative structure, there is no cost to parents for specialized school placement if it is the school setting deemed appropriate by the IEP team. Although there is no cost to parents, funds must be transferred from the state or local district to the specialized school when the child is enrolled there.

A local school district representative, either the special education director or someone such as a school psychologist who has been appointed by the district, must participate in deciding whether a student will attend a specialized school, and must agree that the specialized school is the

DEFINING "LEAST RESTRICTIVE ENVIRONMENT"

It is difficult to determine a least restrictive environment. We needed to prove that the county where we lived could not provide the same quantity and quality of services that the Maryland School for the Blind could provide. This is a challenging task and takes some time and effort.

As new, young parents, my husband and I felt intimidated and unknowledgeable. My advice to others who feel like that: Get over this feeling quickly! It seemed so simple to us that, of course, the program that would be least restrictive for Matthew would be one in which everyone in the school specializes in visual impairments. Physical and occupational therapists would be on staff. There would be speech and language teachers, O&M teachers, social workers, nutritionists, psychiatrists, and teachers of students with visual impairments all in one wonderful place. The best part would be the other children with visual impairment and their parents. We would not be alone anymore. This was how I defined *least restrictive environment*.

The county, however, believed that fewer services, provided by very qualified people who were stretched thin with heavy caseloads, serving Matthew alone in our house, was the least restrictive environment. They also suggested having him attend a center-based program with a teacher who did not have a vision background, with other children, none of whom was visually impaired and some of whom used wheelchairs or other motorized equipment—which seemed to us to be a safety concern for Matthew.

What happened? Well, Matthew started Maryland School for the Blind in October of that year and stayed there for five productive years.

My husband and I were not intimidated by the professionals at the table, and we made sure our voices were heard. Did we as parents have all the data we needed to prove our point?... No! But we trusted our gut instincts as parents of this very special young man and did not leave the decision solely up to the professionals.

My last bit of advice to parents: Read, read, read everything you can find about your child's visual impairment and how it will affect his or her development, and trust yourself, along with the professionals who work with your child. Become a member of the team!

*Sheri Davis
Mother of an 18-year-old son
with Leber's congenital amaurosis
Lutz, Florida*

appropriate placement for him or her. If the team agrees, then there is no cost to the family for the child to attend a specialized school. In a few situations, schools will accept private or family payment for students who are not referred by their districts. For most students the decision to enroll the child in a specialized setting is agreed on by both the family and the district representatives after the IEP is developed, although this agreement may require extensive time for meeting and sharing perspectives.

Education in the Home

Education in the home encompasses home schooling of children from preschool through high school based on their family's preference, as well as that of medically fragile students whose health may prevent them from attending local schools.

In a few cases, students receive their main educational services in their own home. Some families see home schooling as a way to use their time efficiently, maintain strong connections between child and family, and minimize contact with inappropriate behaviors of other students. If a family is considering this option for a visually impaired student, they should consider what services are available for their child related to his or her visual impairment. Occasionally parents will enroll in courses themselves and become certified to teach visually impaired children. If the child is a braille reader or needs to learn braille, parents who are teaching at home will need to be proficient in braille.

In some school districts, teachers of visually impaired students may visit the home to provide services when families educate their child at home. In other districts, the parent must take the child to a school or public building where he or she will receive specialized educational services. If families are considering home schooling, they should talk with school personnel about how their child will receive the specialized services he or she needs related to his or her visual impairment.

Infants and young preschoolers may receive their educational services in the home because this is the natural setting for early learning. The family will be the primary teachers in the early years, and the learning goals will be described on an Individualized Family Service Plan (IFSP). (See Chapter 2.) The main role of the teacher of visually impaired students for children of this age is to support the family in their educational role and to guide them in appropriate activities to enable the child to learn new skills in his or her home.

In a few cases, students are educated at home because their medical and physical needs make it difficult for them to be transported to school or to have contact with other students due to medical risk. In these cases, a home teacher will come to the home to work with the student, and the IEP goals will be carried out in collaboration with the family. If possible, the educational team should consider efforts to connect the child with his or her classmates and age mates via telephone calls, videotapes, or contacts with siblings. These can all provide some social opportunities that are limited when a child is homebound due to his or her physical condition.

There are many variations among the four main types of placements. Educational time in a regular classroom, resource room, specialized settings, and home schooling have often been combined in various ways to meet the needs of students whose personal characteristics or geographical location makes it difficult to access specialized services related to visual impairment. Families need to keep in mind when they are trying to figure out what situation they want for their child that the goal is to find the best way to meet their student's specific and individual educational needs.

It often seems that the greatest limitation to a visually impaired child's education is time. That is, when one skill is being emphasized, there seems to be no time to work on a different one. Families and professionals need to decide what is most important for that child at a particular time and to identify the setting in which that education can best take place. The educational team must make sure that the setting selected provides a balance of academic, social, and practical learning and that the environment allows for collaboration among the family and professionals to enhance the child's opportunities for effective learning.

KEY CONCEPTS IN DETERMINING PLACEMENTS

In considering the appropriate placement for their child, parents will find it helpful to be aware of the terms used in federal and state law to describe educational settings. As noted earlier, a continuum or range of placement options must be available for visually impaired students to ensure that they receive appropriate services throughout their educational years. This requirement also includes the opportunity to change placements when a different setting is needed to obtain an appropriate education. It is also important to realize that the law requires an appropriate placement rather than the best placement, which means that if the school can provide services related to visual impairment in the local school district, families and advocates will need to show why these services are not appropriate if they wish a child to receive services elsewhere.

Least Restrictive Environment

"Least restrictive environment" is the term used to describe placement in the setting in which the child can be provided with an appropriate education and maximum contact with nondisabled peers. For most children this will be their neighborhood public school or the school the child would be expected to attend if he or she was not in need of special education. If it is not, the IEP must state the reason why this setting does not constitute an appropriate placement. This policy is described in the Least Restrictive Environment section of the Individuals with Disabilities Education Act (IDEA Section 612(a)(5)(A):

> To the maximum extent appropriate, children with disabilities, including children in public and private institutions or other care facilities, are educated with children who are not disabled, and special classes, separate schooling, or other removal of children from the regular educational environment occurs only when the nature or severity of the disability of a child is such that education in regular classes with the use of supplementary aids and services cannot be achieved satisfactorily.

Continuum of Services

As mentioned earlier, continuum or range of services describes the various settings that may be considered for students with disabilities, ranging from those that allow for contact with nondisabled peers to those that do not. Under IDEA, public school districts must provide the setting that meets the student's educational needs. For visually impaired students of any age, educational settings should reflect individual needs; the least restrictive setting may not always be with classmates who are nondisabled if an appropriate education cannot be provided in the regular classroom. For example, if a child learns best in small groups with maximum exposure to braille and specialized technology, a separate classroom or specialized school may be the least restrictive environment.

In considering which option will provide the best combination of learning opportunities, you will want to consider how your child might respond in different settings due to his or her individual characteristics.

- **Does he enjoy having many children around, and does he find their company rewarding? Can he keep on task even when others are talking or moving around?** If so, a classroom in a public or private school that includes a large number of students of varying abilities may be an interesting learning setting where he can benefit from a busy and stimulating environment.

- **Does she need to learn many skills related to visual impairment, such as braille, daily living skills, or O&M? Does she learn best when she understands just what will be taught and when a clear structure for learning and practice is provided?** If so, a classroom with a small group of students and a low ratio of adults to children in a specialized school or resource setting may help her learn more efficiently.

- **Does he need to explore and practice with real materials in order to learn? Does he want to move around a room, touch, or look**

closely at features of the environment and manipulate materials with his hands? If so, you may select a smaller classroom setting that is rich in materials and has physical spaces arranged for easy access. In addition, you will want to consider whether the setting provides opportunities to learn through activities in the community.

- **Does she change activities and get to know new people easily? Does she accept or enjoy unexpected events?** If so, a regular classroom or a preschool with plenty of chances to make choices may be interesting and stimulating for her.

- **Is he most successful when he has a predictable schedule where the same events take place regularly, and where routines are followed consistently? Does he need a specialized form of communication such as tactile symbols that can be presented and practiced consistently?** His needs might be met in a regular classroom with a small number of students and several adults to assist, but he may learn most effectively in a specialized setting where routines and symbols of communication are very consistent.

No setting will be an ideal fit for a child; the opportunity to observe the students and activities in a school or classroom can help parents to consider which classroom characteristics will present a challenge and which will be comfortable or appealing for their child.

QUESTIONS ABOUT PLACEMENT

Because there are advantages and disadvantages to each setting, parents may be ambivalent about the best educational placement for their child. That placement may also vary during the child's school years because his or her needs change. It should be reviewed annually. Every local school district cannot offer every option because of the number of students whose needs are to be met; for example, resource rooms for students with visual impairments are available in some mid-size to larger districts, but in smaller districts there are not enough students with visual impairments of a similar age to form a resource room. Students may need to travel to a nearby district or school if they need to receive part of their educational experience in a resource room setting. "Advantages and Disadvantages of Common Educational Placements" lays out some advantages and disadvantages of the different settings for a number of educational options and other concerns that parents may have.

The characteristics of schools that are important for children without visual impairments are also important for the student with a visual impairment. All families want assurance that their children's schools are safe environments with good supervision, well-educated teachers, a challenging

Advantages and Disadvantages of Common Educational Placements

Considerations for Families	Type of Placement			
	Regular class	Special class	Special school for visually impaired students	Home school
Family and community issues				
Advantages	Attends school with friends and neighbors	Remains in community	More physically safe and secure setting	Family participates in all learning
Disadvantages			Must travel from home and sometimes live at school	Student and family do not have contact with other perspectives
Curriculum issues				
Advantages	Maximum contact with state-required curriculum	General curriculum can be adapted for child's needs	Curriculum may emphasize skills related to visual impairment	Family can influence curriculum according to their priorities
Disadvantages	Limited time and focus on skills related	Classroom teacher may not be familiar with	Curriculum may not emphasize state curriculum as much	Parent teachers may not have background in

(continued)

Advantages and Disadvantages of Common Educational Placements *(Continued)*

Considerations for Families	Type of Placement			
	Regular class	*Special class*	*Special school for visually impaired students*	*Home school*
	to visual impairments	visual im-pairments	Students may not have breadth of subjects at high school level	teaching methods and subject matter, including skills in visual impairment
	Classroom teacher may not be familiar with visual impairments			
Social issues				
Advantages	Contact with nondisabled peers in natural setting	Contact with nondisabled peers can be planned according to times of day	Contact with peers and role models who are visually impaired	Family can plan social contacts with children who are positive friends and role models
Disadvantages	Little or no contact with other students who have visual impairments	Some classmates may have disabilities that do not provide appropriate models of behavior	Little or no contact with nondisabled peers	Limited opportunities for social problem solving and dealing with difficult personalities

Service delivery issues

Advantages	Services can be planned in a context with other students	Services can be provided in a less distracting environment	Services are more likely to be provided by professionals who are experienced with visual impairments	Family has contact with service providers, ensuring generalization of skills
Disadvantages	Services depend on availability of teacher of students who are visually impaired and administrator support	Services in visual impairment depend on availability of teacher of students who are visually impaired and administrator support	Services may be separated from regular curriculum and community	Specialized services might not be available in the home

Equipment and materials issues

Advantages	Student may learn more complete responsibility for own materials	Materials can be introduced or created by experienced special educators	Materials and technology for visually impaired students are more likely to be freely available	Family can develop and become familiar with learning materials
Disadvantages	Some materials may be late or unavailable	Some materials may be late or unavailable	General technology may be limited to that which is most accessible	Family may be unaware of materials available to students with visual impairments

and relevant curriculum, and a positive learning environment. Although school personnel in the district and at the specialized school as well as state department of education personnel can provide information about the characteristics of various settings, parents are best served by exploring the options in their community and establishing their own priorities. They may find it helpful to talk to other parents and to specialists in special education who are reachable through parents' groups and the national organizations advocating for special education and for students who are visually impaired (see the Resources section of this book for more information). The questions in the following sections represent some common concerns of families when they are considering the different placement choices available.

Who Makes the Decision?

Ultimately, the members of the IEP team, including the parents, make the decision about where a child should be educated. Families are important members of the team, and their perspective often has an impact on the thinking of other team members. However, it is important for all team members to provide information based on their experience and assessment of the child's needs so that the team considers all options carefully.

The child's own school district is responsible for providing an appropriate education for the child, and in that capacity the district must agree that a placement is appropriate. Often district personnel do not describe the range of educational options. This omission may occur because they do not have the information or forget to bring it up; occasionally it may be because they do not think another placement is appropriate for a child and are concerned about costs that the district might incur. Families should ask about what settings are available for their child. They can make an appointment to speak with the special education director or another knowledgeable administrator in the district if they want more information or have specific questions about placements. School district representatives should encourage families to express their concerns and questions regarding placement, to observe the students and teachers in different educational settings, and to talk with professionals and families who can provide information. If your district does not discuss placement options, it is important to ask what options are available and what information they can provide about different placements. "Questions about Placement Options to Ask School Districts" provides a list of questions that parents may want to ask.

What Is the Least Restrictive Environment?

Sometimes educational personnel or parents automatically assume that the least restrictive environment always means that a student with a visual

Questions about Placement Options to Ask School Districts

The following are some questions about the various placement options for your child that you can ask school district personnel or your IEP team to help determine the best situation to meet your child's specific needs.

1. What placement options are available within the district for students with visual impairments?

2. What factors are considered in making decisions about placement?

3. How many visually impaired students are in the district? What types of placements are they educated in?

4. What kinds of preparation do regular educators receive to work with students who have special needs? To work with those who are visually impaired?

5. How many educators in your district are certified as teachers of visually impaired students? As orientation and mobility specialists? How do you decide how much service students receive from these specialists?

6. What is the process for referral to a specialized school setting? How are referral decisions made?

7. Who is the district's contact at the nearest specialized school for visually impaired children? How can I obtain information about their services?

8. How do teams decide if the place where my child will receive an appropriate education is other than the general education classroom?

9. How are decisions made about general education classroom placements for students with special needs?

impairment or other disabilities should be fully integrated into a regular classroom. However, although federal law requires IEP teams to come up with a plan that allows students to have contact with their nondisabled peers to the maximum extent that is appropriate, it also acknowledges that the team needs to identify a placement that is able to provide the child with an appropriate education and can meet the child's individual needs. Although most children benefit from education with nondisabled children of their own age, in some cases there are greater benefits to be gained from a separate setting—whether it is a special classroom in another public school or a specialized school for students with visual impairments. If a separate setting is chosen, the educational team must be able to demonstrate that this arrangement is necessary to the child's education. Reasons for choosing particular placements for a child can be gleaned from "Advantages and Disadvantages of Common Educational Placements."

What Is an Appropriate Education?

All parents want the best education for their child, but the law does not require that program and placement decisions be based on what is best. School districts are only required to provide an appropriate education, meaning that the child will have access to the specialized instruction, services, and accommodations needed for him or her to participate effectively in the regular education curriculum. This reality can be difficult to understand, since families want their children to have the highest quality education possible. However, defining "best" would be very difficult, given the variations in how people evaluate quality. It is the role of the IEP team to define what each child needs to learn and to make sure that it is provided in the least restrictive environment.

A poor classroom teacher or too few computers in the classroom would not be reasons to declare that a child with a disability is being denied an appropriate education. These kinds of inadequacies are problems related to the general quality of education and affect all children in the class. However, the lack of availability of a teacher of students who are visually impaired or the lack of necessary materials in braille needs to be rectified, because each of these may prevent a child from receiving even a minimally appropriate education.

Can a Placement Be Changed?

Many students attend different types of schools during their school years, as their educational needs change. Some specialized schools will enroll students for short-term placements, especially those who need intensive work in a particular skill area such as O&M or braille reading. In other instances, students may attend two different types of placements in the same school year—perhaps a regular preschool in the morning and a specialized preschool for visually impaired students in the afternoon.

A change in school placement can be made by the decision of the IEP team, usually at a regular IEP meeting. IDEA requires that parents be involved in any decision to change placement, and, unless the parents agree, the child has a right to continue in the existing placement until the new placement has been determined by the team. If parents place their child in a private or separate setting without the agreement of the educational team, or if the parents fail to inform the IEP team that they reject the public school placement or fail to give written notice to the school before removing their child, they may be required to pay the educational costs unless they can prove that the school district did not offer a free and appropriate public education. Sometimes the school or family wants to change a placement at a time other than the regular IEP meeting; in this case a special meeting of the team can be arranged by the district's special education director to make the decision.

How Can the Quality of Education Be Determined?

Educational options for visually impaired students vary, and families and professionals have different priorities for learning. For this reason, one person may view an educational program as very successful but another person may find it insufficient.

The most important factors about a child's education are not determined by setting. Consistency of instruction, curriculum, amount of instructional time, opportunities for active learning, and quality of instruction all influence effective learning as much as the classroom setting. Effective and ineffective education can take place in any setting.

When Is Educational Setting Determined?

A student's IEP must be written and developed before placement is determined. When all team members have discussed what kind of educational program the child needs, then the team can consider where that program can be provided. Often the discussion of placement becomes easier when all members recognize the child's most important educational needs.

Sometimes the discussion of educational placement becomes the focus of the IEP conference. Team members should keep in mind that their most important decision is what the child needs to learn. If a separate or specialized educational placement is recommended, it is because the child needs to learn something that cannot be taught in the regular school setting. Examples of such specialized learning needs for visually impaired students might include daily living skills, braille, use of assistive technology, social skills, and career and vocational skills.

What if I'm Not Satisfied with the Team's Recommendations?

Families have the right to due process regarding disagreements about placement, just as they do for any other area of their child's special education. Due process is the legal procedure required for school districts to address a parent's concerns or disagreements with the educational program of a child who is receiving special education, as specified under IDEA. Before following the formal steps of due process, it is important to be sure that all members of the team have heard and understood one

WHEN IS PLACEMENT DETERMINED?

A child's placement is determined at many different times during his or her education. Our son Matthew has taken advantage of every placement on the continuum, from regular education classrooms to homebound services. Of course, when a child is being initially evaluated, his or her placement is one of the most important decisions to be made. The initial process is one of the most stressful times a family can go through: dealing with the diagnosis and all the new information thrust at them. Take your time during this process. Let the professionals know when you need extra time to think and process all that is going on. This is the time when you will want to learn as much as you can about the educational options available in your area. Visit all the placement options you can, both public schools and schools for the blind and visually impaired. Doing all of this will help you make an informed choice.

Once the initial placement decision is made, your child's IEP team must meet at least once annually to review his or her goals and objectives and the placement. If, for any reason, you want to discuss a placement change, or any other issue related to his or her IEP, you can call an IEP meeting whenever you feel it's necessary.

When making any placement decision, always use the IEP as a guide. If a child requires many related services, such as occupational or physical therapy, speech and language services, or family counseling, then the placement should match those needs. If your local public school cannot provide those services, placement there would not meet the *least restrictive environment* requirement. Your child would be restricted because he or she would not have the opportunity for the services that would best meet his or her needs.

A placement never needs to be permanent. If issues come up that require a review of your child's needs and placement, then address them immediately. Matthew's Tourette's syndrome became progressively worse, to the point where he could not be in a regular education setting without disrupting the class or experiencing excessive stress himself. We advocated for temporary homebound services for him, while we worked with his doctor. He spent five months as a homebound student, keeping up with his academics and continuing to see his teacher for students with visual impairments every day when she came to our home.

Sheri Davis
Mother of an 18-year-old son with Leber's congenital amaurosis
Lutz, Florida

another. Chapter 10 of this book, on negotiations and advocacy, high-lights some ways of approaching differences in perspective. If the first discussion of placement was uncomfortable and if unexpected informa-tion was presented, additional meetings should be scheduled so that the family can discuss the issues that arose after giving them some thought. If there is still no agreement about placement, then the family can initiate a due process hearing.

If a family is requesting what might be considered a more restrictive placement, such as a specialized classroom or school, they should be pre-pared to describe why this is necessary in order for their child to receive an appropriate education. The desired placement must be able to offer education that cannot be provided in the setting preferred by the school district. As noted earlier, problems related to the general quality of educa-tion that affect all children in the class would not be reasons for a change of placement. However, if the current setting lacks the services needed by a student with visual impairments, this would be a reason to consider a change in placement.

ENSURING THE MOST APPROPRIATE PLACEMENT FOR YOUR CHILD

Parents can take a number of practical steps to help their child obtain a placement in which his or her educational needs are appropriately ad-dressed and about which they feel comfortable.

- Talk with the child's classroom teacher and other professionals indi-vidually before the IEP conference. Like parents, professionals may be uncomfortable with the large group setting and may be more will-ing to consider your needs and interests in an individual conversa-tion. You can then be more aware of each person's viewpoint before the conference, and you can better understand why he or she holds particular points of view.

- Visit and observe the classrooms and settings that might be appro-priate for your child. Make an appointment to talk with the teachers or administrators about each setting and to ask questions that are of concern to you.

- Talk with parents of older children who are visually impaired. Ask them about their experiences with different educational settings, and ask them to describe the advantages and disadvantages of each for their child. When you talk with other parents, be sure to consider that your child's needs and your priorities may be different from those of other parents and children.

- Contact the parent information center in your state and other parent groups or advocacy organizations for visually impaired persons (see Chapter 1 and the Resources section of this book for more information), and talk with personnel there about how they support parents in their efforts to obtain the placement they see as best for their children. Many states have a Pilot Parents organization or another organization that can be located through the parent link on your state department of education's web site. Parent organizations such as the National Association for Parents of Children with Visual Impairments (NAPVI) can also be helpful in finding local advocacy assistance for your child. Arrange to take an advocate with you to your child's IEP conference if you are unfamiliar with the law or uncomfortable with your knowledge of educational options.

- Keep copies of your child's educational progress reports in one place so that you can provide evidence of where he or she has made progress and where he or she has experienced difficulty. If there are areas in which progress has been limited, you can then support this with data. If a specific area of concern is not being addressed, make a videotape of your child that shows the skill that concerns you. For example, showing your child trying to dress or to feed himself can help to convince the team that he or she needs specific instruction in daily living skills.

POINTS TO REMEMBER ABOUT PLACEMENT

When you consider the variety of placement options that are available for your child, the key point to remember is that the decision should be based on his or her own particular needs. Therefore, think carefully about the advantages and disadvantages that each possible setting will have for your own child. Consider the goals that the IEP team has set for the year and whether your child would work toward them best in a regular classroom or a more specialized setting. Remember, however, that if you prefer a specialized setting, a clear educational rationale is needed.

Finally, keep in mind that placement does not determine the quality of the educational program. Although no program is perfect, the appropriate placement can provide an opportunity for students to learn in an environment that balances appropriate educational services with a challenging educational plan. With collaboration among family and school personnel, a child can be educated in settings that allow him or her to learn the skills to support the best quality of life throughout school and into adulthood.

Notes

1. N. Barraga and J. Erin, *Visual Impairments and Learning,* fourth edition (Austin, TX: PRO-ED, 2000).
2. S. Lewis and C. B. Allman, "Educational Programming," in C. Holbrook & A. J. Koenig (Eds.), *Foundations of Education: History and Theory of Teaching Children and Youths with Visual Impairments*, Vol. 1 (New York: AFB Press, 2000), pp. 218–259.

For More Information

G. S. Pugh and J. Erin, *Blind and Visually Impaired Students: Educational Service Guidelines* (Watertown, MA: Perkins School for the Blind in cooperation with the National Association of State Directors of Special Education, 1999).

R. Riley, *Educating Blind and Visually Impaired Students: Policy Guidance from OSERS* (2000). Available on the Texas School for the Blind and Visually Impaired web site: www.tsbvi.edu/agenda/osers-policy.htm.

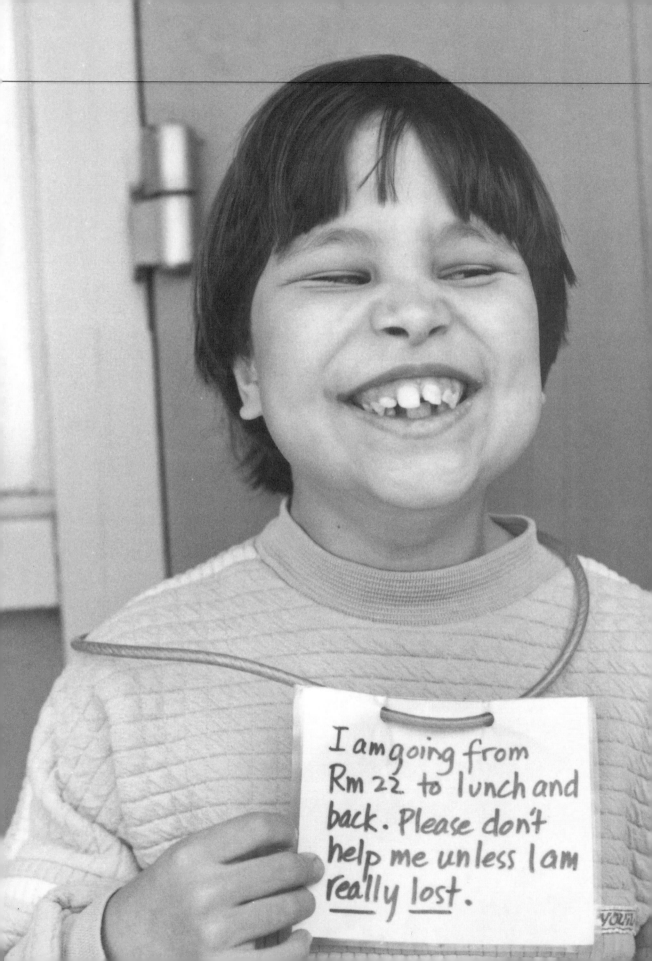

CHAPTER 8

Additional Disabilities: Special Considerations for Classroom and Community

M. Beth Langley

If you have a child who has other disabilities in addition to a visual impairment, you face all the challenges described elsewhere in this book and possibly some others as well. Your child may need a unique combination of supports that involve obtaining services from a variety of different professionals, and you may find yourself trying to juggle and coordinate the efforts of many people to help your child. You may also find that the professionals who can assist your child in one area—with developmental delays or a physical condition, for example—may be very knowledgeable about that area but may not always be familiar with the impact of visual impairment or the needs of visually impaired students. Likewise, teachers of students who are visually impaired may not know much about your child's other disabilities. For these reasons, it is especially important for family members of a child with multiple disabilities to collect, organize, and share information, understand the child's educational needs, and learn how to be an effective coordinator and advocate.

Like all other parents, the parents of children with visual impairments have certain overriding concerns: How will my child succeed in school? Make friends? Have a happy and successful life? If you are a parent of a child who is visually impaired and has additional disabilities, you in all likelihood have a whole other set of concerns and questions in addition to those experienced by parents of children with visual impairments alone.

SEPARATING THE LABEL FROM THE CHILD

One of the big issues facing parents of children with disabilities is finding out what other physical or mental disabilities their child may have. Often it is a matter of time, since some problems don't show up until the child is older. Sometimes the vision disability may not be noticed for a while, either. Some feel that it is best to identify all the disabilities a child may have as soon as possible, in order for the child and family to receive all the necessary services. From a family or parent's perspective, this can be devastating. As the list of disabilities or challenges grows longer, parents wonder how they will cope, and how the family will survive with a child who has so many needs. It becomes harder to see what a child can do, when the focus is on all the things he or she may need help with.

It is also very important to remember that a label of one type of disability or another does not predict a child's future! Parents of children with significant multiple disabilities can tell many stories of terrible predictions made by well-meaning medical professionals or teachers that turned out to be completely wrong. Labels serve a purpose: They allow parents and other caregivers access to services and access to funding. But it can be very difficult for a parent, especially a new parent, to separate the label from the child. Many of us have experienced all the negative stereotypes attached to persons with disabilities. Our experiences have not always been positive, and they leave us fearing for the future of our children.

How do we as parents change the perceptions that other people have of persons with multiple disabilities? We can make sure that our children get the services they need to succeed to the best of their abilities. It is impossible, and unfair, to limit services based on an unknown future. As parents, we know that our children will change, but we don't know how. We do know that they are entitled to services that will help them learn and that are based on assessment of their individual needs and abilities.

Kate Aldrich
Mother of a 24-year-old son with retinopathy
of prematurity and multiple disabilities
Santa Rosa, California

ADDITIONAL DISABILITIES, ADDITIONAL CONCERNS

Parents of children with disabilities besides visual impairment in general have additional concerns about their children's education, socialization, and mastery of the skills of daily living. The often-complex needs of their children require understanding, appropriate identification, and a range of special education services provided by a variety of professionals.

Vision

A student's inability to move or to sit in certain positions may affect how he or she uses vision. His or her medications taken to treat an additional disability, or a fluctuating medical state, may interfere with his or her use of vision.

Communication

A student's difficulties with hearing or speech may require that he or she use special systems of communication (such as touch cues, American Sign Language, tangible symbols, or electronic communication devices). People who interact or work with the student, including educators, therapists, and his or her fellow students, need to know how to communicate with him or her. Children also need to have ways of communicating their needs, preferences, and feelings. And parents need ways of finding out what is happening in school, since their children often cannot relay that information to them.

Tasks of Daily Living

Students with multiple disabilities may need special help with feeding, or special equipment, devices, and assistive technology (such as adapted spoons and cups, communication devices, or environmental control devices) to help them access and control their toys, educational materials, and the environment. They often need many examples and opportunities to practice functional skills, such as dressing and self-feeding, within natural, relevant, and meaningful contexts of their daily lives. In addition, multiply disabled children may be highly dependent on consistent routines, prompts, and cues to understand what they are to do throughout the day.

Health and Safety

Students who are multiply disabled may require medical procedures during the school day or experience seizures that school staff must know how to manage. Procedures need to be established for handling medical emergencies during school. School staff need to know how to recognize signs that may indicate a child is experiencing symptoms such as pain, difficulty breathing, or seizure activity.

Socializing

Students with multiple disabilities may need significant support to interact appropriately with other children and to establish friendships because they may have limited communication skills, limited shared experiences, or difficulties knowing how, when, why, and with whom to converse. Some may use maladaptive or stereotypic behaviors, such as hand flapping, to communicate frustration, boredom, pain, excitement, or sensory overload. These behaviors may be difficult for others to understand or may be interpreted as unfriendly or even threatening.

Mobility

Multiply disabled students may need special handling and positioning strategies and special equipment such as customized walkers or wheelchairs or adapted mobility devices to get around the environment.

Education

Students who are multiply disabled often need extensive modifications to the curriculum. Your child may need a number of services in addition to vision-related services, requiring coordination and communication among many professionals. "Roles and Responsibilities of Team Members and Other Specialists" describes some of these other professionals and their services.

Parents' questions and concerns change as their children's needs and circumstances change over the child's lifetime, but some will always remain the same, regardless of age or surroundings. As the parent of a teenager with multiple disabilities, I, like you, worry with each new environment and transition my child encounters, and agonize over the endless series of decisions about his education. But, through teamwork, labor-intensive planning, the help of many others, and some of the strategies described in this chapter, we have also experienced many successes throughout his school career. Throughout the process of educating your child, it will be helpful for you to involve the efforts of other informed people and also to find some support for yourself. You can do this through other parents, concerned educators, and local and national organizations dedicated to the concerns of people with visual impairments and other disabilities (see the Resources section at the back of this book for more information on these organizations).

Roles and Responsibilities of Team Members and Other Specialists

The educational team for a visually impaired student with other disabilities includes family members, professionals, paraeducators, and the student, just as it does for any other student with special needs. Team members will determine and implement educational goals for the student. Regular communication among team members is important to ensure consistency in the instructors' roles.

The following is a brief summary of the professionals who may participate in working with visually impaired students with additional disabilities, and of their roles and responsibilities. This list is similar to that in Chapter 1, but some of the specific responsibilities and some of the personnel may be different for a student with multiple disabilities.

REGULAR CLASSROOM TEACHERS

Regular classroom teachers are responsible for implementing the objectives that are part of the standard curriculum. In addition, they will work with students on objectives related to specialized skills, such as social skills or daily living skills, when these can be integrated into the standard curriculum. When the student spends most of the day in the regular classroom, the regular classroom teacher may coordinate the educational plan. When a student has visual and multiple disabilities, the classroom teacher and paraeducators will work closely with the teacher of students who are visually impaired to find ways in which the student can participate in classroom activities.

TEACHERS OF STUDENTS WHO ARE VISUALLY IMPAIRED

Teachers of students who are visually impaired work with the student and with other team members, when appropriate, to implement educational goals related to visual impairment. For example, when a student with low vision needs to use vision to locate his or her own coat or when a blind student needs to use touch to recognize tactile symbols, the teacher of students with visual impairments may work with the student on this skill or may work with others in teaching the skills. These teachers will be involved in assessment, planning, and instruction to meet the needs of the student related to his or her visual

(continued on next page)

impairment. They may work through consultation with family members and professionals, or through direct instructional activities.

SPECIAL EDUCATORS

Special educators work with students on educational needs related to their disabilities, either in a resource room or within the regular class. When a child requires significant services related to special needs, the special educator might be the primary teacher who coordinates the educational plan. He or she is often the primary instructor of academic skills as well as for goals related to the student's special needs. Working closely with the teacher of visually impaired students and assigned paraeducators, the special educator will decide who will implement activities with visually impaired students.

ORIENTATION AND MOBILITY (O&M) SPECIALISTS

O&M specialists work with the educational team to create plans pertaining to a student's ability to relate to the environment, travel independently, or otherwise move within it. They work with the student to implement those goals. They also determine the most efficient and independent means of travel for the student. Even a child who is not independently mobile can learn to control travel by using tactile cues, signals, and requests to participate in decisions about his or her movement and travel. The O&M specialist may also provide in-service training and recommendations to the educational team and families.

PARAEDUCATORS

Paraeducators assist in implementing the educational program by carrying out classroom routines with children as assigned by the teacher, preparing individualized materials, providing additional practice on skills as needed, ensuring students' safety, and facilitating social opportunities for students. The consistency and effectiveness of the paraeducator can make the difference in whether or not a child achieves established goals. It is important that team members provide the support and information necessary to prepare paraeducators. In most cases, paraeducators are more effective when assigned to classrooms or groups than when assigned to individual students. Too much assistance on an individual basis may allow students to accept help for tasks that they can do themselves.

RELATED SERVICE PERSONNEL

- Physical therapists train teachers and parents in positioning and handling; facilitate developmental motor skills, more normal movement, and gait patterns; and assess for, recommend, and/or assist in the fabrication and adjustment of orthotics, braces, wheelchairs, and other adaptive positioning or movement equipment.

- Occupational therapists prepare the child to accept and adjust to a more typical array of sensory experiences related to feeding, dressing, and learning through touch; facilitate developmentally appropriate upper extremity function, hand skills, and motor planning abilities; assess for, recommend, design, and fabricate splints for hand positioning or function and other adaptive equipment or aids needed for performing tasks of daily living.

- Speech therapists facilitate the development of early communication behaviors; instruct parents in how to read and facilitate their child's communicative potential; facilitate functional developmental communication behaviors; and assess for, recommend, design, and implement instruction in alternative forms of communication, including objects of reference, calendar systems, gestures and signs, and augmentative communication devices. They also work to encourage a broader array of sound production, improved speech intelligibility, and facilitate oral motor skills in preparation for both speech and feeding.

- Intervenors/interpreters are paraprofessionals trained in facilitating communication between a student who is deaf-blind and his or her environment and in ensuring that the student actively participates in all instructional opportunities.

- Adaptive physical education teachers have specific training in accommodating physical education activities for students with disabilities.

- Registered, licensed vocational nurses provide assistance with or management of medication, extraordinary medical procedures including catheterization, suctioning, gastrostomy tube feedings, intravenous medications or nutrition, and breathing treatments and,

(continued on next page)

in general, ensure the child's medical stability and safety during the instructional day.

- Behavior specialists are teachers with training in how to assess for, design, and manage a variety of interfering behaviors through the development and implementation of a functional behavioral assessment and plan. They may recommend changes in the environment, the instructional demands, and levels of prompts, and proactive means for preventing interfering or maladaptive behaviors as well as reinforcement strategies for encouraging desired behaviors.

- Transition specialists are teachers whose expertise is in the assessment and development of work/vocational opportunities for student's specific interests. They may be responsible for the arrangement of vocational training sites, for personnel to accompany the student to and from the sites, and for transportation between school and work site.

- Job coaches are teachers skilled in coaching a student through the steps required to fulfill the demands of a job selected to match the student's interests.

Each member of the educational team can serve as a resource in the area of his or her specialty.

Adapted from J. N. Erin, *When You Have a Visually Impaired Student with Multiple Disabilities in Your Classroom: A Guide for Teachers* (New York: AFB Press, 2004), pp. 12–17.

THE ROLE OF THE FAMILY

Most families' basic requirements for their children who have multiple disabilities are that they be safe and comfortable; learn to be as independent as possible; be able to communicate; be appreciated, respected, and loved; and have opportunities to be a full-fledged member of their community throughout their lives. The family is the key ingredient in achieving this "bottom line."

Children and youths who have one or more disabilities in addition to a visual impairment are considered to have multiple disabilities. Somewhere between 40 and 70 percent of individuals who have a significant visual impairment also have some combination of other disabilities.[1] These might include developmental delays; mental retardation; neurological dysfunction (including seizure disorders); postural and movement disorders;

sensory integration deficits; hearing impairment; regulatory, social-emotional, and behavioral disorders; and, in rare cases, behaviors and characteristics that fall within the spectrum of autism disorders. Given the many possible combinations of disabilities, their causes, and the visual and functional abilities of the youngsters in this group, the extent of the challenges they encounter and their needs are equally diverse.

Many children with multiple disabilities may have relatively minimal needs, which can be met through universal design accommodations at home and in the community, such as ramps and wider doorways, and the use of low vision devices, such as magnifiers or monoculars, or alternative communication systems such as the use of gestures, signs, pictures, or electronic speech systems. Others may require extraordinary environmental and material adaptations (splints, braces, or other equipment), assistive technology (adapted braillers, communication aids, computers, switches, or environmental control devices), continuing medical interventions, and support of the integrated expertise of many different professionals and agencies. For children with multiple disabilities overall, the ability to use their vision or other senses, control their surroundings, communicate with others, and interact socially can change with each significant life transition or even in different environments. What most children and youths with multiple disabilities have in common is the pervasive, multiple, and interacting effects that the combination of visual and other disabilities have on their ability to access, perceive, and process information and act on it to exert control over their environment.

Regardless of the nature or extent of a child's disabilities, the most important factor in a child's success in reaching his or her full potential—aside from his or her medical stability—is the efforts of the family to provide appropriate and sufficient life experiences and to obtain the necessary strategies, means, and services. A second crucial factor is the creativity of professionals and caregivers and their willingness to think beyond the traditional strategies and interventions used with visually impaired children and youths.

The expression "It takes a village to raise a child" is never more true than when applied to a child with multiple disabilities. In this case, you as the parent need to be the leader of the village to make sure that social, cultural, family, and individual preferences, needs, and goals are taken into account. A child's parents or primary caregivers need to be the ultimate "case managers" for their child—the ones who make sure the child is getting all the different services he or she needs and coordinate the different service providers to make sure they're doing what they're supposed to do. You have been the most consistent factor in your child's life and have the advantage of observing which factors and influences over time and in different environments are most likely to evoke specific desirable behaviors (such as communication or movement), which sets of circumstances have contributed to your child's successes, and which have served as barriers to progress or more functional performance. You are in the best position to recognize and interpret your child's behavior and to know when it is typical and when intervention is needed.

All the members of the "village" are important and essential, but you, the caregiver, are the most important to model expectations and attitudes toward your child. While in the community, you may need to model what you expect of your child in that setting by, for example, asking him or her, "Can you hold the door for the next person?" or cuing "Hold your hand out—you have some change coming." Communicating and demonstrating your child's competence and abilities will send a critical message both to your child and the professionals and others who interact with your child.

A crucial skill will also be asserting your leadership role with a variety of teams. One is the educational team that serves your child through early childhood programs and formal school years. Another is the community team that will need to support you and your child throughout the life span, and includes neighbors, friends, acquaintances, and friendly interested parties such as librarians and local shopkeepers. Another is the transition team that will guide your child into life after school.

As you are working on behalf of your child, you yourself will need support. Chapter 1 contains suggestions you may find helpful. Assistance may initially be provided by your family, friends, or a doctor or religious leader in your community who may know other families with children who are visually impaired. Contact your local agency serving people who are visually impaired or ask your physician or pediatrician, early interventionist, or even the local librarian to assist you in finding contact information for a support group geared to your child's disabilities. Another parent, most usefully one who has a child older than yours and who has already been through what you are experiencing, is an invaluable resource. The Resources section of this book, and Chapter 1, provide more information on how to find an appropriate agency or family support group.

As your child proceeds through the educational process and into adult life after school, you will be faced with many decisions about instructional and other options, strategies, techniques, and therapy and intervention recommendations. You will be called upon to explore, investigate, and question each consideration from the point of view of what you know about your child, your family, and your resources. Many of these decisions will be expedient and made with relative ease and confidence. Others will be time-consuming, heartrending, and laborious and may need to be continually revisited. Either way, your best tools are knowledge; a positive, confident, persistent, and unwavering attitude; and a willingness to model—to demonstrate in action to others—what you know and believe. Deep breathing and a good sense of humor are also very effective!

OBTAINING SPECIAL EDUCATION SERVICES

Children with multiple disabilities are entitled to the same services and supports as students whose only disability is a visual impairment, as guaranteed by the federal Individuals with Disabilities Education Act (IDEA). These services include support from a teacher of visually impaired students, access to orientation and mobility (O&M) services, and a learning media assessment (an evaluation to determine whether your child will do better with braille, print, another format, or some combination for obtaining information). To receive vision-related services, children with multiple disabilities must meet certain medical and functional criteria. These are determined by reports from eye care physicians and a functional vision assessment: an evaluation of how a child uses vision in real-life situations and of how the visual impairment may compromise independence, mobility and educational progress. (See Chapters 1, 3, and 6 for more information.) However, the Individualized Family Service Plan (IFSP) or Individualized Education Program (IEP) teams, of which you are an integral member, typically determine which services children are eligible for and how they are delivered. (See Chapter 4 for more information on the IFSP and IEP.)

To find out how to obtain services, the family of a child younger than 3 might typically contact a local early intervention agency or a program for visually impaired persons. However, a good place to start is with your local "child find" agency, especially if the child is age 3 or older, as explained in Chapters 1 and 2. IDEA requires the states to identify children in need of special services as early as possible, in a process referred to as "child find." Throughout the United States, local school districts, under the state departments of education, function as child find agencies.

In addition, the law requires each state to have a lead agency specifically for early intervention services, and this agency may or may not be the same as the child find agency in your state. The location of lead agencies for early intervention services within state governments varies from state to state. They are usually located, however, in the state department of health, human services, education, or rehabilitation. You may hear these lead agencies called "Part C" agencies, referring to the section in the legislation that describes them. (See Chapter 2 for more information on early intervention services.)

Local school districts are important sources of information, as are directors of special education and supervisors of programs for visually impaired students, agencies and organizations for people who are blind or visually impaired, and state schools for blind students. A helpful resource for locating the Part C agency in your state, the state department of education, organizations and special schools for blind students, and other services is the *AFB Directory of Services for Blind and Visually Impaired*

Persons in the United States and Canada, which is available in print and also online at www.afb.org under the "Where Can I Find?" service finder.

Once your child has been found eligible for services from a program for the visually impaired students, a teacher of visually impaired students must be an integral member of the intervention team, even if only on a consultative basis. The other team members will be your child's classroom teacher, therapists, and others in the educational or early intervention team, including yourself. "Role of the Teacher of Visually Impaired Students Serving Children with Multiple Disabilities" provides guidelines for what you may expect of the teacher of students with visual impairments when your child has multiple needs. (The role of this teacher is also explained in more detail in Chapter 1.) The frequency and intensity of vision-related services should be determined by your child's needs and may increase, at least temporarily, with each major transition from one school placement to another or from one environment to another until he or she becomes competent in the new endeavor or setting. The roles of the teacher of visually impaired students and other instructional personnel are often not mutually exclusive. They should overlap so that the efforts of all are directed toward helping your child achieve the goals set forth by the IEP team.

SETTING GOALS

Once your child is entered into a vision service program, the next step will be to establish goals and determine what kinds of services he or she needs. This determination will be done in an IFSP or an IEP meeting, depending on your child's age. The more prepared you are, the better you will be able to help the team identify and meet your child's specific needs. Organizing important information about your child to share with other members of the educational team (see Chapter 4) is essential, as is identifying your child's significant needs and gathering information to support your perspective.

Faced with a complicated set of decisions to make, you may be tempted to hand them over to the early interventionist or the teacher of visually impaired students. After all, don't the professionals know best? But no one professional can have all the answers for meeting the particular needs of your child, especially when the multiple and interacting effects of visual impairment and additional disabilities need to be addressed. Teachers and therapists are faced with the same decisions you are about what strategies are best and may be most appropriate given your child and family situation. The instructional or educational setting also needs to be considered, as explained in Chapter 7. One question is the extent to which your child will be educated with typically developing

Role of the Teacher of Visually Impaired Students Serving Children with Multiple Disabilities

In working with a student with multiple disabilities, the role of the teacher of visually impaired students and the variety of services provided are similar to those listed in Chapter 1, but the teacher may use his or her specialized expertise in a number of different ways. He or she will:

- Keep a record of how and what your child sees and the visual behaviors with which your child may need some help.
- Determine the influence that posture and environmental elements like illumination and contrast have on how your child uses his or her vision in the classroom and in other activities.
- Help your child to learn alternate ways of accomplishing tasks (compensatory skills) that are appropriate to his or her stage of development, such as the use of the sense of touch to explore and identify objects and the use of hearing to assist in orientation.
- Identify activities and situations throughout the day in which vision or an alternative modality such as touch is essential for your child to use to complete a specific task and determine what needs to be altered, adapted, designed, or constructed to allow your child the same access to an activity as his or her sighted classmates.
- Collaborate with you and other professionals who work with your child to ensure that everyone uses a consistent approach in such areas as facilitating movement and communication and behavior management strategies.
- Participate in your child's assessment for and design of an augmentative communication system (an alternative system of communication including manual signs, pictures, symbols, or an electronic device, for example), if needed, by providing information about your child's specific needs for contrast, placement, style, size, complexity, and proximity of objects, pictures, or symbols and the range and angle of the system's display that will best accommodate your child's visual abilities.
- Consult with you and your child's O&M specialist and therapists during the design, adaptation, and instruction in the use of a

(continued on next page)

manual or power wheelchair, if that is appropriate to meet your child's needs. His or her expertise with your child will ensure that your child can use his or her vision when moving or that your child's chair design facilitates orientation, scanning, and detection of landmarks, obstacles, and drop-offs. This helps to maximize your child's safety and that of others in his or her school and the community.

■ Maintain records that assist in documenting your child's progress and in making decisions about when to change, adapt, or continue current IEP goals, objectives, and/or instructional strategies.

students. You will also need to consider a wide range of issues in deciding appropriate services and placements, including such factors as your child's attention span and medical stability, need for one-to-one instruction, access to therapies within a specific context, ability to transition from one activity or class to another, and extent to which he or she functions in large groups with other children. A strategy or program that you heard was beneficial for another child who has needs and abilities similar to your child's could be just the approach needed. However, this needs to be determined after a careful examination of the needs and abilities of your particular child.

Priorities for Services

Prior to any IFSP or IEP meeting, try to gather information from all the professionals who work with your child as well as insight from friends and family members who know your child best, and from other parents of children who have disabilities. Once you have that information, weigh your needs and resources. This information can help you prepare a list of the areas and items that are most important to you for your child's education, as well as the skills and goals you wish to discuss during the IFSP or IEP meeting.

You may find a number of other steps helpful before the meeting:

● Share any updated information with members of your child's educational team, such as new medical findings, changes in medication and possible side effects of the new medication, or recommended interventions or equipment.

● If possible, prior to the meeting, observe your child in the settings in which he or she receives instruction or therapeutic services so that you are familiar with what is being emphasized and why, as well as how frequently your child receives certain interventions.

- List what you want your child to be able to do that will lead to greater independence, allow your child to participate in a broader range of family and community activities, interact more effectively with other children, and learn more efficiently given his or her visual limitations.

- If your child already has an IFSP or an IEP, review the specified services, goals, and benchmarks so that you can discuss progress and the continued relevance of the goals and services for your child.

- If this is not your first IFSP or IEP meeting, be prepared to express your concerns about any aspect of your child's services, including how and where they are delivered (one to one, in a group, in individual therapy suites, in the classroom) and about what specifically is being taught.

- Also be ready to ask, if appropriate, how your child's visual limitations are being addressed throughout all aspects of the services or interventions (classroom, therapy, music class, outdoor play, physical education) and what accommodations are being made so that your child can participate to the maximum of his or her ability.

- In addition, if your child uses specially designed equipment or materials, be prepared to discuss how they are being used in each setting in which they are appropriate; also be ready to ask team members who have demonstrated success to offer suggestions to other colleagues.

- If your child is currently receiving services in a self-contained classroom within a school or in a school that serves only children with special needs, ask the team to address how they can support your child's interaction with typically developing peers.

- If your child will transition to another setting, request specifics on how information about your child's needs will be shared with staff in the new setting and how your child will be prepared for the transition.

As noted in other chapters, you may invite anyone to these meetings, and your child should always be an active participant as well, as appropriate for his or her age. Chapter 4 contains more information on how to prepare for these meetings, including additional practical suggestions.

At the IEP or IFSP meeting, you should state what you want your child to be able to do or help your child convey his or her desires, preferences, and needs based on what you have observed and experienced with your child. The other participants should help you pinpoint the skills that will contribute to the achievement of each behavior or goal. It is important to limit the goals to a critical few that will truly make a difference for your child and your family. The professionals on the educational team should design their objectives and approaches to meet those goals. For example, if your child is a toddler, you may want him to learn to find a toy or his bottle when it rolls away, search for and grasp small finger foods and his spoon, communicate his needs and preferences, and initiate social interactions with members of your family. If your child is older, you may want her to play with everyone else on the neighborhood playground's equipment, learn to get a drink of water, and manage her own toileting needs.

The teacher of students who are visually impaired; O&M specialist; occupational, physical, and speech therapists; and classroom teacher should facilitate and reinforce skills and design accommodations that will enable your child to reach the specified goals. When all team members are working toward the same ends—that is, integrating their efforts, rather than focusing on separate goals related only to their own disciplines—it is easier to achieve the goals that have been designated.

When considering proposed goals and intervention strategies for your child, it is helpful first and foremost to decide whether what is being suggested will be functional: Will it help your child do something he or she really needs to do and be less dependent on others, either immediately or in the long term? Such goals might include learning to feed him- or herself with a spoon, manipulate the hardware to open any kind of door, climb safely up steps, manipulate various faucet handles, or write his or her name in some manner. Because children with multiple needs may require extraordinary time, effort, and continuing support in the development of skills to acquire as much competence and independence as possible, essential skills and abilities need to be targeted as early as possible. They then need to be built upon and refined (according to the child's abilities and needs) through broadening experiences. For example, your child's learning to introduce him- or herself to others can be initiated and practiced in the classroom, then expanded to be used schoolwide with adults and other students. Then he or she can use this skill outside of the school, as you go on shopping expeditions or to social events together.

Although circumstances may arise that will alter the goals and objectives for your child, beginning to work early on the goals and skills you consider important is of the greatest importance. Therefore, thinking through why a particular skill may be considered necessary is helpful for you in preparing for school meetings. A good way to think about whether a proposed behavior or skill is functional is to ask yourself whether someone else would have to do it for your child if he or she cannot do it independently. The "Intervention Priority Checklist" is a helpful form that you and other educational team members can use as a tool to set goals and priorities; the example shown here illustrates how it is used.

Once the IFSP or IEP team has decided on specific goals and supporting objectives, it will also need to decide the following:

Sample Completed Intervention Priority Checklist

Intervention Priority Checklist

Name: _Jessica James_   Date: _February 3, 2006_

Completed by: _Mr. and Mrs. James, grandparents;_
Mr. Preston and Ms. Chang, Teachers

Directions: List each skill or objective in the spaces across the top. Answer each
question for each skill or objective listed.

Ratings: 3 = Strongly agree   2 = Agree   1 = Somewhat agree   0 = Disagree

Criteria	Cup Drinking	Using a Spoon	Toilet Skills	Move to Activity	Make Choices	Communication	Play with Toys	Finger feeding
Learning this skill is a family priority.	3	3	0	3	3	3	3	2
The activity or activities in which the skill is required are preferred by the child.	2	2	1	2	2	3	3	3
The skill increases the child's ability to interact with people and objects during daily activities.	3	3	1	3	3	3	3	3
If this skill is not learned by the child, someone else will be required to do the task for him or her.	3	3	3	3	3	3	1	3
This skill can be applied across a variety of activities and/or environments.	3	3	3	3	3	3	3	3
This skill occurs frequently enough to ensure multiple opportunities to practice and learn it.	3	3	2	3	3	3	3	3
This skill can be encouraged and reinforced in a natural and meaningful way during daily activities.	3	3	2	3	3	3	3	3
This skill can be easily elicited during different activities.	3	3	2	3	3	3	3	3
The child can acquire the skills in the designated period.	2	1	2	3	3	3	3	2
The skill and characteristics of the task match the child's strengths and desires.	1	1	2	2	3	3	3	2
Total score (Possible total score = 30)	26	25	18	28	29	30	28	27

Reprinted from D. Chen (Ed.), *Essential Elements in Early Intervention: Visual Impairment and Multiple Disabilities* (New York: AFB Press, 1999), p. 315.

- what other supports need to be in place, such as materials; equipment to enhance your child's use of vision, mobility, and positioning; and environmental arrangements.

- the need for assistive technology.

- instructional approaches and strategies to be used.

- instructional personnel and related services (physical, occupational, or speech therapies) that will need to be involved, and instructional minutes (time devoted to each activity) for related and supportive services such as O&M or services for deaf or hard-of-hearing children. Once instructional minutes are determined, the frequency your child is seen will depend on his or her needs.

- methods for collecting data on your child's progress, additional needs, and need for changes in his or her programs.

- consideration of the type of instructional environments (with disabled classmates or with other children without disabilities), the amount of time in each setting, and the process for integrating your child with classmates who do not have any disabilities.

A sample portion of an IEP showing an annual goal and related short-term objectives and benchmarks for an approximately 3-year-old child with severe, pervasive disabilities and cortical visual impairment resulting from shaken baby syndrome is shown here.

Related Services

The topic of related services (see Chapter 5) is particularly important for students with multiple disabilities. Determining and planning the appropriate related services that your child will need is a crucial consideration of the IEP team. The unique services that your child may need may include services typically provided to children with visual impairments, such as O&M training, but may also include services relating to other areas, such as communication development, physical or occupational therapy, mental health concerns, and behavioral issues. It is particularly important for you to be specific about the needs and issues that relate to your child's multiple disabilities. In that way the IEP team can address all the services that will make an educational program successful and appropriate for your child.

The IFSP or IEP process is also the time to discuss any other extraordinary needs and procedures that ensure your child's safety and competence, because the key personnel who work with your child should be present for these meetings. Information you will want to share at this time, and which you will also want to provide to your child's school, may include:

Sample IEP Goal

Pineapple County Schools

EXCEPTIONAL STUDENT EDUCATION (ESE) DEPARTMENT
INDIVIDUAL EDUCATIONAL PROGRAM (IEP)
GOALS/OBJECTIVES/BENCHMARKS

Student progress will be measured by teachers and related service providers. Progress reports will be provided to parents each grading period, indicating the child's progress toward achieving the annual goals and the extent to which this progress is sufficient for the student to meet the goals by the end of the year. Parents will receive either copies of goals pages OR an IEP Progress Report. The IEP team will meet to address any lack of expected progress.

Student #: 0006011974   Date: 6/19/06

Measurable annual goal:

Domain A—Curriculum and Learning Environment

Anthony will demonstrate progress in coordinating eyes with toys, hands, and objects in the environment 20% over baseline as measured by the Family-Centered Approach to Functional Skills Assessment when provided with developmentally appropriate toys and experiences, physical facilitation, appropriate illumination and contrast, and multiple working positions.

1 2 3 4 5 6
Mastery ☐☐☐☐☐☐
Goal Accomplishment ☐☐☐☐☐☐

Progress: Each marking period is rated for mastery and for anticipation of meeting the goal by IEP end. See KEY below.

PERSON RESPONSIBLE FOR COORDINATING TRANSITION SERVICES, IF APPLICABLE:
P. SANCHEZ

Short-term objective or benchmark:
Anthony will demonstrate progress in directing his gaze to toys as they are positioned within his visual field in order to locate them for play.

Short-term objective or benchmark:
Anthony will demonstrate progress in directing his gaze toward people as a request for more of a favorite game or to initiate an interaction.

- a description or demonstration video of how your child communicates—for example, using an augmentative communication system or the signs your child understands

- strategies you use in getting your child to communicate

- techniques you have found that make it easier to feed your child or perform other daily activities, and your child's behaviors and preferences in this area

- techniques you employ to meet your child's medical needs, such as ways to suction your child's tracheotomy or manage gastrostomy tube feedings that are the most comfortable

- how the program or school should handle any medical emergencies, including whom to call, how medical personnel should gain access to the school and whom they should contact, who will accompany your child to the hospital, and any other related information that will be critical at such a time.

KEY INSTRUCTIONAL PRINCIPLES

A number of key principles can be followed to maximize the effectiveness of the education of children with multiple disabilities. When families and professionals are aware of these principles and work together, each individual following the same procedures with a child both at school and at home, the collaboration is a powerful influence that supports skill building, growth, and development. For example, it is particularly clear and reinforcing for a child when everyone who interacts with him or her communicates or performs an activity the same way. A number of other principles are helpful as well.

In general, children and youths with multiple disabilities learn skills most effectively when what is being asked of them makes sense from their point of view. Compensatory skills are ways of using other senses or adaptive strategies to supplement limited vision (checking the level of liquid in a cup with one's fingers) or circumvent obstacles caused by it (using a cane to guide mobility). Many of the approaches and strategies for teaching visual and compensatory skills that have proven effective with students who have multiple disabilities focus on the following:

- using natural environments—those in which children of the same age who do not have disabilities are typically found

- teaching skills in the context of functional and important real-life activities—such as practicing taking shoes on and off

- expecting the child to perform age-relevant skills—for a toddler, drinking from a cup; for a middle schooler, conversing about his or her favorite interests

- teaching and reinforcing skills in a variety of activities, situations, and environments—using the drinking fountain at school, operating the water dispenser on the refrigerator at home, and asking for a drink of water at a neighbor's house

- eliciting visual skills that are naturally related to each other: a child using tracking to find a toy, fixating on it, and shifting his or her gaze to the teacher's face to indicate he or she has made a choice.

Instructional strategies that teach related, functional skills within routines that occur naturally are especially effective. For example, a toddler might learn to shift his or her gaze back and forth between brightly colored bowls that contrast with their contents to choose what to eat and then visually search for his or her spoon.

Other concepts and strategies commonly used in interventions with children and youths who have multiple disabilities are summarized in "Terms Relating to Instructional Concepts and Strategies Used with Students with Visual Impairment and Multiple Disabilities." You should expect these concepts and strategies, as well as others that have been proven and accepted for use with visually impaired students, to be incorporated into your child's intervention goals and programs.

The effect of multiple disabilities on development and learning is not an additive one—it's not that a child has a visual impairment *and* a cognitive challenge *and* physical limitations. The effects of the disabilities are combined, interactive, and far-reaching, with one disability influencing and compromising how the child processes and compensates for another disability. For example, if your child had a significant vision loss only, he would learn to compensate for his limited vision by using his hands and gaining information through touch. However, if your child has a neurological disorder such as cerebral palsy in addition to the visual impairment, her sense of touch may not provide her sufficient information, or she may be highly sensitive to tactile information and avoid touching a variety of substances and textures, especially if they are unfamiliar. Because of these multiplicative effects on learning and integration of information, it is not unusual for children with several disabilities to have problems processing a variety of information that comes in through all sensory channels. For this reason, visually impaired children with additional disabilities frequently have difficulties with sensory understanding, generalization, and knowing how to interact with others, especially peers. These areas need to be addressed as early as possible to minimize their effects on learning and to support development of more effective adaptation. Many of the skills

Terms Relating to Instructional Concepts and Strategies Used with Students with Visual Impairment and Multiple Disabilities

Parents may encounter the following terms in discussions of the concepts and strategies that have been found to be effective in interventions with students with multiple disabilities. They may be incorporated into reports and documents concerning your child, and may be part of your child's intervention goals and programs.

CONCEPTS

Age relevant (or age appropriate): Your child should be expected to demonstrate and have the opportunity to participate in the same behaviors, skills, and activities that are appropriate for nondisabled children or youths of the same chronological age.

Assistive technology (also called **adaptive technology**): Products that people with disabilities use to gain access to environments and activities in which their participation would otherwise be limited. Technology can be relatively simple (low-tech), such as the enlargement of the handle of a spoon with foam, or a single switch device for communication; or more complicated (high-tech) such as a multilevel electronic communication device, software that translates print into speech or braille, or a power wheelchair that allows its user to stand upright.

Functional: Critical for independence, a term often used to describe skills, often designating activities that someone else would have to do for an individual if he or she could not do it for himself or herself. Feeding oneself is a functional behavior; stacking six textured cubes is not.

Natural environment: A context or environment in which children of the same age would typically be found if they did not have a disability. Examples include the home, school, playground, and local supermarket.

Routine: A natural sequence of events that occurs on a predictable and frequent basis, has a beginning and an end, and can be signaled with a consistent set of natural cues, such as putting a backpack in preparation for going to meet the school bus.

Universal design: Principles that ensure that products and environments are accessible to everyone. Examples of universal design are electronically operated doors, elevators, ramps to streets and buildings, and adjustable-height tables.

STRATEGIES

Community-based instruction: Using this approach, children are taught a consistent set of functional and related skills in an age-relevant community setting over a period of time. This enables them to function as independently as possible within that or other similar settings. This type of training may be used to teach skills of daily living, employment, or leisure activities. A field trip is not considered community-based instruction, as it is typically only a one-time exposure to a selected environment or activity.

Discrepancy analysis: A method of deciding what kind of adaptation is necessary for a child to be able to perform a particular task he or she cannot do independently. A discrepancy analysis begins by breaking down a particular task into its most basic steps. The child's performance of the task is reviewed to determine which steps he or she can already do and which steps need to be taught. The discrepancy between the child's existing skills and the needed skills is used to determine whether some form of assistance or adaptation is needed for the child to learn to perform the task.

Embedding: A method that creates opportunities to acquire targeted skills that are integrated into naturally occurring routines and meaningful contexts and activities throughout the day. For example, benchmarks on your child's IEP can be incorporated into her lunchtime routine through embedding: visually scanning to find her spoon, communicating "more" by giving the empty cup to her teacher, or practicing mobility skills by taking her empty tray to the appropriate place in the school lunchroom.

Functional context vision training: A systematic approach for teaching a child to use his or her residual vision to accomplish a specific task, exert control, or receive preferred consequences. The first steps in this model are to select an age-appropriate, functional task and determine which aspects of the task depend on visual attention. Repeated prompts are then systematically provided to encourage the child to pay visual attention, and the task is completed or the desired consequence is offered only if the child attends visually. An example would be giving an infant a serving from his spoon once he directs his gaze toward it.

(continued on next page)

Natural cues: Signals that are naturally present within the child or the environment and that elicit spontaneous and appropriate behavioral responses from a child. They may be sensory, physiological, or contextual. The smell of pizza serves as a natural cue to elicit movement toward the dinner table; the rumble of a motor in the garage is a natural cue that alerts your child that her favorite brother is home.

Individual curriculum sequencing (ICS): This curricular approach promotes the learning of a group of skills that are related to each other by natural, functional, and environmental properties. It assumes that the learner is an active participant and addresses the generalization of behaviors. An example would be the child learning to pull on her sneakers so that she can go to gym rather than as an isolated skill. The model incorporates two or more materials, settings, activities, and instructors into each instructional sequence; for example, the cashier in the cafeteria might ask "What is your name?" and the gym teacher might ask "Is your name José?" This approach also elicits two or more variations of a targeted response. Other aspects of the approach include distributing the teaching of skills across the instructional day, using functional and age-relevant materials and natural cues, and teaching skills at appropriate times.

Partial participation: A strategy for ensuring that a child has age-relevant and appropriate opportunities to take part in the same experiences as his or her nondisabled peers. In this approach, a child who may not be cognitively or physically able to participate in and respond to a situation independently receives the least assistance needed from a peer or adult companion or is helped to participate in the activity, at least on a partial basis, by some form of low- or high-tech assistive device or compensatory adaptation. For example, if an infant cannot move on her own, an adult facilitates her rolling closer to another child so that she can play with him.

Wait time: Additional time (based on a student's individual needs) given to a student to respond, for example, to a natural cue, specific request, or directive before receiving a prompt or additional information.

that are compromised, especially communication, may best be encouraged within social interactions because of the isolation a significant vision loss may impose.

In the process of teaching skills, certain issues are particularly important for children who have multiple disabilities that include visual impairments. Three aspects of instruction need to be emphasized: sensory development, generalization, and social closeness.

Sensory Development

Sensory development or enhancement typically consists of a group of strategies designed to help a child acquire and master skills in obtaining information from his or her senses and, in turn, learn. It is an important area of intervention for children and youths with multiple disabilities since the perception of sensory information is often impaired by their disabilities. Providing sensory experiences to children who are visually impaired can enhance and strengthen their ability to use their functional vision; help them acquire and master compensatory skills using touch, hearing, smell, and taste (such as directing their gaze to a toy placed in their hands, or using the smell of detergent to indicate where to put laundry in the washing machine); and engage them in acquiring functional skills that will help support important life activities.

Even children with significant physical or mental challenges have innumerable natural sensory experiences throughout the day. In working with your child's educational team, you can reinforce their efforts to help your child develop his or her awareness of information obtained through various senses. You provide tactile information to your child each time you wash his hands and face, allow him to touch and finger small bites of food placed on his tray, dry him off, and dress him. Your child will become aware that it is bath time from the sound of running water, know that his brother is home by the sound of tires squealing in the driveway, and realize that dinner is ready from the beep of the microwave. The feel of sand underfoot will alert your child that she is at the beach. Your child's teacher of students with visual impairments can help you select toys that will enhance your child's use of vision, touch, and hearing based on his or her developmental needs and ability to process the input from his or her senses. Emphasizing natural sensory opportunities will become second nature to you once you realize how much you already do that is functional.

Sensory integration refers to your child's ability to understand and make sense of what he or she sees, hears, touches, and feels and to react appropriately to that sensory information (lining up at the door when the fire alarm goes off, for example, or walking to the bathroom when sensing one's bladder is full). Children who have difficulty with using sensory information appropriately, who may be excessively sensitive to sound and touch or any other sensory stimulus, or who may not be able to tease out which sensory information is important at the moment (shown, for example, by not being able to write one's name because one is distracted by a noise outside) may have a dysfunction in sensory integration. If you have concerns about your child's ability to process different forms of sensory information, ask your physician or teacher of visually impaired students to refer you to a pediatric occupational therapist. He or she will be trained in helping you identify concerns about sensory integration and maximizing your child's abilities to use his or her arms and hands for play, self-care activities, and learning.

Generalization

Generalization of skills refers to the ability to use skills in situations other than the ones in which they are first learned. Students with limited vision, cognitive challenges, and additional sensory or motor impairments usually need many different examples and experiences in order to learn and integrate thoroughly skills that their sighted classmates learn incidentally or can figure out just by watching the people and objects in their environments. The following examples demonstrate the importance of generalization:

> Jason had learned to turn the water on and off at school so he could wash his hands independently. However, when his class visited the new fast food restaurant, he needed help to wash his hands because the hardware on the bathroom sink was different from that of the sink in his classroom.

Jason had not yet learned to generalize his knowledge of one set of faucets to sinks in other situations. In addition, although a child may perform a skill smoothly in isolation, he or she may not use it as efficiently when calling on it in more natural settings, amid other distractions.

> Hamida's family and baby-sitters and the staff at her school provided innumerable practice sessions for her to use her augmentative communication device to practice singing "Happy Birthday" for an upcoming birthday party. She proudly responded to the cues of her parents, teachers, and even the mailman by locating and pressing the appropriate adapted button that activated the song that she was "singing." Once at the party with her 4-year-old friends, however, Hamida was so overwhelmed with all the sensory experiences and so delighted with her friends' singing that she was distracted from joining in with the help of her device.

Children with multiple disabilities need repeated practice in many different situations to be able to generalize skills to other settings and contexts. Families and professionals can coordinate their efforts to provide opportunities for repetition and practice. To support the generalization of skills and maximize your child's ability to learn by ensuring consistency among everyone who interacts with your child, it is essential for you to share information on how your child communicates and behaves and, as well, for you to reinforce skills he or she learns in school.

Social Closeness

Social interactions are particularly crucial in the development of basic skills for young children with visual impairments and other disabilities. The importance of opportunities for social closeness cannot be underestimated, regardless of a child's ability to communicate. Being able to bond with and trust family, other children, and other individuals with whom the child has frequent contact, also referred to as social closeness, is critical for the development of functional communication as well as for motivation to explore, move, and learn.

Because it is so important that your child have frequent and multiple interactions with others throughout the day, any program that uses techniques or equipment that isolates your child from social learning experiences—such as placing the child in a box-like space intended to promote initiative in moving and exploring and the development of memory but that prevents interactions with others—needs to be examined carefully to make sure that it does, in fact, benefit your child.

Toddlers and preschoolers, in particular, should have opportunities to acquire and master skills in settings where attaining the skills leads immediately to social interactions with others and to opportunities for communication. Such skills may include learning to direct one's gaze toward a playmate and then shift it to a desired toy to indicate the desire to play with that toy together or learning to crawl toward a group of playmates, signaling a desire to play. Both skills lead to the end result of interaction.

The Gonzales family is able to help their son learn necessary skills in a socially rich context full of opportunities for mutual social and communicative exchange:

Mr. Gonzales enjoys placing José in his adapted chair that helps him sit as his father shaves so José can be near him. He and José push the button together to squirt the shaving cream onto the seat's tray. While Dad shaves, José has a nonresistant surface against which to move his hands and wiggle his fingers. He loves hearing his Dad sing and tries to join in. He especially loves it when the water splashes from Dad's face as he rinses it and onto his own. Afterward, José loves the deep pressure to his arms, legs, and cheeks that his Dad applies as he cleans off the shaving cream and sings a made-up song in Spanish in which he mentions the names of various body parts to help José learn them.

José's mom puts him in his high chair when she cooks so that he can listen to the sounds of the kitchen. Sometimes he helps by stirring or activating the electric can opener with a switch, and playing with a few frozen string beans or some of the mashed potatoes for dinner on his tray. His mother also finds it comforting to know that he is productively engaged while she is busy with other tasks.

CRITICAL FOCUS: COMMUNICATION AND MOVEMENT

In addition to sensory understanding, generalization, and knowing how to interact with others, communication and movement typically are areas that require significant intervention for children who are visually impaired and have multiple disabilities. Being able to move independently and communicate effectively are critical abilities to achieve some measure of control over one's life and environment. For this reason, parents of children with multiple disabilities need to work with their child's educational team to make sure their child's needs for communication and movement are addressed and essential skills are developed. Many students who are multiply disabled require alternative strategies, including the use of assistive technology, for mobility and communication, such as a wheelchair, sign language, or an augmentative communication device. Some parents may be reluctant to allow their child to use such alternative means of moving and communicating, particularly when the child is very young, for fear that the child will not have the opportunity to learn more "natural" skills or the way in which everyone else who is not disabled performs a given activity. However, using assistive technology has important benefits for children with disabilities. It allows them to have immediate control over some aspects of their life, offers them a degree of independence appropriate to their age, and gives them the opportunity to interact with and explore their environment.

Using alternative strategies doesn't mean that a child is not exposed to other appropriate movement or communicative behavior. Alternate strategies should always be used together, to undergird and reinforce each other. For example, teachers and parents may speak words aloud as they use sign language or other augmentative communication strategies with a child. Regardless of the system or way in which your child communicates, be sure to discuss with your child's educational team the ways in which you can encourage his or her attempts to communicate, help him or her build better communication skills, and work collaboratively with other team members on specific skills and goals.

Encouraging Communication

Children who have multiple disabilities that affect their ability to speak usually need to use more than one mode of communication, such as facial expressions, gestures, signs, vocalization, and augmentative devices. They may use objects, idiosyncratic gestures, signs, adapted switches that can record voices and are activated by a single movement, vocalizations, facial expressions, and body postures to indicate their preferences, make choices, or convey what they are feeling, need, or want. As with other types of intervention, learning a variety of ways to communicate is best taught within naturally occurring and motivating social situations, such as learning the sign for ice cream when eating it in the ice cream parlor as well as at a class party.

A child's each and every attempt at communication should be recognized and honored. The more severe a child's physical impairment, the more subtle his or her communicative behaviors may be. Subtle movements may carry significant communicative intent, as when your daughter tightens her muscles and straightens her legs to convey that she really doesn't want to do something. A primary goal is to shape these movements so that they are recognizable and readable by everyone and, if possible and appropriate, accompanied by communication, such as that provided by activating a switch that initiates verbal output. A wide range of augmentative speech output devices are appropriate for use by students with significant visual impairments. A child's communication needs typically change as he or she grows or develops, due to such changes as the need for a greater variety of symbols to express him- or herself or to be able to talk about additional topics. His or her augmentative supports also should change, and you should be an integral decision maker in that process. (Resources that will help you learn to identify, expand, and support communication behaviors when your child has multiple challenges are listed at the end of this chapter.) Opportunities exist throughout the day to encourage your child to communicate, such as showing your daughter how to give you her spoon to ask for "more" or offering your son two toys and allowing him to communicate his preference by handing you the one with which he wants to play.

As your child's caregiver, you are in the best position to appreciate fully the range of your child's communicative behaviors. You spend the most time in the greatest number of settings with your child. Because you can tell the difference among the most subtle of behaviors suggesting his or her communicative intent, make a note of every behavior that has potential or consistent communicative intent. Include what the behaviors typically mean; where they are most likely to be used; and whether they are physical behaviors, signs, and ways in which your child uses augmentative devices and systems, or his or her personal signs, such as arms moving in a swimming motion to ask, "Time to go to the pool?" This information should be shared with and explained to anyone who has consistent contact with your child on a continuing basis to ensure that everyone is up to date on what to encourage and expect. The following situation illustrates how a parent's knowledge of her child and how she communicates provided educational staff with insight about her abilities:

> Tanya is 12 years old and her vision consists of light perception only; she is also severely mentally handicapped. Tanya's mother picked her up early one afternoon from the music class she and her classmates participate in as part of the school curriculum. She prompted her daughter through hand-under-hand modeling (letting Tanya put her hand on her mother's to feel her demonstrating the sign) to ask her teacher in sign language, "May I go?" As she approximated the three signs and proceeded to take her mother's arm to leave, the music teacher expressed her astonishment at Tanya's skill, stating that she had no idea that a child who was blind, and Tanya in particular, could sign. As a result, she and Tanya's other teachers began to expect more of her and also began to plan a different level of instruction.

Motor Skills

Just as communication takes many forms for children with multiple disabilities, their mobility behaviors can be varied as well. They may move around within their environment in a variety of ways, depending on the setting, safety issues, and their health status, motor abilities, age, and level of independence. The same teenager might walk independently within his home, with a sighted guide during family events in unfamiliar environments, with a cane when walking in the mall with friends, and with a shopping cart in the grocery store. At other times he might use a wheelchair, for example, when traveling for long distances or in crowded environments such as an amusement park.

As you do with communication skills, you can help your child learn mobility skills in the course of everyday activities. It is important to encourage mobility in situations where moving independently is both functional and motivating, so that the child has a need and a logical reason to move. For example, if your toddler needs significant support even to roll over, she should be encouraged to roll to retrieve a toy that has moved out of reach, toward her siblings' voices to engage in a gentle game of wrestling, or toward her high chair when it is time to eat. As she rolls, she is receiving vestibular information that will help her use her vision, prepare her system for better control of her head, and improve and maintain an appropriate level of alertness. Although encouraging her to roll on her own may seem to take more time and effort than just carrying her, not only will your back thank you, but you will also be promoting the same motor behaviors that her therapists work on. In addition, you are sending the message to both your child and other family members that she is capable of participating successfully in all aspects of family life.

To practice mobility skills, many children on the verge of walking can push around a weighted child's doll stroller or grocery cart. For older visually impaired children, sessions in a swimming pool can facilitate walking and management of steps. When a child in a wheelchair is not able to move on his or her own, O&M lessons should focus on reinforcing participatory behaviors. These include recognizing auditory, tactile, or visual landmarks in the home, school, or community, and doing chores or running errands such as finding and putting away toys, getting a drink of juice, or finding the ice cream case in the grocery store. Communicative behaviors that indicate where the child wants to go need to be focused on as well. If your child can propel his or her own wheelchair, talk to your child's O&M specialist about adapting the wheelchair, the environment, or both with devices that alert him or her when the wheelchair comes near an obstacle or drop-off.

If your child is ambulatory but lacks the cognitive or motor coordination skills necessary for use of a traditional cane, he or she may benefit from the design and use of an adaptive mobility device, often referred to as a precane. These devices are custom-made from polyvinyl chloride (PVC) pipe to fit your child. A precane affords stability, symmetry, and protection from obstacles by providing a barrier in front of and on both sides of your child. It can be adjusted or reconstructed as your child's needs and size change and may be either a transitional device to a more standard cane or one that is needed permanently. Choosing options and devices for mobility requires a collaborative effort among therapists, mobility specialists, and parents, and, as a student approaches vocational age, job coaches and vocational specialists as well.

THE TRANSITION YEARS

Every parent is concerned about his or her child's future. We all want our children to lead happy, successful, and satisfying lives, but many of us find that the topic of when and how our children will leave home fills us with unease and concern. When a child has multiple disabilities, the subject may be a worrisome one. Despite any personal emotional turmoil it may at first cause, it is important for you to help your child consider what kind of work or life he or she might pursue, and to begin doing so early on. Using the end of elementary school as a timeframe by which you make tentative decisions about what your child may want and need to know and do to prepare for the future can be very helpful—for both of you. Above all, it gives your child sufficient time to work on acquiring the appropriate skills. Given his or her medical status, the range of opportunities available, advances in technology, and exposure to a variety of experiences in the community, it is likely that these plans will change over time. As much as possible, however, your child needs to be engaged in a variety of life-skills instruction and community-based experiences, especially throughout the middle and high school years. These experiences will help him or her develop confidence and capabilities and prepare for the world outside your home. Life-skills instruction focuses on involving the student in a number of practical and meaningful experiences intended to develop the vocational, transportation, self-management, household, communication, and leisure skills he or she will need to function as independently as possible.

By the time your child is 16, you both need to start thinking in a more formal way about what he or she will be doing in the years after high school. Age 16 is the age at which schools are required to begin putting plans for transition into a student's IEP. "Transition" is the term used to refer to the time when a student leaves high school and enters the next phase of his or her life. (Although Chapter 9 contains a great deal of information about the transition process that you will want to consult, this chapter focuses on the implications specifically for students with multiple disabilities.) There are a number of ways in which you can prepare for this momentous time.

You may want to begin by assembling what is called a transition portfolio: a collection of material that details important information about your child to assist and prepare those who will be involved in the transition process along with you and your child. Collecting this information helps to ensure continuity of service and successful strategies. It provides everyone with essential knowledge of your child that is needed to prepare appropriate goals and plans for the future. Information that may be part of such a portfolio includes the following:

- medical information
- need for physical supports or positioning strategies, such as supported sitting in a specially designed chair
- educational programming suggestions (adaptations and supports)
- expressive and receptive communication methods, such as whether your child uses signs, an augmentative communication device, or gestures
- mobility options, including use of a wheelchair or precane
- problem-solving techniques

- behavior management strategies, including effective cues, preferences, and reinforcers

During the transition years, more of a student's time will be spent on vocational or career education and learning specific skills that have been identified by the IEP team as important in preparing for life after school. The following guidelines outline suggested scheduling for vocational education activities for youngsters with multiple disabilities:[2]

- **during elementary school:** 45 to 60 minutes a day spent in vocational or career awareness exploration
- **for 12- to 15-year-olds:** two hours a day spent in training in community-based job sites
- **during middle school:** one to two hours a day spent in community-based experience
- **for 17-year-olds:** 50 percent of the day spent in community-based job training
- **during high school:** 80 to 90 percent of the day spent in vocational training and development of placement-related skills in areas such as money management, travel training, social interaction, greeting skills, and picture or gestural communication.

Life Skills and Community-Based Experiences

Learning life skills is a crucial part of making the transition to independent adult living. But teaching life skills is very difficult in a classroom enclosed within four walls. Although these skills can appropriately be fostered and reinforced within a school building, the variety and quality of instruction are not the same as when the teaching is done in the community, where students will ultimately need to live and function. The effort may be harder and more complex when a school takes students into the community, and many variables must be considered, reconsidered, and subjected to troubleshooting, not the least of which are issues related to transportation, personnel, and medical concerns and equipment. However, opportunities to learn in natural settings are well worth this effort because they promote generalization and encourage the student to respond to natural rather than artificial cues. It is easier to learn how to shop for milk by finding it in the dairy section at the supermarket than by "playing store" with an empty carton on the shelf in the classroom.

Try to think about the types of skills that typically developing sighted children learn incidentally through day-to-day experiences. Often, children with visual and other disabilities must learn these skills through direct, systematic teaching. Children learn life skills as they grow through naturally occurring learning activities within the home. Preschool children who are visually impaired can use life skills such as setting the table and washing clothes to foster motor skills, concepts, communication, and independence. As students get older, however, ingenuity, creativity, and outside-the-box thinking may be needed to provide opportunities for learning the skills needed to make the transition to adult living, and the help and support of the student's school must be enlisted.

An example of an ambitious exercise that would teach students many different skills and expose them to numerous real-world experiences would be one in which you the parent work with teachers at your child's school to set up a thrift shop open to school personnel and students. It could also be open to the surrounding community, depending on the resources available. Such an enterprise would allow students to use a variety of low-tech devices (such as a talking calculator or simple switch to operate a stapler that closes customers' shopping bags) to participate, to their ability, in efforts to recruit, clean, sort, organize, price, and sell thrift shop items. They might also obtain experience in traveling independently by purchasing city bus passes to visit discount and home improvement stores to buy items for cleaning, sorting, and packaging, as well as a variety of laundry supplies for washing, folding, and hanging clothing. Other jobs that can be practiced might include the use of specialized software to make advertisements and signs and to announce special sales and prices and the use of other equipment such as price and date stamps, paper shredders, money sorters, and adapted talking calculators. Money collected might be used for community leisure activities or volunteer work such as buying flowers and gardening equipment to plant flower beds at a nursing home, or saved for additional purchases needed to run the thrift shop. Other less extensive and complex options include participating in Meals on Wheels programs to deliver food to elderly people, washing teachers' and students' cars, assisting with collating and stapling flyers for upcoming parent-teacher association meetings or neighborhood businesses, and small-scale housekeeping, gardening, or landscaping jobs at the homes of school staff and friends.

Because you know your child's preferences, skills, and interests the best, talk with your child's teachers and therapists or guidance counselor to help brainstorm opportunities that allow your child to use his or her talents while learning independent work skills. For example, if your child loves pets, contact a local pet store to see if he or she can help feed the rabbits or hamsters.

Some school districts have established collaborative efforts with local college communities for multiply disabled students to participate in music, swimming, fitness, and weight-lifting classes in addition to using the college's media center. These are examples of programs accomplished through the integrated efforts of instructional personnel and families. The efforts result from extensive planning, time, and energy, but by participating in activities, your child can acquire skills that can lead to productive learning and living experiences.

Planning for the Future

One of your essential responsibilities in the transition process will be to help your child with decisions about what he or she will do once your child no longer of school age. Although this process will be formally initiated when your child is 16 with the writing of the transition IEP (see Chapters 4 and 9), you can help your child begin to identify preferences, dreams, strengths, and potential barriers prior to the IEP meeting. As with any teenager or young adult, your child's preferences and hopes for the future may change as he or she is exposed to additional training opportunities and a variety of community interactions. In addition, as your child nears graduation age, different options may be available than were possible earlier.

Nevertheless, having an idea early on about what your child would like to do in the future allows time to refine that goal and to determine which supports and resources might be needed and what experiences provided to ensure that dream. The following suggestions can help guide your decisions during the initial stages of transition planning:

- Think carefully about what activity, environment, or interaction brings out the best in your child. When is your child the most competent?

- Consider when your child is the happiest and the most motivated.

- Together with your child, explore and brainstorm the kinds of work or activities she would like to do or environments in which she prefers to be. Come up with a list of possibilities where and how this might happen. For example, if your child loves animals, she may work in some manner in a veterinarian's office, help out at a local zoo, volunteer at the local animal shelter, or offer to walk pets of elderly neighbors or residents at an assisted living facility.

- Once you have identified the possibilities, begin to identify the supports and skills that would need to be in place for them to be realized. For example, in order to work in a pet store, does your son need a job coach or the assistance of an occupational therapist to teach him how to open cages and carry a water bowl with both hands? Or a mobility specialist to teach him the routes he needs to know to get the food, take it to the pet cages, and go to the front of the store to wait for transportation?

- Bring this information to IEP meetings, where teachers, therapists, and other educational professionals will help you and your child identify the skills he or she will need to work on in school to be successful within the specific context you have identified.

- As the activities and goals are identified for your child, therapists and teachers should work together with you to analyze the environment to determine options that may be appropriate for your child. They will also help to delineate what skills are needed, what skills will need to be adapted, and which support personnel may need to be in place.

- Invite friends and acquaintances from the business or college community who know your child and his or her needs to the transition IEP meetings. Often these individuals make astute and profound observations and suggestions and are not limited by thinking in more traditional ways. They also frequently have contacts that can facilitate various aspects of your child's ambitions.

In addition, as explained in "Tools for Making Decisions About Transition Beyond School," there are formal tools available to help you explore in a systematic and thorough way your child's strengths and preferences. They also help to delineate skill and support needs and what needs to be done when and by whom in order to realize your child's hopes and plans for life after school.

The benefit of this kind of intensive planning is that it allows the student to try out aspects of the plan before leaving school through experiences in school or in the community. Then, based on feedback from the experience, changes can be made to the plan or other options explored to fit the student's needs, preferences, and abilities. In helping their child experiment with different activities to hone a variety of possible skills, parents will find that comprehensive planning, appropriate supports, and the willingness to explore a variety of different options are key ingredients.

The Community

It is important for your child to be out and about in the community: going to the supermarket, the library, the movies, restaurants, department stores, the "Y," and all the other places young people his or her age go. This is particularly true during the transition years as your child prepares for adult life. Consistent and frequent participation in community activities allows neighborhood storekeepers and clerks, other youngsters, and other community residents to become familiar with your child and his or her personality, style of interacting and communicating, abilities, and needs for assistance. Engaging your child with the world at large in this way does place considerable responsibility on you, however. For the engagement and participation to provide your child with the experiences you hope he or she will have, you will need to involve your child in activities that require him or her to carry out the skills that you wish to be developed. Also, you may find yourself needing to help people modify their usual expectations about behavior and to model for others how to encourage your child to behave in

Tools for Making Decisions about Transition Beyond School

One way to make decisions about what your child will need and do after graduation from high school is to use a formal process specifically designed to look at his or her lifestyle options, dreams, and possibilities. Ideally, this process should be set in motion from two to five years before your child's anticipated date of graduation in order to plan a transition to post-school environments and activities.

Various formal tools and established procedures have been documented to help parents of students with multiple disabilities with the process of transition. The use of a formal transition tool generally entails several meetings of a group of individuals (including the student) who have valuable information about the student or about aspects of his or her goals or objectives. This group can include family members, friends, neighbors, teachers, doctors, and other people who know and care about the student. Typically, each of these individuals responds to a specific set of questions intended to detail the "dream"—that is, the vision that the student and the group come up with for the student's future. The student's strengths, obstacles to fulfilling the dream, and critical supports that would be needed to attain the goal are explored by them. The process might include the following:

1. Identifying your child's dreams and preferences
2. Describing your child: his or her personality, strengths, needs, health status, motivators, and likes and dislikes
3. Clarifying your child's needs and supports
4. Identifying people and strategies needed for your child to realize the dream
5. Describing your concerns and apprehension about the future
6. Outlining timelines and action plans for realizing the dream
7. Assigning responsibilities and roles to integral members of your child's educational or community team

Using this process results in a map of outcomes intended to guide those responsible for ensuring the realization of the student's plans and dreams for the future.

Following are examples of some specific planning tools (see "For More Information" in this chapter for further details). Each has its own process, strategy, and outcomes.

(continued on next page)

- Person-Centered Planning
- Making Action Plans (MAPs)
- Planning Alternative Tomorrows with Hope (PATH)
- Choosing Outcomes and Accommodations for Children (COACH)

the desired manner. Your interactions with your child show everyone else what to expect from your child, how to communicate, and what they need to do to elicit the same degree of competence that you have elicited. Essentially, you will find yourself in the continuing role of performing what might be termed a discrepancy analysis: determining what your child needs to do in a particular setting, what he or she can do, and what assistance he or she needs, in each setting in which you typically find yourselves.

When your child is a teenager and young adult, the task of helping him or her to participate as much as he or she is able in order to fit in becomes more difficult and complex. Given what others of this age group are doing while your child may continue to need help with even the most basic of skills, supporting participation in typical environments becomes complicated. Teenagers and young adults are shopping by themselves, hanging out with friends, volunteering or working in some capacity (baby-sitting and mowing lawns around the neighborhood, for example), and often helping others in community settings. For your child's sake, along with the support of your friends, neighbors, and IEP team, you will want to foster relationships with nondisabled students near your child's age both to provide companionship and to facilitate your child's participation in the same age-appropriate activities. Sometimes, this process will take much planning, modeling, and teaching. Often, however, through simple exposure, these relationships will emerge naturally with just minimal encouragement from you. Teenagers in a youth group at your place of worship often are a source to find someone to play a game of basketball or take your child for a walk or to a movie. Adaptive sports organizations pair children with disabilities with their nondisabled peers. Your local college may also have a "buddy" program that pairs disabled and nondisabled children for social outings and events.

FINAL THOUGHTS

As the parent of a child who, in addition to near-total blindness (light perception only), has severe multiple disabilities (cerebral palsy, seizure disorder, profound mental retardation, and he is nonverbal), I have, in

BECOMING PART OF THE COMMUNITY

Store clerks, pharmacists, the lifeguard at the YMCA, the folks at the mailing store, fellow churchgoers, the bank tellers, and even the librarian have all eventually learned how to address my son, how to read his signals, what his preferences and interests include, and how to encourage his active participation. They have accomplished these feats because they have had many opportunities to observe, react, receive feedback, and try again; they have reasonably good memories; and they are astute observers of how I engage with and respond to him. After several very well intentioned efforts, the librarian has learned that my son reads print although he is visually impaired, and acknowledges his preferences for mystery and humor in his selections. Store clerks announce that his change is ready, give him the paper money, wait patiently as he places it in his pocket, and then offer the coins by supporting his hand with theirs as they release the change into it.

The pharmacist calls out when we enter, "Hey, Eric, it's Ann. Come to pick up your prescriptions?" and she rattles the bag to orient him to which window to approach. Many of these people just have natural talent and have needed no prompting from me!

I have also come to appreciate greatly the power of a credit card. The young clerk at our local consumer electronics store probably had never encountered such a disabled young man. He desperately scanned the area in hopes of recruiting another sales agent to talk to us. When Eric used his wrist communicator (which plays prerecorded voice responses) to share his name and interest in CD players, the clerk immediately grabbed the nearest player and, in compressed speech, relayed to me all its advantages. I offered Eric the headset and suggested he "listen" and try it out. When I asked, "Would you like to try another?" he removed the headset and extended it to the young man. We tried several CD players. When Eric made his selection from two options, the clerk directed us to the CDs while he rang up the sale. Eric selected several, and we returned to pay for his purchases.

The clerk immediately was "awed" by the fact that Eric had selected (by pure coincidence!) the same CD as the demo in the headsets. An immediate bond was established. He turned to me with the total amount owed and asked how I wanted to pay. Eric extended his credit card, and

(continued on next page)

the young clerk was momentarily silenced. When he returned the card to Eric, he also extended the electronic pen for him to sign the display. Since the electronic display would not accommodate his name stamp, I assisted Eric to sign his name. By the time we left, the clerk extended the package to Eric's hand, stating, "Here ya go, dude. Enjoy!" As Eric accepted the package and began to walk out, I heard the clerk exclaim, "Awesome!" So little effort, so much gained.

Modeling what one needs to do to elicit communication and social exchange and to facilitate engagement is the key to community acceptance and initiative. Whatever setting we are in, I make sure that Eric is seen as competent by offering him choices (he couldn't care less whether he eats fish strips or fillets or whether we buy the tan shorts or the black ones). I enlist his assistance with tasks such as paying for goods, putting groceries on the conveyor belt, loading the milk into the cart, or stamping his own name on checks or on the sign-in form at his physical therapist's office.

In addition to perceiving Eric as competent, the community also needs to see him in the role of helping. Eric "offers" to return a grocery cart for an elderly man, holds the door open for others, is a greeter at our church, retrieves items from the top shelves for a fellow customer, walks the dogs of residents who can no longer do so at his grandmother's assisted living facility, and recycles newspapers at the neighborhood facility. Yes, he needs someone's help to do all this, but the bottom line is that he does do it. When he was younger he partially participated in pushing his peers at the playground on the tire swing, showed another child how to fasten his seat belt on a plane, and filled glasses with ice at church picnics.

Yes, I still notice the stares of others who are not as lucky as our community neighbors to have had frequent interactions with him. When the opportunity arises, he and I are happy to share with children who want to or do ask about his disabilities. Before a child can be dragged away by a parent embarrassed that she asked a pointed question about Eric, I inform her, "You were so clever to observe that . . ." What parent can ignore praise doled out to his or her child? These parents additionally learn something as a result.

And, yes, Eric and I boldly go into the women's toilet facility when we are without another male. People notice but seem to realize why he is there, and it has never been an issue. One saintly woman in a very long line at the Houston airport kindly offered to stay with Eric while I used the facility. When I graciously thanked her and explained that he also had to go, she replied that she never thought of that!

Since he became a teenager, Eric has adopted a very age-appropriate attitude that is not always appreciated by others. Although he has no real words, his body actions and vocalizations speak clearly. When he has a meltdown in the community because a preferred song from the piped in music is ending or because a routine he anticipated is interrupted, I can no longer verbally reprimand him because it merely escalates the situation. Now, to distract and calm him, I have learned to respond, "I know you really liked ___, that was a great song," or "You thought we were going to the pool but we need to stop by the cleaners quickly." His screeches momentarily cease so I can escort us to a less conspicuous place but, nevertheless, we have created an incident.

How others react depends on my attitude and show of confidence. My verbal behavior is intended more to help them understand why he is upset than to provide him with feedback at that moment.

M. Beth Langley

general, found the community to be kind and empathetic, and I have found a variety of methods effective in ensuring that my son, Eric, displays his competence in a variety of community settings.

However, as the parent of a youngster with multiple disabilities, I have had my share of heartbreak too. Over the years, I have worried about each new situation, but my fears are usually quickly tempered by other kind and gentle souls who take the initiative to make sure that Eric is safe, productive, and happy. In our role as parents, worry is what we do. But we also can appreciate the successes that come as a result of teamwork, effort, labor-intensive and systematic planning and modeling, and supportive school and community networks. Judiciously skeptical but cautiously optimistic, we as parents live to hear our children being addressed with a greeting like, "Hey, man, let's hit the gym." And to have the words not be ours.

Notes

1. S. W. Teplin, "Visual Impairment in Infants and Young Children," *Infants and Young Children*, Vol. 8 (1995), pp. 18–45.

2. P. Wehman, W. Wood, J. M. Everson, R. Goodwyn, and S. Conley, *Vocational Education for Multihandicapped Youth with Cerebral Palsy* (Baltimore: Paul H. Brookes Publishing Co., 1988).

For More Information

R. Blaha, *Calendars for Students with Multiple Impairments Including Deaf-Blindness* (Austin: Texas School for the Blind and Visually Impaired, 2001).

S. Burgstahler, "Conquering the Jargon Jungle: Technology Terms a Parent Needs to Know," *Exceptional Parent*, 32 (7) (2002), pp. 62–64.

D. Chen, "Parent-Infant Communication: Early Intervention for Very Young Children with Visual Impairment or Hearing Loss," *Infants and Young Children*, 9 (2) (1996), pp. 1–12.

D. Chen, "Interactions Between Infants and Caregivers: The Context for Early Intervention," in D. Chen (Ed.), *Essential Elements in Early Intervention: Visual Impairment and Multiple Disabilities* (New York: AFB Press, 1999), pp. 22–54.

D. Chen and J. E. Downing, *Tactile Strategies for Children Who Have Visual Impairments and Multiple Disabilities: Promoting Communication and Learning Skills* (New York: AFB Press, 2006).

M. Demchak and R. Greenfield, "A Transition Portfolio for Jeff, a Student with Multiple Disabilities," *Teaching Exceptional Children*, 32 (6) (2000), pp. 44–49.

J. Dote-Kwan and D. Chen, "Developing Meaningful Interventions," in D. Chen (Ed.), *Essential Elements in Early Intervention: Visual Impairment and Multiple Disabilities* (New York: AFB Press, 1999), pp. 287–336.

J. E. Downing, *Teaching Communication Skills to Students with Severe Disabilities* (Baltimore: Paul H. Brookes Publishing Co., 1999).

J. N. Erin, *When You Have a Visually Impaired Student with Multiple Disabilities in Your Classroom: A Guide for Teachers* (New York: AFB Press, 2004).

D. L. Fazzi, "Facilitating Independent Travel for Students Who Have Visual Impairments with Other Disabilities," in S. Z. Sacks & R. K. Silberman (Eds.), *Educating Students Who Have Visual Impairments with Other Disabilities* (Baltimore: Paul H. Brookes Publishing Co., 1998), pp. 441–468.

K. A. Ferrell and D. W. Muir, "A Call to End Vision Stimulation Training," *Journal of Visual Impairment & Blindness*, 90 (1996) pp. 364–366.

M. Giangreco, C. Cloninger, and V. Iverson, *Choosing Outcomes and Accommodations for Children (COACH): A Guide to Educational Planning for Students with Disabilities*, second edition (Baltimore: Paul H. Brookes Publishing Co., 1998).

P. Greenhill, M. Lee, and L. MacWilliam, *Movement, Gesture, and Sign Supplement: One Hundred Adapted Signs. An Interactive Approach to*

Sign Communication for Children Who Are Visually Impaired with Additional Disabilities (London: Royal National Institute for the Blind, 1996).

L. Hagood, *Communication: A Guide for Teaching Students with Visual and Multiple Impairment* (Austin: Texas School for the Blind and Visually Impaired, 1997).

M. D. Klein, D. Chen, and M. Haney, *Promoting Learning Through Active Interaction: A Guide to Early Communication with Young Children Who Have Multiple Disabilities* (Baltimore: Paul H. Brookes Publishing Co., 2000).

J. E. Korsten, D. K. Dunn, T. V. Foss, and M. K. Francke, *Every Move Counts: Sensory-Based Communication Techniques* (Tucson, AZ: Therapy Skill Builders, 1993).

M. Lee and L. MacWilliam, *Movement, Gesture, and Sign: An Interactive Approach to Sign Communication for Children Who Are Visually Impaired with Additional Disabilities* (London: Royal National Institute for the Blind, 1995).

M. S. Moon, M. Grigal, and D. Neubert, "High School and Beyond," *Exceptional Parent,* 31 (7) (2001), pp. 52–57.

B. Mount, *Person-Centered Planning* (New York: Graphic Futures, 1992).

J. Pearpoint, M. Forest, and J. O'Brien, *PATH: Planning Alternative Tomorrows with Hope* (Toronto, ON, Canada: Inclusion Press, 1992).

J. Pearpoint, M. Forest, and J. O'Brien, "MAP's, Circle of Friends, and PATH: Powerful Tools to Help Build Caring Communities," in S. Stainback & W. Stainback (Eds.), *Inclusion: A Guide for Educators* (Baltimore: Paul H. Brookes Publishing Co., 1996), pp. 67–86.

K. E. Wolffe (Ed.) *Skills for Success: A Career Education Handbook for Children and Adolescents with Visual Impairments* (New York: AFB Press, 1999).

CHAPTER 9

Transition: Planning for the World Beyond School

Karen E. Wolffe

When you are busy raising a child, you may find yourself with little time to think concretely about your child's approaching life as an adult. However, we all know that time passes quickly. Sooner than we can anticipate, a child's high school years come to an end. For this reason, it is important for parents to begin early to plan for their child's life beyond school. You will want to start exploring the topic yourself and also to engage your son or daughter in conversations and activities that will begin to help him or her think about life as an adult. This process of planning for the future is particularly important when your child has a visual impairment or other disability.

The word "transition" is often used to refer to movement from one phase to another and to the adjustment that such a move involves, such as a move from one job to another or from one period of life to another. Children experience a transition as they move from preschool to elementary school, from middle school to high school, or from high school to college or work, for example. The transition discussed in this chapter focuses on the process of planning and preparing for what a young person will do when he or she leaves high school and moves into the adult world. That may mean going on to postsecondary education such as college, other career training, work, or life in the community outside the family.

TRANSITION: WHAT IT MEANS

The transition from childhood and dependency to adulthood and independence is a pivotal change for all of us that takes place over a long period of time. However, at the end of high school, the process of moving from child-centered environments to adult roles and responsibilities receives particular attention from special educators and rehabilitation specialists for a number of reasons. First, in order for children with special needs to move into independent, successful adult lives, their families typically need to consider a number of questions and plan arrangements and realities beyond those addressed by families of children without disabilities. Second, when children with special needs leave high school, the special education services that they have been receiving in school and that have been supportive to them and their families come to an end. Determining a direction for the next stage of their lives, and organizing the arrangements and, possibly, necessary services in support of this direction, involve deliberate, well-thought-out, careful plans. For children who are visually impaired and for children with other disabilities, this process of planning and implementing goals for growing up and assuming the rights and responsibilities of adulthood is not only essential—it is legally mandated.

Although being concerned about a child's future is a given in parenting, as the parent of a child who is visually impaired, you may find yourself grappling with a number of concerns about how your son or daughter will manage college, a job, or the many activities involved in finding and managing a home. When children reach their teenage years, these concerns may seem daunting, but life planning should not be left to chance. One of the more effective ways for parents to manage their own emotional concerns or anxiety successfully while helping support their children's well-being is to prepare their children for adult life after home and high school. Planning can go a long way toward helping a child prepare for the world at large.

TRANSITION PLANNING: AN ESSENTIAL SPECIAL EDUCATION SERVICE

Transition planning for life beyond school is a process that parents and students may find similar in some ways to other facets of educational planning. That is, it involves parents, students, and professionals in a collaborative effort. It is based on an assessment of the student's needs and appropriate goals for him or her and includes an effort to put in place necessary plans and supports to help the student meet those goals. Finally, it is a process mandated by the Individuals with Disabilities Education Act (IDEA). "Transition: An Overview" describes this overall process.

Transition: An Overview

TRANSITION: WHAT DOES IT MEAN?

The term "transition" refers to the period of time that a student spends preparing specifically for life after leaving the public school system.

WHEN DOES IT START?

The transition process is required to be detailed and included in your child's IEP not later than the first IEP in effect when the child is 16 and updated annually thereafter. For students with multiple disabilities or greater needs, the process can be initiated as early as the IEP team deems necessary to maximize the likelihood of the child's success.

WHAT'S SUPPOSED TO HAPPEN?

The educational team (that's your child, you, and the school personnel and related service providers) is supposed to determine what services your child needs (classes, community-based experiences, information, training, and others) to be successful in the environment (college, vocational training, work, home, dorm, or apartment) he or she intends to move into following public school. There is no prescribed list of services that the school must provide—these services are specific to each child's IEP, based on the assessment of his or her abilities, needs, and life goals. (See "Transition IEP Checklist" later in this chapter for the kinds of services you should anticipate being on your child's IEP.)

WHO'S RESPONSIBLE FOR WHAT?

The student's educational team is responsible for case management (overseeing the student's educational program). The team members are responsible for providing or ensuring instruction in the basic academic courses (English, math, science, geography, civics, history, and so forth). In addition, they are responsible for providing or ensuring training in disability-specific skills—skills and adaptive techniques that the student needs to develop because of his or her visual impairment to help him or her participate equally in academic learning and live independently. These disability-specific skills are taught as part of what is referred to as the expanded core curriculum for children with visual impairments (see Chapter 1 for more information on this topic). They include instruction, as needed, in reading and writing with braille or the use of optical devices, orientation and mobility (O&M),

(continued on next page)

social skills, independent living skills, career education, assistive technology, recreation and leisure, visual efficiency, and self-determination. School personnel are also responsible for evaluating your child's progress in these areas.

Families are responsible for the health and well-being of the student and for participation as part of their child's educational team. They need to attend and contribute to the IEP meetings, including the meetings that establish the student's transition services plan. As part of this process, they need to let both the student and the educational personnel know what their hopes and dreams are for their child. In addition, parents should be able to articulate how they will support their child emotionally or with monetary assistance following graduation from high school or when he or she leaves the public school system. Children may have expectations of their parents or caregivers that may need to be clarified as part of the transition process. If your child has multiple disabilities or a severe cognitive impairment, you may also need to assume the role of advocate so that you can present his or her wishes and desires for life beyond school to the service providers who will help you implement an after school program for your child.

The student who does not have cognitive or other impairments that prevent him or her from doing so is responsible for his or her own life plan. While the student is still in school, this means selecting courses that will enable him or her to pursue life goals such as going to college or working in a particular career. It means that your child needs to consider what he or she is good at doing, likes doing, and values (health, wealth, fame, fortune, family, friends, independence, security). He or she needs to compare these realities to careers of interest to find the best matches. While still in school and living at home, it is important that the student participate in work activities—both volunteer and paid jobs are important to experience. Finally, the student needs to express the plan he or she has in mind at the IEP meeting so that his or her desires can drive the transition planning process.

Other entities, such as public and private vocational rehabilitation agencies or organizations or agencies that serve people with developmental disabilities, are responsible for providing information about their services and making those services available when contracted or hired to do so. (See "Agencies that Provide Services for Adults" at the end of this chapter for further information about the types of agencies outside the public schools that are available to provide services to young people with visual disabilities.)

It is both helpful and important for families to understand that transition services are part of the support that their child who is visually impaired is entitled to receive while in school. Under the provisions of IDEA, the educational team needs to plan and provide transition services that offer the extra assistance that children with disabilities may need in school to navigate the passage into adulthood and to participate fully in all aspects of adult life. In addition, team members need to ensure that no gaps exist in needed services for a specific young person.

Federal law under IDEA requires that schools undertake specific transition activities for children with disabilities. These activities are outlined in an Individualized Education Program (IEP), tailored to each special education student, called a transition IEP. (Chapter 4 provides more information on IEPs and on transition IEPs.) The formal transition process begins around age 16 (or younger, if appropriate due to a need for more advanced planning or a student's multiple needs). The transition IEP is updated annually until the student completes high school or reaches age 22 (in most states), when a student with disabilities must leave the public special education system. During the transition process, the student, the student's family, the IEP team, and, when appropriate, other professionals who provide certain services for adults explore options for the future. Together they decide on a plan for the student to learn skills and receive services designed to facilitate a smooth and seamless transition from school to inclusion in all options available to people without disabilities. Some of the options that the team may consider include:

- enrollment in postsecondary education or training (such as college or vocational training).
- competitive employment, which includes jobs available on the open labor market that are sought after by people with and without disabilities; or supported employment, which is designed for students and adults with disabilities who may need some initial assistance on the job to learn the tasks required of them or other help. These supportive services are typically provided by a job coach or trainer.
- supported or independent living outside of the family's home.
- participation in community activities, including recreation, leisure, and social activities.
- access to other community services, including transportation and health care.

As a parent, you can assist your child in a number of ways during the transition process. In a sense, you have been preparing your child for this process from earliest childhood, as you built a foundation of skills, values, and ways of behaving that he or she needs in order to grow up and assume adulthood. Simple tasks, such as learning to take care of oneself and one's personal possessions, are among the first steps in this process. What you need to know and do to support your child further as he or she embarks on the transition from school to life beyond your home is discussed in this chapter. The chapter also provides information on what you can expect in the way of support from school and other service providers working with your child.

THE TRANSITION PLANNING PROCESS AT SCHOOL

As already noted, transition requirements for students with disabilities are spelled out in the law. In preparation for the student's transition from high school, his or her goals must be explored; for example, goals related to the next environments where he or she will study, work, and live. A number of fundamental and critical questions need to be asked at this time, such as Does the student plan to attend college or participate in other training following high school? Does the student plan to work and, if so, doing what? Can the student live on his or her own? Does the student plan to live in his or her own apartment or a college dormitory? The student's IEP by age 16 must contain a statement of transition services that the school will provide, including the high school courses or activities the student needs to participate in to achieve his or her identified goals for life after high school. Overall, the IEP team needs to connect the student's specific annual goals to the goals the student and the team have identified for the future. Examples of annual goals might be completing Advanced Placement courses for college or participating in vocational education or life skills program designed to teach the student self-care skills related to such areas as grooming and hygiene, planning meals and cooking, taking care of possessions, and using money and credit or debit cards.

To make sure that your child's preferences, interests, and goals are addressed in the IEP, you will want to keep both school records and your own documentation of the areas in which your child performs best. This is particularly important if your child is unable to communicate his or her own interests and abilities easily to the IEP team. You may also want to collect materials and keep your own records and notes to be sure that the services identified on your child's IEP as critical have been provided.

If your child is able to do so, you may also want to encourage your child to collect both school records and information about his or her achievements and community work. This kind of documentation is useful when applying for paid work or postsecondary training programs and application forms need to be completed. For example, your child may have participated in scouting activities, community service, or volunteer work, or have demonstrated skills in the performing arts, athletics, or computer gaming and technology. Or he or she may have received high marks in certain classes in school. These examples of interests and abilities are important to identify and often help with selecting the course of study or work that a young person will pursue following high school.

Determining Interests, Activities, and Needs

School faculty members and guidance staff are also supposed to help with identifying young people's interests, abilities, and goals. Their efforts may involve testing your child. Students are tested frequently to determine the level of their academic skills. In the case of students who receive special education services, they may be assessed to determine their specific needs for transition services. If you feel that such testing would be beneficial for your child, ask your child's primary teacher or the school counselor to recommend vocational or transition testing at the annual IEP meeting. However, it is important to understand that specific assessments for students in transition are not required in most states (other than any exit or proficiency exams that may be required of all graduating students).

What is encouraged, if needed, as a transition service under IDEA is a functional vocational evaluation. This type of evaluation is a process that includes collecting information from a variety of sources about a student's interests, abilities, values, personality traits, work habits, and areas of need. The information sources can include school records and reports relating to extracurricular activities, coupled with observations of the student in school or at work. Informal assessment tools such as interviews with the student, family members, teachers, and employers; observations at school, work, or in the community; and monitoring of work-related behaviors such as attendance, punctuality, and cooperation are used extensively in a functional vocational evaluation. Formal assessment tools are also used to determine what the student's vocational potential may be. As your child is the focal point of the functional vocational evaluation, he or she will be expected to participate, if appropriate, in an interview to discuss interests, abilities, and goals for postsecondary activities. If your child is unable to speak for himself or herself, you or other members of your child's family or extended support system may be interviewed in this process to determine your child's interests, abilities, values, and areas of need.

The types of formal tests used to determine students' vocational interests and abilities vary widely, and parents—in fact, the entire educational team—need to consider the results of such tests with caution. Most of them are not designed for or norm referenced (evaluated) on students with visual impairments. (See Chapter 3 for more information on this topic.) However, formal tests can provide some interesting information that can help with career exploration and guidance related to appropriate courses of postsecondary study.

Specifying Services

As already noted, by the first IEP after your child reaches age 16, the IEP must detail the specific transition services that will be provided for him or her and identify who will provide them. The school does not have to provide all the services a student may need. Other agencies in the community and agencies that provide services for adults may be identified on the IEP as service providers. Community-based agencies, such as public and private rehabilitation agencies, may be asked to provide training in assistive technology, independent living skills, or social skills, or be asked to make arrangements for a student to try out different work experiences.

Rehabilitation agencies serve adults with disabilities who are interested in work but whose disabilities constitute a handicap for work. It is not enough simply to have a disability to qualify for rehabilitation services, as is the case in qualifying for special education services. An individual must also be able to indicate how the disability inhibits or prohibits him or her from going to work. For example, a person who loses an arm has a disability, but if the work that person does is as a social worker the loss of an arm does not constitute a vocational handicap. In contrast, if the person who loses an arm is a pianist, that loss would be considered a vocational handicap. (For more information on rehabilitation agencies, see Appendix A, "Agencies that Provide Services for Adults," at the end of this chapter.)

There is a second expectation in rehabilitation: that the services provided will, in fact, enhance the likelihood of the individual going to work. Historically, rehabilitation programs were established to help adults with adventitious disabilities—those acquired in adulthood, as the result of injury, illness, or trauma, not those present from birth—in returning to work after sustaining an injury. It is important to be aware of this background in order to understand the very different approaches that rehabilitation agencies use in determining who is eligible for services in comparison to the educational system. In general, adults with disabilities apply for services from rehabilitation agencies and must be determined eligible according to these two criteria: that there is a disability and that the disability constitutes a vocational handicap. There is a reasonable expectation that, with the provision of rehabilitation services, the individual will go to work.

Your child will need to apply for rehabilitation services if he or she is 18 years old, unless you retain legal responsibility as his or her guardian.

Without such guardianship, you can only attend meetings with the rehabilitation counselor and your child with your child's permission: your child is the client or consumer of rehabilitation services, not you. However, before a child is age 18, the parent or legal guardian may act on behalf of the child and make inquiries about what rehabilitation services are available and might be obtained by him or her. Some states have rehabilitation personnel (counselors, teachers, case workers, mobility instructors, and assistive technology instructors) who can work with children as well as adults; in other states these services are only available to adults. In addition, there are both public (government-funded) and private (supported through donations) rehabilitation agencies. To find agencies or organizations that might be helpful in your state you can consult the *AFB Directory of Services for Blind and Visually Impaired Services in the United States and Canada* (see the Resources section for more information). Adult services vary widely from state to state. For your soon-to-be-adult child to benefit from them, you will need to do some exploring and shopping around, much as you will need to do if your child plans to attend college or enroll in a vocational training program.

Depending on the state, transition plans may be written into the students' regular IEPs or may be separate documents (sometimes referred to as an Individualized Transition Plan) and attached to the IEP as an addendum. Either way, the transition plan is considered as an integral part of the IEP. As with any IEP, the transition plan must be updated annually or more often if needed. As Chapter 4 indicates, IEPs can be substantial in length. A portion of a sample IEP showing a summary statement on transition can be seen in Appendix B at the end of this chapter. To help you keep track of the various steps involved in transition planning, the accompanying "Transition IEP Checklist" provides a list of the IEP transition process and what you can expect from your child's school.

Involving the Student

Transition planning is to be done with students, not for them, or to them. This principle means that your child will be asked to attend the IEP meeting and to participate in the creation of his or her IEP when planning transition activities (this invitation is required by law). Under IDEA, students and their families are considered members of the educational team. As soon as your child reaches an appropriate age (when in late elementary or early middle school or junior high school, depending on his or her level of maturity), he or she may be asked to begin attending IEP meetings. You may initiate the invitation—just let the other team members know that you wish to include your child so that no one is surprised. Involvement in the IEP process may help your child clarify his or her interests

Transition IEP Checklist

Parents or guardians of students who are visually impaired can use this checklist to monitor transition planning and make sure that appropriate services and considerations for their child are put in place. If the items included in this list are not provided, parents may find it helpful to contact their child's primary teacher or case manager to request them or bring them up for discussion during the IEP meeting.

BEFORE THE FIRST IEP MEETING

After the student turns 16 (or younger, if determined appropriate by the IEP team):

☐ My child received an invitation to his or her IEP meeting to establish a transition plan.

☐ I received an invitation to his or her IEP meeting to establish a transition plan.

☐ The invitation included the following information: when the meeting will be held, where the meeting will be held, and who else has been invited to attend. Participants might include the teacher of students with visual impairments, related service providers (O&M instructor, occupational or physical therapist, school psychologist, or others), general education teachers, representatives from community agencies such as public and private rehabilitation personnel, and others as appropriate.

☐ The invitation indicated that one of the reasons for the meeting is to put together a statement of transition service needs or a statement of needed transition services.

☐ My child and I are prepared to attend this IEP meeting. We have given thought to his or her postsecondary training, employment, and living goals. We have also considered his or her present strengths and weaknesses in the general education (academic) curriculum as well as in areas of disability-specific skills (braille, use of optical devices, assistive technology, etc.).

AT THE IEP MEETING

☐ My child's IEP includes a statement of his or her current performance related to the skills he or she will need to transition successfully from public school to defined post-school environments (for example, college, vocational training, work, or independent or supported living). [Note: This statement of your child's present levels of educational performance should include how the child's disability affects involvement and progress in the general curriculum.]

☐ My child's IEP includes a statement of needed transition services, including

   ☐ Instruction at school or in the community to prepare for postsecondary academic or vocational goals.

   ☐ Related services, such as O&M, career counseling, or training with assistive technology.

   ☐ Community experiences, such as volunteer work, shopping for groceries, and travel to community facilities (library, hospital, recreation centers, and so forth).

   ☐ Employment or other post-school objectives, such as participation in vocational skills training courses, college or university programs, or apprentice or internship programs.

   ☐ Instruction in daily living skills (learning how to take care of oneself and one's possessions).

   ☐ A functional vocational evaluation that considers my child's interests, abilities, values, work personality, and needs.

☐ The activities listed on the IEP are presented as a coordinated set of activities (responsibility for the activities is shared by school personnel, staff from other agencies, my child, our family, and other interested parties). [Note: When appropriate, a statement of the interagency responsibilities or any needed linkages should be included.]

☐ The activities listed on the IEP seem likely to help my child succeed in meeting his or her post-school goals.

☐ The IEP includes a statement of how my child's progress toward annual goals will be measured and how I (we) will regularly be informed of progress toward the annual goals and the extent to which that progress is sufficient to enable my child to achieve them by the end of the year.

☐ At least 1 year before my child reaches the age of majority under state law, the IEP includes a statement that he or she has been informed of his or her rights under IDEA and an explanation of what rights, if any, will transfer to my child on reaching the age of majority.

and desires, make the educational program and the IEP process more meaningful, involve your child actively in decisions concerning his or her life, and help nurture a sense of responsibility and maturity. All of these, in turn, will assist in your child's development as an independent adult.

In planning for transition, you may want to assist your child in preparing for this important activity by spending time before the IEP meeting discussing his or her goals for the future and helping your child understand the importance of planning for life beyond high school. Find out as much as you can about what dreams and aspirations your child has by talking to your child about his or her interests and thinking about your own observations of interests and abilities your child has displayed. Help your child think about the classes he or she is currently enrolled in and what additional classes or activities would help your child best when considering work or college and adult life in general. What help, now and in the years before he or she leaves school, will provide your child with the skills, knowledge, and other preparation he or she might need to succeed in life?

If you and your child discuss these issues before attending IEP meetings, your child will be better prepared to discuss them with you, school staff and educational team members, and professionals such as rehabilitation counselors (or other adult service providers) while actively and effectively participating in the meeting. Rehabilitation counselors or certified vocational rehabilitation counselors are the case managers—the coordinators or overseers—of the public rehabilitation system. They assist eligible clients or consumers with the career exploration, preparation, and placement. (Chapter 8 contains more information on how parents can help prepare their children for transition and identify their interests and preferences.)

PREPARING EARLY FOR LIFE BEYOND SCHOOL: WHAT FAMILIES CAN DO

In many ways, the activities that your child engages in at home and the skills you teach your child are as important, if not more so, than the lessons that he or she learns in school and through participating in other activities such as sports and social events. Preparing for life as an adult requires both the academic skills taught at school and the personal and social skills typically taught at home. Some of the more important and valuable steps that you can take as a parent to prepare your child for life beyond school are showing him or her attitudes and ways of behaving as part of your daily lives that will be of help in the future.

Because being a parent can be one of life's most rewarding experiences, but also one of the most challenging, you may want to find other people to talk to about ways of helping your child move toward a happy, successful, and independent life. Others who can be helpful might include other parents, your child's teacher of visually impaired students, and members of support groups and national organizations for people who are visually impaired and for parents of visually impaired children. (The Resources section of this book describes organizations, publications, and other sources of information and help.)

Convey High Expectations

Parents are the first and most consistent teachers that their children will ever have. You set the stage in many ways for how your child approaches the transition process and life as an adult—and life in general. If you have always expected your child to perform to the best of his or her ability, your child is more likely to be prepared to work with your family, the educational team, and other professionals to prepare plans for the future and act on them. If, for example, you assume that your child can and will do the same chores and activities that other children do, he or she is likely to be better prepared for the independent life planned during the transition process. If, however, you have assumed that your child needs help from other people to participate in most activities, your child may come to believe that he or she cannot be independent. In such cases, your child may find it difficult to prepare for the transition from childhood into adult roles and responsibilities.

Conveying high expectations for children and young people is important for their sense of self-esteem, and this is true for all children, whether they have a disability or not. As already noted, they may need to learn different ways of performing certain activities, may take a little longer initially to grasp concepts and skills, and may need more explanation and hands-on demonstrations in some instances than sighted children. But their families need to express the expectation that they can and will learn the concepts and perform the skills that their friends, siblings, and others their age are performing. Although some children with additional disabilities may not have the same level of general understanding and acquire the same skills as nondisabled children their age, parents and teachers need to expect them to achieve to their potential by challenging them to do the best that they can. In this way, all children, including those with visual and other disabilities, are treated with respect and dignity for their abilities and potential and will have a better chance of achieving that potential.

Conveying high expectations and expecting that a child can do more rather than less may not always be easy for any parent. But it is both healthy and helpful for a child to know that he or she is competent at many things. If you see that your child cannot perform a particular task, it is appropriate to step in and help him or her to learn that skill, but parents and teachers need to be patient and give visually impaired children a chance to respond and to act before we jump in and do things for them. Children with visual impairments—in fact, all children and adults, too—learn best when they are allowed to try skills and determine for themselves whether the behavior or skill works for them. Before answering your child's questions, ask for his or her ideas or thoughts on the subject. If you don't always provide the answers, your child will learn more quickly how to problem solve. If you expect your child to be a problem solver, it reinforces the idea that he or she is capable. (Chapter 8 includes the experiences of a student with multiple disabilities and his parent in activities and relationships that allow him to develop his own competence.)

Encourage Responsible Behavior

One of the primary ways in which all children can learn to be responsible is by performing chores at home. Children with visual impairments are no exception. From early in their lives, children need to be asked to pick up after themselves and put their things away: toys, clothes, and books. They gradually need to assume more and more responsibility as they get older: helping their parents with basic housekeeping such as sweeping, vacuuming, washing and drying dishes, and doing the laundry. And they need to be taught how to perform basic tasks such as making a bed and then be expected routinely to apply the skills they have learned. In some instances, they may need to learn other ways to carry out a task that their parents or siblings do using their sense of vision. In this way they will learn how to take care of themselves and begin to manage their own belongings and environment.

For example, children who are blind or visually impaired cannot sort their laundry into whites and colored clothes using their vision. But various systems can be used to help them mark their clothes to indicate what color a garment is: brailled tags or differently shaped buttons sewn into their clothes, for example. Parents can discuss with the teacher of students with visual impairments how to teach their children ways of doing certain activities. It may seem time-consuming and even inconvenient to have children with visual impairments do household chores, because they may do them differently from their parents or siblings and may take longer to do them. However, having children participate as responsible members of the family will be of great benefit to them and will help them keep up developmentally with children their same age. A child who learns how to master certain chores can also later be encouraged to do them for extended family members or neighbors in need of occasional help and discover a way in which to make some pocket money, leading to independence in another way.

Recognize the Importance of Incidental Learning

One of the most important ways in which you as the parent of a child with visual impairments can help your child prepare for adult life is to recognize that he or she cannot learn incidentally from the environment—that is, just by casually observing the world. Sighted people scan the environment constantly, without conscious thought, and learn what is going on close at hand and in the distance. They see how people are dressed and how they live and behave. Many children with visual impairments are at an information disadvantage compared with their sighted peers. They need the people in their lives who care about them to tell them about what they are missing visually. This information may include items like the latest fashion trends, other people's use of gestures, how things that can't be touched work, how objects look that are too distant to touch or see with limited vision, and how those new things compare to things that are familiar to the child.

From a Parent's Perspective

FITTING IN

The first thing people noticed about Nathan was the cute outfit and darling shoes. Only much later did they notice he didn't focus his eyes. By then, the "sweet" outfit had already won. People weren't uncomfortable because they had already identified Nathan as "such a cute baby . . . such a sweet outfit." He "fit in." When his disability was noticed, it didn't seem so bad.

Call it egotism or call it survival, but after that experience, I always made sure that Nathan was well dressed when we went out into the community. I wanted people to see him first, not the disability. Like it or not, when we "fit in" we are more accepted. Clothes provide a way for us to be like everyone else. Ask any teenager.

I still make sure that Nathan wears the latest clothing styles, that his hair is cut like his peers', that he looks "cool." It's important to him to fit in, to receive compliments from others, to be noticed in a positive way. It's important for me, too. Dressing like everyone else is one way to foster acceptance.

Susan Singler
Mother of a 24-year-old son with retinopathy of
prematurity and additional disabilities
Nashville, Tennessee

To learn about things that can't be seen, children with visual impairments require detailed verbal descriptions of them and the opportunity to touch and explore, whenever possible, the item being described. Parents and family members play an important role in the lives of children with visual impairments as they describe what they see happening in the world around them. They bring their child into close proximity so that he or she can experience the world through touch, smell, and, when possible, remaining vision.

Foster Social Skills

Incidental learning is particularly important for building social skills, which are the ways in which we all behave when we are with other people. Through incidental learning, most people determine what behaviors are acceptable to others. Although some social rules are often announced out loud, such as "Cover your mouth when you cough!" children often learn to follow social rules when they see how others behave and watch the reactions of those around them when they don't follow the rules. Frowns speak volumes to children. Without seeing the reactions of others, children with visual impairments may not realize the negative consequences of not behaving in a socially acceptable way. Adults in their lives need to speak their feelings in reaction to social missteps, for example, "Please give me a chance to answer after you ask a question instead of continuing to talk," or "Please cover your nose when you sneeze."

Another aspect of building social skills that relies heavily on incidental learning for sighted children is learning nonverbal communication skills and gestures. Children who are blind or visually impaired may need to be shown how to gesture appropriately. They may need hands-on instruction to learn how to wave hello and good-bye, shrug their shoulders to indicate that they don't understand something, and shake their heads to indicate "yes" or "no." Likewise, they won't be able to see the facial expressions of others and therefore will need to receive positive reinforcement from those who care about them when they make the appropriate expression, or be corrected when they don't. Practicing both gestures and facial expressions as games or when reading stories that lend themselves to these kinds of activity when children are young can be fun and helpful as well. When children arrive in preschool and kindergarten, they will be more easily accepted into classroom activities and social interactions if they understand how their facial expressions and gestures are seen by those around them. Teachers of students with visual impairments can offer parents suggestions and guidance on how to help children become aware of these important behaviors that will help them become socially accepted throughout their lives.

READY OR NOT . . .

Everyone around your child is changing, just as she or he is, and we need to recognize that. Parents of children with visual impairments need to be their fashion advisors, not just fashion police. It's up to us to make sure they look like their peers. It's up to us to make them aware of what is on display at the mall, in the electronics store, and over the counter at McDonald's. All of this is part of our job of helping them see.

Our children have a significant disadvantage entering the workforce—the attitudes of others. It will possibly be their *greatest* challenge—how to help others see that while they may not see, they can still *do*.

In order for parents to prepare our children, we have to be their eyes. How do they eat? How do they look? Head up? Confident handshake? Forward movement? Etiquette at meals and in greeting others? Posture? Clothing? Our children may not see the effect of these things—but others do.

So, for parents the question is, What current daily living skills need some help at this particular time in this particular place? What braille, cane, dog guide, fashion, or etiquette skills could use some work, given this time and place?

Beyond these questions, though, I found a larger question looming— what about the next step in school and what happens then, job or career, or life? Sometimes I would get so focused on the next grade or year or doctor's appointment, I would forget the reason for all of these meetings—transitioning to adulthood, just like every other child.

Transitions are going to happen whether we are ready or not. When we periodically update not only braille, but also the total package, we prepare our children for a more normal life of work, love, and friendship.

Kevin E. O'Connor
Father of an 18-year-old son with Leber's congenital amaurosis
Long Grove, Illinois

If youngsters have not learned these social lessons during childhood, they will need to be taught them as they approach graduation from the public school system. They are part of what make a successful transition into adulthood possible. Social skills, including the understanding of nonverbal communication skills and appropriate facial expressions, are critical to building friendships and relationships with people outside of the immediate family. For example, having appropriate social skills can make the difference between getting or not getting a job. In addition, a person with or without a disability is far more likely to find satisfactory employment through a network of friends and personal acquaintances than any other way.

Encourage Career Awareness

Incidental learning not only contributes to an individual's understanding of social life, it also contributes to an understanding of the world of work. Just by watching people in their daily lives, sighted children learn what jobs are being performed by those around them, what tools the workers use, what uniforms workers wear, and where they work. Students with visual impairments need considerable input on this topic because so much of this information is visual. They need to know what occupations their parents and family, neighbors, friends, and people in the community perform. The more that their families share with them about the work involved in various jobs, tools and technology used in different professions, and careers that exist in today's world, the better will be their understanding of the working world. When possible, they need to be able to explore environments through the sense of touch. For example, visiting a firehouse and touching a firefighter's hat, axe, truck, hose, and other tools and equipment, and having a chance to talk with the firefighters there is to see some of the realities of that profession without vision. If all a child has ever seen is a toy truck or has only heard about firefighting in stories, the ideas he or she may have of firefighting may not be realistic. In addition to learning about jobs that are obvious in the community, such as those of firefighters or store clerks, visually impaired children will benefit from being told about the jobs "behind the scenes" that support the more overt roles. For example, the dispatcher's job, the mechanic's job, and other support positions that may not be mentioned in stories or made apparent on class field trips need to be described. As they move through childhood, children and teenagers will benefit from going into different work settings when opportunities present themselves and talking with the people employed there. Having a chance to ask about the job duties and tools or equipment used help students understand the different kinds of work that people do. It gives each child a chance to nurture his or her own curiosity and possible interest in work.

Through incidental learning, sighted children and teenagers identify adults in the community, on television, or in movies that they emulate or strive to be like. For children with visual impairments, it is not always easy to find successful adults with visual conditions similar to their own. However, by contacting national organizations for people who are visually impaired and speaking with teachers of students with visual impairments, parents may be able to locate young and older adults who are visually impaired, are pursuing work successfully, and who are willing to speak with children about what they do. Another valuable resource for parents and children is CareerConnect (www.afb.org/careerconnect), a database maintained online by the American Foundation for the Blind, which connects people with mentors—visually impaired individuals who are working successfully and who are willing to discuss their work and the technology they use in performing it.

Offer Realistic Feedback

Parents can help their children in the transition from childhood to adult life, and can contribute to their development in general, by providing them with realistic feedback. Do they behave, dress, and act their age and in a way that is socially and otherwise acceptable? Do they complete the same kinds of chores at home and in the neighborhood as other children do? Do they complete the chores in the way in which they need to be performed, or are they left undone? Do they know current trends and participate in events that are part of the social scene? Parents who can praise their children for behavior that is appropriate and for work that is well done, but also give them helpful feedback on how to improve or correct their behavior, are providing them with information their children need to be successful outside their homes. If children are sheltered from certain realities, they may be surprised when they go to college or begin work, where their parents' standards will be replaced by the standards of professors and employers.

Encourage and Help Identify Interests

In general, parents can help their children, whether visually impaired or not, to begin to develop their own interests and possible future careers in a number of ways. By being aware of what their children seem to enjoy and providing repeated opportunities for that enjoyment, by noticing what their children do well or have an ability or aptitude for and commenting positively on that aptitude, and by providing children with a wealth of different direct experiences—visits to friends and family, family vacations, trips to local community events and places, from stores to farms, libraries, and museums—parents can help their children discover what they like to do and what they might want to do after school. As children approach young adulthood, various resources are available to provide additional information that helps them to analyze their interests, abilities, values, and work personalities. Two helpful resources for students with visual impairments and their families are CareerConnect (www.afb.org/careerconnect) and *Navigating the Rapids of Life: The Transition Tote System.* (See For More Information at the end of this chapter.)

There are many ways in which you can encourage your child to develop his or her interests and explore career possibilities (Chapter 8 contains additional suggestions for parents):

- Help your child connect with the people in his or her life to discuss what their hobbies and work are. Ask friends and family members if they would discuss their work with your child, and if they would be willing to have your child visit them on the job. In addition to friends and family, members of your community such as your family doctor or veterinarian, car mechanic, or neighborhood librarian are great sources of information and support to your child in these explorations. Conversations and relationships with people who know your child can in time lead to opportunities for part-time work that can further help your child decide what he or she would like to think about as a career.

- Ask your child's teacher of students with visual impairments for suggestions on how to encourage and support your child in interests you've observed that he or she has. Numerous organizations for visually impaired people focus on specific activities for both work and leisure and can provide information, such as the United States Association for Blind Athletes, National Association of Blind Lawyers, and United States Braille Chess Association. Some of these organizations can be found through the *AFB Directory of Services for Blind and Visually Impaired Persons in the United States and Canada* (see the Resources section of this book for more information) and through Internet searches.

- Contact national organizations of parents and for people who are visually impaired to explore possibilities such as conferences or meetings and individual contact with visually impaired adults who are performing work of interest to your child and who can act as role models.

FOCUSES FOR PLANNING

When you begin planning for your child's future after school, you may find it helpful to organize the large, and perhaps intimidating, topic of transition into smaller, more manageable areas or parts that are described in more detail in this section. By thinking about your child's interests, abilities, and needs in each of these areas, you can help to ensure that more thorough planning and appropriate arrangements, services, and supports have been considered in each vital area affecting your child's life as an adult. Begin planning early, so that you can anticipate and help your child prepare while he or she is still in school and can more easily obtain helpful transition services.

Here are some of the kinds of questions you might want to start by asking and the areas they relate to:

- **Postsecondary education and training:** Will my child continue his or her education, or pursue some other kind of training directly after high school?

- **Housing and living arrangements:** Where will my child live after high school?

- **Transportation:** How will my child get around and travel independently?

- **Work experiences:** Will my child work directly after high school, and, if so, in what kind of work?

- **Social relationships, recreation, and leisure:** How will my child have a satisfying and happy life as an adult after high school?

Activities related to each of these areas could be included in your child's IEP as transition-related objectives or services. For example, your child might have an objective on the transition IEP to determine whether to attend a local community college after high school graduation. A service that could be provided might be a campus visit with the orientation and mobility (O&M) instructor to investigate transportation options and determine the ease with which the campus can be navigated using a long cane or optical devices. "Tools for Making Decisions about Transition Beyond School," in Chapter 8, contains information about specific tools to help families who are planning for their visually impaired child's future.

Postsecondary Education and Training

Many young people graduating from high school or leaving the public school system continue their studies in colleges, universities, or other postsecondary training. If your son or daughter plans to attend a college or university, he or she may need to complete specific high school courses required by the school he or she wishes to attend. Your child can investigate what courses the college or university requires, and then meet with a high school guidance counselor to ensure that he or she is scheduled for those classes.

Applying for college is a complicated process. In addition to consulting with your child's guidance counselor and teacher of students with visual impairments, you may wish to consult some of the numerous books available in libraries and bookstores on the topic. To prepare for choosing a college or university and completing applications, your child may also wish to enroll in helpful courses offered by the Hadley School for the Blind (see the Resources section of this book). These include correspondence and distance education courses specifically geared for visually impaired students and their families. *College Bound: A Guide for Students with Visual Impairments* also contains extensive information on choosing and applying for college, as well as some of the skills your child will need to negotiate a college education. Another resource for students planning to continue their education beyond high school is the *Transition Activity Calendar for Students with Visual Impairments.* This resource provides in a checklist format information to consider, starting in junior high school, as your child prepares for college. (See "For More Information" at the end of this chapter.)

If your child doesn't plan to attend college, he or she may want to participate in training opportunities in the community after high school. Whether your child wants to attend a gourmet cooking school or take massage therapy classes, he or she will need to prepare instructors and staff about the techniques, materials, or devices he or she uses while studying, such as a magnifier or electronic notetaking device. Your child may want to explore ahead of time any training that is of interest to find out what coursework will be required, what tools are being used, and what instructional materials will need to be accessed. When considering a specialized training program, it is important to find out if the school or program has a placement program for graduates. If so, ask what their placement rate is. It is also helpful to find out whether the instructor has ever worked with a visually impaired person. Questions such as whether materials are available in alternative formats other than print and whether assistive technology is used in libraries or classrooms are important too. Your child may have to explain to staff the accommodations and modifications needed for him or her to participate actively in the programs. Preparing this explanation is an important activity in itself for transition, and the information can be used and updated whenever your child applies for training programs or work opportunities in the future.

Transition activities that can help in the preparation for postsecondary training may include the following:

- Studying and preparing for the SAT or ACT examinations that are required of applicants to many colleges.
- Learning notetaking skills (with both low-tech tools such as paper and pen or slate and stylus and high-tech tools such as electronic notetaking devices).
- Learning or refining organizational skills.

- Improving effective listening and study skills.

- Becoming familiar with audio, electronic, or Web-Braille books such as those available from Recording for the Blind and Dyslexic, the Library of Congress National Library Service for the Blind and Physically Handicapped, Bookshare, or other sources of materials in alternate media for visually impaired persons (see the Resources section of this book for more information).

- Locating and purchasing materials (bold-lined or braille paper, felt-tipped pens, cassette tapes, CDs, DVDs, notebooks, three-ring binders, file or report folders) for school projects independently.

- Developing competent computer skills and a knowledge of assistive technology devices and how to use them.

- Conducting research online while working with assistive technology such as speech output devices or screen enlargement programs to access Internet sites, use search engines, and understand how to navigate web sites.

- Preparing to explain and request or advocate for accommodations or modifications necessary for participation in learning or work environments.

- Practicing how to explain the ramifications of living with a visual disability to strangers and acquaintances such as professors, classmates, or coaches.

College Bound: A Guide for Students with Visual Impairments contains information on how to build such essential skills and a wide range of other topics related to students and families in the process of applying for and starting college.

As your child approaches the end of high school, you both need to be aware that the services provided under IDEA will come to an end. You will need to plan accordingly and become familiar with a new world. While students are in elementary or secondary school, their rights to certain educational services are guaranteed under IDEA, and an IEP clearly explains all their services and educational goals. Once they are in college, the accommodations and services to which they are entitled are mandated through Section 504 of the Rehabilitation Act of 1973 and the Americans with Disabilities Act of 1990 (ADA). These laws have different provisions from those that covered students in kindergarten through 12th grade, and colleges do not necessarily have to provide the same services as high schools do. Once in college, the job of documenting disability and arranging for accommodations falls to the student him- or herself (see "After High School, the Rules Change").

It will be to your child's benefit to become familiar with rights and responsibilities under these laws and to gain a clear understanding of

After High School, the Rules Change

College is different from high school in many ways, and it's not just that the classes are more advanced or that students may be living on their own. In college, students with visual impairments, like their sighted classmates, need to take a lot more responsibility for their own education as well as for other aspects of their day-to-day life. Students with disabilities will need to advocate for themselves to get any special services or accommodations they need.

The following side-by-side comparisons show some of the differences in the laws that cover special educational services for people with disabilities and how responsibilities for these services change after high school.

Public High School	*Postsecondary Educational Institution*
Governing law: Individuals with Disabilities Act (IDEA), which guarantees a free, appropriate public education.	Governing law: Section 504 of the Rehabilitation Act of 1973 and the Americans with Disabilities Act (ADA), which provide for accessibility and reasonable accommodations to prevent discrimination on the basis of disability.
The law covers students ages 3–21 or until they meet regular high school diploma requirements.	The laws cover students with disabilities regardless of age. Schools may not discriminate in recruitment, admission, or after admission solely on the basis of a disability.
School attendance is mandatory.	Students decide to attend and will probably pay tuition.
Districts are required to identify students with disabilities through free assessment and the Individualized Education Program (IEP) process.	Students are responsible for identifying their disability and providing current documentation. They must be their own advocates.
Students receive special education and related services to address needs based on an identified disability.	Formal special education services are not available.

Services include individually designed instruction, modifications, and accommodations based on the IEP.	Reasonable accommodations may be made to provide equal access and participation. Schools are not required to make accommodations that modify essential elements of the curriculum, program, or activity or pose an undue burden for the school.
Individual students' needs based on the IEP may be addressed by program support for school personnel.	No formal program support for school personnel is provided.
Progress toward IEP goals is monitored and communicated to the parent(s) and/or the student.	Students are required to monitor their own progress and communicate their needs to instructors.
Schools assist in connecting the student with community support agencies if so identified as a transition need according to the IEP.	Students are responsible for making their own connections with community support agencies.
Parent involvement is encouraged.	College staff are not permitted to disclose information about students, even to parents, according to the federal Family Educational Rights and Privacy Act (FERPA).

Adapted from E. Trief and R. Feeney, *College Bound: A Guide for Students with Visual Impairments* (New York: AFB Press, 2005), pp. 53–56; source adapted with permission by Disabled Student Services, California State University at Fullerton.

what accommodations are legal and appropriate. However, you and your child may be reassured to know that these laws prevent discrimination on the basis of visual impairment. There are several important sources of up-to-date information about legal rights that your family may find helpful:

- The Office for Civil Rights in the U.S. Department of Education has information on both the ADA and Section 504 at www.ed.gov/policy/rights/guid/ocr/disability.html. This office also publishes helpful information such as "Students with Disabilities Preparing for Postsecondary Education: Know Your Rights and Responsibilities," available both online and in print.

- For more information about the Americans with Disabilities Act of 1990, see www.ada.gov.

- For more information about Section 504 of the Rehabilitation Act of 1973, see www.hhs.gov/ocr/504.html.

Housing

Some young people will continue to live at home after leaving school and some may live in dormitories or apartments while attending college or other postsecondary training. Sooner or later, most will live away from home. Types of living options and choices for a student will vary, based not only on personal desires but also on geographic locations (rural or urban), the availability of transportation, nearness to work or training, amount of supervision and care needed by the student, relationships with siblings and other family members, nature and severity of the student's disability, and money available from earnings or other sources. Your child's competence in daily living skills, skills for community participation, and age-appropriate social skills are additional factors to consider in analyzing the type of living options that will be available to your child when he or she becomes an adult.

Although your child probably will not know as a teenager exactly how or where he or she wants to live as an adult, a useful activity in transition planning can be selecting a particular living arrangement and preparing—and acting out—a practice plan for a hypothetical future. Areas for discussion, coaching, instruction, and practice include how to find an apartment, prepare a budget that includes rent, sign a lease, make a deposit and pay the first month's rent, connect telephone service, pay electric bills, locate transportation services, buy furniture (either new or used), make simple home repairs, stock the kitchen, buy linens and towels, and the many other tasks related to living independently for the first time. You may choose to do these kinds of activities with your child or you may request that such activities be included on your child's IEP.

At home, you can help your child understand some of the aspects of living independently by sharing information about how much it costs to run your household and the amount of energy and time it takes the members of your family. You may want to have your child help you with paying bills, maintaining your home and yard, and shopping for groceries, household products, and yard equipment. You can involve your child in obtaining the services you need for your home, such as those supplied by plumbers, electricians, and carpenters. Whether your child is planning on living in a college dormitory or his or her own apartment, visiting the actual location, planning for practical arrangements, and orienting your child to the living space and surrounding area are important parts of preparing for independent life. While your child is still in school, consulting with his or her teacher of students with visual impairments and O&M instructor can be an essential part of this preparation.

If your child will not be able to live independently following school and will need fairly extensive supervision and support, housing options could include a group home, supported apartment, or an intermediate care facility for mentally retarded individuals. In such cases, it is very important to have a representative from your local developmental disabilities agency at the IEP meeting when housing transition services are discussed. If a representative is not listed on the invitation you receive in advance of your child's IEP meeting and you think one needs to be present, call and ask the IEP coordinator or your child's teacher to help with getting someone there. Funding for these types of housing may be available in your state, but it may be necessary for your child to have received a diagnosis of a developmental disability.

Although your child may not need housing outside your home for several years, if he or she will need an intermediate care facility or supported housing, it is important that you, your family, and the school locate resources as soon as possible (you may even want to start this process while your child is still in elementary school), since eligibility may require documentation and possible assessment of your child. It can be helpful to contact several organizations who operate group homes to determine what skills residents are expected to have in order to be accepted. These skills can then become transition IEP goals related to future housing options.

Group homes are residential programs designed to house between three and eight adults with severe disabilities in a home setting within the community. Most group homes are funded through state departments of mental health and mental retardation. They typically provide room and board, skills training, support services in such areas as money management and other personal needs as necessary, and monitoring of health needs. A key aspect of group homes is that the supervision of residents is supposed to be based on individual needs and residents have written habilitation plans, which are similar to IEPs and spell out the activities and goals for them. Visiting group homes so that you and your child can understand what future options are available is a valuable experience. Some group homes have open houses for families and potential residents. Whenever possible, it is important that other members of the IEP team, including teachers and related service providers, also visit the group homes.

Supported living facilities are designed to allow an individual with disabilities to live in a home of his or her choosing and receive assistance from service providers as needed. Training and support may focus on such skills as money and time management, meal planning and shopping, O&M, integration into community and recreational activities, or any other service deemed necessary for independent or semi-independent living. State or federal funding may be used to pay for living in a supported living facility if an individual is eligible through Social Security, Medicare or Medicaid, or another source. Individuals with disabilities are encouraged under state programs to use funding to purchase services from individuals of their choosing, such as neighbors, family, or friends, who are referred to as "natural supporters."

For young adults with the most severe or profound disabilities, or those who need a structured setting, *intermediate care facilities for mentally retarded individuals* may be available. These facilities are administered through state departments of mental health and mental retardation and funded by Medicaid. They provide housing, medical services, and some skills training. All facilities must be fully accessible for people who are disabled and require a high ratio of staff to residents. Admission to such facilities often involves a wait, and space is limited to those individuals with the greatest need for support.

Transportation

By the time transition planning begins when your child is 16, he or she is best served by being able to travel safely, efficiently, and independently at school, at home, and in the neighborhood, just like his or her classmates without disabilities. Although the O&M instructor is the person from whom your child will learn these skills, you, as your child's parent, are often the one to decide whether or not your child uses the skills learned. Will you allow your son or daughter to travel independently using a cane or optical devices, or use community transportation such as buses or subway systems? Or will you allow your child to travel only with you as a sighted guide or in your car? As with many other activities in life, building confidence in one's mobility skills and becoming expert at them requires practice in using them. If you are concerned about your child's ability to travel independently, you may want to observe him or her during a mobility lesson to educate yourself about his or her level of expertise, or perhaps observe your child from a distance as he or she is trying out new travel skills.

The need to solve transportation dilemmas (whether to walk, ride the bus or subway, take a taxi, or drive with a friend or parent, for example) never goes away for young people and adults with visual impairments. Driving a car is rarely an option for people who are severely visually impaired (except in the most unusual of circumstances, in which an individual who is legally blind may have adequate residual vision to drive using bioptic aids).

Travel Cost Analysis

1. List all the ways you can get to one place in the column on the left.
2. Score each method according to cost, time, and independence:

   1 = An advantage

   2 = Neither an advantage nor a disadvantage

   3 = A disadvantage
3. Add the scores together and write the total in the column on the right.
4. Choose the type of transportation that has the lowest score.

Activity: Going to the mall to shop for clothes.

	Cost	Time	Independence	TOTAL
Ride with a friend	1	1	2	4
Take a cab	3	2	1	6
Ask parents for a ride	1	1	3	5
Take the bus	1	3	1	5

Adapted with permission from J. N. Erin and K. E. Wolffe, *Transition Issues Related to Students with Visual Disabilities* (Austin, TX: PRO-ED, 1999).

You can teach your child a simple way of evaluating transportation options that can be used during adult life as well. To make good decisions about available transportation choices, young people can actually chart their options and analyze a final solution. With this method, you assign a numerical value to each possible method of travel according to its cost and convenience and the independence it provides. You then tally the scores for each option to determine the most desirable one: the option with the lowest score. The "Travel Cost Analysis" shown in this chapter is an example. In this instance, riding with a friend seems to be the best choice for getting to the mall, with the lowest score of 4. Taking a taxi appears to be the least viable option, with the highest score of 6. By teaching your child an objective strategy for thinking through transportation situations, you can help him or her with an important life skill.

Other ideas and strategies for preparing your child to manage without the use of a car for getting about in the community include the following:

- Matching the money your child saves toward a transportation fund (much as you might do if he or she were going to buy a car).

- Allowing your child to take the classroom portion of a driver's education course so that he or she can learn the rules of the road and be an informed passenger.

- Using public transportation with your child whenever possible.

- Encouraging your child to help you with car maintenance so that he or she will be able to help friends who offer him or her rides.

- Keeping your child informed about the expense of operating a car and insisting that he or she contribute toward the cost of gas or tolls when riding with friends.

- Providing an alternative significant event as a psychological "rite of passage" for your child when other young people are getting their first driver's licenses. This event could be a trip across town or across state by bus, or an airplane trip to visit a friend from camp, a grandparent, or another significant adult or family member, so that your child will also feel that he or she can be an independent traveler.

Work Experiences

A critical aspect of the most important aspect of any transition plan is career exploration and preparation for employment through work experiences. Young people with disabilities who work while they are still in high school in either paid or volunteer positions are more likely to work as adults than those who do not work during school. An effective way of ensuring that your child is a desirable and employable potential worker is to include activities on his or her IEP that focus on initiating career exploration, acquiring job-seeking skills, and obtaining work experiences.

Another appropriate transition goal for your child's IEP is for your child to know and be able to describe to others the types of job modifications and accommodations that will be necessary for him or her to be competitive with co-workers who are not visually impaired. Job modifications and accommodations may include special lighting, glare-reducing computer shields, optical low vision devices, enlarged text, braille labeling, assistive technology (such as a computer with speech or braille output), tactile markings on office equipment to allow the visually impaired user to find the required settings, and other equipment or tools relating to your child's visual status or additional disabilities. The earlier that a student learns to evaluate his or her own needs in various situations and explain this information to others, the more likely it is that he or she will be able to explain them and request appropriate accommodations in training and at work—and to do so clearly and with a degree of comfort and assurance. Your child's teacher of visually impaired students can consult with you on the best ways for your child to learn how to meet his or her own needs in this area. It is a skill that will be helpful throughout life.

Work Preparation

At-school, after-school, and summer employment are crucial for building the skills and experience that will set your child apart from other children who simply attend classes and relax at home or with friends after school. These early work experiences set the stage for successful work experiences as an adult. In school, your child may be able to work as a student volunteer assisting with office and clerical tasks, helping in the school cafeteria, selling tickets for athletic events, or lending a hand in the mailroom. Some schools, often special schools for children with visual impairments, also offer paid jobs for students after school and in the summer. Students in vocational classes studying occupations in industries such as food service, horticulture, and maintenance can often get paid part-time jobs after a period of training in which they acquired the necessary basic skills to perform the jobs. Finally, in some states, collaborative agreements between educational and rehabilitation agencies provide paid summer work experiences for youngsters with visual impairments.

Although some young people who are visually impaired are able to obtain work experience on their own, many youngsters, like many sighted students, need the assistance of caring adults to obtain their first jobs. Parents, teachers, and rehabilitation counselors often help students with visual impairments find their early work experiences.

It will still be important, however, for your child to understand the process of how to obtain a job and to make a commitment to following through on work responsibilities. As a parent, you will want to see that your child learns about the activities and skills involved in looking for a job while in school so that he or she can find employment after graduation. For example, does your child know how to find job openings, apply for jobs, interview successfully, and dress appropriately for the kind of work he or she wants to do? Although in this country, state rehabilitation agencies provide training and assistance in job placement for people with disabilities, the assistance and individualized attention available is limited. It is not the same as the daily contact with teachers that a student receives while he or she is still in high school. To determine the level of support available through your state or local rehabilitation agency, you can request that a representative of the agency be present whenever possible at IEP meetings at which transition is being discussed. You can also request through the IEP process that your child be included in career exploration activities and job-seeking skills classes, and be engaged in actual job placement programs in which school (and sometimes rehabilitation) personnel help students find jobs.

For youngsters with multiple disabilities, summer and after-school jobs can be successful with the support of a job coach. Job coaches are on-the-job trainers who work with a student at a job site to help him or her learn the duties of a job and provide any necessary supports for successful interaction between the young person, the employer, and his or her co-workers. Ideally, the job coach works with the student's co-workers to help them understand how to provide support to the student as well. In this way, co-workers provide what are known as natural supports after the job coach finishes his or her involvement at the job site. Working with a job coach is referred to as "supported employment." Job coaches may be provided by the school while your child is entitled to special education services and then later by either rehabilitation or developmental disabilities agencies. If your child has multiple disabilities or is developmentally delayed, having an agency representative present at an IEP meeting who has knowledge of supported employment services can be extremely helpful. Your child's lead teacher or the school counselor should be able to help you identify agency resources if you don't know where to find someone knowledgeable in these areas.

Technology

Mastery of the computer is essential to many aspects of employment, postsecondary education, independent living, and community participation for everyone. Computers have become a basic tool used widely for obtaining information, communicating with others, conducting personal business, spending leisure time, studying, and working. Use of the computer and related assistive technology tools—special hardware and software adapted for use by people who are visually impaired—needs to be introduced and taught to the student who is visually impaired at the same time comparable skills are taught to his or her sighted classmates. Summer or weekend technology training seminars provided by rehabilitation agencies and other specialized service agencies can be essential in helping your child add to his or her computer skills. Under IDEA, your school should assess your child's needs for assistive technology and provide appropriate training as a mandated or required area of instruction.

Young people who are skilled computer users are ready to be part of today's workforce and society. It is therefore important for students to know which technology tools are most appropriate for use with their studies and how these tools can be used in the future as part of their work or career path. It is also useful for them to know how their specialized tools are similar to and different from computer and other equipment used by their sighted classmates. This knowledge will help them meet their own needs in life after school, when college professors, vocational training instructors, and future employers are not likely to be familiar with assistive technology used by visually impaired individuals. As the users of this technology, visually impaired students and employees will become the experts in these new environments. As a rule of thumb, students are best prepared if they have learned the following:

- What assistive technology is crucial for them to succeed in school and future work
- Where to obtain this technology: who the primary manufacturers and distributors are, how to reach those vendors, what the equipment costs initially and to maintain, and where to go for help with procurement and training
- How to operate their computer and other technology equipment with the off-the-shelf programs that they will be using in future training and work
- How to maintain their equipment and devices, as well as how, when, and whom to call for technical assistance
- How to download software updates and install them
- How to solve minor problems or tackle glitches that occur
- When to use back-up skills such as writing with a braille slate and stylus or using cassette recorders to "read" material, in case a device crashes or runs out of power.

Although becoming skilled in the use of technology may seem daunting, technology is an exciting area. The use of specialized equipment can provide your child with powerful abilities whose development needs to be encouraged. The use of technology and advances in the development of assistive technology have provided people who are visually impaired with opportunities and expanding ideas and information that did not exist several decades ago. Because of this, successful visually impaired individuals are typically users of technology. In addition to learning about technology in school, students can obtain information about it in a variety of ways, from discussing the subject with their teacher of students with visual impairments, contacting the state school for visually impaired students (many schools have expert instructors on staff), joining clubs and interest groups, exploring information available from national organizations for visually impaired persons, and investigating the computer training programs listed in such sources as the *AFB Directory of Services,* to browsing resources such as CareerConnect and *AccessWorld*, an online technology magazine.

Recreation, Leisure Activities, and Social Relationships

Recreation and social activities are an essential part of a full and successful adult life. Exploring choices for recreation and leisure in your community can be included as an objective on your child's IEP. For example, when planning and writing goals for mobility lessons, a young adult can request orientation to the local mall, theater, or community athletic fields. Finding out what community-based recreation and leisure activities are available and how to access and participate in those activities can also be included on your child's IEP as a transition-related activity.

By participating in recreation and leisure activities with nondisabled students, such as sports, performing arts, and social events, students who are visually impaired can both gain skills and nurture relationships that will help them to be included in other aspects of adult life. For all of us, social activities are where we find the people with similar interests and abilities who become our friends and acquaintances. They form our personal network, and most people, including those with disabilities, find employment through networking. Whenever possible, students with multiple disabilities also need to be encouraged to participate in their communities, to help them develop independence and relationships outside their families (see Chapter 8 for more information on this topic).

THE ROLE OF OTHER ORGANIZATIONS IN TRANSITION PLANNING

Although the primary responsibility of the school is to provide students with academic and daily life skills that will enable them to move successfully from school to adult environments such as work, a school is not equipped to be a job placement center, rehabilitation center, or independent living center. However, the school needs to help you and your child plan for obtaining these services, should he or she need them. Each state has its own network of agencies, and in some states separate agencies handle specific services for people who are visually impaired or have developmental disabilities (see the appendix, "Agencies that Provide Services for Adults"). The faculty and staff at your child's school can help you and your child identify and become connected with agencies in the community that can provide needed academic, vocational, social, or daily living services after your child graduates from or leaves high school. In addition to requesting information from school staff and your child's educational team about services for visually impaired adults and who provides them in your state and community, you and your child may want to research independently what services are available to help support your child. You may want to investigate local vocational rehabilitation programs where adults with disabilities traditionally receive services and training they may need to prepare for employment, such as career exploration, job placement, or help with postsecondary education and training. "Tips for Life Beyond School" lists a number of other items to consider at this time.

As already noted, as your child approaches the end of high school, it is particularly important to know that rehabilitation services and other adult services differ considerably from educational services provided to children in this country. First, educational services are mandated or required by the federal government, and all children are accepted for these services. Special education services are supplemental or supportive of the general education system and are available only to children with a disability, but all children under age 22 in the United States are mandated to receive a free, appropriate education. Rehabilitation services, however, are based on eligibility and are not mandated for any group. Individuals must apply for services without a guarantee that they will be accepted.

Second, educational services are provided free of charge to children and youths, but many adult services, including some private rehabilitation services and postsecondary education opportunities, are provided on a fee-for-service basis only. Colleges, universities, and other postsecondary training programs charge tuition or require a fee from applicants. Public rehabilitation services are provided free to those who meet certain criteria for financial need, which can vary from state to state. In some instances, services are provided on a sliding-fee scale in which people pay according to their income level rather than having to pay a set fee. For these reasons, parents cannot assume that all adult services will be available to their children without expense.

Third, schools typically cannot terminate services to your child (this can only happen under the most extreme circumstances), but adult agencies can terminate services if a recipient is uncooperative, fails to meet graduation criteria, or doesn't perform well and responsibly. While eligible for special education services, students receive everything they need to benefit from their education from the school or school-based personnel. The school is the de facto case manager that coordinates or oversees a child's education. As adults, however, students will have to find and apply for services from a variety of service providers and, if they are able to do so, will be expected to be their own case managers and to coordinate those services.

If your child is unable to function independently due to a cognitive impairment or multiple disabilities, any services he or she receives when leaving the public school system will be handled by a number of different

Tips for Life Beyond School

■ As soon as your child begins to travel independently or with friends, it is important that he or she obtains a picture identification card. Your local department of motor vehicles provides this service. A state-issued picture ID is also required to cash checks, pick up insured mail, travel by air or rail, and perform many other activities, and you may want to help your child obtain this card at an earlier age.

■ If your child plans to attend a college or university, he or she may need to take the SAT, ACT, or other admissions test. If such tests are required, it will be important to notify the testing authority of your child's need for any accommodations (braille, large print, or audiotaped materials; extended time for test taking; or use of magnification devices or other optical devices such as a video magnifier, or closed-circuit television) well in advance of the test date.

■ Colleges and universities have offices of disabled student services, and many provide a range of important on-campus assistance to students with disabilities. Have your child find out if the school he or she is considering has a disabled student services office and make contact with them.

■ Driving is usually not an option for students with severe visual impairments. For that reason, decisions about where to study, live, and work following high school need to take into consideration alternatives to driving, such as public transportation and proximity to services such as grocery stores, medical and dental facilities, and entertainment.

■ At age 18, your child can apply for Social Security benefits (SSI) that may be used to help him or her make the transition from childhood into adulthood. He or she may contact the Social Security Administration (SSA) office in your community for enrollment forms and information and to determine what benefits he or she may be eligible to receive.

■ Your child can consult the SSA's *Red Book,* a guide to employment support for individuals with disabilities under Social Security disability insurance and supplemental security programs, to understand Social Security benefits and responsibilities for reporting earned income fully. This publication is available online at www.socialsecurity.gov.

■ If your child is not going to be able to live independently in the community, sign up for supported living options well in advance of the date you hope to see him or her move out of your home.

■ If your child is not going to be able to make decisions independently, be sure to complete the necessary paperwork to assume full or limited legal guardianship or determine who will become your child's legal guardian when he or she reaches the age of majority.

agencies. You may need to act as the case manager or retain an independent case manager to deal with the array of service providers and agencies with which you will need to coordinate services. Independent case managers can be found through your medical insurance carrier, local human services organizations such as those for people with developmental disabilities, or home health agencies. An important component of transition planning is determining which services your child is likely to need as an adult. These might include housing, transportation, work, opportunities for socialization, training, medical care, personal assistance, or other related services. While your child is in school, you and the other members of the IEP team need to begin to set those up so there will be no gap in services. Services available to adults with multiple disabilities will vary from community to community. However, most communities have basic services available to adults with disabilities that include finding and funding postsecondary training options, locating transportation and housing, and providing help with securing work and medical and related therapeutic services. If your child will require extensive support beyond school, it is advisable not to wait until he or she actually needs these adult services to learn more about them. If you are your child's legal guardian, you or a case manager will need to research what's available to your child and apply for services as early as possible. Even if your child will not need extensive services from agencies working with adults with disabilities, such as vocational rehabilitation, the sooner the needed services are identified and initiated, the better the likelihood that they will be in place when you and your child need them.

LOOKING TOWARD THE FUTURE

To make a successful transition from school and home to adulthood, students who are visually impaired and their parents need to work collaboratively with the student's educational team and other professionals who provide services to adults. Coordination, cooperation, and information sharing will allow the team to identify the services that the student needs in order to achieve his or her life and career goals.

A parent advocates best for his or her child by understanding that child's abilities as well as his or her needs during this process. With thoughtful planning, persistence, knowledge of services that will help their child, willingness to encourage independence, and support from other helpful parents and informed professionals, parents can help their children begin their lives as competent young adults. A central task in this process is perhaps the hardest task of all faced by a parent: letting go! By helping your child begin to assume responsibility for the future, to the extent possible, you are supporting your child's potential and starting him or her on the road to feelings of competence, well-developed skills, and life as an independent adult.

For More Information

American Foundation for the Blind, *AFB Directory of Services for Blind and Visually Impaired Persons in the United States and Canada*, 27th edition (New York: AFB Press, 2005).

R. N. Bolles, *What Color Is Your Parachute?* (Berkeley, CA: Ten Speed Press, 2004).

J. Dote-Kwan and J. Senge, *Preparing for College and Beyond: A Guide for Students with Visual Impairments* (Los Angeles, CA: Braille Institute of America, 2002).

J. N. Erin and K. E. Wolffe, *Transition Issues Related to Students with Visual Disabilities* (Austin, TX: PRO-ED, 1999).

L. McBroom, *Transition Activity Calendar for Students with Visual Impairments* (Mississippi State: Mississippi State University Rehabilitation Research and Training Center on Blindness and Low Vision, 1966).

S. Z. Sacks and K. E. Wolffe (Eds.), *Teaching Social Skills to Students with Visual Impairments: From Theory to Practice* (New York: AFB Press, 2006).

E. Trief and R. Feeney, *College Bound: A Guide for Students with Visual Impairments* (New York: AFB Press, 2005).

K. E. Wolffe, "Transition Planning and Employment Outcomes for Students Who Have Visual Impairments with Other Disabilities," in S. Z. Sacks & R.K. Silberman (Eds.), *Educating Students Who Have Visual Impairments with Other Disabilities* (Baltimore: Paul H. Brookes Publishing Co., 1998).

K. E. Wolffe, "Career Education for Children and Youths with Visual Impairments," in A. J. Koenig & M. C. Holbrook (Eds.), *Foundations of*

Education: Instructional Strategies for Teaching Children and Youths with Visual Impairments, Vol. 2 (New York: AFB Press, 2000).

K. E. Wolffe (Ed.), *Skills for Success: A Career Education Handbook for Children and Adolescents with Visual Impairments* (New York: AFB Press, 1998).

K. E. Wolffe and D. Johnson, *Navigating the Rapids of Life: The Transition Tote System* (Lexington, KY: American Printing House for the Blind, 1997).

Agencies that Provide Services for Adults

Agencies that provide services to adults with disabilities are often an important part of planning for a student's life after high school. These agencies may be found through the student's educational team, local government information services (some communities have community service directories; reference librarians in local public libraries can provide information on them), the Internet, or telephone directories. In addition, various agencies that serve persons with visual impairments in each state and nationally can be found through the *AFB Directory of Services for Blind and Visually Impaired Persons in the United States and Canada*. (See the Resources section at the end of this book for many of the agencies mentioned here.) The following section provides an overview of these agencies for parents whose children may come in contact with or seek agency services.

VOCATIONAL REHABILITATION AGENCIES

There are public and private vocational rehabilitation agencies in all the states and territories of the United States. The federal government funds public rehabilitation agencies (and, in some instances, state or local entities also contribute funding). They are classified into two general types: those referred to as "general" agencies, which provide vocational and independent living services to people with all kinds of disabilities; and those referred to as "specialized" or separate agencies, which provide services only to people with specific disabilities, such as blindness or deafness.

Whether there is a separate or general rehabilitation agency that serves people who are visually impaired varies by state. The terms "rehabilitation agency" and "vocational rehabilitation" agency are often used synonymously because the outcome goal for the individuals in most of these programs is work. Rehabilitation agencies serve adults with disabilities and vocational needs—they can help with job leads, instruction in job-seeking techniques, adjustment-to-disability counseling, job coaching services, disability-specific skills training, assistive technology, or medical services. However, not all agencies can offer a full array of services—everything depends on their funding, staffing, and whom they are able to serve. When in doubt, contact your local rehabilitation agency and ask what they can offer.

In addition to state agencies and departments of rehabilitation and vocational rehabilitation, private rehabilitation agencies exist that are supported by private donations and programs, such as the United Way. They often serve specific populations, but in some instances serve people with disabilities in general. Some private agencies serving people with a range of disabilities include Goodwill Industries, The ARC (formerly the Association for Retarded Citizens), UCP (United Cerebral Palsy), and Easter Seals. Private agencies serving individuals who are blind or visually impaired (and, in some instances, those with other disabling conditions as well) include National Industries for the Blind facilities, often referred to as Lighthouses for the Blind, and community-specific organizations such as the Cincinnati Association for the Blind, Greater Pittsburgh Services for the Blind, and the Foundation for the Junior Blind in Los Angeles. You may want to investigate your state and local services to determine what's available nearby. If you don't know what's available or need assistance with this research, your local reference librarian is a source for help.

Adults with disabilities are not automatically served by rehabilitation agencies. Individuals who want services or require an advocate (if the individual is cognitively impaired or unable to act independently) must apply for services. Eligibility for vocational rehabilitation services is based on two factors: The disability must be an obstacle to the individual's ability to work, and the services provided must be reasonably expected to result in the individual's going to work. In other words, to be eligible for federally funded rehabilitation services, your child must have a disability that inhibits or interferes with his or her ability to go to work, and the agency personnel must realistically expect that he or she will go to work after receiving vocational rehabilitation services.

Although most public rehabilitation agencies make their services available at little or no cost to the consumer (your child), some are unable to meet the needs of all the disabled people who apply for services. They have established what are called orders of priority for service provision. This means that your state rehabilitation agency may have a list of disabling conditions and an order of severity that dictates who will be served first.

Private rehabilitation agencies often require a fee for their services that may be paid by the individual seeking services or, in some instances, by the state rehabilitation agency sponsoring the individual. For example, in some states, the services of a rehabilitation teacher (sometimes referred to as vision rehabilitation therapy services), an instructor who works with an adult to teach home and personal management techniques or communication skills such as reading and writing with braille, are only available through private rehabilitation agencies, and the state rehabilitation agency contracts with the private agency for those services for its clients.

In some states, job placement services are contracted out to private agencies and paid for through fee-for-service agreements with the state rehabilitation agency. Again, the key thing for parents to understand is that it is important to investigate the local community and state to find out what's available and from whom in regard to adult services. The uniformity of service structure that exists in the area of educational services is not present in the area of rehabilitation.

Once your child has reached the age of legal majority, he or she will be expected to apply for any rehabilitation services that are desired. You are not allowed to act on your child's behalf, unless you are the legal guardian and your child is unable to apply for services independently. If your child applies for public rehabilitation services and is accepted, he or she will enter into a contract with the rehabilitation agency that specifies what services will be provided, how long the services will be provided, the anticipated goal for employment (outcome), and your child's responsibilities. This contract is called an Individual Plan for Employment (IPE). If your child applies for services through a private rehabilitation agency, a similar contract will spell out what services are to be provided and who will be responsible for paying for them.

INDEPENDENT LIVING CENTERS

For adults with disabilities who need community services, such as housing, or help with mobility, activities of daily living, and attendant care, but do not expect or are unable to go to work, independent living centers may be of assistance. Independent living centers throughout the United States provide services to adults with all disabilities. They are frequently staffed and run by people with disabilities who have lived in the community and know local conditions, government regulations, and services available for people with disabilities.

OTHER ADULT AGENCIES

In addition to general and specialized public rehabilitation agencies, a number of other public agencies provide services to people with disabilities. Some of these provide services to individuals who may not be able to pursue vocational goals. Or, the agencies may be set up to help persons with disabling conditions that may or may not be an impediment to employment but interfere with full participation in society. For example, some state agencies provide services to people with developmental disabilities, mental health concerns, cognitive impairment (mental retardation) or other disabling conditions such as hearing impairment. The federal agency that provides financial assistance for unemployed or needy people with disabilities is the Social Security Administration; Medicaid offers medical assistance to individuals with disabilities. There are also federal agencies that provide housing assistance, protection and advocacy, or other services not necessarily directly related to visual impairment.

There are also many private rehabilitation facilities. These facilities provide care and therapeutic interventions for individuals with such conditions as spinal cord injury; traumatic brain injury; and chronic medical conditions such as diabetes, substance abuse, and mental health disorders. Although the majority of these do not work specifically with individuals with visual impairments, if your child needs their services you may want to negotiate for contracted services (under such a contract you might pay for services out-of-pocket, through insurance, or receive assistance through a scholarship or grant) that meet your adult child's needs for vision-related services. These might include, for example, orientation and mobility (O&M), instruction in braille or the use of optical devices, or career counseling. To find these adult agencies, you may want to request information from a public agency rehabilitation counselor or consult the Internet or telephone directory for your community.

ADULT BASIC EDUCATION AND POSTSECONDARY TRAINING

Programs in most communities offered through local school districts, community colleges, or adult literacy programs provide adult basic education classes. Although these classes are typically designed for people without disabilities, there is a requirement under the Americans with Disabilities Act (ADA) that such services be made accessible to individuals with disabilities. Some rehabilitation agencies and facilities offer assistance to individuals with visual impairments who are working toward acquiring a certificate of general educational development (GED) or need assistance with English as a second language. In addition, the Hadley School for the Blind (see Resources) offers free correspondence courses that include high school classes, adult basic education instruction, training in disability-specific skills such as braille, home and personal management, and self-esteem and adjustment to blindness.

POSTSECONDARY ACADEMIC AND VOCATIONAL TRAINING

High school guidance counselors and college offices for disabled student services can provide basic information to students about what schools and services meet their needs. For information specific to postsecondary academic settings that support students with disabilities, including information about financial aid, you may want to visit the George Washington University HEATH Resource Center's National Clearinghouse on Postsecondary Education for Individuals with Disabilities (see Resources). In addition, the college preparatory courses from the Hadley School for the Blind offer information to parents and students with visual impairments that can help with choosing a college or university and making a successful transition into such a postsecondary program.

Training programs other than colleges are also available in communities throughout the United States, and they are required under the ADA to make their programs accessible to students with disabilities. To find training programs in specific areas of vocational skills, you may find that the Internet is your best source of information. If you do not have Internet access, your local public library can help.

Bryant County Schools
Individualized Education Program (continued)

Student Name <u>Marie Rosado</u> ID# <u>123-45-6789</u> Date <u>4-23-06</u> Page <u>8 of 9</u>

TRANSITION

For students who will become age 16 and above during the current school year, transition service needs may be addressed through components of the IEP that focus on the student's course of study. Provide a general description of the student's course(s) of study.

<u>Marie attends all general education classes for academic subjects and receives instruction in braille, daily living skills, vocational education, and orientation and mobility from a teacher of students with visual impairments and an orientation and mobility specialist.</u>

Diploma <u>✓</u> Standard _____ Special [☐ Option 1 ☐ Option 2] ___ NA

For students, beginning at age 16 (or younger), a statement of needed transition services for the student and a statement of interagency responsibilities or any needed linkages must be included. If the indication is that no services are needed, the team must indicate the basis on which this decision was made in the space provided below.

Required

Instruction   <u>Marie will take academic classes required for a standard diploma with appropriate supports.</u>

Community Experience   <u>Marie will develop travel skills in unfamiliar environments within the community.</u>

Employment   <u>Marie will continue to explore career options, personal aptitude, and career development strategies.</u>

Postschool Adult Living   <u>Marie will develop knowledge and skills related to setting up and maintaining an apartment.</u>

Daily Living Skills   <u>Marie will develop alternative methods to perform tasks of daily living, including cooking, cleaning, and shopping.</u>

Transfer of Rights

CHECK (✓) if the student has been informed of transfer of rights at least one year prior to reaching age of majority. Indicate the date when the student was informed.

<u>✓</u> The Student has been informed.   Date of notification <u>4-23-05</u>

Responsibilities and/or Linkages for Transition Services.

The person's signature below indicates willingness to provide support(s), service(s), or skill(s) that relate to the Transition Plan.

Individualized Education Program (continued)

Student Name _Marie Rosado_ ID# _123-45-6789_ Date _4-23-06_ Page _9 of 9_

Division of Blind Services	Provide instruction in living skills	Mike Duffy
Agency Represented	Responsibilities	Agency Representative's Signature
Agency Represented	Responsibilities	Agency Representative's Signature
Parents	Responsibilities	Parent's Signature
Student	Responsibilities	Parent's Signature

Functional Vocational Evaluation _No services needed at this time_

Date of notification _4-23-05_

Responsibilities and/or Linkages
Division of Blind Services Provide instruction in living skills _Mike Duffy_

Adapted from S. Lewis and C. B. Allman, "Educational Programming," in M. C. Holbrook & A. J. Koenig (Eds.), *Foundations of Education: History and Theory of Teaching Children and Youths with Visual Impairments*, Vol. 1 (New York: AFB Press, 2000), pp. 254–255.

NOTES

CHAPTER 10

Negotiation and Advocacy: Parents as Key Players

Mary Zabelski and Susan LaVenture

One of life's central concerns for most parents is making sure their children receive a good education. The families of children who are visually impaired share the same interests, hopes, and fears regarding their children's education as families whose children are without disabilities. Every child has strengths, needs, and preferences that his or her family wants to have respected by the school system. And, often, parents may find themselves in opposition to what a school provides, based on their perception and appreciation of those qualities in their child.

When a child has a visual impairment or other disability, the level of involvement of his or her parents in educational decision making is different from that of parents whose children are not disabled. Federal and state laws and regulations governing educational programs for students with disabilities have recognized the important role of parents in the special education process. In fact, special education laws and regulations in this country enable parents to participate in meetings, discussions, and assessments of their children. Also, because professionals who have not specialized in work with visually impaired students may view the needs of children with disabilities as unfamiliar and more unusual and complex than those of children without disabilities, parents frequently need to educate school staff and other members of educational teams about the needs of their child with a visual impairment. For these reasons, taking an active role as a parent in the education of your child is a critical ingredient in the quality of his or her educational experience.

WHY ADVOCACY?

In a perfect world, all the specialized services that the educational laws entitle our children to receive and that have been described in this book would always be available and easily obtainable. In this real world of ours, however, the full range of necessary services may not be available unless you as your child's parent or guardian first request them, point out their importance, and then actively work on acquiring them—that is, unless you "advocate" for them. This is true for many reasons.

In general, state departments of education and local school districts may not have the funding and staff to do everything that parents would like to have done for their children, disabled or not. In particular, there is a widespread and long-standing shortage of specially trained and certified teachers of students with visual impairments in this country. It has been estimated that at least twice the number of these teachers are needed to meet today's demand for services. This shortage means, in practice, that many parts of the United States do not have a teacher on hand to provide the range of services explained in this book. In addition, because the number of visually impaired children is relatively small in the school population, a child with a visual impairment may be the first visually impaired child to receive educational services in a given school district, particularly in rural areas. When this is the case, school administrators and teachers will be unfamiliar with providing appropriate services and knowing which specialized services are necessary to educate your child who is visually impaired.

What these realities mean is that parents cannot assume that their local public school will automatically provide an appropriate education for their child. Although it is true that a school's failure to provide a child with such an education cannot be legally justified on the basis of a lack of qualified teachers—under the law, the school system is expected to do what it takes to make a teacher available—it is essential for parents to be knowledgeable about the types of specialized services and accommodations their children may need so that they know what to request. Requesting services on behalf of one's child is a first step in advocacy. As a matter of fact, you may find that you need to become your child's best advocate by working on behalf of your child, to make sure that the specialized educational services guaranteed under federal laws are actually available in your state or local school district so that your child can reach his or her full potential. You may also find that this role comes naturally to you.

LOOKING AHEAD TO OUR CHILDREN'S NEEDS

When my daughter, Cara, was entering the seventh grade, I asked if she could learn to write her name in cursive handwriting. Since she was totally blind, no one had ever attempted to teach her handwriting skills. She wrote and read braille. Evidently, nobody thought that handwriting skills were necessary for her. However, I thought that as she grew up and became more independent, she would need to sign her name to a variety of documents, such as her voter registration form, apartment lease, checks, credit card receipts, and other everyday items. Her teacher of students with visual impairments told me that she was overloaded with students on her caseload and would try to work on this skill when she could. She wasn't sure she could get to it. I let it pass. The whole school year went by, and the skill was never introduced. My attempts to teach Cara were not successful; she had too much homework after school. As it was, I was often her reader, her library research assistant, and her proofreader. She had no extra time for me to teach her handwriting.

At her eighth grade IEP meeting, I was prepared. I explained that every other student in the class could write their names and that it was an essential skill. I insisted, in a pleasant but firm manner, that acquiring handwriting skills should be put into the IEP, and it was. Cara learned how to write and sign her name because I was there to advocate for this skill. The regular classroom teacher would never have thought of teaching this skill, nor would this person have any knowledge of how to teach it. The teacher of students with visual impairments had the training but did not have the time. Many teachers are not going to look ahead to the skills that a person who is blind or visually impaired may need to become a successful working adult. We as parents must look ahead to the future, and to the skills our children need for their successful transition into adulthood.

Mary Zabelski
Mother of an adult daughter with retinoblastoma
President
National Association for Parents of Children with
Visual Impairments
Chicago, Illinois

WHAT DOES ADVOCACY MEAN?

When most people hear the word "advocacy," they may think of the focused efforts, even struggles, of concerned citizens who take action to influence government programs and policies. Although many parents engage in this level of advocacy, organizing together to bring pressure to bear on policymakers and government officials, advocacy can also take place on a more direct and personal level. Advocacy means trying to make something happen. It means making the case that something is important and needs to be done. When families advocate for their children, this is in fact what they are doing—presenting information and making requests in a focused way to ensure that something important gets done. Being an effective advocate may seem an intimidating task, but it does not require specialized skills or extraordinary capabilities. The most important ingredients are a knowledge of your child, an understanding of his or her needs, and a familiarity with the law that governs your child's access to special education services.

In advocating for their children, families bring these ingredients to bear on another factor: the school system. Therefore, another important ingredient is the relationship that they come to have with key educational staff members who work with them and their child. Cultivating a positive relationship with your child's school district and its relevant staff members will be of great help to you in your role in the educational process. If you, your child's teacher, and the school district can nurture a good working relationship, everyone can work cooperatively together. By showing that you are an active participant as a team member in the process of developing your child's Individualized Education Program (IEP), you can gain respect from school personnel. You can demonstrate your involvement by attending all IEP meetings (contact the team in advance if you need to reschedule due to other demands) and by keeping in good, consistent communication with school personnel between IEP meetings. Call or e-mail other team members to keep informed about how your child is doing in class and to ask if you can back up their efforts by supporting IEP goals at home.

By presenting clear reasons for your requests, providing accurate and helpful information to other members of the educational team, acknowledging the viewpoints of others, and pressing your points persistently but politely, you can help bring others to see your point of view and thus meet your child's specific needs. In doing so, you become a productive and effective advocate for your child.

BECOMING AN EFFECTIVE ADVOCATE

Some practices and principles you can follow that will help you be a successful advocate are described here.

Know Your Child

As this book has explained, as your child progresses through the educational system, you will need to acquire knowledge and information about the educational issues facing your child. To be a successful advocate, you need to know your child's special needs and how they affect his or her learning. You also need to be aware of your child's rights and be familiar with the services available in or through the school he or she attends. As an equal participant at the meetings to determine your child's eligibility for special education services and the details of his or her IEP, you can have a strong voice in the planning and implementation of specialized instruction and supportive services. If you are unsure of the meaning of specific terms, specialized language, the appropriateness of your child's program, or what program options might be available, do not hesitate to ask questions and voice your concerns in a positive manner. Sometimes, you may find it helpful to bring another knowledgeable person or advocate with you to team meetings for support.

Prepare for Meetings Thoroughly

In addition to being informed and involved in the educational process, you will need to organize and plan for your meetings. If you share letters, medical information, and other reports with school personnel, it will enable them to understand your child and his or her needs better and help them provide the most appropriate services. It will also help them understand your point of view. Always keep a copy of these items in a folder, notebook, or other easily accessible place. You can keep a written log or chronological record of the meetings, milestones, events, and important conversations you have had with teachers and other school personnel related to your child's educational program. Keep all documents, notices and correspondence that you feel are important, such as IEPs, reports, notices of meeting dates, and evaluations together with your log or journal. Chapters 1 and 4 provide more information and suggestions on planning for IEP and other meetings and keeping good files for important documents and records.

Nurture Relationships

To come to a good working relationship with school staff, include teachers, paraeducators or aides, and therapists who work with your child in your efforts to communicate, provide information, and establish connections.

Try to become familiar with the names, roles, and responsibilities of each person who works with your child in school. You might find it helpful to make an appointment to meet with these individuals from time to time so that you can ask any relevant questions regarding your child's specialized program, inclusion in the regular classroom, and any other related services.

ADVOCACY AND NEGOTIATION: CORE ISSUES

When you are new to the special education system you may think that the professionally trained teaching staff on your child's educational team automatically know what is best for your child. As this book has pointed out before, this is not necessarily the case. Most preschool, elementary, and high school teachers have received minimal if any training that will help them understand the modifications and accommodations that are essential for students who are blind or visually impaired, deaf-blind, or multiply disabled, and what students might need in order to access or use their textbooks and materials properly and in a similar way to their nondisabled classmates. Remember that you have more information about your child's medical issues and any visual and medical diagnoses than the school personnel do. You may, in fact, have the best handle on how your child's visual limitations affect his or her learning.

If you are not quite sure about the effects of your child's visual impairment, your child's teacher of students with visual impairments is a good source of information regarding a particular eye diagnosis and how it affects your child's classroom work. Your child's ophthalmologist, optometrist, or low vision specialist may also be a source of important information. Ask these specialists for a copy of your child's latest eye examination report or evaluation. You can then bring this to IEP meetings along with other helpful information and documents. Also remember that any concerns or questions you have may be answered by contacting your child's teacher, the teacher of students with visual impairments, and the special education director of the school district. By becoming involved in your child's educational program, you will over time gain knowledge, experience, and confidence about how to work with the system.

As your child's advocate, you may find that you have to deal or bargain with your child's school district or local school to acquire necessary services for him or her. Such services may include specialized teaching from the special education teacher, teacher of students with visual impairments, orientation and mobility (O&M) instructor, or other therapists with specialties in occupational therapy, physical therapy, speech therapy, or nursing. You may find that you need to arrange, or "negotiate," for services through discussions with the local educational personnel. Sometimes the services will not be readily available. When this is the case, you will need to present your request in writing or through meetings with educational staff, the school's principal, or the special education administrator of the district. The sample letters provided in Appendix A of this chapter provide some examples of how to present your request clearly and in writing to appropriate staff members.

From a Parent's Perspective

WHAT "NEGOTIATION" CAN BE

Surprises sometimes do happen. Early in his school experience, our son, who is visually impaired, was attending a private Montessori school, as his brother had done. He was receiving vision services from the school district at the private school a few times a week from an itinerant teacher of students who are visually impaired.

One year the public school district representative told us that our son now had to go to them, receive services at their location—at 7:30 in the morning—and that "we'd find a place in the new school that would probably work." We questioned this change at the Individualized Education Program (IEP) meeting and were told that this was the policy. When it came time to sign the IEP, we said that prior to signing it, we'd like to wait and talk it over. This response met with some resistance, and some increasingly anxious phone calls from the district representative, over the next few weeks.

Finally, the assistant superintendent called one day and, with some exasperation in his voice, asked, "What do you want?" I replied that I only wanted my son seen as he had been, at his own school. "Is that all? Well, fine!" was the reply.

Although many situations were not handled as simply as that one, we learned who the real decision-maker was in this case. And we learned never to agree unless we really agreed, or at least had had a full hearing.

Kevin E. O'Connor
Father of an 18-year-old son with Leber's
congenital amaurosis
Lake Grove, Illinois

Know the Law

Advocacy and negotiation both involve presenting information to influence others and making efforts to persuade people to your point of view. If advocacy is making the case that something, such as certain services for your child, is important, negotiation is the actual give-and-take discussion in which you attempt to obtain those services. In undertaking these efforts, knowledge of federal and state educational laws is a "must" for you to acquire. The Individuals with Disabilities Education Act (IDEA) is the most important law with which you can become familiar. IDEA protects your child because it applies to children whose disability interferes with their ability to learn.

From time to time, IDEA is reauthorized, meaning that Congress reviews this law, often amending it by adding, strengthening, eliminating, and even watering down some particular areas. Keeping current on these changes can help to prevent problems during informal meetings and negotiations. It is essential that you have updated knowledge about any changes in the law so that you can make informed decisions as you negotiate for services for your child. Information on changes is available through sources such as parent support groups, national organizations advocating on behalf of people who are visually impaired, and state parent training and information centers that are led by parent mentors, as well as at government web sites, including http://idea.ed.gov. These information centers are supported by the U.S. Office of Special Education Programs, as mentioned in Chapter 1; the Resources section of this book provides more details on these sources of information.

Through membership or by contacting these organizations, you can gain information, support, and confidence as you address your child's educational issues or specific needs. For example, the National Association for Parents of Children with Visual Impairments (NAPVI) is a national support group offering information, sharing resources, and providing parent training and support. NAPVI has many state chapters throughout the United States and can help parents and families locate support services in their areas. It also provides parent training regarding IDEA and helps parents become informed about the laws that regulate the education of children who are blind, visually impaired, deaf-blind, or multiply disabled. It is also important to remember that when IDEA is about to be reauthorized, as it is every few years, we as parents and voters should be active in letting our elected representatives hear from us so that they will actively support needed specialized services and provisions.

Understand the IEP Process

Along with knowledge about IDEA, parents need to understand the central role played by the IEP in their child's education (Chapter 4 discusses the IEP in detail). Creating the IEP involves the processes that determine the program to meet your child's educational needs. Based on an evaluation of your child's educational performance levels, the members of the IEP team set annual goals and, depending on your circumstances, short-term objectives or benchmarks (see Chapter 4). These are written into the IEP. The specialized, related therapeutic services that your child needs also will be listed in the IEP. For example, your son or daughter may need the services of a teacher of students with visual impairments and an O&M instructor to learn safe travel skills. The IEP would indicate how much time per week or per month your child will receive these services. The school then must adhere to the number of minutes indicated in the IEP by providing these services for the duration specified on this document.

For children under 3 years of age, the Individualized Family Service Plan (IFSP) is the central working document that spells out the services they and their families will receive and the goals toward which they will be working. IFSPs are family centered, in recognition of the family's essential role in the life and development of a young child. They include goals and objectives that involve the family, and families have direct input into their creation to reflect their specific child and family needs. (See Chapter 2 for more on IFSPs.)

Here, in the essential delineation of services for your child, is where your knowledge of IDEA and the IEP process is invaluable. Your awareness of how your child's visual limitations affect his or her learning can be brought to the table. The specialized services and accommodations designed to meet your child's needs should be written into the IEP, along with instructions for their implementation, details on who will provide them, and the amount of time they will be provided per week.

Be Knowledgeable about Direct and Indirect Services

In addition to your understanding of the law and the IEP process, knowledge of the difference between direct and indirect services is fundamentally important. Direct and indirect service time provided by a specialized teacher or therapist is usually listed on your child's IEP in specific hours or minutes per week, or even per month or semester. Direct service refers to the actual face-to-face time a teacher or therapist spends with your child. For example, if the school has agreed to provide a teacher of students with visual impairments to work directly with your child to help him or her master reading skills in braille, the IEP would list the number of minutes per week of contact and would specify this as the provision of direct service. If, in another case, the role of the teacher of students who are visually impaired is to adapt the classroom physically to accommodate a child with a visual impairment; order classroom materials in your child's preferred reading medium, such as braille; and help the classroom teacher transfer lessons and tests to the format needed by your child, such as braille, large print, or audiotape, the services could be specified as indirect, because they are in effect consultant time provided to the school faculty. This indirect service time also needs to be specified on the IEP.

As a parent, it is important that you review your child's IEP and consider whether the amount of time it documents to be given to direct and indirect minutes reflects your child's needs. If, for instance, your child is just learning to read in braille, 30 minutes per week of direct service from a teacher of students with visual impairments is probably not enough time. Children need daily instruction in reading when they are learning. In such a case, you may need to request additional IEP direct service minutes as needed during your IEP meeting. Once your child masters the basic skills, these minutes may be able to be reduced. If you are uncertain about how much time might be needed to address your child's current needs, consulting with the teacher of students with visual impairments, a parent group, or the special school for blind and visually impaired students in your state (see Chapters 1 and 7) will be helpful.

Presenting your case in a calm, positive, and knowledgeable manner, indicating your child's need for direct instruction at this time with persistence, is part of the negotiating process. A constructive approach can be important in maintaining relationships with school staff that you can use to your child's best advantage when making future requests. Some possible ways in which to discuss services and your child's needs are presented in "Pop-Up IEPs for Parents and Advocates," Appendix B to this chapter.

THE IMPORTANCE OF PARTICIPATING IN MEETINGS

Your Role as Team Member

School districts are required by law to include you as a parent in discussions regarding your child's evaluations (for more on evaluations and assessments, see Chapter 3). They are also required to invite you to meetings to determine your child's eligibility for special education services, plan your child's IEP, and discuss where your child will receive these services. Because of these requirements, the school must send you a written notice or contact you in a timely manner to arrange for mutually convenient meeting dates and times. To be an active participant and successful advocate for your child, you need to be prepared. Good communication skills—an ability to explain your point of view clearly and in a way others can understand—good listening skills, and respect for the opinions of others can be effective tools for you during meetings with your child's educational team members and other school personnel. Remembering these principles will be helpful too:

- Prepare yourself ahead of time.

- Try to be positive, direct, and confident in your comments and feed-back.

- Make an effort to remain calm and in control of your feelings during discussions with other team members.

- Try to stay involved in the processes that result in your child's edu-cational program. You are a member of the educational team, and your opinions and concerns are very important.

It is essential to realize that a regular classroom teacher who does not yet know your child may not be familiar with your child's visual disability and how to provide the special services your child needs because he or she has not had specialized training in working with students with visual impairments. For this reason, the regular classroom teacher and special education teacher should both participate in discussions about classroom services. Perhaps you can arrange for a meeting to discuss your child's vi-sual impairment, its effect on learning, and other issues with these two professionals before the formal IEP meeting of the entire team.

If your child has difficulties in school because he or she is not receiv-ing needed specialized services, or his or her services need to be changed, you will need to speak up and request them. IEPs and IFSPs are required to be created jointly, by school personnel, service providers, and parents working together as a team. The IEP or IFSP must be written and agreed upon by you before your child can begin to receive special services. It needs to be reviewed annually (or more often if needed) to make sure that the program it spells out is working for your child. You have the right to call for a meeting to review the IEP if you have concerns. Your child may have unique needs that only you as a parent can see. Exercising your rights as the parent of a child with a disability can make a tremendous difference in the services provided to your child.

In order to maximize your child's opportunities within the school sys-tem that he or she is a part of, try to remember the importance of work-ing in a positive manner with school personnel. Although the law guarantees you an essential voice in the education of your child, in reality, school and other educational staff can fail to cooperate with you on a day-to-day basis if they see you as an obstructionist or as a complainer. For example, you may not be invited to attend meetings, or they may re-fuse to grant appointments to you when you request them. However, they will be willing to accept you as a part of the "team" and value your im-portant contributions to the process if you approach school personnel in a positive way. That might include complimenting them for your child's successes as well as offering to help with any problems or areas of concern where more effort needs to be made to encourage your child's progress, such as asking what you may be able to do at home with your child to reinforce skills that he or she is learning in school.

Get the Most Out of, and Add the Most to, IEP Meetings

When you first attend IEP meetings for your child, you may feel nervous, anxious, and hesitant to speak up. Feelings such as these are natural and understandable. Sometimes, school personnel and the other professionals at a meeting may use educational and therapeutic terms that are unfamiliar to you. Don't be afraid to ask questions that will help you to become better informed. If you don't understand what a term means, you may not understand how something is meant to benefit your child. If you continue to ask for clarifications, meeting participants will learn that they should use plain language and terms familiar to nonprofessionals, rather than "insider" therapeutic vocabulary or jargon.

Try to obtain support for yourself from other parents, parents' groups, and national organizations devoted to the needs of people who are visually impaired (see Chapter 1 and the Resources section of this book for more information), especially if you feel you need encouragement or help to continue attending meetings as a strong advocate for your child. Over time, as you continue to provide important information about your child in a level-headed and productive way, and present yourself as concerned and informed, most faculty and support service staff will begin to see the value of your input and ideas.

If you feel intimidated about attending meetings, consider bringing another person to help you advocate for the services your child needs. Other parents who have similar issues and concerns may be available to assist you, either to consult with you prior to the meeting or by coming with you. You can also arrange with representatives from parents' groups to attend IEP meetings with you if you feel unsure at first. As you attend more meetings, you may find that the process gets easier. You will become more familiar with what takes place and more successful in working with the other members of your child's educational team.

Try also to remember that it is a good idea to bring medical records and previous educational records to the meeting, especially if there is any disagreement among the team members regarding how your child's disability can affect his or her learning. As already mentioned, keep a notebook or file of previous evaluations, IEPs, and report cards. Write down your questions and concerns ahead of time so you don't forget any relevant issues you may want to discuss during the meeting. Chapter 4 provides numerous suggestions on how to prepare for IEP meetings and work effectively at those meetings. It also includes a useful appendix of responses parents can use to frequently heard comments during meetings, as does this chapter. Some of those suggestions are included here:

ADVOCACY = PASSION PLUS KNOWLEDGE

Advocacy is most effective when passion and knowledge are combined. As parents, we are the most passionate of the team members charged with the education of our children. We must also become knowledgeable about what our kids need, what they deserve, and what they have a right to. We can and should advocate, without apology, for those services that will give them an equal footing with their sighted peers to achieve success in all parts of their lives.

The benchmark for me, as Jameyanne's mother, has always been to look around at what sighted children her age are doing: crawling, riding a bike, reading, skiing, math, walking with friends to the bus stop, working at the computer. I have been told in meetings that Jameyanne gets "the best services" and that she is doing so much better than most blind children. But our children's performance should not be compared to other blind children. It should be compared to their sighted peers. It is the expectation that we as parents should have of our child's performance.

When Jameyanne was in the third grade, her classmates were working in the computer lab while she did nothing. The system wasn't accessible to her, and she had no adaptive skills. For a full year, we kept requesting and insisting that the school provide assistive technology—specialized computer hardware and software that our daughter could use—while we privately hired a technology teacher to teach her at home. As she worked and succeeded at home with specialized software known as JAWS, she was unable to work alongside her classmates in the school computer lab. It was disgraceful!

After consulting with an attorney, we started more serious negotiations with the school to provide the instruction we knew our daughter needed, and had a right to, to be included in computer work at school. The meetings were long and often contentious, but we knew that IDEA was behind us. We also knew that a free and appropriate education included all the elements of the expanded core curriculum [see Chapter 1 for information on this curriculum]. We shared the information with the district as we gathered it, and finally the discussions turned into IEP pages. Many good ideas will simply not be implemented if they are not written into the IEP. If we know what we are entitled to (the law), and

(continued on next page)

we communicate that in the spirit of respect and cooperation (the passion), then we will persevere in the best interests of our children.

We have worked very hard, chosen our battles, saved our outrage for the truly outrageous, and sought to show our gratitude for the things that got done well. Through our advocacy, we were able to turn around a bad situation, which was worthy of due process action, and make an education for our daughter on par with her sighted peers in her school and in the community.

The technology consultant continues to teach Jameyanne new skills and also works with her teacher of students who are visually impaired and the teaching assistants to teach them and offer support. Jameyanne is now fluent with using the Internet and other processing functions, and e-mailing her visually impaired and sighted friends. She uses a BrailleNote with a refreshable display and a talking braille calculator, and is now learning to use a talking graphing calculator for next year's advanced algebra course in her sophomore year of high school. She is also learning to solve her own technical problems with customer service representatives from technology equipment companies, to put her on the path toward transition and independence.

One of the bonuses of having worked hard over the years is to hear from other parents and from the district technology coordinator how much the district has learned about assistive technology. Working to make accommodations for Jameyanne has brought the whole district to a new level of expertise in helping other children with visual impairments and other disabilities.

Time passes quickly. But we, as parents, have been given the charge to advocate for what we know our children need and deserve. Although it is sometimes difficult and tiring, it is also a badge of honor: Doing what needs to be done for our children identifies us as concerned and productive parents.

The relationship with Jameyanne's school has evolved into a team relationship, as it should be to be productive. But I continue to be involved, informed, and on "the front lines" because I have the greatest amount of passion when it comes to her education.

Mary E. Fuller
Mother of a 15-year-old daughter with aniridia glaucoma
Concord, New Hampshire

- Review your role in and the main principles of the IEP process prior to the meeting.
- Request your child's test scores and evaluation data from all appropriate professionals before the meeting.
- Know who will attend the meeting.
- Communicate with the classroom teacher on a regular basis.
- Write down questions or concerns ahead of time.
- Write down your priorities.
- Bring any updated medical information with you.
- Keep a notebook or file of previous evaluations and educational records and bring it with you.
- Bring a friend, relative, or other advocate if you feel intimidated or nervous.
- Ask for clarifications if you don't understand terminology being used by other team members.

Sometimes, there may be disagreements between you and the school personnel regarding instructional methods, service delivery, and the specialized services needed for your child to receive an appropriate education. For example, you might feel that your child needs daily services from the teacher of students with visual impairments, while the school wants your child to receive weekly services or use the services of a classroom aide instead. Another example might be that you want your child to receive reading instruction in braille and in print, while the district insists that your child should read in large print only.

Under IDEA, states establish a system of procedural safeguards to protect the rights of children and their parents and to provide procedures for resolving disagreements that may occur between parents and the school. If you as a parent have tried to work with the school district and there are conflicts that do not seem to be resolved, you have protection and the right to file a complaint with the state education agency or department or to file a formal due process complaint to request an administrative due process hearing. Ultimately, a due process hearing may be needed to resolve disagreements about the amount, type, intensity, frequency, or location of services. However, if it is possible, it is better to attempt to work through areas of disagreement informally through the IEP process, the discussions that you have with other team members at meetings, and informal dispute resolution.

Perhaps you can explain tactfully and persuasively why you feel that your child would benefit from receiving certain services. Producing current assessments and evaluations, including functional vision assessments or low vision examination reports, is very important in these situations. Conferring with your child's teacher of students with visual impairments and other specialized teachers or therapists ahead of time can also be an important strategy. If you have a working relationship with the classroom teacher and the teacher of students who are visually impaired, you can all discuss these issues and requests before the general IEP meeting. Strategies such as these are less expensive and less stressful on you, your child, and school personnel than going through the more formal due process hearing, which can involve the added work and expense of contracting with attorneys to represent you.

WHEN YOU CAN'T REACH AGREEMENT

Although you and the local school personnel may try your best to come up with the right services and placement for your child, there may still be some difficulties or problems. Ideally, families and schools work together to help children with disabilities. However, differing opinions sometimes turn into disputes. When this happens, there are some steps you can take to resolve these issues informally:

- Talk to the school staff, principal, and district special education director informally.

- If you disagree with an identification, diagnosis, or the results of an evaluation that has been made to determine if your child is eligible for special education services, you can request another eligibility meeting or an independent evaluation at no cost to you.

- If you disagree with the educational placement or services that have been suggested, you can request another IEP meeting to discuss these issues.

If informal talks with the school district do not resolve the issues to your satisfaction, more formal action may be necessary, including these possibilities:

- *a state compliance complaint*: a written notice from a parent or organization to the state education agency describing violations of IDEA and requesting an investigation

- *mediation*: a voluntary process in which both parties—parents and representatives of the school district—meet with a trained, impartial person who serves as a mediator

- *a resolution session*: a mandatory meeting of parents and other IEP team members to discuss a complaint and its resolution within 15 days of the receipt of a due process complaint

- *a due process hearing*: a formal presentation of both sides of a dispute by parents and school district before a hearing officer who will decide the matter and issue findings of fact and conclusion

If these procedures become necessary, you will need to request them formally in writing. Some sample letters you might use as templates when writing to request an evaluation or reevaluation, an independent educational evaluation, an IEP review, or a due process hearing are provided at the end of this chapter. For example, you may wish to request an independent educational evaluation (conducted by a professional such as a vision specialist or psychologist outside the school system) if, based on your knowledge of your child, you believe that the evaluation provided by the school district does not give adequate or accurate information about your child's needs and abilities.

Filing a State Compliance Complaint

If you believe that your local school district has not complied with the law regarding your child's educational rights under Part B of IDEA, you can file a complaint with the state department of education in writing. (A state complaint can also be filed by another individual or an organization and must be filed within a year of the violation.) The letter must include a statement indicating why you think your child's educational rights have been violated, facts supporting that statement, and your signature as the party complaining. You need to include the child's name and address, the name of the student's school district, the nature of the child's problem, relevant facts, and a proposed resolution of the problem. A copy of the complaint must be sent to the local educational agency, or school district.

Once your complaint is received, the state education agency has 60 days to carry out an on-site investigation, if it decides that is necessary. The agency gathers additional information, provides the school district with the opportunity to respond to the allegations, and provides an opportunity for you and the school district to engage voluntarily in mediation. If an agreement is not otherwise reached, the state education agency will provide you and the local school district with written notification regarding its findings, any actions that need to be taken, and the time frame in which any action must be taken.

Using Mediation

You can request mediation if you continue to have unresolved issues or concerns regarding the special education program or the related services your child is receiving. Mediation is a voluntary process in which parents or guardians meet with the local school district personnel to resolve any conflicts with the help of an impartial, trained mediator. During the mediation process, parents and representatives from the local school district meet together to discuss the existing problems and any alternative solutions that might serve to alleviate the impasse. This service is provided by the state at no cost to the parent or the local school district.

Mediation will attempt to establish and clarify the issues, determine any point of agreement, and offer solutions to resolve the disagreements. It requires the full participation of both parties and can terminate if one side decides not to participate in the process.

Only persons who have the authority to act on behalf of a child and the local school district can be included in mediation. Mediation activities must take place in absolute confidentiality. No records are kept of the actual discussions. Only the names of the participants are recorded, the dates and location of the mediation, and a summary of the outcome. Discussions may not be used by either party in a due process hearing if one takes place later. An agreement or resolution reached by the parties to the disagreement through the mediation process is set forth in a written, legally binding mediation agreement.

Requesting a Due Process Hearing

If you and your child's school district are unable to resolve your conflict, despite mediation and other attempts at resolution, due process may be your next course of action. An impartial due process hearing is an administrative hearing set up to resolve disagreements between you and the school district.

When a Due Process Complaint Is Appropriate

You have the right to file a due process complaint to request a due process hearing if the school district refuses to initiate, provide, or change the following, or proposes to do so against your will:

- Identification of your child's disability
- Evaluation of your child's needs and strengths
- Determination of your child's educational placement
- Provision of a free and appropriate public education, special education, and related services

The school district may also file a complaint to request a due process hearing to do the following:

- Obtain parental consent for the initial evaluation of a child.
- Prove that the district's evaluation was appropriate.

It may also request a due process hearing in these circumstances:

- If a parent refuses to provide written consent for a reevaluation of his or her child
- To move a student to a temporary alternative educational setting for up to 45 days for behavior believed to be dangerous to the student or others

In most cases, a due process complaint must be filed within two years of when you knew about the action you are complaining about.

How to Raise the Volume: A Summary

If you feel that your child is not receiving the services he or she needs and is entitled to, don't hesitate to request them. It is more effective to begin in a cooperative manner, building on established positive relationships with the members of your child's educational team. Should you continue to feel that your child's needs are not being met, steps to remedy this are available that serve to raise the volume of your concern in incremental steps:

1. Work on creating positive relationships with your child's classroom teacher, teacher of students with visual impairments, orientation and mobility (O&M) instructor, school principal, and any other staff members who provide therapeutic services.

2. To the extent possible, attend school meetings and assemblies and special events to demonstrate your interest in and support of your child and his or her school.

3. Learn about the Individuals with Disabilities Education Act (IDEA), and any recent amendments, so that you are familiar with your child's right to a free and appropriate education.

4. If you notice your child experiencing a school-related problem or have other issues with his or her education, ask the classroom teacher for a meeting (invite the teacher of students with visual impairments or other teacher or therapist, if needed). Ask for the teacher's input and suggestions. Try to keep the atmosphere of the meeting informal, positive, and collaborative.

5. If such meetings are unsuccessful, request in writing a meeting with the school principal or district special education director. Always ask for results from any assessments or evaluations in writing, if these are relevant to your concerns. List your concerns to bring to the meeting, and save a copy for your files.

6. Provide the principal or district special education director with the latest eye reports from your child's ophthalmologist or low vision optometrist, with the narratives describing how the eye diagnosis affects your child's learning in the classroom, and any recommendations for adaptations and accommodations. Bring other updated medical records and assessment as needed also. This information should be available to all the members of your child's educational team.

(continued on next page)

7. If you feel intimidated, bring a knowledgeable friend, other informed parent, or an advocate for support to this and other meetings. Remind participants that you are all working as a team for your child's best interests.

8. If you disagree with the school's evaluations for your child in academic and therapeutic areas, you may request an independent evaluation at no expense to yourself from the district, performed by independent, experienced evaluators.

9. If you can't reach agreement on aspects of your child's IEP, you can take advantage of the formal dispute-resolution procedures described in this chapter, including initiating a state compliance complaint, requesting mediation, and filing a due process complaint to request an impartial due process hearing.

10. Some parents seek additional assistance by contacting their local state or congressional representatives, to make them aware of the issues.

Filing a Due Process Complaint

To request a due process hearing, you must file a written due process complaint with your local school district superintendent and the state agency or department of education. Your letter must include the name and address of your child; the school your child attends; the reason for the hearing request (a statement of how your child's rights are being violated); and the resolution being sought. Make sure to keep a copy of this letter for your records.

After receiving your request for a due process hearing, the state education agency will appoint a hearing officer and give written notice to you and the school district. Your due process complaint must meet certain requirements, known as "sufficiency." The school district has 15 days to challenge your complaint, in writing, for failing to include the proper information. If it is challenged, the hearing officer will determine within 5 days whether the complaint is sufficient, and will notify both the parties in writing of the decision. Within 10 days of receiving a state due process complaint, the school district (or parent, if he or she is the recipient of the complaint), must send the other party and the hearing officer a written answer addressing the issues raised in the complaint.

Both you and the district may request (in writing) one hearing officer substitution if needed within five days of receiving the notice. You might request a substitution of a hearing officer if there appears to be any conflict of interest. For example, the hearing officer cannot be a state or local education agency employee and must have the knowledge and ability to understand laws and regulations as well as legal interpretations. This will give him or her the capability to hold the hearing and to make a decision in accordance with the law.

Resolution Sessions

Before a due process hearing is scheduled, the local education agency, or school district, must convene a resolution session. This preliminary meeting involves the parents, relevant members of the IEP team, and a representative of the school district with decision-making authority. The session must be convened within 15 days of receiving notice of a parent's due process complaint. During the resolution session, the parents discuss their complaint and the local school district is provided an opportunity to resolve the complaint. The representatives of the school district may not include an attorney unless the parent is also accompanied by an attorney. The resolution session may be waived if the district and the parents agree in writing, or if they agree to use mediation. If an agreement is reached at the resolution session, the parties must sign a legally binding agreement, and this document is legally enforceable in any state court or United States district court. A party may void the agreement within 3 business days.

Due Process Hearing

If the school district has not resolved the problem within 30 days from the receipt of the parent's due process complaint, a due process hearing may occur and the applicable time lines for due process will begin. There are very specific time lines throughout the process of the procedural safeguards, from the initial written notification of a complaint by the parent to the final due process hearing. Parents must be aware of these time lines and adhere to their requirements to make sure they are taking all the necessary steps to ensure the success of their case.

When a due process hearing is held, both parties have certain rights, including the right to present evidence and call witnesses, to legal representation or support from other persons having knowledge of the rights of students with disabilities, to prohibit evidence that was not made available at least five days prior to the hearing, to a verbatim record of the hearing, and to findings of fact and decisions. Both parties also have the right to a written decision, the right to request a clarification, and the right to appeal the decision in court. The student has the right to be placed in school if he or she has not yet been admitted, with parental consent, and the right to remain in his or her current placement unless both parties agree to another arrangement.

Parents also have the right to be informed of the procedures available to request a due process hearing, low-cost or free legal services, and an interpreter for deaf persons or of the primary language in the home at public expense, and to have the child present at the hearing. Parents are also entitled to request that the hearing be open to the public and have the right to recover reasonable attorney's fees if they prevail in the hearing or the court action.

Because a hearing can be complicated and difficult, you may want to ask someone else, perhaps an advocate or attorney, to help you prepare for the hearing and possibly attend with you. It is not necessary, but it can be helpful and reassuring. The school can assist you in locating free or low-cost legal services if you request this in writing. Also, each state has parent training and information centers that provide information on advocacy and legal services (see Chapter 1). National parent support groups, such as NAPVI, or state affiliate chapters of organizations such as NAPVI, the American Council of the Blind, or the National Federation of the Blind, can also provide assistance through training about the rights of students with disabilities.

FINAL THOUGHTS ON ADVOCACY

Although many parents may feel that advocacy is not something they would comfortably undertake, you may find that requesting services and arguing persuasively for them on behalf of your child is a natural, almost automatic, outgrowth of your love and concern for your child. You may experience a range of feelings, some of them negative, about meeting with many professionals, pressing your viewpoint, and staying informed about your child's educational situation. And you may sometimes feel tired and discouraged. Try to keep in mind that all these feelings are natural—and that you should not doubt the power you possess to make the difference in your child's life and educational career. By remembering that you are a key player whose voice and opinions need to be heard, you can help your child travel the journey through the school years to a successful future. In their desire for the success of this journey, all parents and children are alike.

For More Information

C. Cortiella, "NCLB and IDEA: What Parents of Students with Disabilities Need to Know and Do" (Minneapolis: National Center on Educational Outcomes, University of Minnesota, 2006); available online at http://education.umn.edu/nceo/OnlinePubs/Parents.pdf.

P. W. D. Wright and P. D. Wright, *Wrightslaw: From Emotions to Advocacy: The Special Education Survival Guide* (Hartfield, VA: Harbor House Law Press, 2002).

REQUESTING (REFERRAL FOR)
AN EVALUATION
AND/OR REEVALUATION
(Sample letter)

Your Address

Your Phone Number

Date

Mr. /Ms._____
          (Superintendent or Principal)

District Address

Dear_____:

I am the parent of_____, whose date of birth is
_____, and who is a student in the
_____grade/school. I am referring my child
for a special education evaluation/reevaluation for the following reason(s):

(List your reasons here.)

1.
2.
3.

I understand that if the school district accepts my referral request, the
district must obtain my written consent prior to conducting the
evaluation/reevaluation. I also understand that this letter starts the
60-day timeline.

Finally, I understand that if the school district turns down my request, the
district will provide me with a written explanation of the reasons for not
conducting an evaluation/reevaluation.

Thank you.

Sincerely,

(Your name)

(THIS LETTER MAY BE HANDWRITTEN)

REQUESTING AN INDEPENDENT
EDUCATIONAL EVALUATION
(Sample letter)

Your Address

Your Phone Number

Date

Mr. /Ms._____
      (Superintendent)

District Address

Dear_____:

I am the parent of_____, whose date of birth is
_____, and who is a student in the
_____grade/school.

I am requesting that the school district agree to pay for an independent evaluation of my child. I believe the district's evaluation was not appropriate because (examples: it did not identify the specific special education services needed to help my child; it did not use the correct evaluation instruments; it has not helped develop an appropriate program for my child).

(List your reasons here.)

1.
2.
3.

I understand that if the school district turns down my request, the district must immediately request a due process hearing. I would appreciate it if you would contact me at your earliest convenience to let me know whether the independent evaluation will be provided or when the hearing will be scheduled.

Thank you.

Sincerely,

(Your name)

                    (THIS LETTER MAY BE HANDWRITTEN)

REQUESTING AN IEP REVIEW
(Sample letter)

Your Address

Your Phone Number

Today's Date

Mr. /Ms._____

         (Principal or Counselor)

Name of School
Address of School

Dear_____:

I am the parent of_____, age
_____, who is a student in grade_____
at_____School. I think that there should be a
change in my child's Individualized Education Program (IEP). I am
requesting a meeting to talk about this and to consider changes in the IEP.
I understand that if the school district agrees to convene an IEP meeting, it
must provide the 10-day notification of conference. I also understand that
if the school district does not agree to convene an IEP meeting, it must
provide written notification of its refusal, including an explanation of the
reason why no meeting is necessary. These notifications must be provided
within ten (10) days after the receipt of my request.

I am providing three (3) times and dates that I am available to meet with
the IEP team. Please provide me with a written response of the IEP team's
availability within ten (10) school days of the date of this letter.

Thank you for your time and attention to this matter.

Sincerely,

(Your name)

cc: Principal of School

(THIS LETTER MAY BE HANDWRITTEN)

REQUESTING A DUE PROCESS HEARING
(Sample letter)

Your Address

Your Phone Number

Date

Mr. /Ms._____
(Superintendent)

District Address

Dear_____:

As provided for under IDEA, I am requesting a due process hearing on behalf of my (son/daughter/ward) _____, whose birthdate is _____. My child currently attends _____School.
The hearing is requested to resolve differences over (state the specific reasons for the request) and I will be requesting that the hearing officer order the following remedy (be specific).

_____
_____
_____
_____
_____
_____
_____
_____
_____

Please contact me at (phone number) _____
if you have any questions or want more information.

Thank you

Sincerely,

(Your Name)

(THIS LETTER MAY BE HANDWRITTEN)

Pop-up IEPs for Parents and Advocates

Are you dreading your next Individualized Education Program (IEP) meeting? Are you already in disagreement with your IEP team or your school staff over needed services for your child? If so, you are not alone. This appendix provides examples of some "conversation stoppers" that parents may hear when advocating for their children with the IEP team. It gives you information on what the "real" issues underlying these responses might be, some respectful but effective responses you can be prepared to give, and a look at specific areas of the laws as they relate to educating children with disabilities. These can all assist you in getting your IEP team meetings moving again in a more positive direction. The replies may be useful not just in IEP meetings, but in other discussions and conversations about your child, too.

These samples and suggestions were originally prepared as an interactive, online resource for parents by the National Center on Low-Incidence Disabilities. Visit the Center's web site at http://nclid.unco.edu/ to see these suggestions in their original form and to read more extensive portions of the law as it applies to the education of children with visual impairments.

"It's not reasonable to expect the classroom teacher to describe everything to your child. She has 30 other students."

What's Wrong with This Statement?

This statement communicates that making certain accommodations for your child may be seen as beyond what the teacher can be reasonably expected to do. Overworked teachers, who are managing crowded classrooms, completing paperwork, and attending meetings, may feel that doing any additional work is beyond what they can handle. However, children who are blind or visually impaired have the right to access all of the information available to sighted students in order to participate fully, meaningfully, and successfully in the classroom. The level of effort required to include a student who is blind or visually impaired is frequently overestimated by educators unfamiliar with teaching students with visual impairments. Giving teachers specific examples of how to describe lessons they might think of as "visual" can help them feel more comfortable in meeting the needs of all children in their classroom, regardless of their abilities.

Possible Responses

1. "We understand that what we're asking may seem challenging at first, but it really isn't as involved as you might think. If you verbalize what you're writing on the board, Christine will be able to follow along independently. For example, if you were writing the names of the months on the board, you would simply say, 'September, capital S, lower case e-p-t-e-m-b-e-r.' With a little practice, verbalizing information becomes a natural process that benefits all students in the class, since everyone learns in different ways and at different rates. Plus, Christine will be included and able to follow along with her peers instead of having to wait for delayed, individual assistance. Christine's teacher of students who are visually impaired will also be able to offer specific tips and strategies."

2. "I know that it seems very involved at first. Last year, Sam had Mr. Menendez along with Mrs. Liang. Both teachers were unfamiliar with the process and had concerns similar to the ones you're expressing. After working with the teacher of students who are visually impaired, however, both teachers quickly picked up an ability to provide information both visually and audibly. They did an excellent job of creating a successful learning environment for Sam. At the end of the year, both teachers told us that they felt their experience with providing information audibly improved their teaching and increased their understanding of the different learning needs of all their students. I'm sure both teachers would be happy to share their experiences with you. May I ask them to call you?"

Where the Law Supports Your Responses

Federal Regulations: Section 300.119(a)(b) Technical assistance and training activities; Section 300.156 (a) Personnel qualifications
IDEA 2004 (Public Law 108-446): Section 601(c)(5)

Positive Steps You Can Take

- Meet with your child's teachers as early in the year as possible.
- Make sure your child's classroom teacher and teacher of students who are visually impaired have made contact and are communicating with each other.
- Ask the teacher of students who are visually impaired to set up an in-service training opportunity for the teachers and school staff to demonstrate appropriate adaptations and answer any questions.

- Parents, in conjunction with a teacher of students who are visually impaired, can demonstrate how to describe visual information without disrupting the flow of a lesson. Modeling adaptations for teachers can illustrate that the level of effort to include students who are blind or visually impaired is not as great as teachers might have thought.

- Have your child's previous teachers or related service providers who were effective talk to your child's new teachers about their experiences.

- It is important for the classroom teacher, the teacher of students who are visually impaired, and you to work as a team. Parents and teachers of students who are visually impaired can answer questions and offer support. Provide new teachers with a reasonable amount of literature and resources about including students who are visually impaired or blind in their classroom. As parents, you can provide information that is unique to your child. Be clear, concise, and specific about how you would like teachers to accommodate your child.

- Teach your child to be a confident and respectful self-advocate in asking for descriptions of visual lessons by approaching the teacher or raising his or her hand (like anyone else) when he or she does not understand something.

- Arrange to visit the classroom for a morning or a day to observe how things are going and offer helpful suggestions (check to make sure your child is comfortable with this as well). If you have suggestions, set up a meeting with the teacher of students who are visually impaired and the classroom teacher. Always start constructive criticism or feedback by offering positive comments, praise, and/or encouragement for any effort that they have made.

- If you disagree with the IEP, make sure to include a written statement noting your objections. Unless indicated otherwise, signing the IEP indicates attendance but not necessarily agreement.

"We were excited to discover how well your child can see!"

What's Wrong with This Statement?

Partial vision can be complex and/or fluctuating; therefore, it is easy to draw incorrect conclusions about how children see their environment. There is an important distinction between children's ability to *see* something and their ability to *understand* it accurately. Just because children see something does not mean that they are able to see things clearly or in their entirety (whole objects), or that they see everything in the same way all of the time. Lighting, contrast, size, distance, spacing, clutter, fatigue, and medications can dramatically alter what a child can see in any given situation. Many children use their partial vision very well. This does not mean that they are fully sighted, however; accommodations are still necessary.

Possible Responses

1. "We feel good when Mirella can see things, too. Unfortunately, it's hard for us to tell what she sees without conveying to her that we doubt her ability in fully understanding the item or concept. Often she tells us she sees something and then we realize later that she didn't see as much as we had thought. We don't want her to feel bad by questioning her ability to understand something. And we want to make sure she knows that seeing is not the only way to know something. We describe things to her and encourage her to get information for herself by asking questions and getting up close to objects so she can explore them using all her senses. By doing these things, we've helped her gain better understandings of items and concepts within her environment."

2. "Whenever Marco relies exclusively on his vision to do things, whether it's walking, reading, or playing, we find he becomes extremely fatigued within a very short time. His experience with the activity can turn from enjoyment to hard work. This causes him to feel frustrated and give up. We're all happy when Marco uses his vision successfully. Still, we also know that he needs to have nonvisual ways to do things, too; ways that help him maintain his stamina as tasks become longer and more complicated. This will allow him to continue to enjoy what he is doing and engage in activities for longer periods of time."

3. "We never discourage Abby's use of vision. But there are times and conditions when using touch or hearing is more effective for her than using vision alone. We encourage her to determine what works for her in each situation and to ask questions if she doesn't understand or needs assistance. We want her to learn that all her senses are valuable and she should use the techniques that work the most efficiently, effectively, and safely in different situations."

Where the Law Supports Your Responses

Federal Regulations: Section 300.306 (c) (1)(i)(ii) Determination of eligibility
IDEA 2004 (Public Law 108-446): Section 601(c)(5) and Section 602(3)

Positive Steps You Can Take

- Work with your child's teacher of students who are blind or visually impaired to educate the school staff about the efficiency and effectiveness of nonvisual techniques. Provide examples of how persons who are blind or visually impaired use such techniques effectively.

- Educate school staff about the multifaceted dynamics of low vision. Provide examples of when your child has seen things inaccurately due to partial vision, which may have resulted in a safety hazard or development of an incomplete concept. Personal examples enhance staff members' ability to understand and realize why what you are telling them is important.

- Arrange for the staff to meet at least one person with low vision who successfully uses both visual and nonvisual techniques to maintain gainful employment and live and travel independently.

- Help your child become comfortable with nonvisual techniques by giving him or her lots of practice with them at home. Don't place a higher value on techniques that use vision. Instead, place the value on effectiveness, efficiency, safety, and independence.

- Teach your child to speak up when he or she cannot see something, doesn't understand something that is being presented visually, or is visually fatigued.

- If a technique doesn't work well for your child, help him or her find another way. Encourage your child to discover what works by offering the various tools or methods with a positive attitude and lots of chances for practice.

- Educate your child and teachers to recognize common signs of vision fatigue and to know what to do if they occur. These signs include headaches, neck or shoulder strain, general tiredness, blurry or reduced functional vision, nausea, or rubbing the eyes frequently. Possible alternatives include switching to a nonvisual technique, such as braille or auditory reading, alternating between near and distance viewing tasks, adjusting lighting, using optical aids, or briefly resting the eyes.

- Ask the teacher of students who are visually impaired to conduct a functional vision evaluation to help determine under what conditions and with what aids it would make sense for your child to use his or her residual vision. This professional can also conduct an assessment to determine your child's primary and secondary learning media.

- If you disagree with the IEP, make sure to include a written statement noting your objections. Unless indicated otherwise, signing the IEP indicates attendance, but not necessarily agreement.

"We think the cane could pose a hazard to other students. We'd like your child to leave it at the door or in the locker."

What's Wrong with This Statement?

The proper use of a long cane will not cause a hazard but can actually prevent hazardous situations from occurring. The cane identifies a child as having a visual impairment so that others can respond appropriately. Like vision, the cane provides a preview of what is out in front and enables the child to detect objects, identify drop-offs and other changes in elevation, and walk confidently at a normal speed. Furthermore, the cane helps a child develop spatial concepts and environmental awareness. The child must be taught to take personal responsibility for the cane and use it appropriately for safe and independent travel.

Possible Responses

1. "According to Ellie's formal orientation and mobility evaluation the cane is a necessary tool for her safe and independent travel. In fact, she's building life-long skills that will enable her to negotiate a variety of environments independently."

2. "Jan needs her cane in the same way that a student in a wheelchair needs wheels or a student with myopia needs eyeglasses. She uses it for safe and independent mobility. Not allowing her to use her cane in the halls and classroom will compromise not only her safety but also her understanding of the environment. In addition, her IEP can't be considered implemented if she's not allowed to use her cane."

3. "Kumar's cane is a respectable and necessary tool that enables him to move about safely, independently, and age appropriately. For example, it would be demeaning as well as inconvenient if he had to wait for someone to "take" him to the bathroom. He's been trained in the proper use of his cane and should be expected to use it properly. The O&M specialist would be glad to discuss any concerns you have."

Where the Law Supports Your Responses
Federal Regulations: Section 300.105(a) Assistive technology
IDEA 2004, (Public Law 108-446): Section 601(c)(5); Section 602(1)(A)

Positive Steps You Can Take

- Your child's O&M specialist will teach proper use and storage of the cane in a variety of environments. You can support these efforts by encouraging your child to use the cane whenever he or she leaves the house.

- Collaborate with your child's O&M specialist to educate school staff about the cane and its importance for your child's safe and independent mobility.

- Get to know adults who are blind or visually impaired who are skilled in the use of a long cane. If possible, arrange a visit to your child's class to educate classmates and staff.

- Enable your child to communicate to others how important the cane is through role playing or practicing some simple statements such as: "The cane is my eye on the ground," "My cane bumps things so I don't," "The cane lets me see what's out in front of me. It's an extension of my body," and "The cane locates things and gives me a few steps to react."

- Have the school celebrate White Cane Safety Day (October 15th).

- If you disagree with the IEP, make sure to include a written statement noting your objections. Unless indicated otherwise, signing the IEP indicates attendance but not necessarily agreement.

"Your child doesn't seem to want to use any specialized devices" (e.g., a cane, braille, optical aids, assistive technology, etc.).

What's Wrong with This Statement?

When specialized tools (such as a cane, braille, optical aids, or assistive technology) have been deemed appropriate and necessary based on the results of assessment, the use of these tools cannot be avoided just because the child does not like them. Just as some children do not like math, they are still required to take it because it is a life skill. Students may not want to use tools that are different from what their classmates are using or may not want attention drawn to their visual impairment, but they still need to learn these life skills. Children may also resist the use of specialized devices because they have not yet mastered the skills and may find using them difficult. School and home can work together to help children understand the value of these devices, overcome any reservations, and provide multiple opportunities for guided practice in their use.

Possible Responses

1. "We're also very concerned about Jamal's reluctance to use his optical aids and we're trying to figure out why he doesn't like to use them. Perhaps they're not helping his visual access as much as we had hoped, or perhaps he needs more practice so that he can use them more quickly and comfortably. We're working with his teacher of students who are

visually impaired and his O&M specialist to assess the situation and perhaps provide more training and practice."

2. "It sounds as if it would be helpful to educate Fatima's classmates about special tools she will be using. Perhaps we could do a workshop with the class. I know some adults who are blind or visually impaired who are very skilled in the use of a variety of aids and techniques. They would be happy to come and visit Fatima's class at a time that's convenient for you."

3. "Sometimes it's hard for Jessica to be the only student who uses specialized tools. It would be beneficial for her to spend some time with others who use similar devices. Perhaps she needs to be introduced to other students with visual impairments in the district. We've also enrolled her in a summer camp for students who are blind or visually impaired. We hope this will increase her motivation to use these tools but, in the meantime, we think instruction needs to continue."

Where the Law Supports Your Responses
Federal Regulations: Section 300.105(a) Assistive technology; Section 300.324 (2)(iii)
IDEA 2004 (Public Law 108-446): Section 601(c)(5); Section 601(d)(1)(A); Section 602(1)(A)

Positive Steps You Can Take

- Work with your child's teacher of students who are visually impaired and O&M specialist to educate school staff about the efficiency and effectiveness of using specialized devices and skills. Share examples of persons who are blind or visually impaired who use a variety of tools effectively.

- Have staff meet at least one person who is blind or has low vision who is gainfully employed and lives/travels independently.

- Children can be encouraged toward the goal of regular, comfortable, and proficient use of specialized techniques and tools. Consider having your child take responsibility for his or her own achievement as a goal in the IEP.

- Help your child become comfortable with using specialized skills and devices by introducing and encouraging their use at home. Provide opportunities for lots of practice!

- Have your child's teacher work closely with the teacher of students who are visually impaired and O&M specialist to come up with solutions and strategies that might encourage your child to "like" his or her devices, or at least see the value in their use.

- If you disagree with the IEP, make sure to include a written statement noting your objections. Unless indicated otherwise, signing the IEP indicates attendance, but not necessarily agreement.

"We don't normally recommend a cane for children this young."

What's Wrong with This Statement?

More and more today, children who are blind or visually impaired are given a cane as soon as they can walk. For younger children, the cane fosters independent exploration that piques their curiosity and, in turn, encourages more exploration. The cane enables children to walk without fear or hesitation, and with no more collisions than are experienced by other sighted children their age. It fosters age-appropriate confidence and independence and increases safety. The introduction of the cane should not be determined by age but by a formal orientation and mobility evaluation. By kindergarten, average children who use a cane are able to walk with confidence and understand and carry out proper cane etiquette in the presence of others and in close quarters. The longer children go without the use of a cane, the more likely they will develop inefficient adaptive strategies (such as foot shuffling) and will view the cane as more stigmatizing than helpful.

Possible Responses

1. "We notice that Anya walks hesitantly and with fear. She's also had a few nasty bumps and falls. We think a cane would be a great help to her. We'd like to work together with you on helping Anya learn proper cane use and become a more safe and confident traveler."

2. "We've read articles that talk about how much young children learn when they can move independently and explore. The articles also suggest that early cane use reduces fear and promotes motor development. We realize this approach may be different from the way you were trained and represents another point of view. But we hope you're willing to consider this information and to conduct an assessment before we make a definite decision."

3. "We're not only concerned that Gabriel move safely but also that he can get around like the other kids his age. How will the other kids view him as an equal if they have to lead him everywhere?"

4. "We understand that you were trained not to give a child Paulina's age a cane. However, we need to discuss what's right for Paulina. We think she's ready for a cane and definitely needs one to move about safely on her own. Instead of using pre-cane devices (such as push toys), we feel it's more appropriate for Paulina to learn how to use a cane in different

situations. Of course, she'll be expected to use it in a safe and appropriate manner. We think it's important to work with an orientation and mobility specialist to complete an appropriate assessment and determine how best to begin working on her cane skills."

Where the Law Supports Your Responses
Federal Regulations: Section 300.105(a)(b) Assistive technology
IDEA 2004 (Public Law 108-446): Section 614(d)(3)

Positive Steps You Can Take

- Collaborate with your child's O&M specialist to educate the school staff about the efficiency and effectiveness of a cane. Give examples of persons who are blind or visually impaired who use a cane to travel effectively and independently.

- Help your child become comfortable with using the cane by introducing and encouraging its use at home. Provide opportunities for lots of practice!

- The school district is not responsible for purchasing a cane for your child, but they often do while the child is receiving orientation and mobility instruction. A white cane can be purchased from a variety of sources. (See the Resources section at the back of this book.)

- If you disagree with the IEP, make sure to include a written statement noting your objections. Unless indicated otherwise, signing the IEP indicates attendance, but not necessarily agreement.

"We're sorry. We're not going to be able to provide a one-on-one aide to care for your child like you do."

or

"Of course your child will need a personal aide. We can't expect our teachers to do all that extra work."

What's Wrong with This Statement?

Children who are blind or visually impaired learn a series of skills that enable them to perform the tasks of life using methods that do not require unimpaired vision. The goal is for children to practice and master these skills in order to acquire and master age-appropriate self-sufficiency. A classroom aide would not have to "care for" such a student.

In the classroom, children who are blind or visually impaired have specific learning needs, and if the classroom teacher cannot meet these needs alone, a paraprofessional may be necessary. However, the paraprofessional should not take on the role and responsibilities of the teacher. With guidance from the classroom teacher, as well as from the teacher of students who are blind or visually impaired, paraprofessionals can perform essential tasks, such as adapting educational materials or reinforcing the use of specialized skills.

Assigning an improperly trained paraprofessional to your child may limit your child's access to competent instruction from a certified teacher, separate your child from classmates, or interfere with the classroom teacher accepting responsibility for your child's learning. If the IEP team determines that a paraprofessional is a necessary support, it is important to make sure that the paraprofessional understands his or her role. The role, time allotment, and specific duties of any paraprofessional must be determined according to the individual needs of your child, and then clearly delineated in the IEP.

Possible Responses

1. "I'm sorry, there seems to be a misunderstanding here. We do not want someone to "take care of" Adira. Quite the opposite. We're working very hard at home to ensure that she will be able to take care of herself in an age-appropriate manner. We'd like the expectations of and training for independence to continue at school as well. A classroom aide should provide support only during times that Adira most needs it. The goal is not to make her dependent on a person but rather to have that person available to facilitate her independent access to the environment."

2. "Perhaps we haven't communicated clearly why we see the need for an aide. Roberto is not yet as independent as his peers. It's hurting him socially, academically, and emotionally (especially in regard to his self-esteem and self-confidence). We feel there needs to be an intense and, we hope, brief effort to bring him closer to performing at the same level as his peers. We'd like to include a specific goal of increasing independence while gradually reducing the need for an aide. We'd like to get it in the IEP right away."

3. "We feel the need to have an aide in the classroom at this point to provide individual help to Emily on occasion. But Emily must learn to pay attention and respond directly to the teacher. We'd like the emphasis to be on moving the aide into a more 'background' position as soon as possible. Then she could concentrate on adapting materials that will enable Emily to participate in the classroom and have academic success. We, of course, would expect that the classroom aide would get direction for adapting materials from Emily's teacher of students who are visually impaired."

Where the Law Supports Your Responses

Federal Regulations: Section 300.34(a) Related services; Section 300.43 (a)(1) Transition services

IDEA 2004 (Public Law 108-446): Section 601(c)(5); Section 602 (33); Section 614(d)(3)

Positive Steps You Can Take

- Communicate respectfully, positively and clearly what your concerns are regarding the educational need for a paraprofessional.

- Expect independence and give your child practice, practice, practice at home. The more your child can practice caring for him- or herself at home, the more skilled and confident he or she will become at school. Expect your child to learn to "do it myself."

- Request that the school provide training to the paraprofessional on promoting independence for children who are blind or visually impaired. The goal is for this person to facilitate access and independence, not to "do things for" your child.

- Make sure the paraprofessional has access-to-your child's teacher of students who are visually impaired and O&M specialist, and knows your child's strengths as well as his or her educational and independence goals.

- Paraprofessionals supplement, not supplant, the classroom teacher. Make sure your team knows and understand this!

- If you disagree with the IEP, make sure to include a written statement noting your objections. Unless indicated otherwise, signing the IEP indicates attendance, but not necessarily agreement.

"We're concerned about your child's safety. We can't let him (or her) be involved in that activity because we don't want him (or her) to get hurt."

What's Wrong with This Statement?

Blindness or visual impairment should never be the reason that children do not participate in an activity. Children who are blind or visually impaired learn a series of skills that enable them to accomplish tasks with impaired vision. In addition, adaptations can be made to various activities so that children who are blind or visually impaired can take part. Some individuals assume that children with visual impairments are more fragile, and that everything in the environment is an inherent danger to them. Unfortunately, overzealous attempts to protect children who are blind or visually impaired from physical harm may teach them that they are incapable and helpless. Children repeatedly exposed to such beliefs are susceptible to learned helplessness and negative self-fulfilling prophecies. Conversely, children who are given opportunities to learn skills and participate in a variety of activities with appropriate adaptations gain competence and confidence and increase their knowledge base and understanding of fundamental concepts.

Possible Responses

1. "We understand that marching band is competitive and that you don't want any student to get hurt. However, we know that many children who are blind or visually impaired around the country have been safe and successful in participating in marching band. We're researching strategies that have worked for other children. As we learn, we will share with you what we discover."

2. "Ling is only as vulnerable as the other children are when they are not paying attention. She's had bumps and bruises growing up, just as other children. We don't want to limit her experiences to protect her from those minor scrapes. She'll be fine."

3. "Brian should have no problem performing on stage. It would be helpful to let him orient himself to the stage and to mark the spot where he is supposed to stand with heavy-duty tape. After that he should be able to find his mark independently. His part and the actions of his character don't need to be altered to compensate for his blindness."

4. "Swimmers who are blind or visually impaired can compete safely by having a spotter use a long pole to tap the swimmer on the head, shoulder, or back as they near the wall. Wrestlers who are blind or visually impaired can compete safely with each other by maintaining physical contact and touching fingertips whenever they're standing. People who are blind or visually impaired compete in track by running along a guide wire or running with a guide. People who are blind or visually impaired participate in archery by using verbal descriptions, physical guidance, and positioning guides."

Where the Law Supports Your Responses
Federal Regulations: Section 300.1 (a)(b) Purposes; Section 300.107(a)(b) Nonacademic services; Section 300.117 Nonacademic settings
IDEA 2004 (Public Law 108-446): Section 601(c)(5); Section 602(33); Section 614(d)

Positive Steps You Can Take

- Comments like this might also be heard in the setting of community or religious activities, or among extended family members. Let others know the confidence you have in your child and his or her abilities by sharing positive comments.

- Make sure your child can "walk the talk" by having high expectations, providing many opportunities to practice skills, and expecting independence at home.

- When your child is about to try something new, the two of you can explore ahead of time how people who are blind or visually impaired participate safely in that particular activity. Then share this information with the sponsor, instructor, or coach so that appropriate adaptations can be prepared.

- Collaborate with the teacher of students who are visually impaired, the O&M specialist, and other teachers or coaches who have successfully taught other children who are blind or visually impaired to do the activity your child is interested in. Encourage your child to talk to the teacher or coach.

- Remind yourself that you may have felt the same way before you knew about the skills and tools for blindness and visual impairment. Now that *you* know better, encourage and reassure anyone expressing doubt as many times as needed, with a smile on your face.

- If you disagree with the IEP, make sure to include a written statement noting your objections. Unless indicated otherwise, signing the IEP indicates attendance, but not necessarily agreement.

"Don't worry, she's doing fine. It's normal for children who are blind to be a year or two behind."

What's Wrong with This Statement?

Blindness or visual impairment itself does not cause children to be behind in academic areas. Academic achievement can be affected, however, by circumstances such as low expectations and not having books and materials in accessible formats. On the other hand, achievement can be positively affected by having age-appropriate expectations, accessible materials, good training for teachers and paraprofessionals, early intervention, and consistency between home and school. If your child is behind academically, a careful assessment of all areas including the child's prior learning experiences and opportunities can help identify the reasons why. It can be helpful to consider the following questions: Have his or her tactile learning opportunities been limited? Is large print being used when braille might make your child more productive? Has you child had enough O&M instruction and practice? Have expectations been appropriately high at home and at school? Work with your child's teacher of students who are blind or visually impaired to find answers to these questions.

Possible Responses

1. "Let's keep our focus on how Autumn's IEP goals compare to the state standards for eighth grade. How can we ensure that the goals and services we're talking about today will help her achieve what the state standards require of all eighth graders?"

2. "The assessment shows that Sammi is about two years behind in his academics, even though everyone agrees that he should be able to keep up with his class. Let's put together a remediation plan with goals for each month so that we make sure he catches up in every subject."

3. "I'm concerned that we're not expecting as much from Khalid as he's capable of. I admit that I think we haven't given him as much independence at home as may be possible, but I'd like to change that and see if Khalid improves. I'd like the bar to be raised at school too. We really need to work together on this."

Where the Law Supports Your Responses

Federal Regulations: Section 300.324(a)(i)-(iv) Development, review, and revision of IEP

IDEA 2004 (Public Law 108-446): Section 601(c)(5)

Positive Steps You Can Take

- It's important to have age-appropriate expectations at home as well as at school. Always look for opportunities to promote learning and independence for your child. Be careful not to step in and help too soon. Make a conscious effort to let your child work things out.

- If you suspect that your child has an additional disability, make careful observations regarding areas in which he or she struggles as well as strategies that have worked. Write these down to share with the IEP team. Even if your child has additional disabilities, you can still have high expectations and provide appropriate learning opportunities and experiences.

- Have your child spend time with peers and adults who are blind or visually impaired who can act as positive role models.

- Get connected to other parents whose children with visual impairments experienced typical development. Find out what worked for their children.

- Fill in the visual gaps for your child. Ask questions to see where the gaps are and then provide experiences to fill them in. Has your child ever touched the roots of a plant? Does she know applesauce isn't red and some apples are green? Does he know what facial expressions and gestures mean socially? ~~Go out on field trips. Go for walks (take~~ the cane!) and stop to smell, touch, and listen.

- If you disagree with the IEP, make sure to include a written statement noting your objections. Unless indicated otherwise, signing the IEP indicates attendance, but not necessarily agreement.

"Sorry, our school is not equipped with and does not have the money for the assistive technology your child needs."

What's Wrong with This Statement?

Many school districts are struggling with shrinking budgets. However, by law the school district must provide your child access to a free, appropriate public education. This includes equal access to the same learning materials and activities as his or her sighted peers. Students needing specialized technology such as adapted computers with braille display, screen magnification, large print software, speech output, or tactile graphics are entitled to these adaptations by law. The school district is responsible for the cost of the needed technology.

Possible Responses

1. "Joshua is currently unable to use the classroom computer. He must have the same opportunity to access the information and technology as his sighted peers. I'd like to request an assistive technology evaluation so that we can determine what his needs are and what technology could benefit him."

2. "Eva's assistive technology evaluation identifies her technology needs and provides recommendations for specific programs and devices. We all want to give Eva the opportunity to keep up with her classmates. I'd like the evaluation results to be included in her IEP, including the recommendation for training on the equipment for Eva and her classroom teacher."

3. "I can appreciate the dilemma that you face in these times of budget cuts, but we're here to focus on Bradley's need for accessible classroom materials and we know that the law requires the school to provide that access. Bradley needs this specific modification in order to keep up with his class and complete his work independently.

4. "It's really a matter of prioritizing the money that the district does have, and for our conversation today, this isn't about money, this is about equal access. Antonia needs adapted computer technology to work in the computer lab with the other students in her class."

Where the Law Supports Your Responses
Federal Regulations: Section 300.105(a)(b) Assistive technology
IDEA 2004 (Public Law 108-446): Section 601(c)(5); Section 602 Definitions; Section 614(1)(A)(i) Definitions

Positive Steps You Can Take

- Various assessments can be used to determine your child's need for assistive technologies that enable her to access the curriculum. These include assessments of functional vision, learning media (braille, large print, regular print with low vision devices), and independent living.

- Consult with other agencies and schools for the blind or visually impaired to learn about the variety of assistive technology devices available.

- See if your state instructional materials center or assistive technology center loans programs or devices to children who are blind or visually impaired. Districts may be more willing to purchase a device that has been shown to be effective for your child.

- You may also want to suggest alternative funding sources to your district, such as corporate donations, Medicaid, private donations, and agencies for the blind.

- Introduce staff to at least one person who is blind or has low vision who effectively uses assistive technology to maintain employment and live/travel independently.

- If you disagree with the IEP, make sure to include a written statement noting your objections. Unless indicated otherwise, signing the IEP indicates attendance, but not necessarily agreement.

"We can't get a certified teacher of students who are blind or visually impaired/orientation and mobility specialist to come way out here!"

or

"Since our teacher of students who are visually impaired/O&M specialist has a large caseload, we can only provide X hours/minutes of services per week."

What's Wrong with This Statement?

Although there is a shortage of teachers and specialists certified in blindness and visual impairment, this does not relieve school districts of their legal requirement to provide highly qualified teachers who are certified to teach specialized skills such as braille, mobility, or assistive technology.

By law, both the type and amount of services provided to children who are blind or visually impaired must be based on individual needs, not staff availability. Since it is crucial for children who are blind or visually impaired to learn the specialized skills and tools that will enable them to participate fully in school and community life, it is necessary for them to have teachers with expertise in these areas. These children have unique learning needs and must be taught by someone with an understanding of how vision loss affects learning and the strategies necessary to address their needs. Teachers of students who are blind or visually impaired are crucial to the overall functioning of school programming for these students. They also perform assessment and evaluation. Therefore it is important that these specialists be included in the planning and implementation of ophthalmological reports and discussion of a student's functional vision.

Possible Responses

1. "We're sure that as educators and professionals you understand the necessity of having certified instructors. We realize that there's a shortage in the field of blindness and visual impairment, and that locating staff may require extra effort. We've heard that other districts have found teachers through job fairs and by offering attractive compensation. Felipe has already lost X hours of instruction that will need to be made up by a certified teacher of students who are visually impaired. We wouldn't want him to get any further behind."

2. "We understand that it may take a few months of intensive effort to recruit someone due to the teacher shortage in this field. However, I'm sure we also all agree that Rachel's education can't be put on hold for that length of time. Let's work together to brainstorm temporary solutions. Perhaps we could contract with a certified teacher of students who are visually impaired from another district, join with another district and share a teacher of students who are visually impaired, or encourage a current district employee to obtain certification as a teacher of students who are visually impaired."

Where the Law Supports Your Responses

Federal Regulations: Section 300.2(b)(2) Applicability of this part to State and local agencies; Section 300.18(b)(1)(i)-(iii) Highly qualified special education teachers

IDEA 2004 (Public Law 108-446): Section 601(c)(5); Section 602 (9) Free appropriate public education

See Maryland court case, *Aaron Richmond v. Calvert County Schools*, August 5, 2002 (available on the National Federation of the Blind's web site at www.nfb.org/fr/fr8/frsf02.htm).

Positive Steps You Can Take

- Acknowledge the shortage while insisting that every effort is made to solve the problem.

- Offer suggestions, such as places to advertise (university programs that train teachers of students who are visually impaired and/or O&M specialists), adding financial incentives, sharing a teacher, or other additional resources.

- If you disagree with the IEP, make sure to include a written statement noting your objections. Unless indicated otherwise, signing the IEP indicates attendance, but not necessarily agreement.

"We don't do things the way they did in your old school, and so we have to rewrite the IEP."

What's Wrong with This Statement?

The IEP process begins with observations and assessment that identify a student's present levels of performance, strengths, and needs. The goals are then designed to address these needs, and finally, the team discusses what program would best meet the identified needs. Listen to what the program has to offer, but remember that the district has a responsibility to look at the former plan and implement it until a new one is formed. Keep in mind that the IEP is not based on what a program has to offer but on the needs of your child.

Possible Responses

1. "We understand there are always differences when a student switches schools and we're very interested in hearing what your program offers. However, we went through a comprehensive assessment process for Ann's current IEP and feel that her teacher of students who are visually impaired and previous classroom teacher created a quality education program. It's my understanding that for now the school is required to continue to implement the existing IEP until a new one is approved by the team."

2. "We don't want to rush into creating a new IEP because the staff has not yet had a chance to get to know Lem. Why don't we try out the existing program for now and meet again in X days/weeks to see if it's addressing his needs?"

Where the Law Supports Your Responses
Federal Regulations: Section 300.320(a)(1)-(7) Definition of individualized education program; Section 300.323(a) When IEPs must be in effect

IDEA 2004 (Public Law 108-446): ~~Section 614(2)(C)~~ Program for children who transfer school districts

Positive Steps You Can Take

- It is best to research potential programs well in advance of any planned move. The quality of education for children with visual impairments varies throughout the United States, as does the quality of all education.

- The IEP should
  - Include the materials, tools, and techniques that will enable your child to participate fully in school lessons and activities
  - Incorporate the individualized instruction your child needs
  - Acknowledge the role of a certified teacher of students who are visually impaired
  - Acknowledge the role of an O&M specialist
  - Indicate how the expanded core curriculum will be addressed
  - Provide specifics regarding literacy instruction
  - Demonstrate a long-term view of education: Work backwards from what you see your child doing at age 25. What skills will be necessary for your child to be successful at age 25?

- If you disagree with the IEP, make sure to include a written statement noting your objections. Unless indicated otherwise, signing the IEP indicates attendance, but not necessarily agreement.

"We did our best to schedule everyone, but the general education teacher is unable to attend."

What's Wrong with This Statement?

The law is very specific about who makes up the IEP team and, therefore, who must be present at the IEP meeting. The absence of any team member (or an inadequate time frame for that member to provide input) can hinder the IEP process. For example, if a child is learning how to use a cane, all team members need to understand and support the development of these skills. If a team member leaves early or is absent, he or she will not have the information necessary to support these skills. In the case that the parents and school agree that a team member may be excused from attending the meeting, his or her input can be provided in writing.

Possible Responses

1. "We think Mr. Fogerty's input is important to the goals we were planning to address today. Let's reschedule for when he's able to attend.

Since my husband and I took off work, we can stay and do some pre-planning with Mrs. Allen and Mr. Wong regarding goals for Jordan in their areas of expertise. That way we will have an outline for some of the goals that we can share with everyone at the actual IEP meeting."

2. "The IEP meeting is the chance for all of us to be on the same page about Laura's educational services and goals. We can't do this if everyone is not here. In the future, we insist that you contact us in advance if you know a team member can't be present for all or part of the meeting. We believe that we all want to plan an educational program that specifically targets Laura's academic needs. There's really no point in spending all this time talking without the entire IEP team present."

Where the Law Supports Your Responses
Federal Regulations: Section 300.321(a)(1)-(7); (e)(1)(2) IEP Team

Positive Steps You Can Take

- Contact your child's IEP team leader in advance if you plan to request goals or services that may require input from someone who does not usually attend your child's IEP meeting.

- Request a parent-teacher conference in advance so you can review issues and information with the general education teacher, thus reducing the amount of time required for his or her presence at the IEP meeting.

- Make sure that everyone who needs to be present is listed on your IEP meeting notice. If a team member is missing from the list, call and find out why and arrange for a new meeting date if necessary. If you do not receive this notice, insist on one for future meetings.

- If a certain team member is notorious for being a "no-show," try to find out why and ask your child's case manager and/or local education agency representative for help in resolving the problem.

- When a team member is excused from attending the IEP meeting, create a plan to share important information he or she missed.

- Be courteous and notify the IEP team leader (e.g., school psychologist) in advance of the people you are bringing with you, or if you have to reschedule the meeting.

- Thank the staff members who come to the meeting. Even if you don't agree with their recommendations, show your appreciation for their participation.

- If you disagree with the IEP, make sure to include a written statement noting your objections. Unless indicated otherwise, signing the IEP indicates attendance, but not necessarily agreement.

"These are the only job training opportunities we offer at this school."

What's Wrong with This Statement?

Children's potential career interests/skills may be neglected because the emphasis of education is placed on the core academic curriculum (i.e., reading, math, science, and social studies). However, for students who are blind or visually impaired especially those who will not be attending college, career education is an important component that needs to be addressed. Individual transition plans tend to be minimal in scope because teachers may have limited time, resources, or knowledge to implement appropriate transition planning. While many districts have transition specialists, they are not typically trained in visual impairment and may inadvertently suggest only jobs that they think people who are blind or visually impaired would be able to do. Instead of selecting careers based on disability, it is essential that transition plans be created around the strengths and interests of the individual child.

It is also important that children who are blind or visually impaired acquire and master the independent living, social, self-advocacy, and job readiness skills that are necessary for them to get and keep a job. Even though many children who are blind or visually impaired are excelling academically, securing employment upon graduation can be challenging because of discrimination or insufficient preparation in independent living skills.

Possible Responses

1. "Maddy loves to sew. She loves the colors and tactile differences of fabrics. I know the school has had her selling candy in the school store for the past two years, but we'd like to see her gain a variety of work experiences. Let's start by identifying job sampling opportunities related to Maddy's interests, such as working at a fabric store or at a clothing store."

2. "Even though Keenan's vocational rehabilitation counselor is unable to provide services until he is 18, she suggested that we begin assessing the services he's receiving and determine when he will lose entitlement to those services. It's important to know which support services will be continuing, which ones will be lost, what the eligibility criteria are for new and potential services, and if we need to sign up for any waiting lists. Keenan wants to move out and be independent, and therefore services need to be coordinated to ensure that he has a smooth transition from school to work."

Where the Law Supports Your Responses
Federal Regulations: Section 300.43(a)(1)(2) Transition services; Section 300.321(b)(1)-(3) IEP Team
IDEA 2004 (Public Law 108-446): Section 613(d)(1)(A)(VIII)

Positive Steps You Can Take

- Consult with the vocational rehabilitation counselor, even if he or she cannot attend the IEP meetings or provide direct services, about steps that can be taken now to smooth your child's transition from school to work.

- Check with the agency in your state that deals with vocational rehabilitation for individuals who are blind or visually impaired to find out age and eligibility requirements.

- Involve your child in the transition planning process to the maximum extent possible. Request that teachers incorporate activities related to career awareness/career skills into the core curriculum.

- Talk to your child as he or she is growing up about various careers and make note of emerging interests and abilities. Get in touch with organizations of blind professionals for job/career ideas.

- With your child, create a list of his or her abilities, strengths, and interests and possible job and career paths that could be a good match. Use this information to discuss with transition personnel. Volunteer work can be a good way to sample job areas.

- If you disagree with the IEP, make sure to include a written statement noting your objections. Unless indicated otherwise, signing the IEP indicates attendance, but not necessarily agreement.

"Some of the braille textbooks haven't come in yet, but we're getting them translated as fast as we can."

What's Wrong with This Statement?

The school district must provide your child access to a free, appropriate public education. All textbooks, readings, daily handouts, and worksheets must be provided in braille, if that is your child's preferred literacy medium, at the same time these materials are available to your child's sighted peers. Without access to the same instructional materials in a format your child can use, his or her progress in the general education curriculum will be limited and he or she may not be able to keep up. Unfortunately, it is often difficult to get materials in braille because of the lag time in book adoption and ordering as well as the fact that it can take up to six months to render a textbook into braille. As a result, many children start, and may even finish, the school year without receiving their textbooks.

An instructional materials accessibility provision was included in the 2004 reauthorization of IDEA. This clause requires that publishers provide a standard electronic file to a central repository (The American Printing House for the Blind) for all textbooks used in K–12 classrooms. It is anticipated that the standard electronic format and the central repository will speed up considerably the process by which printed textbooks can be converted into braille, thus increasing the speed by which they get into the hands of students.

Possible Responses

1. "We appreciate the challenges of working with the district (county or state) system, but we believe that Monique's access to the curriculum can't be compromised. What's slowing down the process of obtaining her textbooks in braille? As parents, we would be happy to call them (e.g., the school board, the central board, the ordering center) to encourage the acceleration of this process."

2. "We need to convene a meeting between Zach's regular education teachers and his teacher of students who are visually impaired to make sure that the worksheets and handout are given to that teacher or to a braille transcriber at least one week before being used in the classroom. We can document this plan in his IEP."

Where the Law Supports Your Responses

Federal Regulations: Section 300.103(c) FAPE—methods and payments; Section 300.105(a) Assistive technology
IDEA 2004 (Public Law 108-446): Section 601(c)(5); Section 612(a)(23)(A) In general; Section 613(a)(6) (A) In general; Section 614(d) Individualized Education Programs

Positive Steps You Can Take

- Braille textbooks should be ordered *at least* 5 to 6 months prior to the beginning of the school year. Convene a meeting with your IEP team members, teacher of students who are visually impaired, or administrator to help with this process.

- Locate a certified braille transcriber in your area. If the textbooks are not ready at the beginning of the school year, your school district can hire this person on a temporary basis.

- Parents should have a print copy of textbooks at home. Print copies of worksheets and handouts should also be sent home.

- Suggest other sources for braille materials such as downloading or scanning books to read on a personal note-taking device with a refreshable braille display. The information may also be available online, thus permitting use of a screen reader.

- Have both your school and your child sign up with the National Library Service for the Blind and Physically Handicapped (this is a service of the Library of Congress; learn more about it at www.loc.gov/nls/).

- Search the American Printing House for the Blind's Louis Database (www.aph.org/) and Bookshare (www.bookshare.org) for a listing of books that are available in alternative formats.

- Work with your state school for the blind to see what protocols they use in obtaining braille materials.

- Find out when textbooks are adopted for the next school year. Contact the local school board or state board to make sure they understand that delays in adoption will mean that children who are blind or visually impaired will not have timely access to textbooks. Because blindness is a low-incidence disability, these professionals may not be aware of this problem.

- If you disagree with the IEP, make sure to include a written statement noting your objections. Unless indicated otherwise, signing the IEP indicates attendance, but not necessarily agreement.

"We don't feel your child needs braille."

What's Wrong with This Statement?

Sometimes parents are told that braille is not appropriate for their child because he or she has enough vision to read print, has a cognitive disability, or has not yet acquired enough reading readiness skills. However, by law, every child who is blind or visually impaired is entitled to learn braille if braille is needed at the present time or might be needed in the future. Learning to read in braille is no more or less difficult than learning to read in print. Your child will undertake it with the same excitement and interest that children might have for any other subject or skill when braille is presented in a positive light, the teaching methods are engaging and appropriate, instruction is consistent, and children are taught to pair their functional vision with their sense of touch. Choosing braille does not mean rejecting the use of print. It is entirely feasible for a child who is visually impaired to use both media. Braille is a literacy tool, whether it is used exclusively or together with print.

Possible Responses

1. "We've been doing some reading about the impact of early braille instruction on later literacy and employment rates. It seems that visually

impaired children with some functional vision who had intensive, early braille instruction showed significantly higher literacy skills and employment rates as adults. We believe that the advantages of early braille instruction far outweigh the disadvantages for Maria. Besides, we've been reading from print/braille books with her, and she loves the idea of reading with her fingers and looking at the pictures with her eyes."

2. "We have a brochure, the *National Agenda for the Education of Children and Youths with Visual Impairments, Including Those with Multiple Disabilities* [available online at www.tsbvi.edu/agenda/national-ppt.htm and at www.afb.org], which describes the legal requirements for providing braille instruction to children with visual impairments. As we understand it, the IEP team must provide braille instruction unless an evaluation indicates that braille is not needed now and won't be needed in the future. Since learning braille can have such a profound impact on our daughter's quality of life, let's make sure we have all the facts before we make the decision."

Where the Law Supports Your Responses
Federal Regulations: Section 300.105(a) Assistive technology; Section 300.324(2)(iii) Development, review, and revision of IEP

Positive Steps You Can Take

- Expose your child and yourself to braille early and often. Picture books with added braille to borrow or buy are available from several sources such as the American Printing House for the Blind (www.aph.org) and BookShare (www.bookshare.org).

- Learn more about braille. The more comfortable you are with braille, the more likely you will be able to make decisions about print, braille, or both based upon facts—not emotions or misconceptions.

- Work with your state or regional library for the blind and local and school libraries to get copies of print/braille storybooks into their collections.

- Contact organizations to see if there is an adult braille reader in your community who can read with and/or tutor your child in braille, demonstrate and talk to your child's class about braille, or tutor yourself and your child in braille.

- Organize a print/braille storybook hour for a group that includes children who are blind or visually impaired and children who are sighted. Recruit a proficient braille reader to read aloud to the group. Your school's visual impairment program, organizations of the blind or visually impaired, or the library for the blind or the local school for the blind or visually impaired might be interested in sponsoring this event.

- Encourage your child's siblings and sighted peers to learn about braille.

- If you disagree with the IEP, make sure to include a written statement noting your objections. Unless indicated otherwise, signing the IEP indicates attendance, but not necessarily agreement.

"We don't normally write that into the IEP."

What's Wrong with This Statement?

The district is legally bound to implement only those services that are written into the IEP. Therefore your child's educational needs must be documented in the IEP. Items to be listed in the IEP include all accommodations and modifications; specialized devices; what, where, when, how much, and how often educational services will be provided; who will provide these services; and skills your child will be expected to master. The following skill areas should be assessed and included as appropriate: alternative skills of blindness and visual impairment such as braille, orientation and mobility, and adaptive technology; social interaction; independent living skills; recreation and leisure; career education; visual efficiency; and self-advocacy skills.

Possible Responses

1. "We feel that everything we agree upon should be written into the IEP. Then the expectations for everyone's part in implementing the goals and accommodations are clear. Having everything documented in the IEP will also help other staff when Anna transitions to middle school and high school and would make it easier for the next school if our family were to move."

2. "It sounds like we all agree on the goals and services that are important for Reggie. Let's think how we can write them into the IEP."

Where the Law Supports Your Responses
Federal Regulations: Sec. 300.324 Development, review, and revision of IEP IDEA 2004 (Public Law 108-446): Section 602(9) Free appropriate public education

Positive Steps You Can Take

- Meet with your child's teacher to discuss areas he or she believes need to be addressed in the following year to help your child function better in the classroom as a learner and a class member. Discuss what worked and didn't work this past year. Take notes and ask the teacher to sign them next to your signature. These can later be attached to or incorporated into the IEP.

- Make a list of areas that you as a parent would like to see improve for your child (if appropriate, create this list together with your child). A few examples include improved reading speed or reading comprehension, social skills, participation in group activities, orientation and mobility skills, and organization skills. Share this list with team members in advance; discuss and fine-tune items before the meeting. Invite team members to suggest items that they feel need to be addressed. Point out that this will help shorten the time at the meeting.

- Work with your child's teacher of students who are visually impaired to circulate a list of special materials, equipment, and approaches that can be included in the IEP.

- Be sure to thank everyone for their participation before and after the meeting.

- If you disagree with the IEP, make sure to include a written statement noting your objections. Unless indicated otherwise, signing the IEP indicates attendance, but not necessarily agreement.

Glossary

This glossary explains some of the common terms that relate to visual impairment and the education of students who are blind or visually impaired. It contains terms used in this book as well as others that you are likely to hear used by members of educational teams or see on students' eye reports and in their files.

accommodations. Arrangements, techniques and materials that change how a child is taught or tested, such as the use of large print or braille materials, or extra time allotted for taking a test.

activities of daily living (ADL). The routine activities that an individual must be able to do in order to live independently, such as dressing, preparing and eating food, and so forth.

acuity. See **visual acuity**.

adapted materials. Materials such as texts, lessons, and other print reading matter that have been prepared in formats such as braille, large print, or electronic files for use by people who are visually impaired.

adaptive technique. A technique or method that helps a visually impaired person perform an activity, such as writing or counting money.

adaptive technology. See **assistive technology**.

alternate achievement standards. Expectations of performance for students with severe cognitive disabilities that may differ in complexity from the state's standards for all children, but that address prerequisite skills.

alternate media. Formats other than regular print for the presentation of information that can be used by people who are blind or visually impaired, such as braille, large print, or audio recordings.

assessment. For educational purposes, the process used to determine a student's current needs and skill levels.

assistive technology. Equipment, especially electronic devices and computer hardware and software, that helps people who are blind or visually impaired obtain information and communicate; includes **closed-circuit televisions**, braille translation software, **braille embossers**, **screen readers** combined with a **speech synthesizer**, screen-enlargement software, and **refreshable braille displays**. Also known as **adaptive technology** or access technology.

assistive technology assessment. The process used to determine what technology tools a student needs to perform successfully his or her current and future educational tasks.

audiobook. A book read aloud and recorded on cassette or other format.

braille. A tactile system for reading and writing, based on a cell-like structure made up of six raised dots used in various arrangements to represent printed letters.

braille embosser. An electronic braille printer that connects to a computer and prints (embosses) braille on paper.

braillewriter. A machine similar to a typewriter that is used to write or emboss braille.

case manager. The professional in the public rehabilitation system charged with assisting eligible clients or consumers with the career exploration, preparation, and placement process; also, more broadly, the individual on an educational team responsible for coordinating the activities and services provided by other professionals.

center-based services. Services provided at an agency, rather than in an individual's home.

child find. A process mandated by federal legislation (see **Individuals with Disabilities Education Act**) to identify children with disabilities or at risk of developmental delays and provide them with early assistance and services.

closed-circuit television (CCTV). A device that magnifies print or pictures using a camera to project an image onto a television screen or computer monitor. Also known as a video magnifier.

core curriculum. The general education curriculum that all students in public schools are expected to master, including language arts, science, mathematics, and social studies.

daily living skills. Abilities (such as methods for personal grooming, household management, and communication) that individuals need to be able to perform tasks for living independently; the skills needed for the routine activities of everyday life. Also called **independent living skills.**

developmental delay. Performance below the level that is expected for a given age, as in cognitive, communication, motor, sensory, and social abilities.

direct service. Services provided by a professional or agency directly to an individual, as opposed to the provision of information or consultation, or referral of the individual elsewhere for services or assistance. Also, as specified on an **Individualized Education Program (IEP)**, the face-to-face time a teacher or other service provider spends with a child delivering direct instruction or other services.

disability. A condition that exists when, in a particular setting, an individual cannot independently perform a specific set of functional activities.

due process. The legal procedure required for school districts to address a parent's or guardian's concerns or disagreements with the educational program of a child who is receiving special education, as specified under the **Individuals with Disabilities Education Act**.

early intervention. Intervening in a child's development to provide support at an early time in his or her life.

early interventionist. A professional who works with infants from birth through age 3 who have disabilities and their families.

electronic notetaker. A portable device with a braille or typewriter keyboard for input, and output in braille and/or speech, that interfaces with a computer, and may also function as a personal digital assistant.

electronic travel aid. A device that gives off audible signals when objects are nearby in the environment, for use by individuals with **visual impairments** to move about or travel safely.

expanded core curriculum. A curriculum that covers the unique, disability-specific skills, such as **independent living skills** and **orientation and mobility skills**, that students with **visual impairments** need to acquire and master to compensate for vision loss and live independently and productively.

facility-based employment. See **sheltered workshop**.

family-centered. An approach in which the family's needs and desires are addressed and the family is treated as an equal participant, choosing the type and frequency of service delivery, the specific related services, and the service provider from a range of options.

functional vision. A degree of vision sufficient to be of use in performing a given task, such as reading or sewing.

functional vision assessment. An assessment of an individual's use of vision in a variety of tasks and settings, including measures of near and distance vision; visual fields; eye movements; and responses to specific environmental characteristics, such as light and color. The assessment report includes recommendations for instructional procedures, modifications or adaptations, and additional tests. Also known as **functional vision evaluation**.

functional vision evaluation. See **functional vision assessment**.

group home. A residential program designed to house a small group of adults with severe disabilities in a home setting within the community

home-based services. Services provided in an individual's home, rather than at an agency or in the community.

incidental learning. Learning gained by observing persons and activities around us within our immediate environment.

inclusion. An educational philosophy that advocates placing students with disabilities in general education classrooms with children who are not disabled for all or part of the school day; often used interchangeably with **mainstreaming**.

independent living program. A program administered by the U.S. Rehabilitation Services Administration that offers **rehabilitation** services to eligible clients who are not candidates for specific services that help people find and maintain a job, such as some persons who have multiple disabilities or elderly persons who are visually impaired.

independent living services. Training in **independent living skills** used in everyday life with the goal of helping an individual to live on his or her own.

independent living skills. Skills for performing daily tasks and managing personal needs, such as those for self-care, planning and cooking meals, maintaining a sanitary living environment, traveling independently, budgeting one's expenses, and functioning as independently as possible in the home and in the community.

indirect service. Information, consultation, or other support provided by a professional or agency to an individual or group, as opposed to the hands-on provision of therapeutic or other services. Also, as specified on an **Individualized Education Program (IEP)**, consultation or other support provided by a teacher or other service provider, as opposed to face-to-face instruction or therapy.

Individualized Education Program (IEP). A written plan of instruction by an educational team, which includes a student's present levels of educational performance, annual goals, short-term objectives, specific services needed, duration of services, evaluation, and related information. Under the **Individuals with Disabilities Education Act (IDEA)**, each student receiving **special education** services must have such a plan.

Individualized Family Service Plan (IFSP). A plan for the coordination of early intervention services for infants and toddlers with disabilities, similar to the **Individualized Education Program (IEP)** that is required for all school-age children with disabilities. A requirement of the **Individuals with Disabilities Education Act (IDEA)**.

Individuals with Disabilities Education Act (IDEA). The federal legislation that mandates and safeguards a free, appropriate public education for all eligible children with disabilities in the United States.

Individuals with Disabilities Education Improvement Act (IDEA 2004). The 2004 reauthorization of the **Individuals with Disabilities Education Act (IDEA)**.

instructional materials center (also **instructional resource center**). Resource centers that provide **adapted materials**, such as **braille** textbooks, large-print books, and texts on tape, for visually impaired students.

interdisciplinary team. Professionals from various disciplines who conduct and share the results of assessments and jointly plan instructional programs. See also **multidisciplinary team**.

intermediate care facility for the mentally retarded. Structured living settings for young adults with the most severe or profound disabilities, or those who need a structured setting. Administered through state departments of mental health and mental retardation and funded by Medicaid, they provide housing, medical services, and some skill training.

itinerant teacher. An instructor who moves from place to place (e.g., from home to home, school to hospital, or school to school) to provide instruction and support to students with special needs.

lead agency. According to the **IDEA Part C** program, the agency in charge of **early intervention** for a specific state.

learning media. The formats and methods that best enable a student who is visually impaired to learn, such as **braille**, **closed-circuit television (CCTV)**, **magnifiers**, and audiotapes.

learning media assessment. An examination of a student's ability to use general learning materials and determination of any specialized formats he or she needs to complete current and future reading and writing tasks.

least restrictive environment. An environment that is adapted only to the extent necessary to maximize learning for a student who is disabled; also, the setting in which a child with disabilities can be provided with an appropriate education and maximum contact with nondisabled students.

literacy. The ability to read and write.

literacy medium. The material or method that a student uses to read and write, including print, braille, and audiotapes.

local education agency (LEA). The administrative agency for the public schools in a given area, such as a board of education.

low vision. A **visual impairment** that is severe enough to interfere with everyday activities and cannot be corrected by ordinary eyeglasses or contact lenses; vision that may be usable to plan and perform daily tasks.

low vision device. A device used to improve the ability of persons with **visual impairments** to use their vision. Low vision devices include **optical devices** such as **magnifiers** and **telescopes** as well as nonoptical devices such as bold-line felt-tip markers.

low vision evaluation or examination. A specialized clinical examination to assess the visual abilities and needs of an individual with low vision.

low vision specialist. An ophthalmologist or optometrist who specializes in the diagnosis and treatment of people with low vision, including the prescription of optical and nonoptical devices.

low vision therapist. A professional who performs **functional vision assessments** following clinical **low vision examinations** and implements the recommendations of the low vision rehabilitation team. The low vision therapist may provide instruction in the use of **functional vision** as well as in the use of **low vision devices**.

magnifier. A type of **low vision device** used to increase the size of an image based on lenses or lens systems; a magnifier may be mounted on a stand, handheld, or mounted in eyeglasses.

mainstreaming. The placement of a student with a disability in a general education classroom with children who are not disabled for all or part of the school day; often used interchangeably with **inclusion**.

mobility. The act of moving or the ability to move from one's present position to one's desired position in another part of the environment; see also **orientation**.

mobility aid, electronic. See **electronic travel aid**.

mobility skills. A set of specific techniques and strategies to help people with visual impairments remain safe while traveling.

modifications. Changes to the standard of learning or performance, or the requirements that a student needs to meet, for a learning task, such as being taught material at a lower grade level, being tested at a lower grade level, or being taught fewer skills in the curriculum at the same grade level.

multidisciplinary team. A team made up of professionals from different disciplines who work independently to conduct assessments of a student, write and implement separate plans, and evaluate the student's progress within the parameters of their own disciplines. See also **interdisciplinary team**.

multiple disabilities. Two or more concomitant disabilities (physical, mental, or emotional) that have a direct effect on the ability to learn.

National Library Service for the Blind and Physically Handicapped. A part of the U.S. Library of Congress that loans free reading materials on tape, on disk, or in **braille** through a network of libraries throughout the country to individuals who are unable to read regular print books because of a visual or physical disability.

natural environments. Environments for the delivery of special education services, defined in the law as settings that are natural or normal for other children of the same age who do not have disabilities.

nonoptical devices or **aids. Low vision devices** that do not involve optics, such as high-intensity lamps or bold-lined paper.

occupational therapist. A professional who uses specific activities to improve an individual's physical, social, psychological, or intellectual development, focusing on the development of fine motor skills and perceptual abilities.

ophthalmologist. A physician who specializes in the medical and surgical care of the eyes and is qualified to prescribe ocular medications and to perform surgery on the eyes. He or she may also perform refractive and **low vision** work, including eye examinations and other vision services.

optical device. Any system of lenses that enhances visual function.

optometrist. A health care provider who specializes in the diagnosis and treatment of refractive errors and other eye conditions, and who prescribes and dispenses eyeglasses or contact lenses, as regulated by state laws. May also perform **low vision examinations**.

orientation. The knowledge of one's distance and direction relative to things observed or remembered in one's surroundings and the ability to keep track of these spatial relationships as they change during locomotion; see also **mobility**.

orientation and mobility (O&M). The field dealing with systematic techniques by which persons who are blind or visually impaired orient themselves to their environments and move about independently. See also **mobility**, **orientation**.

orientation and mobility (O&M) specialist. A professional who specializes in teaching travel skills to persons who are visually impaired, including the use of canes, dog guides, and electronic traveling aids, as well as the use of human guides.

Part B. The part of the **Individuals with Disabilities Education Act (IDEA)** that delineates the provision of **special education** and **related services** to children and young adults between the ages of 3 and 21 years.

Part C. The part of the **Individuals with Disabilities Education Act (IDEA)** that delineates the provision of **early intervention** services for infants and toddlers with disabilities from birth to their third birthday and their families.

physical therapist. A professional who focuses on the development, correction, and prevention of motor problems (those involving muscular movement).

preliteracy skills. Skills that help prepare a child's interest in and ability to read.

procedural safeguards. Methods required under the **Individuals with Disabilities Education Act (IDEA)** that state and local educational agencies must establish to protect the rights of children with disabilities to a free and appropriate education.

refreshable braille display. An electronic device using small pins to display in **braille** the text that appears on a computer or **electronic notetaker**.

rehabilitation. The process of bringing or restoring an individual to a normal or optimum state of health or level of constructive activity; a means of medical treatment and physical or psychological therapy; specifically, the relearning of skills already acquired prior to the onset of a visual disability.

rehabilitation counselor. A rehabilitation professional who serves as a **case manager**, usually at a state agency, and may provide therapeutic counseling.

rehabilitation teacher. A professional whose primary goal is to instruct persons with **visual impairments** to utilize adaptive skills to perform the tasks of everyday life, primarily in the areas of communication, personal management, home management, leisure time, and movement in familiar environments. Also known as **vision rehabilitation therapist**.

related services. Services required under the **Individuals with Disabilities Education Act (IDEA)** to assist a child with a disability to benefit from **special education**.

resource room. A service delivery option designed to support students with **visual impairments** who are enrolled in a general education classroom by providing specialized instruction and support from a qualified teacher who is housed on site.

screen-magnification system. A computer system that electronically enlarges the characters displayed on a computer monitor.

screen reader. A computer program that translates print characters on a computer screen into their sound equivalents as part of a **speech output system**. These sounds are then "spoken" as words by the **speech synthesizer** component of the system.

sensory channel. A sense through which an individual acquires information, such as vision or touch.

sensory integration training. Instruction, often provided under the supervision of an occupational therapist, that helps an individual organize and integrate or process the sensations received by seeing, hearing, touching, and smelling.

sensory training. Instruction that helps a person who is blind or visually impaired develop his or her other sensory abilities to be aware of the environment.

sheltered workshop (also **facility-based employment**). A business that provides jobs for individuals with a disability who may need special assistance to be able to work.

slate and stylus. A portable, lightweight device used to write **braille**. It consists of a frame in which braille paper is placed with rows of small round indentations arranged in the shape of braille cells and a pen-like instrument used to punch indentations into the paper.

special education. Specially designed instruction, provided at no cost to the parents, to meet the unique needs of a child with a disability to receive a free and appropriate public education.

speech output system. A computer-based system that converts text displayed as print into simulated speech.

speech synthesizer. Part of a **speech output system** that provides the spoken equivalent of the print text displayed on a computer monitor.

speech therapist. A professional in the area of communication techniques and speech and language pathology who teaches people to improve their spoken communication.

supplementary aids and services. Supports provided in the regular education class and other education-related settings, including extracurricular activities, to enable children with disabilities to be educated with nondisabled children to the maximum extent appropriate.

supported living facilities. Living facilities designed to allow an individual with disabilities to live in a home of his or her choosing and receive assistance from service providers as needed.

synthetic speech. Reading aloud of text, such as that on a computer screen, produced by a combination of **screen reader** software that can read the text and a **speech synthesizer** that can convert that text into speech.

tactile. Related to or experienced through the sense of touch.

tactile adaptations. Changes of visual materials, including text, pictures, and maps used in the classroom, into a format that can be understood by a student using active touch.

tactile skills. The ability to explore an object systematically, enabling a person to observe all the features of that object by using his or her sense of touch.

Talking Book. A book or other reading material recorded aloud for a listener who is blind or visually impaired.

Talking Book program. A free national library program administered by the National Library Service for the Blind and Physically Handicapped of the Library of Congress for persons with visual and physical limitations. Books and magazines are produced in **braille**, in electronic formats, and on recorded discs and audiocassettes and are distributed to a cooperative network of regional libraries that circulate them to eligible borrowers. The program also lends the devices on which the recordings are played.

teacher of students with visual impairments. A specially trained and certified teacher who is qualified to teach special skills to students with **visual impairments**.

technology device. See **assistive technology**.

telescope. A **low vision** device that uses lenses or lens systems to make small objects appear closer and larger.

transdisciplinary team. See **multidisciplinary team**.

transition Individualized Education Program (IEP). A program, written for a student age 16 and older, that addresses the need for **transitional services** in the areas of employment, education and training, leisure and recreation, and living arrangements. It details proposed activities to achieve desired outcomes, establishes timetables for reaching these goals, and assigns responsibility for providing support to the agencies and individuals responsible for following through on each activity. See also **Individualized Education Program (IEP)**.

transitional services. Assistance, instruction, and planning for an individual who is making a change to a different type of environment and from one system of services to another. Transitional services are required by the **Individuals with Disabilities Education Act** for toddlers who are moving from **early intervention** services to preschool or other appropriate services; and for young adults who are moving from school to community living and employment or from secondary school to higher education.

video magnifier. A computer-based device for magnifying images and projecting them on a computer screen. See also **closed-circuit television**.

visual acuity. The sharpness or clearness of a person's vision; how much detail a person can see, usually measured by a standard eye chart.

visual impairment. Any degree of vision loss that affects a person's ability to perform the tasks of daily life.

vocational rehabilitation. A system of services that evaluates personal, work, and work-related traits and is designed to result in the individual's optimal placement in employment.

Resources

This resource listing provides a sample of the organizations and companies that offer assistance, information, services, referrals, and products related to special education and the education of children who are visually impaired. For more complete listings of service providers, parents can consult the *AFB Directory of Services for Blind and Visually Impaired Persons in the United States and Canada,* available from the American Foundation for the Blind or online at www.afb.org. AFB's Information Center at (800) AFB-LINE (232-5463) also provides helpful information.

ORGANIZATIONS OFFERING INFORMATION, SUPPORT, AND SERVICES

American Council of the Blind
1155 15th Street, NW, Suite 1004
Washington, DC 20005
(202) 467-5081; (800) 424-8666
Fax: (202) 467-5085
E-mail: info@acb.org
www.acb.org

The American Council of the Blind (ACB) is a membership organization and national clearinghouse for information that promotes the effective participation of blind people in all aspects of society. ACB provides information and referral; legal assistance and representation; scholarships; leadership and legislative training; consumer advocate support; assistance in technological research; a speaker referral service; and consultative and advisory services to individuals, organizations, and agencies.

American Foundation for the Blind
11 Penn Plaza, Suite 300
New York, NY 10001
(212) 502-7600; (800) 232-5463
TDD/TTY: (212) 502-7662
Fax: (212) 502-7777
E-mail: afbinfo@afb.net
www.afb.org

The American Foundation for the Blind (AFB) serves as an information clearinghouse for people who are visually impaired and their families, the

357

public, professionals, schools, organizations, and corporations and operates a toll-free information hotline. AFB conducts research and mounts program initiatives to promote the inclusion of visually impaired persons, especially in the areas of literacy, technology, aging, and employment; advocates for services and legislation; and maintains the M. C. Migel Memorial Library and the Helen Keller Archives. It also produces videos and publishes books, pamphlets, the *Directory of Services for Blind and Visually Impaired Persons in the United States and Canada*, the *Journal of Visual Impairment & Blindness*, and *AccessWorld: Technology and People with Visual Impairments*. AFB maintains the CareerConnect web site (www.afb.org/CareerConnect), a free resource for people who want to learn about the range and diversity of jobs performed by adults who are blind or visually impaired throughout the United States and Canada; a National Literacy Center in Atlanta; a National Center on Vision Loss in Dallas; AFB TECH, which focuses on assistive and mainstream technology, in Huntington, West Virginia; a National Employment Center in San Francisco; and a Public Policy Center in Washington, DC.

Association for Education and Rehabilitation of the Blind and Visually Impaired
1703 N. Beauregard Street, Suite 440
Alexandria, VA 22311
(703) 671-4500; (877) 492-2708
Fax: (703) 671-6391
E-mail: aer@aerbvi.org
www.aerbvi.org

The Association for Education and Rehabilitation of the Blind and Visually Impaired (AER) is the primary membership organization for professionals who work in all phases of education and rehabilitation with visually impaired persons of all ages on the local, regional, national, and international levels. AER seeks to develop and promote professional excellence through such support services as continuing education, publications, information dissemination, lobbying and advocacy, and conferences and workshops.

Blind Babies Foundation
1814 Franklin Street, 11th Floor
Oakland, CA 94612
(510) 446-2229
Fax: (510) 446-2262
E-mail: bbfinfo@blindbabies.org
www.blindbabies.org/

Blind Babies Foundation (BBF) provides early intervention services to infants and to preschool children who are visually impaired and their families in Northern California counties, all at no cost to the families.

Blind Children's Center
4120 Marathon Street
Los Angeles, CA 90029
(323) 664-2153
Fax: (323) 665-3828
E-mail: info@blindchildrenscenter.org

The Blind Children's Center (BCC) is a family-centered agency that serves children with visual impairments from birth to school-age.

Braille Institute of America
741 North Vermont Avenue
Los Angeles, CA 90029
(323) 663-1111; (800) 272-4553
Fax: (323) 663-1428
E-mail: info@brailleinstitute.org
www.brailleinstitute.org

The Braille Institute of America provides information, referrals, and materials on the needs of children and adults who are blind or visually impaired and promotes the use of braille as well as supports the provision of adapted materials through a wide range of outreach and direct-service activities.

Center for Law and Education
43 Winter Street, 8th Floor
Boston, MA 02108
(617) 451-0855
Fax: (617) 457-0857
www.cleweb.org

The Center for Law and Education (CLE) is a national support center focusing on the legal rights and responsibilities of students and school personnel and on key education programs and initiatives, including Title I, vocational education programs and school-to-work systems, and special education for students with disabilities. CLE undertakes advocacy efforts, participates in the formulation of legislation and policies at the national level, and provides assistance to students, parents, and educators at the state and local levels.

Council for Exceptional Children
Division on Visual Impairments
1110 North Glebe Road, Suite 300
Arlington, VA 22201-5704
(703) 620-3660; (888) 221-6830
TDD/TTY: (866) 915-5000

Fax: (703) 264-9494
E-mail: service@cec.sped.org
www.cec.sped.org
www.ed.arizona.edu/dvi (Division on Visual Impairments)

The Council for Exceptional Children (CEC) is a professional membership organization of teachers, school administrators, and others who are concerned with children who require special services. CEC publishes periodicals, books, and other materials on teaching exceptional children; advocates for appropriate government policies; supports professional development activities; and disseminates information on effective instructional strategies. Its Division on Visual Impairments focuses on the education of children who are visually impaired and the concerns of professionals who work with them.

Council of Schools for the Blind
North Dakota School Vision Services/School for the Blind
500 Stanford Road
Grand Forks, ND 59203-2799
(701) 795-2708
Fax: (701) 795-2727
www.cosb1.org/members

The Council of Schools for the Blind (COSB) promotes new opportunities for children who are blind and visually impaired; increases public understanding of blindness; encourages efficient management of specialized schools for students who are blind, which educate a diverse population from academic to severely multiply disabled children; and provides information on these specialized schools, many of which offer outreach services for students and their families.

Foundation for Blind Children
1235 East Harmont Drive
Phoenix, AZ 85020-3864
(602) 331-1470
Fax: (602) 678-5819
E-mail: info@the-fbc.org
www.the-fbc.org

The Foundation for Blind Children (FBC) provides a comprehensive system of services for blind and visually impaired children, adults, and their families in Arizona.

Hadley School for the Blind
700 Elm Street
Winnetka, IL 60093

(847) 446-8111; (800) 323-4238
TDD/TTY: (847) 441-8111
Fax: (847) 446-9916
E-mail: info@hadley.edu
www.hadley.edu

The Hadley School for the Blind offers a wide range of free distance education courses through traditional mail or online to eligible students, family members, and professionals.

Heath Resource Center
The George Washington University
National Clearinghouse on Postsecondary Education for
Individuals with Disabilities
2121 K Street, NW, Suite 220
Washington, DC 20037
(202) 973-0904 (Voice/TTY)
(800) 544-3284
Fax: (202) 973-0908
E-mail: askheath@gwu.edu
www.heath.gwu.edu/

The Heath Resource Center is a national clearinghouse on postsecondary education for individuals with disabilities that serves as an information exchange about educational support services, policies, procedures, adaptations, and opportunities at American campuses, vocational-technical schools, and other postsecondary training sources. The Heath Center participates in national conferences, training sessions, and workshops; develops training modules; publishes resource papers, fact sheets, directories, and web site information; and fosters a network of professionals in the arena of disability issues. Heath is one of three clearinghouses authorized by the Individuals with Disabilities Education Act (IDEA) to provide specialized educational information to people with disabilities, their families, and the professionals who work with them. Its free booklet *Financial Aid for Students with Disabilities*, describes federal financial aid programs, state vocational rehabilitation services, and regional and local sources of aid and includes a listing of nationally awarded grants and a pre-college checklist to organize the search for funds.

Helen Keller National Center for Deaf-Blind Youths and Adults
141 Middle Neck Road
Sands Point, NY 11050-1299
(516) 944-8900
TDD/TYY: (516) 944-8637
Fax: (516) 944-7302

E-mail: hkncinfo@hknc.org
www.hknc.org

The Helen Keller National Center for Deaf-Blind Youths and Adults (HKNC) provides services and technical assistance to individuals who are deaf-blind and their families and maintains a network of regional and affiliate agencies. HKNC's National Training Team also offers seminars, on-site conferences, and short-term programs to increase knowledge and support the development of skills specific to deaf-blindness in those working with individuals who are deaf-blind across the country.

Hilton/Perkins National and International Program
Perkins School for the Blind
175 North Beacon Street
Watertown, MA 02472
(617) 972-7228
Fax: (617) 923-8076
www.perkins.org/

The Hilton/Perkins National and International Program works to improve the quality of life for individuals with visual impairments, including those with multiple disabilities, through special projects that support and offer direct service to children, their families, and professionals. It publishes books for families and professionals about the education of children with visual impairments, multiple disabilities, and deaf-blindness and consults on the development of services for children who are blind with multiple disabilities and deaf-blindness and their families in developing countries.

Lighthouse International
111 East 59th Street
New York, NY 10022
(212) 821-9200; (888) 222-9320
TDD/TTY: (212) 821-9713
Fax: (212) 821-9707
E-mail: info@lighthouse.org
www.lighthouse.org

Lighthouse International provides vision rehabilitation services for all ages and operates an integrated preschool program for children who are blind or visually impaired.

National Association for Parents of Children with Visual Impairments
P.O. Box 317
Watertown, MA 02471
(617) 972-7441; (800) 562-6265

Fax: (617) 972-7444

www.napvi.org

E-mail: napvi@perkins.org

The National Association for Parents of Children with Visual Impairments (NAPVI) is a membership association that supports state and local parent groups and conducts advocacy workshops for parents of visually impaired children and youths, including those with multiple disabilities. NAPVI operates a national clearinghouse for information, education, and referral; fosters communication among federal, state, and local agencies that provide services or funding for services; and promotes public understanding of the needs and rights of visually impaired children and youths. It distributes various books for parents and teachers of visually impaired students and produces the quarterly magazine *Awareness*.

National Association of State Directors of Special Education

1800 Diagonal Road, Suite 320

Alexandria, VA 22314

(703) 519-3800

TDD/TTY: (703) 519-7008

Fax: (703) 519-3808

nasdse@nasdse.org

www.nasdse.org

The National Association of State Directors of Special Education (NASDSE) is a membership organization of state directors of special education and others employed in state education agencies who direct, coordinate, or supervise programs and services for the education of students with disabilities. It provides assistance to state education agencies in the delivery of quality education to children and youths with disabilities through training, technical assistance, research, and policy development; offers consultative services; publishes newsletters; and sponsors conferences.

National Center on Secondary Education and Transition

Institute on Community Integration

University of Minnesota

6 Pattee Hall, 150 Pillsbury Drive SE

Minneapolis, MN 55455

(612) 624-2097

Fax: (612) 624-9344

E-mail: ncset@umn.edu

www.ncset.org

The National Center on Secondary Education and Transition is a clearinghouse for information, resources, and publications on secondary education and transition services for students with disabilities.

National Coalition for Parent Involvement in Education
3929 Old Lee Highway, Suite 91A
Fairfax, VA 22030
(703) 359-8973
Fax: (703) 359-0972
www.ncpie.org

The National Coalition for Parent Involvement in Education (NCPIE) advocates for the involvement of parents and families in their children's education and for relationships among home, school, and community to enhance the education of all young people. It advocates for strong parent and family involvement initiatives at the national level; provides resources and legislative information; and conducts activities involving member organizations and their affiliates and constituencies to increase and promote parent and family participation.

National Consortium on Deaf-Blindness
Western Oregon University
345 North Monmouth Avenue
Monmouth, OR 97361
(800) 438-9376
TDD/TTY: (800) 854-7013
Fax: (503) 838-8150
E-mail: dblink@tr.wou.edu
www.ncdbtad.org
www.dblink.org/

The National Consortium on Deaf-Blindness (NCDB) is a federal project that combines the resources and expertise of three organizations: the Teaching Research Institute at Western Oregon University, the Helen Keller National Center, and the Hilton/Perkins Program, Perkins School for the Blind. NCDB provides technical assistance throughout the United States, makes information relevant to deaf-blindness easily available, and promotes personnel training efforts to improve the skills and knowledge of service providers who work with children and youths who are deaf-blind. Activities include national conferences, area meetings, workshops, webinars, individualized technical assistance to states, and information services directed toward families, state deaf-blind projects, educators, early intervention and other service providers, and educational and adult service agencies.

DB-LINK is the Information Services and Dissemination arm of NCDB. DB-LINK maintains an in-depth collection of materials and products pertinent to deaf-blindness that is available to families, teachers, service providers, and the general public. It provides information and referrals regarding deaf-blind children from birth through age 21 and publishes the newsletter *Deaf-Blind Perspectives.*

National Dissemination Center for Children with Disabilities (formerly the National Information Center for Children and Youth with Disabilities, NICHCY)
P.O. BOX 1492
Washington, DC 20013-1492
(202) 884-8200 (Voice and TTY)
(800) 695-0285 (Voice and TTY)
Fax: (202) 884-8441
E-mail: nichcy@aed.org
www.nichcy.org

The National Dissemination Center for Children with Disabilities serves as a national information clearinghouse on subjects related to children and youths with disabilities. It provides information and referral to national, state, and local resources and disseminates numerous free publications. It also offers fact sheets on a variety of disabilities; information packets; and "State Sheets," which list each state's resources for people with disabilities. Parents can call or send in requests for free information or a publication list.

National Federation of the Blind
1800 Johnson Street
Baltimore, MD 21230-4998
(410) 659-9314
Fax: (410) 685-5653
E-mail: nfb@nfb.org
www.nfb.org

The National Federation of the Blind (NFB) is a membership organization that works to improve the social and economic opportunities for visually impaired persons and the understanding of blindness by the general public. NFB provides public education and support services to blind and visually impaired persons, evaluates programs and provides assistance in establishing new ones, grants scholarships to people who are visually impaired; and provides technical training and research support. It publishes *The Braille Monitor* and *Future Reflections,* a magazine for parents; and maintains affiliates in all states and the District of Columbia, as well as the National Organization of Parents of Blind Children.

National Fiesta Educativa
163 South Avenue 24, Suite 201
Los Angeles, CA 90031
(323) 221-6696

Fax: (323) 221-6699
E-mail: info@fiestaeducativa.org
www.fiestaeducativa.org

National Fiesta Educativa works to empower Latino families of persons with special needs through education, training, referral, and information and sponsors an annual conference at the University of Southern California in Los Angeles for parents and professionals for the exchange of ideas and information.

National Industries for the Blind
1310 Braddock Place
Alexandria, VA 22314-1691
(703) 310-0500
E-mail: services@nib.org
www.nib.org

National Industries for the Blind (NIB) enhances the opportunities for economic and personal independence of persons who are blind, primarily through creating, sustaining, and improving employment. NIB operates under the Javits-Wagner-O'Day (JWOD) Act, a mandatory federal purchasing program that enables people who are blind to work and provide products and services to federal and commercial customers. Its web site has a listing of NIB-associated agencies that provide employment and career training opportunities for blind individuals throughout the United States.

National Organization for Albinism and Hypopigmentation
P.O. BOX 959
East Hampstead, NH 03826-0959
(603) 887-2310; (800) 473-2310
Fax: (603) 887-2310
E-mail: info@albinism.org
www.albinism.org

The National Organization for Albinism and Hypopigmentation (NOAH) is a membership organization that provides information on albinism and hypopigmentation, offers peer support, sponsors conferences, and publishes a newsletter.

National Technical Assistance Consortium for Children and Young Adults Who Are Deaf-Blind
Western Oregon University
Teaching Research Institute
345 North Monmouth Avenue

Monmouth, OR 97361-1314

(503) 838-8391

TDD/TTY: (503) 838-9623

Fax: (503) 838-8150

www.tr.wou.edu\ntac

The National Technical Assistance Consortium for Children and Young Adults Who Are Deaf-Blind (NTAC) provides technical assistance to families and agencies serving children and young adults who are deaf-blind. NTAC is a federally funded consortium project of the Teaching Research Institute and the Helen Keller National Center.

PACER Center (Parent Advocacy Coalition for Educational Rights)

8161 Normandale Boulevard

Minneapolis, MN 55437-1044

(952) 838-9000; (888) 248-0822

E-mail: alliance@alliance.org

www.pacer.org

www.taalliance.org

Dedicated to helping parents in Minnesota understand special education laws and obtain appropriate education for their children, the PACER Center engages in a wide range of national assistance and information activities in support of parents and houses the National Parent Centers Alliance and the Technical Assistance Alliance for Parent Centers, a national and regional technical assistance system that develops and coordinates parent training, information, and resource centers throughout the states. It also offers an extensive selection of publications, including several newsletters, as well as workshops for parents of children with disabilities.

Perkins School for the Blind

175 North Beacon Street

Watertown, Massachusetts 02472

(617) 924-3434

Fax: (617) 926-2027

info@perkins.org

www.perkins.org

The Perkins School for the Blind is a specialized school and learning center maintaining a wide range of educational, training, and outreach activities relating to students who are visually impaired, including those who are multiply disabled. In addition to sponsoring conferences and community programs, it publishes materials on the instuction of visually impaired students and related topics.

TASH (formerly The Association for Persons with Severe Handicaps)
29 West Susquehanna Avenue, Suite 210
Baltimore, MD 21204
(410) 828-8274
Fax: (410) 828-6706
E-mail: info@tash.org
www.tash.org

TASH is an advocacy organization for professionals who work with infants, children, and youths who have severe disabilities and their families. It holds an annual national conference and publishes the *Journal of the Association for Persons with Severe Handicaps* and the *TASH Newsletter* and has a committee on early childhood that meets at the annual conference. TASH has state or regional chapters.

Texas School for the Blind and Visually Impaired
1100 West 45th Street
Austin, TX 78756-3494
(512) 454-8631; (800) 872-5273
TDD/TTY: (512) 206-9188
Fax: (512) 454-3395
www.tsbvi.edu

The Texas School for the Blind and Visually Impaired (TSBVI) is a specialized school and learning center that offers online information and resources about visual impairment, instruction, technology, assessment, and a wide range of other topics related to the education of students who have visual and multiple disabilities and publishes professional books, assessments, and curricula.

The ARC of the United States
1010 Wayne Avenue, Suite 650
Silver Spring, MD 20910
(301) 565-3842
Fax: (301) 565-5342
info@thearc.org
www.thearc.org

The ARC of the United States is a national organization devoted to promoting and improving supports and services for people with mental retardation and related developmental disabilities and their families. The ARC works at the local, state, and national levels to promote services, public understanding, and legislation and to foster research and education on behalf of all children and adults with cognitive, intellectual, and developmental disabilities.

United States Association for Blind Athletes
33 North Institute Street
Colorado Springs, CO 80903
(719) 630-0422
Fax: (719) 630-0616
E-mail: media@usaba.org
www.usaba.org

The United States Association for Blind Athletes (USABA) is a national membership association that promotes sports involvement for people who are blind.

Visually Impaired Preschool Services (VIPS)
1229 Garvin Place
Louisville, KY 40203
(502) 636-3207; (888) 636-8477
Fax: (502) 636-0024
E-mail: info@vips.org
www.vips.org

Visually Impaired Preschool Services (VIPS) offers appropriate services to infants, toddlers, and preschoolers who are visually impaired and to their families.

ORGANIZATIONS OFFERING SCHOLARSHIPS

The following organizations provide graduate or undergraduate scholarships to students who are blind or visually impaired.

American Council of the Blind
Scholarship Office
1155 15th Street NW, Suite 720
Washington, DC 20005
(202) 467-5081; (800) 424-8666
Fax: (202) 467-5085
E-mail: info@acb.org
www.acb.org

American Foundation for the Blind
Information Center
11 Penn Plaza, Suite 300
New York, NY 10001
(212) 502-7661; (800) 232-5463
TDD/TTY: (212) 502-7662
Fax: (212) 502-7777

E-mail: afbinfo@afb.net
www.afb.org/scholarships.asp

Association for Education and Rehabilitation of the Blind and
Visually Impaired
AER Ferrell Scholarship Fund
1703 N. Beauregard Street, Suite 440
Alexandria, VA 22311
(703) 671-4500; (877) 492-2708
Fax: (703) 671-6391
E-mail: aer@aerbvi.org
www.aerbvi.org

Blinded Veterans Association
477 H Street NW
Washington, DC 20001-2694
(202) 371-8880; (800) 669-7079
Fax: (202) 371-8258
www.bva.org

Christian Record Services
4444 South 52nd Street
Lincoln, NE 68516
(402) 488-0981
Fax: (402) 488-7582
E-mail: info@christianrecord.org
www.christianrecord.org

Council of Citizens with Low Vision
American Council for the Blind
1155 15th Street NW, Suite 1004
Washington, DC 20005
(800) 733-2258
www.cclvi.org

Foundation for Exceptional Children Yes I Can!
1110 North Glebe Road, Suite 300
Arlington, VA 22201-5704
(800) 224-6830, ext. 462
yesican.sped.org/scholarship/index.html

The Jewish Guild for the Blind
15 West 65th Street
New York, NY 10023

(212) 769-7801
Fax: (212) 769-6266
E-mail: info@jgb.org
www.jgb.org

Lighthouse International Career Incentive and Achievement Awards
111 East 59th Street
New York, NY 10022
(212) 821-9428
E-mail: info@lighthouse.org
www.lighthouse.org

National Federation of the Blind
Scholarships Committee
805 Fifth Avenue
Grinnell, IA 50112
(641) 236-3366
www.nfb.org

New Hampshire Charitable Foundation
37 Pleasant Street
Concord, NH 03301-4005
(603) 225-6641
Fax: (603) 225-1700
E-mail: info@nhcf.org
www.nhcf.org

Recording for the Blind and Dyslexic
Scholarship Office
20 Roszel Road
Princeton, NJ 08540
(609) 452-0606; (866) 732-3585
Fax: (609) 520-7990
www.rfbd.org

VSA Arts
818 Connecticut Avenue NW, Suite 600
Washington, DC 20006
(202) 628-2800; (800) 933-8721
TDD: (202) 737-0645
Fax: (202) 429-0868
www.vsarts.org

COLLEGES AND UNIVERSITIES OFFERING SCHOLARSHIPS

The following institutions provide graduate or undergraduate scholarships to students who are blind or visually impaired.

Fordham University
Director of Financial Aid
33 West 60th Street, 9th Floor
New York, NY 10023
(212) 636-6815
Fax: (212) 636-6018
E-mail: financialaid@law.fordham.edu
http://law.fordham.edu/index.htm

George Mason University
Disability Resource Center
4400 University Drive
Fairfax, Virginia 22030
(703) 993-2774
apollo.gmu.edu/finaid

George Washington University
Disability Support Services
Marvin Center, Suite 242
800 21st Street, NW
Washington, DC 20052
(202) 994-8250
Fax: (202) 994-7610
E-mail: dss@gwu.edu
www.gwired.gwu.edu/dss/ApplytoGW/#7

Vanderbilt University
Department of Special Education
Peabody College
Box #328
230 Appleton Place
Nashville, TN 37203-5721
(615) 322-2249
www.vanderbilt.edu

Western Michigan University
Department of Blind Rehabilitation
3404 Sangren Hall
Western Michigan University

Kalamazoo, MI 49008-5218

(269) 387-3455

www.wmich.edu/hhs/blrh/

SOURCES OF PRODUCTS AND EDUCATIONAL MATERIALS

The following organizations and companies provide a wide variety of specialized products, materials and services for students who are blind or visually impaired.

Ablenet

2808 Fairview Avenue North

Roseville, MN 55113-1308

(651) 294-2200; (800) 322-0956

Fax: (651) 294-2259

E-mail: customerservice@ablenetinc.com

www.ablenetinc.com/

Ablenet creates simple-to-use assistive technology products and educational programs for people with physical and cognitive disabilities.

American Printing House for the Blind

1839 Frankfort Avenue

Louisville, KY 40206-0085

(502) 895-2405; (800) 223-1839

Fax: (502) 899-2274

E-mail: info@aph.org

www.aph.org

The American Printing House for the Blind (APH) administers the federal quota system established under the Act to Promote the Education of the Blind, acting as the official supplier of textbooks and educational materials for visually impaired students below the college level in the United States. It publishes braille, large-print, recorded, CD-ROM, and tactile graphic materials; manufactures a wide assortment of educational and daily living products; modifies and develops computer-access equipment and software; maintains an educational research and development program concerned with educational methods and educational aids; and provides a reference-catalog service for volunteer-produced textbooks in all media for students who are visually impaired and for information about other sources of related materials. APH houses the National Instructional Materials Access Center (NIMAC), the central repository for electronic files of educational materials in this country.

Bookshare.org
480 California Avenue, Suite 201
Palo Alto, CA 94306
(650) 475-5440
Fax: (650) 475-1066
E-mail: info@bookshare.org
http://www.bookshare.org

Bookshare.org is a web-based membership organization that supplies accessible books in digital formats for people with disabilities.

Enabling Devices
385 Warburton Avenue
Hastings-on-Hudson, NY 10706
(914) 478-0960; (800) 832-8697
Fax: (914) 479-1369
E-mail: info@enablingdevices.com
http://enablingdevices.com/home.aspx

Enabling Devices develops affordable learning and assistive devices to help people of all ages with disabling conditions.

Exceptional Teaching Aids
20102 Woodbine Avenue
Castro Valley, CA 94546
(510) 582-4859; (800) 549-6999
Fax: (510) 582-5911
E-mail: ExTeaching@aol.com
www.exceptionalteaching.com

Exceptional Teaching Aids manufactures and distributes educational materials and equipment for visually impaired students, including tutorial and other educational software programs; braille materials for reading readiness, math readiness, and math practice; and books on audiocassette.

Howe Press of the Perkins School for the Blind
175 North Beacon Street
Watertown, MA 02172-2790
(617) 924-3490
Fax: (617) 926-2027
E-mail: HowePress@Perkins.org
www.perkins.pvt.k12.ma.us/area.php?id=9

The Howe Press manufactures and sells a variety of products for visually impaired persons, including manual and electric Perkins Braillers, slates, styli, mathematical aids, braille games, braille-vision books for children, heavy- and light-grade braille paper, and Tactile Drawing Kits.

Independent Living Aids
200 Robbins Lane
Jericho, NY 11753
(516) 937-1848; (800) 537-2118
Fax: (516) 937-3906
E-mail: can-do@independentliving.com
www.independentliving.com

Independent Living Aids provides a wide variety of adaptive products for individuals who are blind or visually impaired.

LS&S Group, Inc.
P.O. Box 673
Northbrook, IL 60065
(847) 498-9777
TDD/TTY: (866) 317-8533
Fax: (847) 498-1482
E-mail: info@lssproducts.com
www.lssgroup.com

LS&S Group offers a wide variety of products for independent living for people who are visually impaired or hearing impaired.

Maxi Aids
42 Executive Boulevard
Farmingdale, NY 11735
(631) 752-0689; (800) 522-6294
Fax: (631) 752-0689
E-mail: sales@maxiaids.com
www.maxiaids.com

Maxi Aids distributes a wide variety of adaptive products and products for independent living.

National Braille Press
88 St. Stephen Street
Boston, MA 02115
(617) 266-6160; (888) 965-8965
Fax: (617) 437-0456
E-mail: orders@nbp.org
www.nbp.org

The National Braille Press provides braille printing services for publishers and other organizations, including the Library of Congress; offers transcription of documents related to school or work; and sponsors a children's Braille Book-of-the-Month Club.

National Library Service for the Blind and Physically Handicapped
Library of Congress
1291 Taylor Street, NW
Washington, DC 20542
(202) 707-5100; (800) 424-8567
TDD/TTY: (202) 707-0744
Fax: (202) 707-0712
E-mail: nls@loc.gov
www.loc.gov/nls

The National Library Service for the Blind and Physically Handicapped (NLS) maintains a national program to distribute free reading materials—classics, current fiction, and general nonfiction—in braille, on recorded disks and cassettes, and in electronic formats to visually and physically handicapped persons who cannot utilize ordinary printed materials. Materials are distributed and playback equipment is lent free of charge through a network of regional and subregional libraries and machine-lending agencies throughout the United States. In addition, NLS operates a reference information section on all aspects of blindness and other physical disabilities that affect reading, and functions as a bibliographic center on reading materials for people with disabilities and organizations that lend reading materials in special media.

Recording for the Blind & Dyslexic
20 Roszel Road
Princeton, NJ 08540
(609) 452-0606; (866) 732-3585
Fax: (609) 520-7990
E-mail: custserv@rfbd.org
www.rfbd.org

Recording for the Blind & Dyslexic (RFB&D) lends recorded and electronic materials and textbooks to people who cannot read standard print because of visual, physical, or learning disabilities.

Seedlings Braille Books for Children
14151 Farmington Road
Livonia, MI 48154-4522
(734) 427-8552; (800) 777-8552
Fax: (734) 427-8552
E-mail: seedlink@aol.com
www.seedlings.org

Seedlings Braille Books for Children is a nonprofit publisher of braille books for children.

SpecialEd Solutions, Inc.
P.O. Box 6218
San Antonio, TX 78209
(210) 828-3785; (877) 324-2533
E-mail: info@SpecialEd.com
http://specialed.com/pages/5/index.htm

SpecialEd Solutions offers products, adaptive mobility devices, and related accessories that teachers of students who are visually impaired, special education teachers, occupational therapists, and parents can use with children who are blind or deaf-blind or have visual or multiple impairments.

WEB SITE RESOURCES

College Board
45 Columbus Circle
New York, NY 10023
(212) 713-8000
www.collegeboard.com/pay

The College Board offers a wide range of information on college planning, information about different forms of financial aid; an online scholarship search; and assistance with completing the Free Application for Federal Student Aid (FAFSA), the financial aid application form for federal and state student grants, work-study, and loans.

Federal Student Aid Information Center
P.O. Box 84
Washington, DC 20044
(800) 433-3243
www.studentaid.ed.gov

This Federal Student Aid Information Center of the U.S. Department of Education offers a wide range of information on every aspect of financial aid for students of all ages. It includes the Free Application for Federal Student Aid (FAFSA)—the financial aid application form for federal and state student grants, work-study, and loans—as well as forms to apply for all types of federal loans. Specific resources for blind and visually impaired students can be found at http://studentaid.ed.gov/PORTALSWebApp/students/english/impairedresources.jsp.

IDEA Partnership at NASDSE
National Association of State Directors of Special Education

1800 Diagonal Road, Suite 320
Alexandria, VA 22314
(877) IDEA Info [877-433-2463]
E-mail: partnership@nasdse.org
http://idea.ed.gov

The IDEA Partnership provides checklists and information on IDEA and No Child Left Behind legislation, success in school, federal student aid, and college planning and preparation.

Project Salute
www.projectsalute.net

Project Salute offers resources for families and services providers on tactile learning strategies for working with children who are deaf-blind or who are blind with additional disabilities.

The National Center on Low-Incidence Disabilities
University of Northern Colorado
Greeley, CO 80639
(970) 351-1061
(800) 395-2693 (Voice/TTY)
www.nclid.unco.edu

The National Center on Low-Incidence Disabilities (NCLID) is an information and research clearinghouse offering a wide range of informational resources and data on special education law, teacher training, and the education of students with vision and hearing disabilities for educators and parents.

Wrightslaw
http://www.wrightslaw.com

Wrightslaw offers in-depth information about special education law, education law, and advocacy for children with disabilities for parents, educators, advocates, and attorneys.

GOVERNMENT AGENCIES

Office of Special Education and Rehabilitative Services
U.S. Department of Education
400 Maryland Avenue, SW
Washington, DC 20202
(202) 245-7468
www.ed.gov/about/offices/list/osers/index.html

The Office of Special Education and Rehabilitative Services (OSERS) supports programs that help educate children and youths with disabilities, provides for the rehabilitation of youths and adults with disabilities, and supports research to improve the lives of individuals with disabilities.

Office of Special Education Programs
U.S. Department of Education
400 Maryland Avenue, SW
Washington, DC 20202
(202) 245-7459
www.ed.gov/about/offices/list/osers/osep/index.html

The Office of Special Education Programs (OSEP) is dedicated to improving results for infants, toddlers, children and youths with disabilities ages birth to 21 by providing leadership and financial support to assist states and local districts. OSEP administers the Individuals with Disabilities Education Act (IDEA), which authorizes formula grants to states and discretionary grants to institutions of higher education and other non-profit organizations to support research, demonstrations, technical assistance and dissemination, technology and personnel development and parent-training and information centers.

Social Security Administration
6401 Security Boulevard
Baltimore, MD 21235
(800) 772-1213
TDD/TTY: (800) 325-0778
www.ssa.gov

The Social Security Administration (SSA) administers the primary federal retirement and assistance entitlement program in the United States and publishes a variety of online and print materials.

U.S. Department of Education
Office for Civil Rights
550 12th Street, SW
Washington, DC 20202-1100
(800) 421-3481
TDD/TTY: (877) 521-2172 (TDD)
Fax: (202) 245-6840
E-mail: ocr@ed.gov
www.ed.gov/policy/rights/guid/ocr/disability.html

The Office for Civil Rights of the U.S. Department of Education provides information and publications on the rights of students under both the Americans with Disabilities Act and Section 504 of the Rehabilitation Act of 1973.

U.S. Department of Health and Human Services
Office for Civil Rights
200 Independence Avenue, SW
Washington, DC 20201
(800) 368-1019
TDD: (800) 537-7697
E-mail: ocrmail@hhs.gov
www.hhs.gov/ocr/

The Office for Civil Rights of the U.S. Department of Health and Human Services is the enforcement agency for Section 504 of the Rehabilitation Act of 1973. It provides information about rights under the act and how to file a complaint.

U.S. Department of Justice
Disability Rights Section, Civil Rights Division
950 Pennsylvania Avenue, NW
Washington, DC 20530
(800) 514-0301
TTY: (800) 514-0383
Fax: (202) 307-1198
www.ada.gov

The Disability Rights Section of the U.S. Department of Justice is responsible for the enforcement of the Americans with Disabilities Act (ADA) and provides information and assistance. ADA regulations, publications, and other materials are available in large print, audiotape, and braille, on computer disk, and in standard print.

FOR FURTHER INFORMATION

Books

American Foundation for the Blind. *AFB Directory of Services for Blind and Visually Impaired Persons in the United States and Canada*, 27th edition (New York: AFB Press, 2005).

Chen, D. (Ed.). *Essential Elements in Early Intervention: Visual Impairment and Multiple Disabilities* (New York: AFB Press, 1999).

Chen, D., & Dote-Kwan, J. (Eds.). *Starting Points: Instructional Practices for Young Children Whose Multiple Disabilities Include Visual Impairment* (Los Angeles: Blind Children's Center, 1995).

Crane, P., Cuthbertson, P., Ferrell, K. A., & Scherb, H. *Equals in Partnership: Basic Rights for Families of Children with Blindness or Visual Impairment* (Watertown, MA: Hilton/Perkins Program and National Association for Parents of the Visually Impaired, 1997).

D'Andrea, F. M., & Farrenkopf, C. (Eds.). *Looking to Learn: Promoting Literacy for Students with Low Vision* (New York: AFB Press, 2000).

Downing, J. (Ed.). *Including Students with Severe and Multiple Disabilities in Typical Classrooms: Practical Strategies for Teachers* (Baltimore: Paul H. Brookes, 1996).

Erin, J. *When You Have a Visually Impaired Student with Multiple Disabilities in Your Classroom: A Guide for Teachers* (New York: AFB Press, 2004).

Ferrell, K. *Reach Out and Teach: Meeting the Training Needs of Parents of Visually and Multiply Handicapped Young Children* (New York: AFB Press, 1985).

Goodman, S. A., & Wittenstein, S. H. (Eds.). *Collaborative Assessment: Working with Students Who Are Blind or Visually Impaired, Including Those with Additional Disabilities* (New York: AFB Press, 2003).

Haring, N., & Romer, L. (Eds.). *Welcoming Students Who Are Deaf-Blind Into Typical Classrooms: Facilitating School Participation, Learning, and Friendships* (Baltimore: Paul H. Brookes, 1995).

Heller, K., Alberto, P., Forney, P., & Schwartzman, M. *Understanding Physical, Sensory, and Health Impairments: Characteristics and Educational Implications* (Pacific Grove, CA: Brookes/Cole, 1996).

Holbrook, M. C. (Ed.). *Children with Visual Impairments: A Parent's Guide*, second edition (Bethesda, MD: Woodbine House, 2006).

Holbrook, M. C., & Koenig, A. J. (Eds.). *Foundations of Education*: *History and Theory of Teaching Children and Youths with Visual Impairments*, Vol. 1 (New York: AFB Press, 2000).

Huebner, K., Prickett, J., Welch, T., & Joffee, E. (Eds.). *Hand in Hand: Essentials of Communication and Orientation and Mobility for Young Children Who Are Deaf-Blind* (New York: AFB Press, 1995).

Huebner, K. M., Merk-Adam, B., Stryker, D., & Wolffe, K. *The National Agenda for the Education of Children and Youths with Visual Impairments, Including Those with Multiple Disabilities—Revised* (New York: AFB Press, 2004).

Kendrick, D. *Business Owners Who Are Blind or Visually Impaired* (New York: AFB Press, 2000).

Kendrick, D. *Health Care Professionals Who Are Blind or Visually Impaired* (New York: AFB Press, 2001).

Kendrick, D. *Jobs to Be Proud Of: Profiles of Workers Who Are Blind or Visually Impaired* (New York: AFB Press, 1993).

Kendrick, D. *Teachers Who Are Blind or Visually Impaired* (New York: AFB Press, 1998).

Koenig, A. J., & Holbrook, M. C. (Eds.). *Foundations of Education*: *Instructional Strategies for Teaching Children and Youths with Visual Impairments*, Vol. 2 (New York: AFB Press, 2000).

Langley, M. B. (2001). *ISAVE: Individualized Systematic Assessment of Visual Efficiency* (Louisville, KY: American Printing House for the Blind, 2001).

Lewis, S., & Allman, C. B. *Seeing Eye to Eye: An Administrator's Guide to Students with Low Vision*. (New York: AFB Press, 2002).

Olmstead, J. E. *Itinerant Teaching: Tricks of the Trade for Teachers of Students with Visual Impairments*, second edition (New York: AFB Press, 2005).

Pogrund, R. L., & Fazzi, D. L. (Eds.). *Early Focus: Working with Young Children Who Are Blind or Visually Impaired and Their Families*, second edition (New York: AFB Press, 2002).

Pugh, G. S., & Erin, J. (Eds.). *Blind and Visually Impaired Students: Educational Service Guidelines* (Watertown, MA: Perkins School for the Blind in cooperation with the National Association of State Directors of Special Education, 1999).

Russotti, J., & Shaw, R. *When You Have a Visually Impaired Student in Your Classroom: A Guide for Paraeducators* (New York: AFB Press, 2004).

Sacks, S. Z., & Silberman, R. K. (Eds.). *Educating Students Who Have Visual Impairments with Other Disabilities* (Baltimore: Paul H. Brookes, 1998).

Sacks, S. Z., & Wolffe, K. E. *FOCUS (Full Option Curriculum for the Utilization of Social Skills) Materials* (New York: AFB Press, 2000).

Sacks, S. Z., & Wolffe, K. E. (Eds.). *Teaching Social Skills to Students with Visual Impairments: From Theory to Practice* (New York: AFB Press, 2006).

Smith, M., & Levack, N. *Teaching Students with Visual and Multiple Impairments: A Resource Guide* (Austin: Texas School for the Blind and Visually Impaired, 1996).

Spungin, S. J. (Ed.). *When You Have a Visually Impaired Student in Your Classroom: A Guide for Teachers* (New York: AFB Press, 2002).

Swenson, A. *Beginning with Braille: Firsthand Experiences with a Balanced Approach to Literacy* (New York: AFB Press, 1998).

Trief, E., & Feeney, R. *College Bound: A Guide for Students with Visual Impairments* (New York: AFB Press, 2005).

2006 Red Book: A Summary Guide to Employment Support for Individuals with Disabilities Under the Social Security Disability Insurance (SSDI) and Supplemental Security Income (SSI) Programs (Baltimore: Social Security Administration, 2006).

Wolffe, K. *Skills for Success: A Career Education Handbook for Children and Adolescents with Visual Impairments* (New York: AFB Press, 1998).

Wright, P. W. D., & Wright, P. D. *Wrightslaw: From Emotions to Advocacy: The Special Education Survival Guide* (Hartfield, VA: Harbor House Law Press, 2002).

Journals and Newsletters

AccessWorld: Technology and People Who Are Blind or Visually Impaired
AFB Press
American Foundation for the Blind
11 Penn Plaza, Suite 300
New York, NY 10001

(212) 502-7651; (800) 232-5463
Fax: (212) 502-7774
accessworld@afb.net
www.afb.org/aw

Awareness
National Association for Parents of Children with Visual Impairments
P.O. Box 317
Watertown, MA 02471
(617) 972-7441; (800) 562-6265
Fax: (617) 972-7444
napvi@perkins.org
www.napvi.org

Deaf-Blind Perspectives
345 N. Monmouth Avenue
Monmouth, OR 97361
(800) 438-9376
TTY: (800) 854-7013
Fax: (503) 838-8150
dbp@wou.edu
www.tr.wou.edu/tr/dbp/

DOTS for Braille Literacy
AFB National Literacy Center
100 Peachtree Street, Suite 620
Atlanta, GA 30303
(404) 525-2303; (404) 659-6957
literacy@afb.net
www.afb.org

Exceptional Children
Exceptional Parent
Teaching Exceptional Children
Council for Exceptional Children
1110 North Glebe Road, Suite 300
Arlington, VA 22201-5704
(888) CEC-SPED; (703) 620-3660
TTY: (703) 264-9446
Fax: (703) 264-9494
service@cec.sped.org
www.cec.sped.org; www.ed.arizona.edu/dvi/welcome.htm

Journal of Visual Impairment & Blindness
AFB Press
American Foundation for the Blind
11 Penn Plaza, Suite 300
New York, NY 10001
(212) 502-7651; (800) 232-3044
jvib@afb.net
www.afb.org/jvib

RE:view
Association for Education and Rehabilitation of the Blind and
Visually Impaired
Published by Heldref Publications
1319 18th Street, NW
Washington, DC 20036-1802
www.heldref.org

Young Exceptional Children
Division for Early Childhood of the Council for Exceptional Children
634 Eddy Avenue
Missoula, MT 59812-6696
(406) 243-5898
dec@selway.umt.edu

Index